$TOCK INVESTING

for

EVERYONE

Other Books in the *Wiley Investment* Series

$TOCK INVESTING

— *for* —

EVERYONE

Tools for Investing Like the Pros

Arshad Khan and Vaqar Zuberi

John Wiley & Sons, Inc.

New York • Chichester • Weinheim • Brisbane • Singapore • Toronto

Library of Congress Cataloging-in-Publication Data:
Khan, Arshad.
    Stock investing for everyone : tools for investing like the pros /
Arshad Khan and Vaqar Zuberi.
        p.   cm.—(Wiley investment series)
    Includes index.
    ISBN 0-471-35731-6 (cloth : alk. paper)
    1. Stocks.   2. Investments.   I. Zuberi, Vaqar.   II. Title.
III. Series.
HG4661.K43   1999
332.63'22—dc21   99-29530

Printed in the United States of America

10 9 8 7 6 5 4 3 2

Contents

Acknowledgments

The writing and production of this book has been a long and challenging project, which could not have been completed without active help from many quarters. To our surprise, help and encouragement were available at every stage of this project. We gratefully acknowledge help from coworkers, business associates, friends, students, strangers on the Internet, and our families.

The help extended by Hitachi's management, in providing the forum and facilities for the 30-member focus group that reviewed this book, is highly appreciated. We also take this opportunity to thank Diana Singer for thoroughly reviewing the manuscript and providing valuable comments. We would also like to thank Kyle Beaird and Brett Bernstein, of Zacks Investment Research, for providing valuable research data and enthusiastic encouragement. Finally, we would like to thank Janice Phelps for her valuable comments and constant encouragement throughout the course of this project.

This project has run very smoothly and for that we have to acknowledge the excellent management provided by Mina Samuels, Editor, John Wiley & Sons.

Introduction

Stock Investing for Everyone comprehensively covers a broad range of topics relevant to stock market investing. It provides powerful tools to those who take stock investing seriously. Its contents, both in breadth and depth, make it a unique publication that fills a void that has existed despite the availability of many stock investing books. Consequently, for many years to come, it will be a valuable and profitable resource for stock market investors.

The book starts off by laying the background, and case, for investing in the stock market. It then provides detailed information on where, and how, to conduct stock investment research. This is followed by an in-depth discussion of the variables influencing stock prices and the widely used methods for valuing stocks.

An introduction to the basics of fundamental and technical analysis is followed by a comprehensive description, and practical interpretation, of stock market variables (or indicators). Indicators covered include earnings per share, moving averages, market breadth, sentiment and economic indicators, and others. Also analyzed comprehensively are the behavior of individual stocks and the overall market. Topics include bull and bear markets, corrections, recognizing a market top (and bottom), bullish and bearish signs, seasonal factors, and so on. Detailed coverage is given to related topics—such as recognizing the behavior patterns of weakening stocks, the art of handling hot stocks, and group/sector monitoring.

The book introduces readers to various investment principles and strategies. It provides step-by-step instructions on how to screen, rank, and select stocks using different investment strategies. It also teaches investors how to conduct comprehensive fundamental analysis on a company—in order to determine if it has the potential to be a good investment. The book covers other important aspects of stock market investing, which often do not get the attention they deserve—such as selling strategies, risk management, and portfolio management.

Finally, in Chapter 20, casual investors are taught the "Express" method in a step-by-step manner. This is a fast and easy procedure for screening stocks and determining their price appreciation potential. Specific real-world examples are provided, with actual data, for different scenarios—such as buying or rejecting a stock. This procedure is ideally suited for the majority of investors who cannot invest the time and effort required to screen and analyze a company prior to buying its stock.

Stock Investing for Everyone is based on the growth investing philosophy. However, a fair amount of coverage has also been given to momentum investing. The reason is that the behavior of momentum players can considerably affect a stock, or even the overall market, in the short term. By understanding how momentum investors act and react, an alert investor will be in a better position to understand what, at times, appears to be the inexplicable behavior of stocks.

By clearly and comprehensively presenting the tools to master the art of stock market investing, the authors invite you to share the enjoyment and profits available to the knowledgeable investor.

$TOCK INVESTING

for

EVERYONE

Chapter 1

Why Invest in the Stock Market

Why Invest in Stocks

Investors have many choices when it comes to investing their hard-earned money. While each investment vehicle has its advantages, the stock market has characteristics that make it the ideal vehicle of choice for the vast majority of investors. The characteristics that define stock market investing are described in the following sections.

Ownership and Liquidity

A *corporation* enjoys a central place in a free market economy. It is the vehicle through which capital is raised, business is generated, and wealth is created. Since the ownership of a corporation is split into small parts (or shares), these shares can be made available to the general public. Thus it becomes possible for any investor (even with very limited funds) to participate in the ownership and growth of any publicly traded company—one whose shares are traded on a *stock exchange*.

A benefit associated with stock ownership is that every shareholder, irrespective of the number of shares owned, gets voting rights. Voting can be required for a number of reasons including the issuance of more shares, approval of an employee stock option plan, and so on. Voting shareholders elect members of the *board of directors* and have the right to attend stockholders meetings. While a small shareholder cannot change the way a company is run, shareholders sometimes do get together to force management to change the way they conduct business.

A very important advantage of owning stocks is that they are very liquid assets (i.e., can be sold very quickly and efficiently). Such transactions take place in the stock market—a convenient and efficient place for getting buyers and sellers together for the purpose of trading.

Price Appreciation and Profit Sharing

Sharing Profits

An investor who buys the shares of a company becomes its shareholder and, therefore, becomes entitled to share in its profits. Profits earned by a company are either distributed as a *dividend* to all shareholders or reinvested in the company. Reinvestment helps a company to grow and build greater value. As the value of the company grows over time, its stock price appreciates. This price appreciation is dependent on many factors such as:

- The company's profitability levels
- Growth prospects
- Overall stock market conditions

While shareholders can share in the profits of a company, they are also exposed to potential losses that an investment can incur due to a stock price decline caused by the company's poor performance, external factors, or other reasons.

Profit Potential

Historically, stocks have been the best vehicle for increasing the value of investments in the long run. In 1995, the *S&P 500* index (a widely used stock performance index) rose 34.11%, followed by a 20.26% rise in 1996. It appreciated 31% in 1997 and 26.7% in 1998. Prior to this period also, stocks have had a comparatively superior performance. According to the *Stocks, Bonds, Bills and Inflation 1998 Yearbook* by Ibbotson Associates, the performance of various investments during the 1926–1997 period, using the value of $1 invested at year-end 1925, was as follows:

Small company stocks	$5,519.97
Large company stocks	$1,828.33
Long-term government bonds	$39.07
Treasury bills	$14.25
Inflation	$9.00

Beating Inflation

Since 1926, stocks have outpaced the *inflation* rate significantly, while fixed income investments have not. In general, it has been observed that the higher the short-term *volatility* of an investment, the greater is its potential to outpace the rate of inflation over time. Based on historical returns, the stock market is the best investment for protection against inflation.

While short-term results may be volatile, stocks have outpaced both inflation and fixed income securities in the long run. Thus, considering the long-term effects of inflation and the uncertainty of future financial needs, it may be even more risky if too "conservative" investments are made.

Understanding Common Stocks

Number of Shares Issued

Every equally valued unit of ownership in a corporation is called a share. The total number of shares issued by a company, which represents the total ownership of a corporation, varies tremendously from company to company. Some companies issue a few hundred thousand shares, while others issue hundreds of millions of shares. Individual investors and/or institutions may own all, or part, of a company by buying its shares.

Volatility and Risk

Understanding Price Fluctuations
Stock prices do not remain static. They can fluctuate every day, hour, minute, and even with each trade. These price fluctuations, and the volatility of stock returns, are well known to stock market observers. The degree to which a stock's price moves up or down, especially in the short term, is described by the term "volatility." For short-term investors, especially traders, price volatility is very important and can be critical at times. However, for long-term investors, price volatility in the near term (days or months) is of far less concern.

Daily, and year-to-year, price fluctuations occur in tandem with changes in the business climate which, in turn, change investors' perceptions. The reason is that the business environment, along with management's successful efforts, is critical to the success of a company. Any positive business development is a plus for the stock price and vice versa.

Effect of Fundamental Factors
In the short term, stock prices are volatile because, at any given moment, many crosscurrents and forces are in play in the stock market, the economy, and the underlying business. Market players constantly try to establish and refine valuations. Changing expectations, hopes, and fears drive these valuations. However, in the long run, these forces are not the determining factors in establishing stock prices. Prices are ultimately determined by fundamental factors such as *earnings* (profits) and dividend

growth. Therefore, even though volatility and price swings characterize stocks in the short term, time and the overriding influence of fundamentals tend to even out these swings in the long run. This makes short-term volatility more acceptable to investors.

Market Volatility

Most investors are aware that stock market averages and *indexes*, such as the *Dow Jones Industrial Average (DJIA)* and the S&P 500 index, fluctuate routinely. These swings may be as high as 3% on a single day. On some days, the swings or drops can be massive. For example, on October 19, 1987, the DJIA dropped 508 points—a fall of 23%. This was followed by a 10.2% rise just two days later.

On October 27, 1997, the DJIA dropped 554 points—equivalent to a 7.18% decline. On October 28, 1997, the DJIA soared 337 points—equivalent to a 4.71% gain. On September 8, 1998, the DJIA surged 380 points—a 4.98% gain. It was the largest one-day point gain ever for this index.

The Nasdaq is more volatile than the DJIA and is characterized by wider swings. Its biggest gain ever was on September 8, 1998, when it rose 6.02%. Individual stocks are also characterized by price swings. The amplitude of these swings can vary—depending on the company, sector, group, and size of the company. For example, many technology stocks routinely swing 1% to 5%, while large bank stocks mirror the market moves.

Confusing Volatility with Risk

Ordinary investors, not too familiar with the stock market, tend to equate the risk of stock market investing with short-term price stability. They consider price volatility to be risky despite the positive long-term prospects, and tend to view investments that retain a stable price, like *money market funds*, to be safe. For an investor parking funds for a short period, viewing risk and safety in these terms is acceptable. However, for the long-term investor, investing in instruments with less perceived risk, such as certificates of deposit (CDs) and cash reserves, actually increases the risk. The reason is that such investments, as historical returns show, do not outpace inflation significantly compared to stocks.

Why Stock Prices Go Up

Supply and demand for a stock determines its price. When demand for a stock increases, its price increases. In other words, when there are more buyers than sellers, the stock price goes up. The reverse also holds true.

In general, three factors tend to attract buyers to a stock and cause its price to rise:

1. Actual increase in *net earnings* (*net profits*)
2. Anticipation of earnings increase
3. General stock market move to the upside

Distribution of Profits

When a company is consistently profitable, there is an increase in its value, appeal and, consequently, its share price. The profits earned are usually disbursed in one of two ways:

▌ Plowed back into the company to enable further growth.
▌ Paid out as dividends to the shareholders.

A company that pays a dividend is considered to be an attractive investment by many income-seeking investors. However, if a company does not earn sufficient profits, it borrows money in order to meet the dividend payout. This is considered a negative for the stock price. When investors value a company, they analyze the level of its profits and dividends. The reason is obvious: A company's total return includes the dividend payout and capital appreciation. For example, if a company's share price increases 10%, and it has a 5% dividend payout, the total annual return will be 15%.

Price Rise Mechanism

When demand for a stock increases, its price is bid up as buyers place buy orders for it. (Similarly, when supply increases and sellers outnumber buyers, the price decreases.) The mechanics of how a price rise works is quite simple: If there are more buyers than sellers, the *ask price* (the lowest price at which someone is willing to sell) will rise. This will raise the bid price. However, if an insufficient number of sellers are enticed to sell, the ask price will rise even more. This process will continue until enough sellers come in to fill all the buy orders and cause equilibrium to be achieved.

As the ask price rises, in this process of trying to reach equilibrium between buy and sell orders, another factor can come into play. Limit sell orders, which are standing *limit orders* from potential sellers to sell at a prespecified price, can kick in. When the ask price rises to the sell order limit price, more sellers are brought in automatically. This happens because the acceptable selling price for such investors is reached and, consequently, their limit orders get executed.

How Stocks Are Affected by Return on Equity

Return on Equity (ROE)

The return obtained on the *book value* of a company's shares is called *return on equity (ROE)*. It is a measure of the return that a company's management is able to earn on the money entrusted to it by its shareholders.

$$\text{ROE} = \textit{Net income earned}/\textit{Shareholders' equity}$$

where Shareholders' equity = *Common stock* + Preferred stock +
Paid-in capital + *Retained earnings*

Simply stated, ROE measures the return generated for each invested dollar. For example, a 12% ROE means that for each $100 invested in the company, the return was $12. From a shareholder's view, ROE is a key return on investment ratio.

Return on equity is also a measure of how fast a company can grow without having to seek additional sources of capital. A high ROE causes the net worth of a business to expand rapidly. In general, a ROE less than 10% is considered unsatisfactory. For a small growth company with good prospects, a ROE of at least 15% is desired. Such a company may have a ROE as high as 40% to 50% for a few years. In 1997, the average ROE for the S&P 500 stocks was estimated to be 17.24.[1]

Relating ROE to a Stock's Price Performance

When a company earns a profit, most of it goes into its retained earnings. These plowed-back profits increase the book value which, being related to its stock price, causes the stock price to rise and rewards shareholders. Usually, a company's stock price is higher than its book value, which is the amount that would be generated if all the company's tangible *assets* were liquidated.

Shareholders of companies generating high ROE have been handsomely rewarded by the stock market. For example, Microsoft's ROE has consistently ranged between 30% and 40%, while its earnings growth has been about 25%. Another standout example is Intel. Its ROE increased from 16.9% to 30.9% over a six-year period (1989–1995). The prices of both stocks appreciated manyfold during this period—as well as in subsequent years.

---

[1]*Investor's Business Daily*, March 30, 1998.

For several decades, the ROE for U.S. companies has shown an upward trend. Since the 1950s, when the ROE was about 10% for the S&P, it has been rising steadily. By 1995, ROE had improved to 17%. This rise is attributed to the heavy use of technology for reducing costs, *profit margin* improvement, and increased productivity. With improving efficiency in the use of stockholder investment dollars, the stock market can expect to continue receiving more inflow of money and, consequently, move higher in the long term.

The Bullish Case for Stocks

The overall trend of the stock market, especially since the 1980s, is up, as shown in Figure 1.1. There is no reason to believe that returns from stocks in the next couple of decades are going to deteriorate. Over the long term, stocks will continue to be the most viable means of accumulating wealth and should remain the core holding of most *portfolios*.

Why the Stock Market Should Move Considerably Higher

Boomer Factor

The long-term trend for the stock market appears to be very *bullish* (i.e., price expected to rise). There are a number of factors leading to this conclusion. One of the most important is the baby boomer factor. There is a growing realization by baby boomers, as well as today's younger genera-

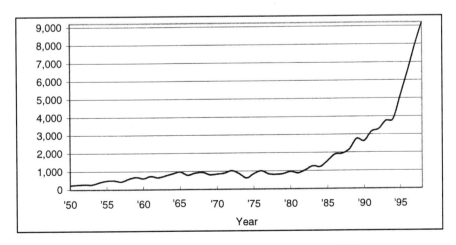

Figure 1.1   **Historical Performance of the DJIA: 1950–1998**

tion, that Social Security may not provide the safety and retirement income that Americans had come to expect. Also, baby boomers are transitioning from the spending to the savings (investment) phase of their lives. They realize that their greater longevity will boost their need for stocks—the best capital growth vehicle. They are also aware that stocks outperform *bonds* and cash in the long term. Hence, baby boomers are expected to pour huge amounts of dollars into the stock market in the next two decades.

The first avalanche of boomer dollars has been one of the pillars of the *bull market* of the 1990s. In 1998, monthly cash inflows into *mutual funds* averaged $13.23 billion. This flood of money is expected to continue flowing for many years to come. Therefore, for the next 20 to 25 years, until the boomers start selling to pay for their retirement, we can expect the stock market to continue its powerful move upward.

Other Bullish Factors

There are a number of other factors that indicate the stock market will remain a good investment in the foreseeable future. These include the following:

- A fundamental change in thinking: Buy-and-borrow mentality of the 1980s has been replaced by moderation and frugality.
- A smaller government, smaller deficit.
- More efficient corporations forced by competitive pressures: Downsizing (lean and mean) mentality is replacing the expansionary philosophy of the 1980s.
- An overall increase in U.S. productivity: ROE in the United States has been trending higher, which makes the stock market more attractive.
- Inflation under control: disinflationary trend has led to lower interest rates, causing returns on alternative investments (CDs, money market funds, and bonds) to be unattractive.
- Global economic boom, which began in the 1980s and is expected to continue well into the twenty-first century:
  More demand for products and services expected in fast growing emerging markets such as China—which has a growing middle class; this will benefit U.S. companies.
  Free market development, and accompanying growth, in the former Communist bloc.

■ A young generation with a different profile:

They are saving more today, about $2,000/year, than the young baby boomer generation did (even though they are making about $2,000 less/year after adjustment for inflation).[2]

Their expectations for what the government will do for them are a lot less.

■ Investing paradigm change: $29.34 billion poured into stock funds in January 1997—more than was contributed in all of 1990[3]; in just the past two years (1997 and 1998), $385.9 billion was invested in stock funds; this continuous inflow into funds must be invested.

Where Stocks are Headed

The most widely used average for monitoring the progress of the stock market is the DJIA. Table 1.1 indicates the years when the stock market, as represented by the DJIA, crossed important psychological barriers.

Long-Term

How much is the DJIA expected to rise? In 1996, when the DJIA was in the 6,000 range, a money manager forecasted a 10,000 DJIA by the year 2000.[4] While that number looked unreal, in actuality it was based on an average annual price appreciation of 18% from 1996 to 2000. If in the next 10 years the DJIA performs as well as it has in the decade prior to 1996, we can expect the DJIA to hit 20,000 by the year 2006.

Table 1.1 The DJIA's Spectacular Rise

Year	DJIA	Year	DJIA
1972 (November 14)	1,001	1997 (February 13)	7,022
1987 (January 8)	2,002	1997 (July 16)	8,036
1991 (April 17)	3,004	1998 (April 7)	9,033
1995 (February 23)	4,003	1999 (March 29)	10,006
1995 (November 21)	5,023	1999 (May 3)	11,014
1996 (October 14)	6,010		

---

[2]*MoneyWorld*, May 1996, p. 4.
[3]*Investor's Business Daily*, February 28, 1997.
[4]Ibid., November 12, 1996.

Using a more conservative appreciation rate, economist Edward Yardeni predicted that the DJIA will rise to 15,000 by the year 2005.[5] Again, while this number seems extremely high, it represents an annual increase of only 9.3%.

Another professional, Don Wolanchuk, forecasts the DJIA advancing to 18,000 by the year 2005.[6] *Timer Digest* has rated him the top timer in 1995, 1991, and 1990. In 1992 and 1993, he was placed second.

Short-Term

It is very difficult for investors, including market professionals, to predict the short-term performance of the stock market. For example, a review of the market forecasts made by 36 market professionals at the end of 1995— of where the DJIA would close at the end of 1996—is very revealing:

▌ Twenty-one predicted a close below 4,900.
▌ Twenty-nine predicted a close below 6,000.
▌ Seven forecast a close of 6,000 or higher.
▌ Only Don Wolanchuk forecast 6,600—which the DJIA reached in-traday on November 26, 1996.

Investors should be aware that a number of factors can significantly affect short-term forecasts. These include higher (or lower) *price/earnings ratio* (*P/E ratio*) or earnings of the DJIA component companies, state of the economy (such as a recession), and turmoil in international markets (such as the Asian economic crisis in 1997).

Who Should Invest in the Stock Market

In general, two classes of people need to invest in stocks. The first group includes those who have already accumulated some money. These people need to protect this capital from the corrosive effect of inflation. The second group primarily includes ordinary working people. These people save money slowly. They need to invest so that their savings will grow over time, while being protected from inflation. Considering that these two groups comprise almost the full spectrum of potential investors, it becomes apparent that most people need to invest in the stock market to achieve financial safety, stability, and independence.

---

[5]Ibid., June 19, 1997.
[6]Ibid., October 22, 1996.

When to Invest in the Stock Market

Timing the Market

Recognizing the Moderating Effect of Time

Investing in the stock market has risks associated with it, especially in the short term. However, time has a moderating effect on stock market risk. As the period for which a stock is held is increased, the chances of losing money are lowered, and the odds of earning a return close to the long-term average are increased. From 1950 to 1997, returns on a one-year investment in stocks have ranged from +83.57% to –25.05% for small stocks, and from +52.62 to –26.47% for large stocks.

However, over a 10-year period, returns for large stocks have varied from 5.9% per year (for the worst 10-year period) to 19.4% per year (for the best 10 years). For small stocks, returns have ranged from 11.5% to 16.9%. Based on these results, it is obvious that stocks should be considered a long-term investment. Both risk and reward should be judged over a period of years—not months or days.

Selection and Timing

There are two critical variables involved in stock market investing: selection and timing. For the long-term investor, selection is a more important factor than timing. On the other hand, timing is more important than selection for the short-term trader with a short investment horizon. A trader, understandably, is always concerned with timing. However, no matter what the investment horizon, every investor must choose a satisfactory combination of these two key variables.

When to Invest

Success in the stock market is not achieved overnight. It needs patience and discipline. For the long-term investor, any time is appropriate to invest regardless of the short-term trend of the market. When it is realized that two-thirds of the time the market goes up, the odds of investing on the way up are greater. However, to be assured of decent profits, an investor must focus on quality companies with strong long-term prospects.

Avoid Missing Powerful Moves

Every bull market has started with a powerful *rally* to the upside. Many investors who miss out on this initial big move wait for a correction (i.e., a market price drop) so that they can enter the market at a lower price. Unfortunately, many times such an anticipated correction does not material-ize. Instead, the market continues to trend higher. Such investors, in ef-fect, try to fight the trend—a losing proposition. Investors need to be aware of the old, but valid Wall Street sayings, "Don't fight the trend" and "The trend is your friend."

Many investors sell out, with the intention of buying back stocks at lower prices, when they think that the market begins to look dicey, overvalued, or overbought. Besides the buy/sell transaction costs in-volved, this timing strategy leaves much to be desired, especially if the market continues its advance. Quite often, the market declines by a small amount before beginning a significant advance. By the time a sold-out investor determines that the rebound is not a temporary bounce, but a solid advance, the market may already have made a sig-nificant move to the upside. Besides missing the solid advance, the in-vestor will also end up paying *commissions* and capital gains taxes generated by the selling.

Many investors trying to time the market miss powerful stock market moves. From April 14 through 22, 1997, the DJIA gained 6.9% in only seven trading days. In just four weeks in April/May 1997, the DJIA rose 15%. Again, in 1998, following a sharp decline, the DJIA rose 27.7% in less than three months.

Investors sitting on the sidelines also missed one of the most powerful moves the market has ever made, which started in November 1994 and continued into late 1995. During the one-year period starting in Novem-ber 1994, the DJIA gained a phenomenal 39%. During calendar year 1995, the DJIA gained 33.45% and the Nasdaq composite gained 39.92%.

Avoid Timing through Dollar Cost Averaging

To avoid timing the market, which is very difficult, *dollar cost averaging* can be used as a viable alternative. This strategy involves buying a fixed dollar amount of stocks at periodic intervals, such as monthly or quarterly, re-gardless of the current price. Since it is assured that the market will gyrate up and down, the dollar cost averaging approach helps eliminate the pos-sibility that all purchases will be made at a high price.

In this strategy, whether the price is high or low, the same amount of money is used to purchase the stock periodically. Therefore, more shares get accumulated at lower prices than at higher prices. When the stock price is low, a greater number of shares are bought, while fewer shares are bought when the price is high. This technique works well for the investor who is:

■ Investing for the long term.

■ Investing in a company with long-term favorable growth prospects.

■ Able to invest relatively large amounts.

The disadvantage of dollar cost averaging is that during bull markets, when money needs to be put in right away, an investor ends up investing rather slowly. However, during weak markets when stocks move up and down, this strategy works quite well. Another disadvantage is that an investor can have relatively fewer funds invested in a growth company when it starts its price appreciation, unless one gets in very early. Also, if a wrong selection is made to start with, the original mistake can be compounded. Finally, due to more transactions taking place, more commissions need to be paid to the *broker*.

Concluding Remarks

Investing in stocks has many advantages, with the most important being capital appreciation and beating inflation. Stocks are the ideal investment vehicle for most ordinary investors to realize superior gains, because returns from stocks are unmatched by other investment alternatives.

A number of very positive factors indicate that the stock market will continue to move higher. Of these, the most important is the baby boomer factor. It will cause large amounts of dollars to be pumped into the stock market for many years to come.

Chapter 2

Stock Classifications

Classification: Why and How

Need for Analysis

A wide variety of companies trade in the stock market. The range of companies includes well-established large companies, medium-sized companies, recently established small companies, and start-ups with few or, in some cases, no products. Investors use many classifications to group these companies in order to analyze and track them.

A company being analyzed for selection, or performance evaluation, should be compared to others in its own group or industry. For example, a fast growing $100-million technology company's performance should be compared to that of a similar-sized company. It may also be compared to an appropriate sector index. For example, it can be compared to the junior growth sector index, whose components are smaller companies of similar size. A small company should not be compared to the DJIA or any of its component companies. The reason is that DJIA companies are well-established companies, generating annual sales in billions of dollars, and any comparison would be equivalent to comparing apples to oranges.

Classification Method Commonly Used

A common way of classifying stocks is through *market capitalization*. Market capitalization is the dollar value obtained by multiplying a company's total number of *outstanding shares* by its stock price. If a company is trading at $20 per share, and it has a total of 1 million outstanding shares, its market capitalization is $20 million. Companies with the largest market capitalization are called large cap, big cap, or blue chip stocks.

No common definition exists, based on market capitalization, on what constitutes small, medium, or large cap stocks. One definition classifies any company with a market cap under $100 million as a small cap stock, while another uses $500 million as the cutoff number for this classification. Typically, a large cap company is defined as one having a capitalization of $1 billion, with a medium cap ranging between $100 million and $1 billion. A small stock is defined by some investors in terms of the stock price being under a certain value—such as $20.

Growth Stocks

What Is a Growth Stock?

A company whose growth rate is appreciably higher than the market average is called a *growth stock*. During a slow economy, such a company continues to perform well because it is less tied to the economic cycle. A growth stock is typically characterized by:

▪ Product or service that is in good demand.
▪ Sufficient profits that can be reinvested for future growth.
▪ Stable or improving profitability trend.
▪ Excellent management.

The increase in profits of a growth company, which rise in tandem with its growth, gets reflected in its share price. A good growth stock generates a high return on *stockholders' equity*. It also provides very good protection against inflation.

Characteristics of Growth Stocks

An investor should analyze the various characteristics of a growth stock prior to buying it. Among the most important characteristics defining a good growth stock are:

▪ Good growth record over the past few years; sustainable future growth.
▪ Growth rate of more than 20%.
▪ If growing at 10–15%, should be ready to accelerate to 25–30%.
▪ Solid *balance sheet*.
▪ Little or no debt.
▪ Leading-edge products; competitive advantage.

- Strong product(s) cycle.
- Future product demand, especially with a single or limited number of products.
- Ability to have pricing flexibility due to good market positioning.
- Financial strength to move into new markets.
- Marketing strength.
- Good management capabilities and depth.

Growth Stocks Benefiting from the Power of Compounding

Growth stock investing highlights the power of compounding, which is underestimated by many investors. They do not realize that a company growing at an annual compound rate of 15% will double in five years. Tripling will occur in just eight years. In 17 years, the company will be 10 times its original size. Consequently, knowledgeable investors buy growth stocks primarily for *capital gains* (i.e., for selling at a profit after holding them for a few years). Growth stocks are intrinsically more profitable than income stocks, and particularly so after tax. However, such stocks are not suitable for all portfolios because of their higher volatility.

Fast growth companies have the potential for both high reward and high risk. Investor expectations for these companies are based on their expectations of increased future profits. If these expectations are met or exceeded, the price appreciation can be significant. However, if expectations are not met, the price drop can be very dramatic and disastrous.

Valuation of Growth Stocks

Growth companies earn a high ROE. They rarely pay out dividends. Most of their *cash flow* is channeled back into the company. This is used for research and development (R&D), leading to the development of new products, expansion into new markets, and so on. A good growth company can often reinvest its own internal cash flow at a 20% or higher rate of return. This results in building the company's value at a fast pace. Reinvestment also has an advantage in that it shields investors from having to pay taxes on dividend payouts. For an investor primarily concerned with income, though, growth stocks are not the appropriate investment vehicle.

Many formulas have been devised to value growth stocks, which are difficult to select and value. In general, they command higher P/E ratios, and lower *yields*, than ordinary stocks. Usually, it is difficult to determine the appropriate P/E for a growth company. Everything else being equal, a company growing at a faster rate should command a higher P/E. Analysts use different criteria to determine the appropriate P/E ratio for a growth company (P/E ratios are explained in detail in Chapter 5).

Risk of Growth Stocks

Growth stocks usually have a shorter performance record, compared to well-established companies, that an investor can evaluate. Therefore, they are more risky. It is not unusual for growth stocks to face occasional set-backs, causing short-term price declines of 20% or more. Initially, the market risk of such companies is high. However, a patient investor with a horizon of four to five years, and good stock selection skills, can obtain tremendous returns with such stocks.

Before investing in growth stocks, one must understand what makes a promising growth company succeed or fail. Also, after a growth stock has been bought, it needs to be closely monitored.

Where to Find Growth Companies

Growth companies can be found in many industries. However, most of them are concentrated in the technology sector, which constitutes about 15% of the U.S. economy and is expected to grow at a 25% annual rate. This sector includes industries such as computers, semiconductors, the Internet, and communications. In the past few years, the groups with the highest revenue growth have been cellular phones, office supplies, local area networks, semiconductor equipment, radio and TV, and computer retailing.

The common factor in the success of companies in these industries is the introduction of new products, in ever shortening product cycles, which have higher profit margins. This is the key ingredient for making their earnings grow rapidly. Such companies spend a large percentage of their *revenues* on R&D—the key for creating new products and, consequently, profits. One of the outstanding stocks of the past two decades, Microsoft, spends 17% of its sales on R&D. This has assured Microsoft of a dominant position in its industry. Eli Lilly and Glaxo Wellcome, very successful drug companies, spend about 15% of their sales on R&D.

Other growth areas are the financial services and health care industries. These areas will benefit from the baby boomers starting to reach their prime saving years and their need, as they move into their middle age and beyond, for more health care.

Where to Invest

Companies riding a theme are mostly, though not always, found in industries growing at an above-average rate. To identify growth industries, one needs to look around and observe trends. The explanation for this is that trend changes affect society for years to come and, consequently, become the key to earning higher profits through companies benefiting from such trends. Once a trend is determined, an investor should pick stocks that are most likely to benefit from that trend.

Benefiting from Themes

It is well known that the economy rides waves of changing lifestyles and innovation. These trends, rather than fads, last for some time, generate growth, and produce stock market leaders. However, these trends are not apparent to most investors for a considerable time. Therefore, one of the most profitable ways to make money in the stock market is to buy a stock that is expected to benefit from a theme, or trend, before most investors become aware of it.

A stock investor who invests in a trend can be reasonably assured of the growth of the industry and, consequently, the company in which the investment has been made. Therefore, every investor should try to identify trends for potential benefit. To ensure exceptional gains, however, one needs to be in early in the theme before it becomes apparent to everyone.

Understanding How a Theme Works

Networking has been one of the more recent themes, still not ended, which has provided tremendous returns to those who invested in it. It is based on increasing productivity—the objective of American corporations in recent years. The driver for this has been the increased competitive environment in which they have been competing globally, and within the United States, in the 1990s.

The networking theme is fairly simple. The first stage of productivity improvement was achieved through the use of personal computers (PCs). To further improve productivity, through the sharing of computer resources, companies started to install networks that linked individual computers. This led to the tremendous growth of networking companies, which provided products that made it possible to link computers at different locations. Also, once the networks were installed, the need for databases (that store data) followed automatically. This led to the tremendous growth of database companies. Investors who correctly read the trend, which has been in existence for over a decade now, and invested in companies like Cisco Systems, 3Com, and Oracle, have been handsomely rewarded.

Future Themes

The following are some trends and concerns that have recently been in vogue and are expected to continue for many more years:

- *Internet*: Dramatic Internet growth has led to new needs and requirements that did not exist just a few years ago. Companies meeting those needs have benefited tremendously. Big winners include America Online (AOL), Netscape, Yahoo, Sun Microsystems, and Cybercash. While hardware and software companies initially benefited due to this phenomenon, we can expect e-commerce leaders to outperform for many years to come.
- *Gene therapy*: With demand for more efficient drugs, at lower costs, expected to continue in tandem with an aging population, this field is expected to see big growth in the years to come. With many companies having invested significant amounts of money in this area in the past decade, this theme is expected to produce many winners in the next decade.
- *High-speed communications*: The demand for information by companies and individuals has grown explosively in the past few years and will continue to do so. Growth will be high both in the United States and overseas. To meet this demand, high-speed communications will be required. Companies in this industry have the potential to be great investments. Ascend Communications and Cisco, innovative companies in this area, have already rewarded their shareholders.
- *Assisted living*: As the baby boomers age in large numbers and live longer, a whole new set of needs will have to be filled. Companies meeting the requirements of an elderly population can be expected to perform quite well in the foreseeable future.
- *Crime, fear, and financial efficiency*: Companies associated with security equipment and services profited handsomely in recent years—which is attributed to the trend for privatization of prisons (financial efficiency) and security concerns arising due to crime and domestic terrorism acts.
- *Computer security*: With computers intruding more and more into our daily lives, and with the growth of Internet commerce, security aspects are increasingly becoming important.

Small Capitalization Stocks

What Is a Small Cap Stock?

The term "small capitalization," or "small cap," refers to small companies with good potential for fast growth in the coming years. Typically, small companies most attractive for investment purpose are those that:

- Offer an innovative new product or service.
- Have captured a niche market.

A subgroup within the small capitalization stocks is "microcap" stocks. Different definitions are used for this classification. For example, one fund manager defines it as the smallest 5% of the stock market. Market Guide classifies a company as a microcap if its market cap is below $300 million. According to this definition, there were 6,481 microcaps (in its database of 9,199 stocks) in April 1999. Small cap stocks, ranging in market cap between $300 million and $1 billion, numbered 1,276—while mid cap stocks (between $1 billion and $5 billion) numbered only 909.

Volatility and Cyclical Performance

In the long run, small cap stocks have produced higher returns than large cap issues. However, in the short term, they can be quite volatile and are characterized by large price swings. It has been observed that small cap stocks generally run in cycles of five to seven years. During this period, they outperform the big cap stocks. Factors that help small stocks outperform include a slowing (or sluggish) economy and a stronger dollar. The ability of small companies to continue strong earnings growth during a slow economy, or recession, makes them more valuable during such periods.

Small stocks outperformed the overall market from 1974 to 1983, when they started to underperform. This continued until early 1991 when they again started outperforming. As can be expected, the upward move from 1974 to 1983 was not straight up. During this period, there were four corrections averaging about 21%. Again, small cap stocks, as measured by the S&P 600 small cap index, rose from 1991 until early 1994. For most of 1994, they were down until they resumed their upward move later in the year. By mid-1995, the S&P small cap index had reached an all-time high as the small caps outperformed the large cap stocks. Since 1996, despite forecasts to the contrary, small stocks have underperformed compared to large cap stocks.

Factors Favoring Small Stocks

Some of the factors expected to fuel the growth and prices of small cap companies are:

- Earnings growth
- Undiscovered companies—industries of the future
- Attractive valuations
- Steadily growing economy
- Stable and low interest rates
- Strengthening of the U.S. dollar
- Political/tax reform

Comparison to Other Investments

For an investor who is not seeking dividend income, small caps can be a relatively attractive and profitable investment compared to large cap stocks. This is based on the historical performance of small stocks. For example, a dollar invested in large cap stocks grew to $1,828 from 1925 to 1997. This is considerably less than the growth achieved, during the same period, by small company stocks that grew to $5,519. Comparisons of historical returns for 10-year periods are shown in Table 2.1.

Table 2.1   **Relative Performance of Investments versus Inflation**

Period	Annual Rates of Return per Decade (Compounded)				
	Large stocks	*Small stocks*	*Long-term bonds*	*Treasury bills*	*Inflation*
1920s[1]	19.2	−4.5	5.0	3.7	−1.1
1930s	−0.1	1.4	4.9	0.6	−2.0
1940s	9.2	20.7	3.2	0.4	5.4
1950s	19.4	16.9	−0.1	1.9	2.2
1960s	7.8	15.5	1.4	3.9	2.5
1970s	5.9	11.5	5.5	6.3	7.4
1980s	17.5	15.8	12.6	8.9	5.1
1990s[2]	16.6	16.5	10.7	5.0	3.1
1988–1997	18.0	16.5	11.3	5.4	3.4

[1]For the period 1926–1929.
[2]For the period 1990–1997.
Source: Ibbotson Associates.

Risk of Small Stocks

Small cap stocks, individually and as a group, tend to be risky. The failure rate among small and emerging companies is disproportionately high. However, they also have the potential for superior rewards. They are leaders in a slow growth environment, when profits are harder to come by, due to their ability to produce earnings at a higher rate than large cap stocks. However, while it is easy to say that small cap stocks outperform, it is not as easy to choose specific stocks that will appreciate in price significantly.

Compared to any large cap stock, a typical small cap stock will have only a few analysts following it. The average small cap stock has only four analysts following it and only two for microcap stocks. This compares to 22 analysts for large capitalization stocks and 10 for mid cap stocks.[1]

In many cases, a company may not be followed by any reputable analyst. Therefore, if no or only a few analysts follow a company and project its earnings, there is a higher level of uncertainty and investment risk due to potentially unexpected, and unpleasant, surprises. However, if such a company reports a positive earnings surprise, the news can propel it to a higher price level in a very short period.

Other Stock Classifications

Blue Chip Stocks

A blue chip company, according to one definition, either has a market capitalization of $1 billion, or it has a market capitalization of at least $200 million and its stock is included in either the DJIA or the S&P 500.

Blue chip companies are well-established companies with solid earnings, regular dividends, and a record of good price performance. These high-priced stocks are less risky. However, their potential for price appreciation is limited. Since these companies are very large, typically with billion-dollar *sales*, they are not expected to grow at the same rate as small and nimble companies. Such companies try to maintain market share rather than emphasize growth. When the overall market performs poorly, blue chips fall by a smaller percentage compared to small stocks. Companies like International Business Machines (IBM), Exxon, and General Electric (GE) are in this category.

---

[1]*Investor's Business Daily*, January 22, 1997.

Cyclical Stocks

A cyclical stock is one whose earnings are very sensitive to the performance of the economy and the business cycle. Companies in this category include Caterpillar, United Airlines, and International Paper. During an economic expansion, when the economy is growing, the earnings of such companies improve. However, during an economic contraction, earnings at these companies decrease significantly. Consequently, when the economy is slowing, investors move to small companies that can expand, and outearn, larger cyclical companies. Therefore, cyclical stocks have been losers, in the past, when economic growth slowed.

Generally, cyclical stocks have benefited the most during economic rebounds. During recessions, cyclical stocks such as paper, autos, and chemicals perform poorly. However, as the economy improves, their performance also improves. Capital goods companies perform well in the mid to late expansion cycle. This happens because demand for capital goods follows an economic recovery after a fairly delayed period. Consequently, such companies reach their peak when the business cycle is mature.

Defensive Stocks

The revenues and profits of some companies are not dependent, to any significant degree, on the economic cycle. Therefore, when the economy slows down or slides into a recession, investors flock to these companies—which are better known as defensive stocks. Such companies, typically in the energy and food industries, are characterized by slow but steady growth. Companies in this group include Exxon, McDonald's, and Archer-Daniels-Midland (ADM).

When the ability of companies to continue generating profits becomes questionable, especially when the economy starts to slow down, investors rotate to defensive stocks. If such companies start to perform strongly when the economy is strong, it indicates potential problems for the economy and the stock market in the not too distant future.

Value Stocks

These are stocks of companies that currently are not performing well. They are the targets of investors seeking stocks that are fundamentally sound but are trading at less than their intrinsic value. These beaten down shares reflect the pessimism of the investor community regarding the company's prospects—at least for the near term. For a value stock, investors already expect bad news in the future. Therefore, any unanticipated positive news or development can make the stock price rise considerably.

Concept Stocks

This refers to companies that are characterized by supergrowth. A "concept stock" company will typically be small and unknown, at the moment, to the investment community at large. It will typically be reaching a mass market with a breakthrough, or blockbuster, product or service. Consequently, it may be able to generate returns of immense proportions. Achieving returns of two to one, four to one, or ten to one are possible with such a company.

Penny Stocks

A *penny stock* is a low-priced stock, generally selling for under $1 per share. The risk associated with penny stocks is extremely high and, therefore, investors should avoid them.

Concluding Remarks

For superior returns, investors should focus on growth companies, which are characterized by an above-average growth rate. Such stocks have superior capital appreciation potential. For achieving success in the stock market, learn to recognize the characteristics of growth stocks.

Pick stocks that are part of a theme or trend. Themes last for some time, generate growth, and produce stock market leaders. Theme companies are typically found in industries growing at an above-average rate. To identify growth industries, just look around and observe trends. Be smart and learn to differentiate between fads and trends. Fads have a short life, while trends last for many years.

Small capitalization stocks should be favored over large capitalization or blue chip stocks—whose fastest growth period is history. Do not screen out small stocks just because they are characterized by higher short-term volatility. To minimize risk, favor companies that are currently profitable and have been so for the past three to five years. Stay away from speculative stocks.

Chapter 3

Stock Research Sources

Introduction to Stock Investing Research

The Equalizer

For individual investors, the investment horizon has changed tremendously in the past 10 to 15 years. Two decades ago, an individual investor had very few tools available for undertaking serious investment research. In the past, while a dedicated investor could perform in-depth research, its utility was limited due to the delay in collecting and analyzing information. Today, investors have access to a host of tools that have placed them on an almost equal footing with professional investors. The catalysts for this change have been:

- The personal computer.
- Easy access to investment material through the Internet and online services.
- Inexpensive and easy-to-use investment software packages.

What Can Be Researched

Using powerful software tools, an individual investor can collect current and historical data within hours if not minutes. For example, it is possible to obtain the following data for any listed stock, as well as other important investment information, within minutes:

- Price and volume data (for a day, week, year, 10 years, or more).
- Earnings of a company (at the very moment the news is released).
- Earnings estimates made by independent analysts (for the next quarter, next year, or even the next three to five years).

■ Company research reports prepared by analysts.
■ Company financial statements.
■ Insider buying and selling activity.

This chapter introduces investors to various investment sources for researching and monitoring individual stocks, overall stock market, economy, business environment, and other factors that can affect the stock market as well as individual stock prices. Since there are so many sources to choose from, selecting the right source(s) to start with can become a very confusing task for new investors. For such investors, it is advisable to start from the list contained in the "Concluding Remarks" section of this chapter.

The information contained in this chapter is not all-inclusive. Investors can be assured that new and innovative research sources, especially on the Internet, will continue to be introduced.

Newspapers and Business Publications

Investor's Business Daily (IBD)

This is an excellent newspaper, focusing primarily on individual stocks and the stock market. It is published five times a week—Monday through Friday. It contains a wealth of stock market, bond market, and mutual funds data, as well as business and economic data. It also contains excellent analysis of market behavior. Provided are features on individual companies, trends, computers and automation, and so on, and useful lessons for investors interested in learning more about how the stock market works. The IBD is a tool that every investor can use.

The Wall Street Journal (WSJ)

This is one of the best sources for keeping investors informed about overall business conditions, the economy, and factors affecting the stock market. It also provides stock market data, though not as extensively as the IBD, and market analysis. A regular reader of the WSJ will always remain well informed about various factors that directly, or indirectly, affect the stock market and the economy.

Trade Newspapers/Journals

Trade publications of various industries and sectors can be tapped for obtaining useful investing information. These publications can provide useful insight into business conditions and industry trends. They can also be a source for technical reviews, identifying companies that are performing well, and monitoring the competition. Quite often, new companies with potential promise, or new products, are mentioned/reviewed in these publications. Therefore, an astute investor can become aware of new products/trends shaping up at an early stage.

Business Publications

Among the well-known publications in this category are *Barron's*, *Forbes*, *Fortune*, *Business Week*, *Money*, and the *Individual Investor*. Using these, an ordinary investor can gain useful insight into the economy, the stock market, and individual stocks. Investors can use these publications to identify promising stocks. These stocks can then be subjected to more rigorous analysis prior to procurement.

Barron's is a weekly publication that provides useful information covering various aspects of the stock market including specific information about individual stocks. It contains a wealth of statistical data. It also carries detailed interviews with market analysts and money managers. *Barron's* and *Forbes* are focused more toward investors who want to buy stocks, rather than limit themselves to mutual funds. *Forbes* and *Fortune* are published biweekly. *Business Week* is published weekly, while the *Individual Investor* and *Money* magazine are published monthly. These publications also have web sites (see Table 3.1).

Information Highway and Electronic Sources

The Internet: World Wide Web (WWW)

Investors can now use cyberspace for stock market research. A number of web sites offer free investment research material (see Table 3.2). Information available includes stock *quotes*, company research reports, company

Table 3.1   **Internet Addresses for Business Magazines**

Barron's	http://www.barrons.com
Business Week	http://www.businessweek.com
Forbes	http://www.forbes.com
Fortune	http://www.pathfinder.com/fortune
Individual Investor	http://www.iionline.com
Money	http://www.pathfinder.com/money

Table 3.2 **Internet Sources for Stock Investing Information**

Barron's	http://www.barrons.com
Bloomberg Personal	http://www.bloomberg.com
Charles Schwab & Co.	http://www.schwab.com
The Closing Bell	http://www.merc.com/cbell2.html
CNN	http://www.cnnfn.com
Dataquest	http://www.dataquest.com
Daytraders Online	http://www.daytraders.com/
Economic reports	http://www.stls.frb.org
EDGAR	http://edgaronline.com
Fidelity Investments	http://www.fid-inv.com
Ford Investor Services, Inc.	http://pawws.com/Ford_phtml
The Hulbert Financial Digest	http://www.hulbertdigest.com
Individual Investor (Online)	http://www.iionline.com/
Intuit	http://www.investorinsight.com
Invest-O-Rama	http://www.investorama.com
Investors Alliance	http://www.freequote.com
INVESTools	http://www.investools.com
J.P. Morgan Risk Metrics	http://www.jpmorgan.com
Market Guide	http://www.marketguide.com
Market Technicians Association	http://www.mta-usa.org/~lensmith
Merrill Lynch & Co.	http://www.merrill-lynch.com
Moody's Investors Service	http://www.moodys.com
Money Pages	http://www.moneypages.com
MSN Investor	http://www.investor.msn.com
Ohio State Univ. Department of Finance	http://www.cob.ohio-state.edu
Online Intelligence	http://www.ozsoft.com
Onramp Access Stocks and Commodities	http://www.onr.com/stocks.html
Pathfinder	http://www.pathfinder.com
The Red Chip Review	http://www.redchip.com
Research Wizard	http://www.reswizard.com
Schwab Select	http://www.schwabselect.com
SchwabNow	http://www.schwab.com
SEC's EDGAR Database of Corporate Information	http://www.sec.gov/edgarhp.htm
SmallCap Investor	http://www.financialweb.com
Standard & Poor's	http://www.stockinfo.standardpoor.com
TradeAlert	http://tradealert.com
Trading.com	http://www.tradingday.com/
Wall Street Journal Money & Investing Update	http://update.wsj.com
Whole Internet Catalog Personal Finance Page	http://www.users.interport.net/ ~gerlach/invest.html
Yahoo!	http://quote.yahoo.com
Zacks Investment Research	http://www.zacks.com

news, earnings news, stock screening and analysis tools, summary of recommendations, investment letters, market summary, investment conferences, historical data, and so on.

The sources in Table 3.3 provide very diverse and comprehensive data and information including quotes, news, charting, stock screening programs, company research reports, general investing information, trading, economic data, and so on. Table 3.4 lists web sites where an investor can place trades.

Online Services

Using commercial online services, investors can obtain quotes, download historical price data, track portfolios, obtain market or company news, trade stocks, conduct research on companies, chat with other investors, scan bulletin boards, and so forth.

America Online (AOL) provides access to a large number of investment sources. Company news, earnings data, company profiles, financial information, and other valuable investment data can be accessed through this service. Useful sources accessible through AOL include Market

Table 3.3 **Internet Sources for Quotes and News**

American Stock Exchange	http://www.amex.com
APL Quote Server	http://www.secapl.com
Bloomberg Personal	http://www.bloomberg.com
Charles Schwab & Co.	http://www.schwab.com
Data Broadcasting	http://www.dbc.com
Market Edge	http://www.marketedge.com
MSN Investor	http://www.investor.msn.com
Nasdaq	http://www.nasdaq.com
North American Quotations	http://www.naq.com
NYSE	http://www.nyse.com
Paragon Software	http://www.interquote.com
PC Quote	http://www.pcquote.com
PRNewswire	http://www.prnewswire.com
Quote.com	http://www.quote.com
Standard & Poor's	http://www.spcomstock.com
Telescan	http://telescan.com
Tradingday.com	http://www.tradingday.com/
Wall Street City	http://www.wallstreetcity.com
World Wide Quote	http://www.wwquote.com
Yahoo!	http://quote.yahoo.com

Table 3.4   Internet Trading Sites

AccuTrade	http://www.accutrade.com	(800) 858-0386
American Express Financial Direct	http://www.americanexpress .com/direct	(800) 658-4677
Ameritrade	http://www.ameritrade.com	(800) 454-9272
Aufhauser & Co.	http://www.aufhauser.com	(800) 368-3668
Ceres Securities	http://www.ceres.com	(800) 669-3900
Commandline PC	http://www.regaldiscount.com	(800) 786-9000
Computel Securities	http://www.rapidtrade.com	(800) 432-0327
Datek	http://www.datek.com	(212) 514-7531
eBroker	http://www.ebroker.com	(800) 553-9513
Empire Financial Group	http://www.lowfees.com	(800) 900-8101
e.Schwab	http://www.eschwab.com	(800) 362-6789
E*Trade	http://www.etrade.com	(800) 786-2575
Fidelity Investments	http://personal.fidelity.com/	(800) 544-8666
Gruntal & Co.	http://www.gruntal.com	(800) 223-6813
J. B. Oxford	http://www.jboxford.com	(800) 500-5007
Jack White & Company	http://pawws.secapl.com/jwc	(800) 753-1700
Lombard Brokerage	http://www.lombard.com	(800) 566-2273
Montgomery Securities	http://www.montgomery.com	(800) 227-4786
National Discount Brokers	http://pawws.secapl.com/ndb	(800) 417-7423
Net Investor	http://www.netinvestor.com	(800) 638-4250
Pacific Brokerage Services Inc.	http://www.tradepbs.com	(800) 416-7113
PC Financial Network	http://www.pcfn.com	(800) 237-PCFN
PC Online Investment Center	http://www.bullbear.com	(800) 262-5800
Piper Jaffray	http://www.piperjaffray.com	(800) 333-6000
Quickway	http://www.quick-reilly.com	(800) 672-7220
Schwab Online	http://www.schwab.com	(800) 540-0667
Siebert Online	http://www.msiebert.com	(212) 644-2400
Smith Barney	http://www.smithbarney.com	(800) EARNS-IT
Wall Street Access for Windows	http://www.wsaccess.com	(800) 487-2339
WallStreet Electronica	http://www.wallstreet.com	(212) 213-8743
Webbroker	http://www.waterhouse.com	(800) 934-4134

Guide, First Call Corporation, and Zacks Investment Research—all of whom provide earnings estimates.

The Strategic Investor is an investment source accessible through Prodigy. It provides detailed company reports on more than 5,000 companies. It also enables stock screening using different investment models. Data provided includes consensus earnings estimates, company-to-company comparisons, and historical financial and pricing data.

Bulletin Boards

There are a number of bulletin boards and newsgroups on the Internet and the online services that one can use for stock research and exchanging information/ideas with other investors. Some popular sites that can be accessed on the Internet are:

- Silicon Investor: http://www.techstocks.com
- StockClub: http://www.stockclub.com
- StockChat: http://www.stockchat.com

The popular sites on the three major online services are Motley Fool (AOL), MoneyTalk (Prodigy), and Investor's Forum (CompuServe).

Broadcast Media

CNBC Cable Television Channel

This cable TV station provides business news and in-depth stock market coverage. It provides very useful investment information and analysis including:

- Financial and business news.
- Stock quotes.
- Interviews with investment professionals, analysts, and senior company executives.
- Economic data.
- Bond market data.
- Market highlights.
- Information about individual stocks making the news on a particular day.
- Other related investment information.

Channel and subscription information can be obtained from (800) 800-CNBC or (800) SMART-TV.

TV and Radio Talk Shows

A widely watched TV financial program is *Wall Street Week* with Louis Rukeyser. This talk show is broadcast, nationwide, on Friday evenings. It is a good source of general information, review, and outlook for the stock market. A number of well-known money managers appear on this show. At times, they provide very useful insight to novice investors.

The weekly *Bob Brinker Money Talk* is a two-hour talk show that can be reached at (800) 934-2221. It is aired nationwide and is an excellent starting point for all types of investors, including stock investors. The program has a web page at http://www.bobbrinker.com.

Some local radio stations provide in-depth reporting of daily stock market action and highlights. One such station is Money Radio in Southern California, which can be contacted at (800) 365-5669. The *Adrienne Berg Show*, on WABC 77 in New York, is another program that potential stock market investors will find useful.

Investment Newsletters and Publications

What Is Available

There are scores of investment advisory newsletters that are published periodically (Table 3.5). Their annual subscription rates range from about $30 to hundreds of dollars. However, most subscriptions are in the $150–$200 per year range. These newsletters reflect a variety of opinions, differing sentiments (*bulls* and *bears*) and investment strategies. They cater to a variety of investment needs ranging from the conservative to the speculative. Most of them analyze, in various depths, the current state of the economy and the stock market. Many also make specific stock recommendations. Some indicate a specific buy and sell price range for individual stocks. In general, if a stock appears in multiple newsletters as a recommendation, it should be considered a good candidate for further investigation.

Obtaining Newsletters

An investor should never buy any investment advisory newsletter without first obtaining a sample issue. Most newsletters provide one or two free issues, if requested. Always ask for an old issue, six to nine months in the past. Analyzing a dated issue can indicate the newsletter's stock market forecasting accuracy and also how its recommended stocks performed. It also pays to check an investment newsletter's performance as rated by the *Hulbert Financial Digest* (HFD), which is available in most libraries, or by the *Timer's Digest*. Some public libraries also subscribe to selected investment newsletters, with the most common one being the *Value Line Investment Survey*.

Table 3.5 Investment Advisory Newsletters

Newsletter	Phone number	Address
Argus Research	(212) 425-7500	17 Battery Place, Suite 1800, New York, NY 10004
Bert Dohmen's Wellington Letter	(808) 545-2243	66 Queen Street, Suite 3801, Honolulu, HI 96813
Blue Chip Advisor	(800) 237-8400	107 Edinburgh South, Suite 207, Cary, NC 27511
Breakthrough Stocks	(800) 832-2330	P.O. Box 4106, McLean, VA 22103
The Cabot Market Letter	(800) 777-2658	176 North Street, P.O. Box 3067, Salem, MA 01970
California Tech Stock Letter	(415) 726-8495	P.O. Box 308, Half Moon Bay, CA 94109
The Chartist	(310) 596-2385	P.O. Box 758, Seal Beach, CA 90740
The Cutting Edge	(800) 433-1528	1217 St. Paul Street, Baltimore, MD 21202
Dick Davis Digest	(800) 422-9299	P.O. Box 9547, Ft. Lauderdale, FL 33310-9547
Dow Theory Forecasts	(219) 931-6480	7412 Calumet Ave., Hammond, IN 46324
Dow Theory Letters	(619) 454-0481	P.O. Box 1759, La Jolla, CA 92038
The Garzarelli Outlook	(800) 804-0938	7811 Montrose Road, Potomac, MD 20854
Ground Floor	(800) 477-3400	Six Deer Trail, Old Tappan, NJ 07675
Growth Stock Outlook	(301) 654-5205	P.O. Box 15381, Chevy Chase, MD 20825
Growth Stock Winners	(800) 832-2330	1750 Old Meadow Road, McLean, VA 22102
The Hulbert Financial Digest	(703) 683-5905	316 Commerce Street, Alexandria, VA 22314
Informed Investor	(800) 723-2400	24040 Camino Del Avion, Monarch Beach, CA 92629
Inside Track	(800) 211-6361	P.O. Box 60019, Potomac, MD 20897-5958
The Insiders	(800) 442-9000	3471 N. Federal Highway, Ft. Lauderdale, FL 33306
Investech Market Analyst	(406) 862-7777	2472 Birch Glen, Whitefish, MT 59937
Investment Quality Trends	(619) 459-3818	7440 Girard Ave., Suite 4, La Jolla, CA 92037
Investor's Digest	(800) 442-9000	2200 SW 10th Street, Deerfield Beach, FL 33442

(Continued)

Table 3.5 Continued

Newsletter	Phone number	Address
Market Logic	(800) 442-9000	3471 N. Federal Highway, Ft. Lauderdale, FL 33306
Marketimer	(914) 591-2655	P.O. Box 229, Irvington, NY 10533
New Analysis Highlights	(603) 647-4870	P.O. Box 10718, Bedford, NH 03110-0718
The Next SuperStock	(301) 215-6341	15779 Columbia Pike, Burtonsville, MD 20866
Oberweis Report	(708) 897-7100	841 North Lake Street, Aurora, IL 60506
OTC Growth Stock Watch	(617) 444-6100	1040 Great Plain Ave., Suite 2, Needham, MA 02192
OTC Insight	(510) 274-5037	P.O. Box 5759, Walnut Creek, CA 94596
Professional Tape Reader	(800) 868-7857	P.O. Box 2407, Hollywood, FL 33022
Prudent Speculator	(213) 315-9888	P.O. Box 1767, Santa Monica, CA 90406
The Pure Fundamentalist	(708) 945-4700	P.O. Box 7084, Deerfield, IL 60015
S.A. Advisory	(801) 272-4761	2274 Arbor Lane #3, Salt Lake City, UT 84117
Shortex	(800) 877-6555	6669 Security Blvd., #103, Baltimore, MD 21207
Small Stock Detective	(800) 832-2330	P.O. Box 4106, McLean, VA 22103
Smart Money	(800) 477-3400	Six Deer Trail, Old Tappan, NJ 07675
Stanton's Market Strategy	(201) 794-1879	23-00 Route 208, Fair Lawn, NJ 07410
Strategic Investing	(617) 332-3323	1905 Beacon Street, Waban, MA 02168
Timer's Digest	(203) 629-3503	P.O. Box 1688, Greenwich, CT 06836
The Value Line Investment Survey	(800) 833-0046	P.O. Box 3988, New York, NY 10008-3988
Wall Street Digest	(813) 954-5500	One Sarasota Tower, Sarasota, FL 34236
Young's Intelligence Report	(800) 848-2132	98 William Street, Newport, RI 02840
Zweig Forecast	(800) 633-2252	P.O. Box 2900, Wantagh, N.Y. 11793

It is also possible to get a five-month subscription to four or five selected newsletters, of your choice, for only $69 in a special deal. This offer, which includes a choice from among scores of newsletters, is often advertised in the *IBD* by the Select Information Exchange (SIE), which can be contacted at (212) 247-7123 or (800) 743-9346.

Evaluating Newsletters

A newsletter should be reviewed prior to ordering to determine if it fits the investor's objective and strategy. The investor's goals, risk tolerance, and market philosophy should match that of the newsletter. If there is disagreement with a newsletter's philosophy, one cannot be expected to agree with its stock recommendations. Therefore, an aggressive growth investor should not subscribe to a newsletter that tracks only big cap stocks or has a value-based approach.

For making a decision regarding a newsletter subscription, an evaluation should be undertaken with the same seriousness that is required for purchasing a stock. Also, one should be selective and subscribe to only one or two newsletters. There is no point in getting repetitious, and expensive, reads on the economy and the stock market. Finally, realize that no advice can substitute for one's own good judgment.

Comparing Newsletters

The monthly *HFD* reports on how much an investor would have gained, or lost, if the various investment newsletters' recommendations had been followed. According to the *HFD*, the top five newsletters for the five-year period through November 30, 1998, on a total return ranking (not adjusted for risk), were:

1. The *Prudent Speculator* (29.4%)
2. *OTC Insight* (20.7%)
3. *Fundline* (19.6%)
4. *Timer's Digest* (19.4%)
5. The *Insiders* (19.2%)

The newsletters with the best record for the past 15-year period, according to the *HFD*, are:

1. The *Chartist* (16.9%)
2. The *Prudent Speculator* (14.1%)
3. *Investor's World* (13.8%)

It should be noted that many respected professionals in the financial newsletter business disagree with the results presented by the *HFD*. The reason is that some newsletters ranked high by the *Timer's Digest* are ranked lower by the *HFD*. This can be attributed to the different ranking methods used by the *HFD* and *Timer's Digest*. Since it is difficult for an investor to determine which ranking is more valid (because only the *Timer's Digest* makes available the basis for its calculations), these rankings should be used with caution. Rankings alone should not be used for making decisions. Instead, any selection should be based on an actual evaluation of the newsletter.

Company Research and Earnings Estimate Reports

Company research reports and earnings estimate reports are the most important sources of investment research material for an individual investor. (See Table 3.6.) The reports prepared by investment research firms are easily available to any investor for a small fee. However, the circulation of reports published by *brokerage* companies, based on research done by their own research departments, is usually limited to their own clients.

A company research report provided to an investor by a broker is typically a package of individual reports from different sources. For example, the company research report provided by Charles Schwab & Co. to its clients includes individual reports from Standard & Poor's Corporation (stock report), First Call Corporation (earnings estimate report), Vickers (insider trading), Argus Research (stock report), and Business

Table 3.6   **Internet Sources for Earnings Estimates**

Analyst Center	http://www.schwab.com
First Call	http://www.firstcall.com
IBES	http://www.ibes.com
Individual Investor Online	http://www.iionline.com/
INVESTools	http://www.tabula.com/
Market Guide	http://www.marketguide.com
MSN Investor	http://www.investor.msn.com
Nelson's	http://www.irnet.com/pages/Nelson.stm
Research Wizard	http://www.reswizard.com
SchwabNow	http://www.schwabselect.com
Standard & Poor's	http://www.stockinfo.standardpoor.com
Yahoo!	http://quote.yahoo.com
Zacks	http://aw.zacks.com

Wire (news stories). The cost of the complete package is under $6. Each of these individual reports can also be obtained directly from the issuing source.

Zacks Investment Research is a good resource for investors desirous of getting the latest research information on a company. It provides a list of brokers whose research departments have produced a research report, in the last 120 days, on a specific company. Another good source is Market Guide, whose key products are based on a proprietary database. Market Guide provides company reports, flexible and customized reporting for more than 10,000 companies, and earnings estimates. Another source for quickly obtaining earnings estimates is CNBC: (900) 225-CNBC.

The following are useful sources of company research and earnings estimate reports for investors:

- The *Value Line Investment Survey*
- First Call Corporation (only earnings estimates)
- Standard & Poor's Corporation
- Zacks Investment Research
- Yahoo! web site (http://quote.yahoo.com)
- Multex.com
- Institutional Broker Estimate Service (IBES)

The *Value Line Investment Survey*

The *Value Line Investment Survey* reports, available in most libraries, provide a wealth of data on about 1,700 individual stocks. Each company report contains data on its historical and recent earnings, price history, price momentum, and risk. It also provides company and industry analysis (Appendix A).

Value Line surveys include two important measurements: Timeliness Rank and Safety Rank. The timeliness measurement focuses on a stock's expected price performance, relative to the overall market, in the next 12 months. Timeliness is rated on a scale of 1 to 5. The timeliness of each stock indicates how it is expected to perform over the next 12 months. Stocks ranked 1 (highest) or 2 (above average) are expected to outperform the market. Those ranked 4 or 5 are expected to underperform the market over the next year. Safety ranking, also on a scale of 1 to 5, indicates price stability. It quantifies the potential risk associated with a specific stock.

The *Value Line Investment Survey* provides additional information such as:

■ Best- and worst-performing stocks in the past quarter.
■ Stocks with the highest price appreciation prospects for the next three to five years.
■ Stocks with the highest, and lowest, P/E ratios.
■ Stocks with the highest return on capital.

Contact information:
Value Line Investment Survey
P.O. Box 3988
New York, NY 10008-3988
(800) 833-0046; (212) 907-1500

First Call Corporation

First Call issues individual company earnings estimate reports that contain extremely useful information for investors. These reports include data pertaining to consensus analysts' recommendations (buy/hold/sell), fiscal year earnings estimates, current quarter earnings estimates, as well as estimate revisions (Appendix B). The First Call earnings estimate report is typically included in the company research report package provided by many brokers to their clients.

Contact information:
First Call Corporation
22 Pittsburgh Street
Boston, MA 02210
http://www.firstcall.com
(617) 856-2459

Standard & Poor's (S&P) Corporation

The S&P Corporation publishes a number of company research reports. The most widely disseminated report, which individual investors should focus on, is the S&P Stock Report shown in Appendix C. This report includes the company's business summary, earnings, financial performance, and historical data. It can be ordered directly from S&P Corporation. Most brokers, as part of their service, also provide it to their clients for a small fee.

The *Outlook* is an S&P newsletter, available in most public libraries, which analyzes the market, trends, and individual stocks. It also includes a forecast of where the market is headed. The *Outlook* evaluates individual stocks, taking into consideration both investment goals and risks. It includes stock lists that rate the best- and worst-performing stocks and stock groups. It also issues buy, hold, and sell recommendations. To rank the immediate price appreciation potential of stocks, it uses a one-star (sell) to five-star (buy) rating system.

Contact information:
S&P Corporation
Equity Research
25 Broadway, New York, NY 10004
http://www.stockinfo.standardpoor.com
(800) 221-5277; (800) 852-1641; (212) 208-8000

Zacks Investment Research

Zacks also publishes company research reports. It is one of the best sources of earnings estimate data available to an individual investor. A Zacks company report, Appendix D, includes the following information:

- Overview of the company's business.
- Summary of sales, net income, and earnings per share history.
- Analysis of earnings per share surprises.
- Overview of analysts' earnings per share estimates.
- Comparison of company's long-term expected EPS growth rate versus its industry.
- Overview of analysts' buy/hold/sell recommendations.

Zacks also publishes the *Analyst Watch*, which is available to individual investors in two formats: monthly and biweekly. *Analyst Watch* includes a list of 150 stocks, called the "Recommended 150," which have ranked highest based on Zacks' stock screening criteria.

Zacks' research covers about 5,400 stocks and includes estimates collected from 2,700 analysts. Along with the hard copy *Analyst Watch*, this information is available to investors on the Internet through a service called Analyst Watch on the Internet (AWI) for a small fee. AWI includes portfolio alerts, company research reports, and custom equity screening. Its custom equity screening function gives investors the capability to interactively screen Zacks' equity database, using any combination of 81 investment criteria.

Contact information:
Zacks Investment Research
155 North Wacker Drive
Chicago, IL 60606
http://aw.zacks.com and http://www.reswizard.com
(800) 767-3771; (800) 399-6659

A Limitation

Earnings estimates are the basis for forecasting the future price appreciation potential of a stock. Hence, it is very important that an investor have confidence in the projected earnings estimates for a company. Therefore, one must be aware of the limitations of the earnings estimates provided by different sources.

A limitation of the earnings estimates provided in the S&P and Value Line reports is that they are based on research conducted by a single company (S&P or Value Line). On the other hand, First Call and Zacks base their reports on data provided by a large number of analysts—who work for different brokerage companies and investment firms.

A typical company's earnings estimate report, from First Call or Zacks, is based on the consensus estimates of 4 to 25 analysts who follow it. Thus the effect of a single wrong estimate on the consensus value of an earnings estimate is usually not significant. Therefore, earnings estimates from First Call and Zacks generate more confidence.

Other Sources

Investment Clubs and Groups

A number of investment clubs have sprouted all across the country. Many of them are good sources of information and investment ideas for their members. Some well-known associations are listed in Table 3.7.

The Investors Alliance is a nonprofit education and research association. Its inexpensive Power Investor for Windows software program is loaded with features including:

■ Stock database screening
■ Company financial data

Table 3.7   **Investment Clubs**

American Association
  of Individual Investors
612 N. Michigan Ave.
Chicago, IL 60611
(800) 428-2244
	The National Association
	  of Investment Clubs
	1515 E. Eleven Mile Road
	Royal Oak, MI 48067
	(313) 543-0612

Investors Alliance 219 Commercial Blvd. Lauderdale-by-the-Sea, FL 33308 (888) 683-1181	National Council of Individual Investors 1900 L Street NW, Suite 610 Washington, DC 20036 (888) 624-4111

- Industry and sector analysis
- Price quotes and charts
- Technical charting
- Technical scan

Company Literature and Press Releases

An easy source to tap for general investment information on a company is the company itself. Every publicly traded company has an investor relations department, willing to provide free information regarding the company—upon request. Typically, they can provide annual and financial reports, 10K and 10Q reports (i.e., detailed annual and quarterly reports that every company submits to the *Securities and Exchange Commission*), earnings releases, news releases, company research reports, analysts' earnings estimates, news articles on the company, and so on. All that an investor needs to do is call, or write, to obtain this information.

Investors need to be careful when reading the *annual report* of any company. Generally, annual reports are written in a very positive tone and do not indicate the depth of problems, if they exist, that the company may be facing. Therefore, not everything said in the report should be taken at face value. Instead, one should read between the lines to find something meaningful.

Miscellaneous Sources for Investment Data, Analysis, and Tools

A number of sources are available to investors for obtaining investment data, analysis, quotes, news, and investment tools. Some of these are listed, along with their web addresses, in Tables 3.2, 3.3, 3.4, and 3.6. For serious investors, a number of investment software products, including stock search programs, are available (Tables 3.8, 3.9, and 3.10). Most of these software programs are in the $100–$1,000 price range. These programs can include the following, as well as additional, capabilities and features:

- Intraday, daily, or weekly stock prices and volume
- Price/volume charts
- Technical indicators
- Creation of custom indicators
- Stock screening using specific parameters

An excellent investment book, containing comprehensive information on a wide variety of investment sources, is *The Investor's Information Sourcebook* authored by Spencer McGowan (New York: New York Institute of Finance, 1995). Most libraries carry this book.

Table 3.8   **Charting, Data, and News Sources**

Alert Technologies	(800) 316-8932
BMI	(800) 943-6036
Daily Graphs	(800) 472-7479
Data Broadcasting Corp.	(800) 551-1322
DTN Wall Street	(800) 475-4755
Investors Alliance	(607) 243-3601
Mansfield Chart Service	(201) 795-0629
Quote Xpress	(800) 603-5465
Quotes Plus	(800) 627-9637
Reality Online	(800) 842-3045
SmartServ Online	(888) 467-3783
Track OnLine	(800) 367-5968
Traders Access	(888) TBSPINC
Worden Brothers	(800) 776-4940

Table 3.9   **Investment, Technical Analysis, and Trading Software**

AIQ TradingExpert	(800) 332-2999
Market Analyzer Plus	(800) 522-3567
Market Guide for Windows	(516) 327-2400
MetaStock (Equis International)	(800) 882-3040
NavaPatterns (Nava Development)	(800) 532-0041
Omni Trader	(800) 880-0338
Online Intelligence	(713) 877-1204
Power Investor for Windows	(888) 683-1181
QuoTrek 7.0	(800) 287-2736
Signal	(800) 824-0960
Stock Investor Pro	(800) 428-2244
StockTools for Windows	(800) 735-0700
SuperCharts	(800) 556-2022
TeleChart 2000	(800) 776-4940
Telescan Analyzer	(800) 324-8246
TickerWatcher	(404) 733-5733
TradeStation4	(800) 328-1265
Wall Street Analyst	(800) 556-2022
Windows on Wall Street	(800) 998-VIEW

Table 3.10   Stock Search Sources and Programs

AAII (Stock Investor Pro)	(800) 428-2244
CompuServe	(800) 522-4477
Dial Data Retriever Program	(800) 367-5968
Dow Jones News/Retrieval	(800) 522-3567
Financial Web	http://www.financialweb.com
Ford Investor Services, Inc.	http://pawws.com/Ford_phtml
Intuit	http://www.quicken.com
Investors Alliance	(888) 683-1181
IQC Corp.	http://www.iqc.com
Market Guide for Windows	(516) 327-2400
Microsoft MoneyCentral	http://www.moneycentral.com
Morningstar (StockTools for Windows)	(800) 735-0700
SchwabNow	http://www.schwab.com
Telescan (ProSearch 5.0)	(800) 324-8246
U.S. Equities Ofloppy	(800) 876-5005
Value/Screen III	(800) 654-0508
Wall Street City	http://www.wallstreetcity.com
Zacks Investment Research	(800) 399-6659

Concluding Remarks

There is no shortage of investment resources for the serious investor. These days, for those who want it, investment data for stocks is literally available at the fingertips. Based on the authors' experience, the most useful sources of information, investment ideas, monitoring, and research data (for individual stocks and the overall market) for an individual investor (with moderate or no stock market experience) are the following:

- Company information and financials (Market Guide).
- Company research reports (S&P, Zacks, and Value Line).
- Earnings estimate reports (Zacks, First Call, and Yahoo!).
- *Investor's Business Daily* for monitoring (stocks, business, and economic conditions) and investment ideas.
- CNBC cable TV for day-to-day market action, highlights, and analysis from the experts.
- *Investor's Digest* and *Dick Davis Digest* for investment ideas and overview (of market and economic conditions).

▮ *Individual Investor* and *Money* magazine for investment ideas and big picture highlights.

▮ Recommended stock lists (Zacks *Analyst Watch*, S&P *Outlook*, *Growth Stock Winners*, and Value Line).

▮ Internet address: http://quote.yahoo.com.

Other web addresses listed in Table 3.2 are also useful research sites. The suitability of a site depends on an investor's information requirements—such as quotes, charting, stock screening, economic data, and so on.

Chapter 4

Factors Influencing Stock Prices

Performance Drivers

Basic Variables

The performance of the stock market is tied to corporate profits, the economy, inflation, and interest rates. In general, any development that increases the risk for a company's future profits will cause its stock price to decline. On the other hand, any development that reduces the risk is bullish for the stock.

Short- and Long-Term Factors

Factors affecting stock prices can be either short- or long-term. In the short term, the impact of fundamentals on stock prices is limited. The factors that significantly influence the short-term direction of stock prices are:

- The market's internal momentum
- Interest rate trends
- Various investor sentiment factors

In the long run, sound fundamentals determine the direction of a stock (as well as the market), because they provide the true basis for valuing individual stocks and the overall stock market.

Internal Factors

A number of business factors directly related to a company's core business affect its operations, business prospects, profitability, and, in some cases, viability. These important factors are described in the following sections.

Products

The ability of a company to sell products determines its revenues, profits, and growth rate. Companies that produce innovative products and continue to do so consistently are generally very profitable. Consequently, they are well rewarded through stock price appreciation. In a dynamic marketplace, a company needs to remain innovative with its product offerings in order to remain successful. A factor investors should note is the company's product line diversity. A company with more products is less vulnerable if one or two products fail. However, on the other hand, one-product companies are more focused and can easily control a profitable niche.

Product Cycle

Companies need to innovate and introduce new products regularly in order to stay ahead of their competition. If a company plans its product releases per market requirements, it can reap good profits. If the product cycle is very strong, with a number of products slated for release in the near future, it can be expected that revenues will grow in line with the products' release. This affects profits and, consequently, the stock price because the market anticipates this revenue growth. Companies such as Intel, which has continued to introduce newer products in ever shortening cycles, have been very well rewarded. On the other hand, companies with poor or delayed product cycles have usually languished and, in many cases, even gone out of business.

Competition

The effect of competition on a stock's price can be significant. The entry of new competition can, in many cases, mean big trouble even for profitable companies. For example, in 1995, Intel decided to enter the chipset market. As a result, Opti, the leading maker of chipsets, almost overnight lost its market to a new but very powerful competitor. Consequently, the company suddenly had to struggle to survive, even though it had been performing quite well. Within a few months, its stock price dropped from $29 to $4.62. Even if a company's competition is not as formidable as Intel, its stock price can be influenced by the products, and product cycle, of competing companies.

Markets: Presence in Growth Areas

The presence, or absence, of a company from growth areas can affect its sales and earnings, as well as stock price. This absence of products can be from either sectors or markets (countries, regions) experiencing fast growth. For example, C-Cube Microsystems experienced phenomenal growth, and profits, in the mid-1990s because its products were introduced in China—a very fast growing market.

Niche/Monopoly

The ability to corner a niche area can be very profitable for a company and its stock price. If a small company has a unique product that serves a profitable niche, its stock will generally perform very well. Similarly, a company controlling a market through either a monopoly or a large market share can also generate hefty profits consistently. This gets reflected in its stock price. An example is Intel, an extremely successful company that, with its high-end microprocessors, has dominated the IBM-compatible personal computer market.

Institutional Presence

Individual investors once held the majority of outstanding stock in the United States. However, in the past few decades, *institutional investors* have displaced them. These include insurance companies, pension funds, investment firms, nonprofit organizations, banks, corporations, and so on. These institutions own a large percentage of the outstanding stock of large cap companies. However, the ownership of small companies by these institutions is limited. When institutions recognize a small company and start buying its stock, its stock price gets a significant boost.

Management

A company's fundamentals are very important in determining how well a stock will perform. However, almost equally important is the quality of its management. Without good management, a company cannot thrive. There are numerous examples of profitable companies being ruined by poor management. When analyzing a company, investors need to note if the following important management characteristics are present:

- Integrity.
- Ability to execute the company's plans.
- Willingness to invest for the future.
- Main focus on making correct business decisions rather than pleasing Wall Street for temporary gain.
- Open communications.
- Record of success.

External Factors

There are a number of environmental factors, external to a company's core business, that affect its operations, business prospects, and profitability. An investor should be aware of these factors, which are described next.

Inflation

Understanding the Background

In the 1970s and 1980s, inflation rose to very high levels. When the inflationary spiral's effect became obvious to individuals and businesses, they started to take advantage of this phenomenon. They used a simple formula: borrow valuable dollars now and repay later with depreciated dollars. Even prudent individuals and businesses went on a borrowing binge—with greater frequency and for larger amounts. The upward inflationary trend continued until 1981, when it was broken due to the combined effects of a recession and fundamental changes in economic policy.

The disinflationary trend change was not apparent to most individuals and businesses for some time. It started getting recognized by 1986, when debt growth began to decrease. The savings and loan (S&L) crisis, a record number of personal and business bankruptcies in the early 1990s, the high unemployment rate during the 1990–1991 recession, and the slow recovery that followed put a further damper on the inflation spiral. Since then the inflation rate, as measured by the consumer price index (CPI), excluding the volatile food and energy components, has been trending downward.

Why Inflation Hurts Stocks

Rising inflation hurts stocks because it is expected that the earnings growth of companies will be insufficient to offset the higher inflation rate. In other words, the value of future earnings will be diluted by inflation and, consequently, stock prices will be negatively impacted. One of the most important ingredients for a successful bull market is investors' perception that inflation has been whipped. Three of the greatest bull markets took place when inflation was under control. The first one occurred from 1921 to 1929, when the Dow gained 504%. The next super bull market was from 1949 to 1966, when the Dow jumped 523%. The third super bull market started in 1982, after the inflation of the 1970s had been brought under control. Also, one of the foundations of the last super bull market, which started in 1990 and ended in 1998, was low inflation.

Influence of Inflation on Interest Rates

Inflation and debt demand strongly influence interest rates. The 1990 recession dramatically decreased debt demand and reduced inflation. Due to this recession, and the disinflationary trend that had started earlier, interest rates declined significantly from 1990 to 1993. Both short-term and long-term interest rates declined. The *prime rate*, the rate that banks charge their most creditworthy commercial customers, declined significantly. It decreased from 10% in 1990 to 6% in 1993. This decline in interest rates led to a significant shift in assets from CDs and money market funds to stocks and bonds. This propelled the stock market higher.

Monetary Policy and Interest Rates

Factors Producing the Monetary Climate

Stock prices are significantly affected by prevailing monetary conditions. Interest rate trends and Federal Reserve Board policy are among the most important factors that determine the stock market's major trend. The trend, once established (either up or down), typically lasts one to three years. The factors that combine to produce the monetary climate are:

- Loan demand
- *Liquidity* in the banking system
- Inflation (or deflation)
- Federal Reserve policy decisions

At the end of World War II, the yield on 30-year Treasuries was under 2%. However, it increased to more than 13% in 1981, when inflation was rampant in the economy, before starting to decline. In the long run, the level of government spending and deficit financing, besides changes in the inflation rate, determines the rise and fall of interest rates.

Effect of Higher Interest Rates

Interest expense is a major expense for most companies. A decline in interest rates reduces their cost of borrowing. Therefore, as interest expense is reduced, profits are increased. Consequently, as investors realize the potential for increased future earnings due to falling interest rates, they tend to bid stock prices higher. On the other hand, if interest rates rise, the opposite takes place—expectations of declining profits cause stock prices to move lower.

During a period of economic expansion and growth, demand for loans picks up; this causes interest rates to rise. Also, when the U.S. government runs up huge deficits, it needs to borrow excessively, which, in turn, puts pressure on interest rates. When interest rates rise, alternative investments become more attractive to investors. Therefore, money starts shifting from the stock market to the bond market, money market funds, and CDs. This causes pressure on stock prices. Conversely, when interest rates move lower, stocks face less competition from other types of investments, especially short-term instruments.

Types of Interest Rates

There are two main types of interest rates—short-term and long-term. Figure 4.1 shows some selected interest rates. They are reported every weekday by the *IBD* and followed by bond and stock market investors. In general, stronger economic growth causes short-term rates to edge up. Long-term interest rates are affected by the inflation outlook, as well as by the interest rate differences between the United States and foreign countries.

The Federal Reserve controls both the discount rate and the federal funds rate (Figure 4.1). The discount rate is the interest rate at which member banks borrow funds from the Federal Reserve. The federal funds rate is the interest rate at which banks borrow from each other in order to meet their reserve requirements. This rate is a key policy instrument. Its level, at any time, is a clear reflection of the Federal Reserve's intentions.

In 1994, the Federal Reserve increased the federal funds rate six times by a total of 225 basis points (2.25%) in order to cool the economy and reduce the possibility of inflationary pressures building up. In 1995, it increased it by another 50 basis points (i.e., 0.5%). These rate hikes indicated to investors that the Fed had effectively changed the interest rate trend. On March 25, 1997, the Fed raised the federal funds rate by 0.25%, to 5.5%, when it appeared that inflationary pressures might build up due to the continuing strong economic growth rate. In 1998, the Fed cut interest rates when it appeared that the economy was slowing and the international economic crisis seemed to be deepening.

Real Interest Rates

To keep interest rates in perspective, many economists closely watch the real interest rate (Figure 4.2). This is the average effective federal funds rate minus the inflation rate. Real interest rates rise when inflation declines and nominal interest rates hold steady.

Role of the Federal Reserve

During a slowing economy, or a recession, the Federal Reserve eases interest rates. This easing stimulates business investment and consumer spending,

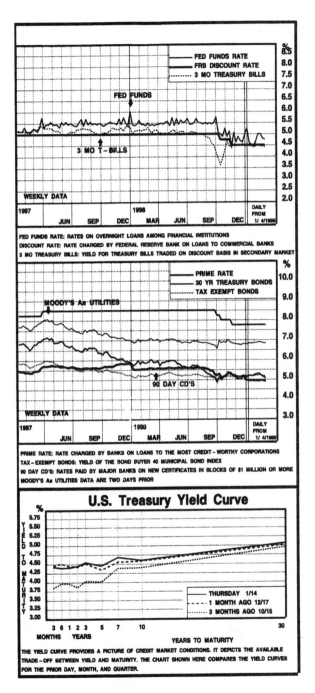

Figure 4.1   Selected Interest Rates

Source: *Investor's Business Daily*, January 15, 1999. Reprinted with permission.

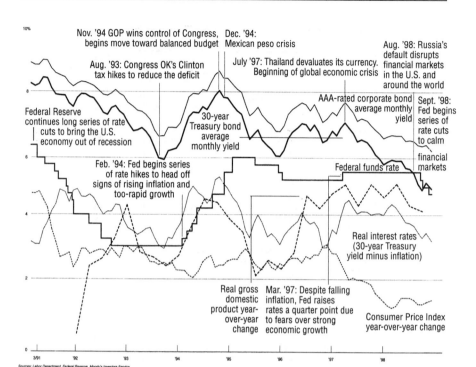

Figure 4.2   **Real Interest Rates**
Source: *Investor's Business Daily*, January 19, 1999. Reprinted with permission.

boosting corporate earnings. During falling interest rates, a flood of cash is shifted into stocks and mutual funds. During such periods, when saving rates are very low, the catchphrase "cash is trash" has often been used. One such period was from 1991 to 1993, when the Federal Reserve followed a very accommodative policy. During this period, which was characterized by massive discount rate cuts, money market rates dropped to their lowest levels in two decades. Also, during this period, the reserve requirement on commercial bank deposits was cut from 12% to 10%. These steps helped end the long recession and propelled the stock market to new heights.

In 1998, at the height of the global economic turmoil, when the U.S. economy started to slow down, the Federal Reserve rapidly cut interest rates three times—which buoyed the stock market. From September through November, the Fed cut the fed funds rate 0.25% three times, which reduced it from 5.5% to 4.75%. In October, simultaneously with the second fed funds rate cut, the Fed reduced the discount rate by 0.25%—giving a strong signal to the market.

The Fed raises interest rates if it thinks that the economy is growing too fast. In February 1994, when it appeared that the economy was growing at a very fast pace, which could lead to inflationary pressures, the Fed started to hike up short-term interest rates. This negatively affected the stock market, which had been rising steadily since the 1990 recession. While the rate hike was small, it was the perception that the interest rate trend had changed, in the negative direction, which put a damper on the stock market.

Federal Reserve Tools

The Federal Reserve has three very powerful tools that it can use, through easing, to boost the economy as well as the stock market. They are:

- Level of reserve requirements of member banks
- Discount rate
- Federal funds rate

Tightening either rate hurts the economy and, therefore, stock market prices. As part of their monitoring activities, investors should track Federal Reserve policies and actions, especially the discount rate, to determine if the Federal Reserve is in an easing (bullish) or tightening (*bearish*) mode. If the interest rate picture is favorable, and the overall market is headed higher, investors can be more confident that their individual stocks will appreciate as well.

Forecasting Interest Rates

By correctly predicting the trend of interest rates, an investor can make a reasonable forecast regarding the future direction of the overall market. A number of newsletters and financial organizations, such as banks and investment firms, attempt to forecast the direction of interest rates using some well-known, as well as proprietary, techniques. An example of forecasting interest rates, based on the 30-year bond yield, is shown in Figure 4.3.

A widely used method for determining whether the interest rate trend is bullish or bearish is based on the spread between the federal funds rate and the yield on the two-year Treasury note. When this spread narrows, it is considered good news for stocks because, in such a case, the Federal Reserve is not expected to raise short-term interest rates.

Some financial magazines also forecast interest rates. For example, the *Individual Investor* magazine forecasts interest rates using a proprietary model. Its model, which includes seven economic and technical variables, attempts to forecast the direction of interest rates six months down the road.

For predicting future interest rates, a variable monitored by analysts is

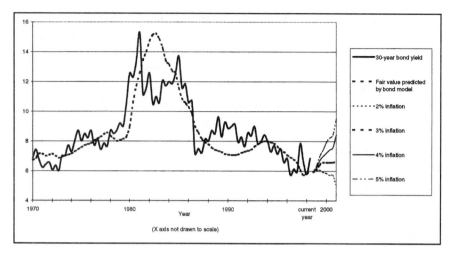

Figure 4.3   Model for Forecasting Interest Rates (Based on Historical Yield of 30-Year Bond and Inflation Rate Forecast)

the performance of utilities—as represented by the Dow Jones Utility Average. This is a good barometer for indicating the future interest rate direction. Typically, if the utility index shows strength, it indicates that interest rates are headed lower. The explanation is that utility stocks are very sensitive to interest rates. If interest rates change, as reflected by the bond market, the change shows up in the Dow Jones Utility Average way before it gets reflected in the overall stock market. Consequently, the performance of utilities is considered to be a leading indicator of the overall market trend.

Bond Market

Bonds are long-term securities, issued by corporations and governments, which pay a fixed interest and are repaid in full at maturity. They move up and down regularly just like stocks (Figure 4.4). Bondholders profit in two ways: firstly, by being paid the interest on the bond, and secondly, if the price of the bond increases. However, the latter is a paper profit unless one is a trader. The value of bonds and, consequently, yield is very sensitive to inflation and interest rates (Figure 4.5). This is explained in the following sections.

Effect of Interest Rates on Bond Prices
Suppose the U.S. Treasury issues bonds at the prevailing interest rate of 8%, and a bond buyer pays the par (stated) value of $1,000. If the interest

Figure 4.4 Long-Term Interest Rate Trend

rate falls to 6%, the price of the bond will rise because its return, 8%, will be higher than that of a new bond. On the other hand, if interest rates rise to 10%, the price of the bond will fall because its 8% return will be less than the current rate.

In general, any factor that causes interest rates to rise is a negative for bonds. The reason is that bond investors worry about higher inflation, and interest rates, eating into their rate of return. A big jump in bond prices often indicates a growing belief that the economy is headed for a weak period (when interest rates are lower). The direction of interest rates can be gauged from charts provided by the *IBD* (Figure 4.1) and the *WSJ*.

Effect of Bond Yields on Stock Prices
The bond yield has a significant effect on the behavior of the stock market—with bond yields and the P/E ratio of the S&P 500 being closely correlated. Since 1982, long-term interest rates have been trending lower, which has been a major factor in the stock market's rise since then (Figure

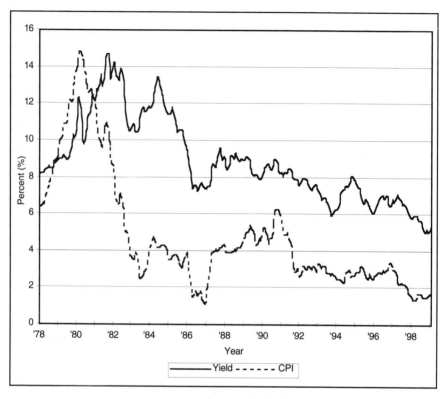

Figure 4.5   Yield versus Inflation—30-Year Bond Yield versus Inflation (CPI)

4.4). In 1995, 30-year bond yields fell all year due to the fast pace of economic growth, which pushed interest rates to the upside. However, in 1996, as the economy started to cool and its growth rate decreased, bond yields reversed direction as shown in Figure 4.4. This was very positive for the stock market, as it moved to new record highs and gained 26% for the whole year.

Bond yields have ranged from a high of 4% to a low of 0.5% above stock market earnings yield during the past 20 years. In general, stocks are considered relatively overvalued when the bond yield exceeds stock market earnings yield by 3% to 4%. Since bonds and stocks are in competition for investment dollars, money flows into bonds from riskier stocks at the higher end of this range. At the lower end, the flow is reversed into stocks.

In 1982, when the stock market yield was 12.5% and Treasury bond yield was 12.9%, the DJIA went up 400 points within a few months. However, in October 1987, the DJIA crashed when the stock market yield was 5.3%, while the Treasury bond yield was 9.1%.

Economy and the Business Cycle

The performance of the stock market is closely related to the state of the economy whose strength determines, to a large extent, the level of profits that companies will earn. During economic expansion and growth, profits continue to rise; this translates into rising stock prices. On the other hand, during a recession, profits are reduced or losses are incurred. This causes stock prices to remain stagnant or go down. Historically, the stock market has forecasted the economy by 6 to 12 months.

Investors should understand the business cycle, which describes the economy's expansion or contraction, since it strongly influences the earnings trend of most companies. As part of this exercise, an investor should monitor economic indicators, which are described in detail in Chapter 10.

Currency Fluctuations

Fluctuations in the value of the dollar against the currencies of countries with which U.S. companies do business can directly impact their profits. Companies without overseas business are shielded from these fluctuations. A weak dollar has both advantages and disadvantages. On the positive side, it makes U.S.-produced goods and services cheaper. This improves the competitive position of U.S. exporters in foreign markets. Profits that they earn in foreign currencies are translated into more dollars, which is the currency in which profits and earnings are reported. On the other hand, a strong dollar negatively impacts companies with overseas sales. A negative effect of a declining dollar is that foreign investors lose the incentive to invest in the United States; at times this can impact the stock market to some extent.

Political Factors

Whenever major political uncertainty exists, either in the United States or overseas, the stock market is affected negatively. This uncertainty can be the result of international or domestic crisis, a president's rising or falling political fortune, upcoming congressional elections or results, or a host of other political factors. For example, in November 1994, a Republican majority was reelected to Congress. When it was realized that Congress was serious about a balanced budget, spending reform, and tax cuts (including capital gains), the market started a big upward move.

In August 1990, the long uncertainty after Iraq invaded Kuwait had a very negative effect on the market, which underwent a *bear market* (declining prices). The 1973–1974 stock market losses coincided with President Nixon's troubles and the 9% increase in inflation during the first year of his second term. Usually, these effects are temporary, since the ultimate factor determining stock prices is profitability. So long as a political event does not affect the basic profitability of a company, especially in the long term, any negative effect usually is temporary.

Supply and Demand: Money Inflow into the Stock Market

The factors cited most often to explain the up and down movements of stock prices are corporate profits and interest rates. An additional factor, just like in any business, is supply and demand. This is the effect of more money chasing fewer shares. Supply can be reduced due to *mergers, acquisitions,* or stock buybacks by the company. Mergers and acquisitions activity hit a record $1.61 trillion in 1998, a 78% increase over 1997, which removed a large number of shares available for trading.[1]

A number of reasons can increase the demand for a stock. One of the most important has been the flood of cash moving into mutual funds in the past few years—which has propelled the market upward. In 1998, $158 billion was pumped into stock funds following an infusion of $227 billion in 1997.

The supply and demand factors and how they affect a stock's valuation are explained in more detail in the following chapter.

Concluding Remarks

There are a number of factors, external and internal, that affect the behavior and performance of stocks. The relative importance of these factors varies. The most important external factors are inflation and interest rates. Other factors include global competition, which is forcing American companies to become more productive, and the political climate, which is forcing Congress to become more responsible fiscally.

Among internal factors, the most important ones are the ability to provide customers with superior and innovative products, as well as the level of competition. However, an investor cannot afford to ignore any factor. Any of the factors listed earlier can become crucial for the profitability, or even survival, of a company. Investors should try to remain informed and monitor all factors. However, the extent of coverage—and the degree to which these factors are monitored and analyzed—can vary significantly.

---

[1]*Investor's Business Daily,* January 4, 1999.

Chapter 5

Valuing Stocks

To be successful in the stock market, an investor needs to understand:

- Factors that make stocks rise and fall.
- How to value stocks.
- Characteristics of good stocks.

If an investor understands these three important factors, success in the stock market will be assured. The first two factors are described in this chapter, while the characteristics of winning stocks are highlighted in Chapter 14.

One of the most difficult questions that an investor has to answer is: "What is the stock worth?" If this question is answered accurately prior to purchasing a stock, significant gains can be reaped. The key is understanding a simple basic principle: A stock is just like any other commodity that can be bought or sold, and is worth only what a buyer is prepared to pay for it. Therefore, it is imperative that every investor understand the following factors—because they determine what other investors are willing to pay for a stock:

- Supply and demand
- Trading factors
- Fundamental factors

Factors Determining Stock Prices

Supply and Demand

Every investor wants to own a stock whose demand exceeds supply, because such a stock will invariably rise in price. However, in order to be able to pick stocks with such characteristics, investors need to under-stand a stock's supply and demand as well as factors affecting them. The reason is that any change in demand and supply, both of which can change at different rates, makes share prices fluctuate. If demand for a stock increases, its price tends to rise. An increase in supply depresses the stock price.

Supply

Stock supply is determined by two factors: the total number of shares is-sued by the company and its trading *volume* on a particular day. The to-tal number of outstanding shares data is readily available to all investors. This number remains fairly steady unless there is a stock *split* or shares buyback by the company. Significant changes in a stock's sup-ply (i.e., in the number of outstanding shares) are always announced by the company.

Not all outstanding shares of a company are available for trading. A company's management, or the founder's family, may own a large number of shares that may be unavailable for trading. Also, company management is often restricted to selling their shares during specific, and small, time windows due to company rules. These factors reduce the supply of stock available for daily trading, which can influence the stock's trading pattern and price.

The actual number of shares available for trading is called the *float*. Over the years, the best price performers have been companies with a rel-atively small number of available shares. During 1998, the average float of the 10 top-performing Nasdaq stocks was only 16.64 million shares.

Demand

For some companies, the demand for their stock is steady. For others, demand can fluctuate significantly and at frequent intervals. If the number of shares available for trading is known, it can indicate the de-mand required to push up the stock price. Stock demand is influenced by many factors, which change constantly. These include factors affect-ing fundamentals (earnings, dividends, acquisitions, economy, etc.), market or group behavior, investor psychology, political news, and other external factors. For example, on December 11, 1996, Intel an-nounced that its plants were operating at full capacity and it expected to enjoy "a pretty healthy growth rate." This indicated to investors that earnings for Intel would continue to improve and, consequently, de-mand for its shares rocketed. Its shares soared $7.75 on double its aver-age daily trading volume.

Trading Factors

Liquidity

Investors want to be in a position to sell a stock immediately, if required. This is an important factor in stock ownership. However, while most stocks trading on the various exchanges have sufficient liquidity, this is not true for all stocks. Some stocks trade only a few hundred, or thousand, shares per day. They can be difficult to sell even during a normal trading day. During a fast declining market, the liquidity of such a stock can become a serious problem, especially if a large number of shares need to be unloaded. With few buyers available on even a normal day, it is possible that a seller may find no buyers when the stock, or the overall market, is declining rapidly. Therefore, in general, it is preferable to buy stocks with a trading volume greater than 200,000 shares per day. Stocks trading less than 100,000 shares per day should be avoided, unless the investor is aware of some special circumstances.

Change in Trading Volume

Any increase or decrease in the daily trading volume of a stock, in conjunction with other factors, can affect a stock's price. This can be attributed to many reasons. In general, heavy pickup in volume along with a price rise, as occurred with Intel's stock indicated earlier, is considered bullish. However, heavy volume accompanied by a price drop is considered bearish. This factor is explained in greater detail in Chapter 8.

Role of Institutions

These days, large institutions have become major investors in the stock market. Before investing in any company, they closely look at its float and average daily trading volume. Typically, they avoid investing in stocks with an average trading volume under 200,000 shares per day. Many institutions use a higher limit, approximately 500,000 shares, because high liquidity ensures that they will be able to exit from a stock quickly. They know that if they dump a large block of shares of a thinly traded company, it can induce a large price drop. Worse still, there may be an insufficient number of buyers, when required, to buy all the shares being dumped.

Company Size

Companies with large floats, with hundreds of millions of outstanding shares, rarely make big price moves due to their inertia. Moving the price of a widely held and heavily traded company like Exxon, with 2.43 billion outstanding shares and an average daily trading volume of 3.96 million shares, requires a tremendous amount of buying and selling. Even during the *Exxon Valdez* oil spill crisis in Alaska, despite very negative news coverage, Exxon's stock price did not move significantly.

Small stocks make big moves. Typically, these stocks have small floats and low daily volume. They are rarely covered by brokerage companies and, hence, have low demand for their stock. When such companies start getting the attention of institutional investors, demand for their shares rises. Consequently, their stock price can rise significantly.

Factors that constrain institutions create an opportunity for the ordinary investor, who is unrestricted by volume and other screening criteria. Such an investor can venture to take advantage of an investment opportunity in a smaller company that may not be open to institutional investors.

Spread Factor

The price that investors pay or receive for a stock is affected by its *spread*. A disadvantage of a thinly traded stock is its larger spread. The spread between the bid and ask prices of small capitalization and low trading volume stocks, typically traded on the Nasdaq, is far greater than for stocks traded on the *New York Stock Exchange (NYSE)*. Large spreads, which can be as high as $1 to $2 per share, negatively affect a stock's price, liquidity, and trading pattern.

Fundamental Factors

In general, four fundamental factors influence the price of a stock. They are:

1. Earnings outlook
2. Dividend prospects
3. Financial condition
4. Comparison to other investment alternatives

In the short term (i.e., days or months) stock prices fluctuate in tandem with investor expectations of earnings and growth. These expectations are very volatile and sensitive to news items (directly or indirectly affecting the company), business conditions, market behavior, and a number of other factors.

The long-term stock price rise (or fall) depends on a company's actual rising (or falling) earnings and dividends, as well as its financial condition. Price/earnings ratios, dividend yields, and price/book value relationships have little short-term relevance to the price trend. However, in the final analysis, they provide the basis of value upon which stock prices rest.

Methods for Stock Valuation

Valuing stocks is not a straightforward exercise because the relationship existing between price and value is very difficult to measure. Also, since other investment opportunities are available for an investor's capital, valuing stocks can become quite complicated. In general, stocks are analyzed and valued using the following four approaches:

1. Investment environment
2. Relative value
3. Performance expectation
4. Intrinsic value determination

Investment Environment

This method is based on comparing stocks with other investment alternatives such as bonds and money market funds. Valuation is based on interest rates as well as the rate of inflation. Both these variables directly influence the relative attractiveness of stocks. For example, if interest rates rise, investors tend to change their asset allocation in favor of bonds over stocks. The reason is that as bond returns increase due to rising interest rates, the difference between bond and stock returns decreases. At some stage, bonds start looking more and more attractive, due to their lower risk, even though still providing a lower return than stocks. At some point, consequently, money starts shifting from stocks into bonds. Generally, investors require approximately a 4% higher return from their equity investments (such as stocks), due to their profits (earnings) risk, than from less risky investments such as bonds.

In addition to allocation between different investment types, investors also switch their funds between different sectors of the stock market based on prevailing conditions. For example, prices of defensive stocks are bid up during a recession, while cyclical stocks are favored during an expanding economy. Therefore, stock valuations can be influenced by the perception of investors regarding the company, industry, and the economy.

Relative Value

This method is based on comparing a stock to others in the stock market in terms of earnings, dividends, or yield. In this method, the value of a stock is compared to a benchmark such as:

▪ An index (S&P 500, Russell 2000, etc.)
▪ Specific industry group

■ Comparable stock group
■ Other stocks

Performance Expectation

This method values a stock based on its expected performance in the next 6 to 18 months. It is based on the expectation that the stock's relative performance will be better than the overall market during the time frame being considered.

Intrinsic Value Determination

This method values a stock based on the individual merits of the company. It attempts to evaluate the true market value of the company and, consequently, its stock price. No consideration is given to its current trading price. In this method, a thorough analysis of the company's financial situation, assets, liabilities, earnings, dividends, management, and other fundamental factors is made.

Valuation Tools

Investors use a number of indicators to measure a stock's value with varying degree of success. These indicators—such as dividend yield, price-to-dividend ratio, price-to-book value ratio, and price/earnings ratio—provide a good reference point for relating a stock's price to its value.

Price/Earnings (P/E) Ratio

The price/earnings ratio, commonly known as the P/E ratio, relates a stock's price to its earnings per share. It is an important *fundamental analysis* yardstick used to value a stock. This valuation tool is used by many investors to determine whether a stock is undervalued or overvalued.

The P/E ratio is calculated by dividing the current stock price by its annual earnings per share (EPS). If the stock price is $40 and the company earned $2 per share for the year, its P/E can be calculated as follows:

$$\$40/\$2 = 20$$

Individual and Collective Market P/E

The P/E ratio can be calculated for an individual stock or the overall market. The stock market's collective P/E ratio indicates the overall market valuation—whether it is overvalued or undervalued. Investors typically use the P/E ratios of the DJIA and the S&P 500 for this purpose.

To calculate the DJIA's P/E ratio, the EPS of all the 30 DJIA components are added and then used in the denominator of the P/E equation. For example, on December 31, 1998, the DJIA index was at 9,181 and the collective earnings of its 30 components were $396.90 per share. Therefore, the market's P/E ratio was:

$$\frac{9,181}{396.9} = 23.13$$

An individual stock's P/E ratio should not be compared to the market's collective P/E. Instead, it should be compared to the P/E of similar companies.

Trailing and Projected P/E Ratio
The trailing P/E ratio is based on past earnings. Using trailing P/E as a measure of value is equivalent to driving a car while staring into the rearview mirror. An investor's focus should be forward-looking since the historical record has limited use. While it is a good measure of past performance, trailing P/E ratio cannot indicate future growth prospects or earnings potential. The P/E ratio reported in most newspapers is based on trailing earnings.

Projected P/E ratio, calculated by using estimated future earnings, is a more valuable valuation tool. It is calculated by dividing the current stock price by the projected earnings per share. Projected earnings are provided in company research reports, which are available to individual investors, and on the Internet. Investors should use projected P/E ratios with care because they are based on earnings estimates, which may later prove to be inaccurate.

It has been observed that not much of a relationship exists between a stock's P/E and its current earnings. Instead, a better correlation exists with projected earnings. The reason is that investors, especially large institutions, have a long investment horizon. Instead of looking at the next year or two, they look as far ahead as three to five years. Therefore, they use the expected higher level of future earnings to perform their valuations.

Relative P/E Ratio
This is a measure of a stock's current P/E ratio compared to its historical P/E ratio. Relative P/E ranges from 0% to 100%, which indicates the

range from an all-time low to an all-time high P/E ratio. If a stock has historically traded in the 10–20 P/E range, a P/E ratio equal to 20 represents a relative P/E of 100%. A current P/E ratio of 14 would represent a relative P/E of 70% (i.e., 14/20 × 100). Some investors prefer this number to be below 50% when evaluating a stock for procurement. A stock trading near the high end of this range is not considered attractive by such investors. They consider such a stock to be overvalued relative to its own history and, hence, more susceptible to a price correction.

Historical earnings and P/E ratios can, sometimes, be misleading because they can be distorted due to adjustments for write-offs, which can be significant. For example, the period 1992–1993, which followed a severe recession, was characterized by widespread restructuring and write-offs by American companies.

What Increases the P/E Ratio

A stock's P/E ratio never remains constant. Since the stock price, which fluctuates daily, is used to calculate the P/E ratio, this ratio also fluctuates daily. As the stock price moves up or down, the P/E ratio moves in tandem with it. Lower earnings increase P/E ratios, while higher earnings reduce P/E ratios. As earnings are released every quarter, which changes the earnings per share number to be used in the calculations, the P/E ratio also changes. A long-term investor does not focus on these fluctuations. Such an investor knows that the stock price, in the long run, ultimately rises in line with the company's increased earnings and financial health.

A high return on equity can account for a higher P/E. Since investors desire a superior return on their investments, they are willing to pay a premium for a company with a high ROE. The P/E ratio can also increase based on the market's perception of the company's future earnings potential. This perception may be based on future earnings estimates provided by analysts following the company, other independent sources, or the company itself. When awareness grows that there is good potential for increased earnings, big money starts coming into the stock and its price starts to appreciate, consequently increasing its P/E ratio.

Effect of Economic Growth on P/E Ratios

In a slow-growing economy, companies find it tough to increase earnings. This is especially true for large companies who see their growth, and earnings, decrease in such an environment. This is in contrast to growth companies who continue to grow at a fast pace even during a sluggish, or contracting, economy. Therefore, during slow economic growth periods, companies that can achieve steady, above-average earnings growth are favored by investors. These growth companies are typically small. Also, their P/E ratios are higher than those of large, well-established companies.

During severe economic contractions, P/E ratios become distorted. As earnings drop during a recession, P/E ratios expand and, in some cases, increase considerably. This causes stock prices to decline until P/E ratios decrease to a level considered a reasonable value—based on expected lower earnings. These low P/E ratios are considered bullish. During the start of an economic expansion, at the end of a recession, stock prices rise faster than earnings. Hence, P/E ratios increase. However, as higher earnings start coming in, P/E ratios decline to more normal levels.

Effect of Inflation and Interest Rates

Among the factors that analysts use when evaluating P/E ratios are inflation and interest rates. Besides nominal interest rates, like the discount and federal funds rates, real interest rates are also used for valuation.

Table 5.1 shows that higher market valuations are linked to lower inflation rates. During periods when inflation has been under control, with corresponding low interest rates, P/E ratios have typically exceeded 16 while often exceeding 18. In 1997, when the inflation rate was 1.7%, the P/E of the S&P 500 ranged from a low of 18.56 to a high of 24.77. On the other hand, during inflationary periods, when interest rates rise and investors are concerned, P/E ratios have fallen below the historical average of 14.

In late 1994 and 1995, the market made an explosive move upward. Based on projected 1996 earnings, the P/E ratio of the S&P 500 increased to 17. However, because inflation was under control, the increase in market valuation did not cause much concern. Therefore, no corrective action was initiated to bring down the market price, which would have

Table 5.1   Effect of Inflation on Valuations

Inflation	Average S&P 500 P/E ratio
Less than 3.5%	16.2
Less than 4.5%	15.3
4.5%–5.5%	15.6
5.5%–6.5%	12.1
6.5%–7.5%	10.0
Greater than 7.5%	8.6

Source: Goldman, Sachs & Co. as noted in IBD, December 9, 1996.

decreased the P/E to normal levels. In contrast, in August 1987, when the market topped, the DJIA's P/E ratio was 22.1. This was a period of rising interest rates. Consequently, it was no surprise that a market correction was initiated, which caused the DJIA to drop dramatically by 22.6% on October 19, 1987. In just two months of the 1987 bear market, the DJIA fell 41%. This resulted in the P/E dropping to a more normal level.

P/E Ratios in Different Industries

A large variation exists in the P/E ratios of companies in different industries. Some industries are characterized by high P/Es while others have low P/Es. The higher the P/E, the more optimistic investors are about the company's future earnings. The level of a stock's P/E ratio depends on the industry to which it belongs as well as its overall growth rate. In the Internet, networking, telecommunications, and computer-related industries, which are growing very fast and have exploding earnings, an investor has to pay a premium for stocks. Such companies have higher risk, with potential for higher reward, and command a higher P/E. On the other hand, a stock in a more established, slow-growth industry will command a lower P/E that will reflect such a company's lower growth rate.

Figure 5.1 shows the P/E of small stocks, as represented by the Russell 2000 index, versus the larger stocks represented by the S&P 500 index.[1] Appendix E lists the P/E ratios of a number of stocks in various industries. Also listed are the corresponding annual earnings growth rates. As is quite obvious, P/E ratios vary in a wide range.

P/E of Growth Companies

The growth rate of a company is reflected in its P/E ratio. The higher a company's profit growth rate, the more expensive the stock is (as measured by its P/E ratio). Growth stocks tend to have higher P/Es, which can range anywhere from 25 to 50 times the annual EPS. This explains why a fast growing company like Oracle traded at a 39 P/E ratio while PG&E Corporation, a large utility, traded at a 17 P/E ratio on December 31, 1998. When investors believe that a company's growth rate will accelerate, they bid the price up. On the other hand, if they believe that the growth rate will decrease, they make the P/E ratio decline by decreasing the stock price.

For growth stocks, a useful valuation guideline is based on comparing the P/E ratio with the earnings growth rate. Basically, the P/E ratio should

---

[1]*Wall Street Journal*, May 19, 1997, p. C1.

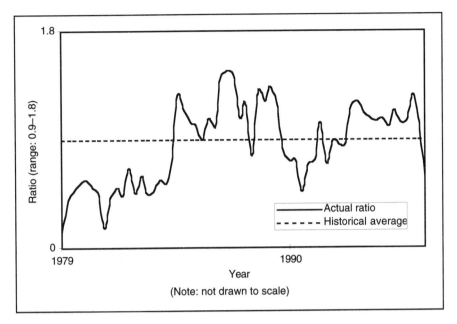

Figure 5.1 Ratio of Small Stocks P/E to the S&P 500 P/E, 1979–1997
Sources: Wall Street Journal, Deutsche Morgan Grenfell, First Call.

be less than the earnings growth rate. For example, if a company's earnings growth rate is 40% and its P/E ratio is 40 or less, many growth analysts consider it reasonably valued. Some analysts allow an even higher P/E, which can be as high as 25% over the growth rate. This is more applicable to high-technology and biotechnology companies. Less aggressive growth investors prefer to buy stocks that are trading at a P/E ratio that is less than 75% of the growth rate. Such investors will consider buying a stock growing at a 40% rate only if its P/E ratio is 30 (i.e., 40 x 0.75) or less.

P/E-to-Projected Growth (PEG) Ratio

Some investors use the PEG ratio to value stocks. It is obtained by dividing a company's P/E ratio by its annual earnings growth rate. For calculating this ratio, the projected P/E ratio is used rather than the trailing P/E ratio, because a growth stock investor pays for the future. If the P/E ratio is 20 and the annual growth rate is 40%, the P/E-to-projected growth ratio is equal to 0.5 (i.e., 20/40). Generally, a stock is considered attractive if this ratio is less than 0.75 and overpriced when it is over 1.25. Table 5.2 compares the valuations by market cap for large, mid, and small capitalization stocks.

Table 5.2   **Valuations by Market Cap (Cap-Weighted Valuations)**

Index	Forward P/E	Long-term growth	P/E-to-projected growth (PEG) ratio
S&P 500 (large cap)	20.7	13.8	1.50
S&P 400 (mid cap)	19.8	16.9	1.16
S&P 600 (small cap)	19.3	18.5	1.04

Sources: Morgan Stanley Dean Witter/*Investor's Business Daily* (March 16, 1998).

This ratio can be calculated using data provided in various company research and earnings reports. For example, as shown on the Yahoo! web page on January 1, 1999, Duke Energy Corp. had a P/E ratio of 18.9 and an earnings growth rate of 25.7%. This was equivalent to a P/E-to-growth ratio of 0.74 (i.e., 18.9/25.7).

Keeping P/E Ratios in Perspective

Value investors avoid investing in companies with high absolute P/E ratios. Typically, they do not buy a stock whose P/E ratio exceeds a certain limit. Growth investors have a different approach. They analyze a P/E ratio in the context of the company's future earnings growth rate. For example, consider a stock trading at a P/E ratio equal to 35. This ratio appears rather high. However, if the company's earnings are growing 45% annually, it is actually trading at a discount to its future earnings. This makes it attractive to growth investors. On the other hand, a stock with a P/E ratio equal to 10 is expensive if its expected annual earnings growth rate is only 5%.

A P/E ratio should never be evaluated in isolation as a simple number. It should be compared to the P/E ratios of similar stocks, usually in the same industry, because these ratios vary significantly from industry to industry. For example, one should not compare the P/E of a fast-growing software company with the P/E of a well-established bank. Generally, computer stocks have high P/E ratios, about 20 or more, due to their high growth rate. However, banks have lower P/E ratios, around 12 to 15, because of their slower growth rate.

Some investors observe a stock's P/E history to determine if it is overvalued. If the company's P/E ratio remains high quarter after quarter, they take it as a sign that earnings are expected to continue growing at a healthy pace. Investors should be careful when using the P/E ratio as a screening tool. If the P/E ratio is analyzed in isolation, it can cause big winners to slip through. For example, in the past 20 years, the average P/E of the top-performing stocks at the start of their biggest moves was 23. These ratios later increased to an average of 55. Thus, investors unwilling to consider high P/E stocks missed selecting the biggest winners.

The Dangers of High P/E

Stocks cannot always live up to investors' expectations. When these expectations are not met, the price drop can be drastic. The higher the P/E of a company failing to meet expectations, the greater the likely price drop. Therefore, an investor should be aware of the risk associated with high P/E stocks—higher risk as well as higher reward.

At times, investors have unrealistic expectations. They expect a growth stock to continue growing at 40% to 50%, year after year. Some companies have done this for many years, but ultimately their growth tapers off. This can occur when investors are not ready to hear the bad news of a slowdown in growth. When this happens, they exit en masse, magnifying the price drop.

The Dangers of Low P/E

A company with a low P/E is considered attractive based on two assumptions:

1. Its stock price will appreciate significantly if its P/E rises to the level of other companies in its industry.
2. Being so low, the stock price has nowhere to go but up.

However, it should not be automatically assumed that a company with a low P/E ratio is more attractive, a better value, or less risky. For example, the P/E may be low due to perceived negative future prospects in terms of earnings potential, growth, competition, and so on. In general, a low P/E should be evaluated in conjunction with the determination of the potential increase, or decrease, in the earnings growth rate.

Using Low P/E to Your Advantage

An astute investor can take advantage of a company's low P/E ratio, if there exists no fundamental reason for it to trade at a P/E ratio that is lower than other stocks in the same group. For example, Informix Corporation was trading at $14.50, with a P/E ratio of 14, in May 1994. At that time, other stocks in the same group were trading at P/E ratios ranging from 30 to 40. With sound fundamentals, Informix was a stock that appeared very inviting to knowledgeable investors. When its new product cycle started on time just a couple of months later, contrary to rumors and investors' expectations, it quickly started trading at P/E multiples equivalent to other companies in its group. In less than a year, the stock doubled.

Historical Valuation Levels

Valuation levels have changed over the years due to the changing business environment. During the late 1940s and early 1950s, the market's P/E ratio ranged between 8 and 12. In the 1960s, it increased to the 15–20 range. Historically, the stock market's P/E has generally ranged between 10 and 22 (Figure 5.2). Typically, when the market's P/E ratio has exceeded 20, the economy has been in the early part of a recovery.

Many bull markets in this century have ended when the P/E ratio rose above 20. When the market topped in August 1987, the DJIA's P/E ratio was 22.1. When the market hit a bear market low in 1982, the average stock was priced at only seven times earnings. The bear market of 1990 took P/E ratios down to an average of 6.5. On July 17, 1998, when the market topped, the P/E ratio of the DJIA was 24.1—a five-year high (Figure 5.3). When the market bottomed on September 1, 1998, the P/E had declined to 20—still high by historical standards.

Historically, the P/E ratio for the S&P 500 has averaged approximately

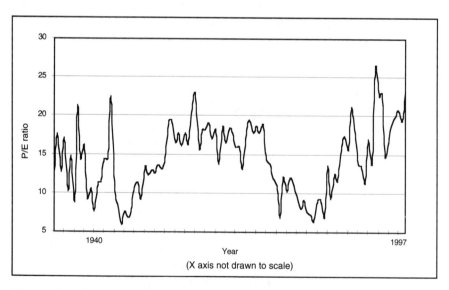

Figure 5.2   Historical P/E Ratio of the S&P 500
Sources: Barron's and the WEFA Group.

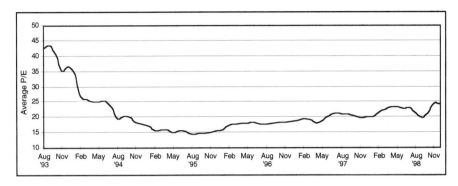

Figure 5.3   DJIA Monthly Average P/E

14. The S&P 500's earnings and P/E ratio from 1977 to 1998 are shown in Table 5.3.

Forecasting Based on P/E
The P/E ratio, by itself, is not always a reliable indicator of the future price movement of an individual company or the market as a whole. However, despite this, it is used by many investors as a tool to forecast the future price level of stocks and the overall market.

For Individual Stocks
For an individual company, its projected annual earnings can be used to forecast the level to which its stock price will rise in the future. The formula used is:

$$\text{Forecasted price} = \text{Current P/E} \times \text{Projected annual EPS}$$

For example, if a company's fiscal 1999 projected annual earnings are $4 per share and an assumption is made that it will maintain its current P/E of 15, the price estimated at the end of fiscal 1999 will be $60 (15 × $4 = $60).

The actual P/E ratio at the end of the forecast period can be higher than its current level, which can result in a higher price level being reached. The actual P/E can also be lower, in which case the price level attained will be lower. For example, if the market accorded the stock a higher P/E ratio, 20, the forecasted price will be $80 (20 × $4 = $80). There can be a number of reasons why the stock, as explained earlier, may be accorded a higher P/E ratio.

Table 5.3 Historical S&P 500 Valuations

Year	Diluted EPS	P/E ratio—high	P/E ratio—low	Dividends per share	Dividend yield %—high	Dividend yield %—low	Book value per share	Price-to-book ratio	Cash flow
1998	37.71	31.53	23.56	16.20	1.69	1.30	209.63	5.85	71.92
1997	39.72	24.77	18.56	15.50	2.06	1.58	190.12	5.10	70.84
1996	38.73	19.55	15.45	14.90	2.49	1.97	181.84	4.07	67.07
1995	33.60	18.50	13.66	13.79	3.00	2.22	174.32	3.53	61.06
1994	29.92	16.12	14.57	12.70	2.91	2.63	158.29	2.90	55.01
1993	21.85	21.55	19.64	12.70	2.96	2.70	149.96	3.11	46.44
1992	18.86	23.40	20.92	12.38	3.14	2.81	149.74	2.91	43.98
1991	16.29	25.60	19.12	12.20	3.92	2.93	158.85	2.63	38.69
1990	21.73	16.98	13.60	12.32	4.17	3.34	153.01	2.16	44.87
1989	22.87	15.73	12.04	11.05	4.01	3.07	147.26	2.40	44.10
1988	23.75	11.94	10.22	9.73	4.01	3.43	141.32	1.97	45.33
1987	17.50	19.24	12.80	8.81	3.93	2.62	134.07	1.84	35.86
1986	14.48	17.54	14.05	8.28	4.07	3.26	126.82	1.91	32.19
1985	14.61	14.51	11.20	7.90	4.83	3.73	125.20	1.69	31.19
1984	16.64	10.24	8.88	7.53	5.09	4.42	122.47	1.37	31.74
1983	14.03	12.31	9.86	7.09	5.13	4.11	116.93	1.41	27.62
1982	12.64	11.31	8.10	6.87	6.71	4.80	112.46	1.25	25.81
1981	15.36	8.99	7.34	6.63	5.88	4.80	109.43	1.12	27.41
1980	14.82	9.48	6.63	6.16	6.27	4.38	102.48	1.33	25.58
1979	14.86	7.49	6.47	5.65	5.88	5.08	94.27	1.14	24.45
1978	12.33	8.68	7.05	5.07	5.83	4.74	85.35	1.13	20.76
1977	10.89	9.83	8.33	4.67	5.15	4.36	79.07	1.20	18.33

For the Market

The basic formula used to forecast the future price level of the overall market is the same as that used for individual stocks.

$$\text{Forecasted price} = \text{Current P/E} \times \text{Projected annual EPS}$$
$$\text{(of the 30 DJIA companies)}$$

To forecast the DJIA for 1999, let us make the following two assumptions:

1. Market P/E will remain at 23, its 1998 year-end level.
2. The 30 companies making up the DJIA will earn an estimated $461 per share.

Therefore, the 1999 forecast for the DJIA will be:

$$23 \times \$461 = 10,603$$

Any price appreciation ultimately accrues from an increase in corporate earnings or an expansion in P/E ratios. The level to which the overall market can be expected to rise is based on the estimated earnings of the 30 DJIA companies. For example, it was estimated in 1995 that the DJIA annual earnings for 1996 would be $399 per share. At that time, the DJIA's P/E ratio was 13.8 and it was estimated by some analysts that the stock would be trading at 5,506 by the end of 1996. This was based on the assumption that the P/E ratio would be maintained at its current level.

The market, however, was undervalued at a P/E ratio of 13.8 because adequate consideration had not been given to two important factors: improving corporate profits and favorable interest rates. Consequently, investors bid the P/E up to 18.9 by mid-December 1996, causing the DJIA to rise to 6,430—far higher than had been forecasted. However, the forecasts of investors who realized that the 1995 P/E was very low, and correctly estimated a higher P/E in 1996, turned out to be quite accurate. Similarly, most forecasts for 1997 turned out to be incorrect, on the low side, because of incorrect assumptions.

Assumptions

It needs to be understood that these price movement forecasts, for individual stocks and the market, are made on the basis of assumptions for corporate profit growth, earnings, and P/E ratio levels. Any projection can be thrown off by factors such as emotional or panic selling, change in the competitive environment, business outlook, business cycle, and so on.

Guidelines for Using P/Es

The following are some guidelines when using P/E ratios:

▪ Current P/E ratio has very little bearing on the future price movements of winning stocks.

▪ P/E ratio based on estimated projected earnings should be used for most analyses.

▪ P/E ratio for a fast-growing young company with exploding earnings can be very misleading and, therefore, can be ignored.

▪ P/E ratio of a winner is generally higher than the market P/E at the start of the stock's major move to the upside.

▪ P/E ratio should be compared to the:
Stock's historical P/E.
P/E of other companies in the same industry.

▪ Favor a growth stock whose P/E ratio is less than the percentage rate at which its earnings are expected to grow (i.e., its projected earnings growth rate).

▪ If institutional ownership is low, a stock's P/E tends to be low.

▪ Beware of stocks with unusually low P/Es; don't buy a stock just because its P/E is low—there may be a reason and it should be investigated.

▪ All things being equal, it is better to buy a stock with a lower P/E.

▪ Do not use P/E as the primary criterion for deciding to buy or reject a stock.

▪ Do not buy a stock with the lowest P/E in a group/industry just because it looks undervalued.

▪ Do not buy a stock just because its P/E is at the historical low of its P/E range.

▪ P/E ratio can become meaningless if a loss is reported; even a single quarterly loss or an extraordinary onetime charge can distort the annual earnings figure and, consequently, the P/E ratio.

Price-to-Book Value Ratio

The price-to-book value ratio is calculated by dividing the stock price by the book value per share of the company. If a stock's price is $50 per share and the book value is $10 per share, its price-to-book value ratio is:

$$\frac{\$50}{\$10} = 5$$

Just like for P/E ratios, the price-to-book value ratio can be calculated for either an individual stock or the whole market as represented by the

DJIA or the S&P 500 (Table 5.3). Since the price-to-book value ratio is dependent on the book value per share, whose rise or fall affects it directly, investors need to understand book value and its limitations. These same limitations also apply to the price-to-book value ratios.

Book Value per Share

Book value per share is a valuation tool commonly used by investors. It is defined as the total of all assets, minus all *liabilities* (i.e., shareholders' equity), divided by the total number of outstanding shares and share equivalents. Book value per share is based on the premise that if a company's stock price is below its book value per share, the stock is undervalued. Hence, such a stock is considered attractive for purchasing. Conversely, a stock is considered overvalued if its price is more than its book value per share. The danger of an overvalued stock is that it becomes vulnerable to a price decline—to a level that will bring it in line with its book value per share.

Book Value Limitations

To understand the importance of book value in terms of the business being evaluated, it should be noted that this ratio varies in a wide range from company to company as shown in Table 5.4. For example, a service-based insurance company will have assets considerably different from an automobile manufacturer that owns large manufacturing facilities. The ratio is

Table 5.4   Range of Price-to-Book Ratios

	Price-to-book ratio	Industry average
S&P 500 average	8.40	
American Express	4.83	5.08
Bank One	3.03	3.70
Exxon Corp.	4.23	4.21
General Electric	7.04	8.52
General Motors	3.19	2.74
Intel Corp.	9.18	8.08
Life Financial Corp.	0.62	2.33
Lindsay Mfg.	2.09	2.41
McDonald's	5.68	4.74
Microsoft Corp.	18.90	15.19
Oracle Corp.	12.40	15.19
Papa John's Intl.	4.74	4.74
Sun Microsystems	8.33	14.24

Source: AOL/Market Guide, January 1, 1999. Reprinted with permission.

also influenced by the size of the company. For example, the average price-to-book ratio of microcap stocks is lower than that of large caps. In January 1997, the price-to-book value of microcap stocks, according to Merrill Lynch & Co., was less than half that of large cap stocks, down from two-thirds about a year earlier.[2] This was a year when large cap stocks considerably outperformed the smaller stocks, which consequently changed the valuation ratios. Therefore, in any analysis, the book value of a company should be compared to others in the same industry.

To keep book values in perspective on a larger scale, it should be understood that the U.S. economy has been changing from a manufacturing to a service-based economy. Corporations are quite different today than they were a few decades ago. Companies can now make more money using fewer assets. Also, many manufacturing operations have moved to offshore sites. Consequently, the average book value is lower now because service companies have lower book values than their manufacturing counterparts.

Book values can be inaccurate, or misleading, because they do not always reflect the true net worth of a company. This is attributed to the use of different accounting methods for items such as depreciation, which can cause book values to vary significantly. Accounting book values can be misleading because they do not reflect:

- ▌ Changes in the market value of assets.
- ▌ Impact of inflation, if any, on assets' value; appreciated assets are recognized only when sold.
- ▌ Real costs of repaying liabilities.

Therefore, when comparing price-to-book values, care should be taken to ensure that the correct basis for comparison is being used; otherwise the wrong conclusions can be reached.

Relating Book Value and Stock Prices
Despite book value limitations, good long-term correlation has existed between book values and stock prices. In the past, the price-to-book value ratio has been a good indicator before the market turned up or down. However, contrary to expectations, its warning signs since late 1990 have not led to trouble for the market.

The price-to-book value of the DJIA is reported daily in the *IBD* (Table 5.5). One of its highest values ever achieved was in June 1987, prior to the big crash, when the price-to-book value ratio was 4.5. One of

---

[2]*Investor's Business Daily,* January 22, 1997.

Table 5.5 Psychological Market Indicators

Psychological market indicator	Current	Five-year				Twelve-month			
		High	Date	Low	Date	High	Date	Low	Date
Ratio of public/NYSE specialist short sales (above 0.6 bullish; below 0.35 bearish)	0.75	2.25	6/14/96	0.56	10/31/97	2.18	9/11/98	0.68	2/20/98
Ratio of price premiums in puts versus calls	0.61	2.57	7/2/97	0.13	8/31/98	1.52	1/11/99	0.13	8/31/98
Mutual fund share purchases/redemptions (X—money market funds)	1.49	2.19	1/24/94	0.98	11/1/94	1.69	2/2/98	1.08	8/31/98
Nasdaq daily trading volume as % of NYSE daily volume	126%	199%	11/27/98	66.5%	12/16/94	199%	11/27/98	79.8%	9/4/98
Number of stock splits in Investor's Business Daily 6000 (prior 30 days)	59	211	6/18/98	40	11/16/98	211	6/18/98	40	11/16/98
New issues in last year as % of all stocks on NYSE	12.8%	33.7%	3/3/94	12.7%	12/24/98	20.4%	5/27/98	12.7%	12/24/98
Price-to-book value of Dow Jones Industrial Average	5.91	6.24	1/8/99	3.24	4/20/94	6.24	1/8/99	4.96	10/1/98
Price-to-earnings ratio of Dow Jones Industrial Average	24.8	26.2	1/8/99	13.7	10/26/95	26.2	1/8/99	19.4	8/31/98
Current dividend yield of Dow Jones Industrial Average	1.66%	2.90%	11/22/94	1.54%	5/14/98	1.96%	10/1/98	1.54%	5/14/98

Source: Investor's Business Daily, January 15, 1999. Reprinted with permission.

the lowest values was 1.06, in January 1983, at the beginning of a bull market. On July 16, 1998, a day before the market topped, the DJIA's price-to-book value was 6.15, a five-year high. The five-year low was 3.24, which was achieved in April 1994.

Depending on whether large cap or small cap stocks are in favor, the level of price-to-book ratios can vary considerably. For example, when small stocks were outperforming in 1983, their price-to-book ratio was at a 25% *premium* to large cap stocks. In 1990, this changed to a 30% *discount*. In December 1996, following a year of underperformance by the small cap stocks, they were again trading at a 30% discount.[3]

Dividend Yield

What Is a Dividend?

Typically, when a company earns a profit, it either reinvests it in the company to achieve future growth or distributes it to the shareholders as a dividend. The payout amount varies according to the level of profits earned and the company requirements (cash flow, debt level, investment needs, etc.). Many high-growth companies do not pay dividends and have no intention of doing so. They prefer to reinvest their profits to fund further growth of the company.

Calculating Dividend Yield

To calculate the dividend yield, the annual cash dividend per share is divided by the stock price. If the annual dividend is $1 per share and the stock price is $20 per share, the dividend yield is 0.05 (i.e., $1/$20), which is equivalent to 5%. This yield is a measure of the percent annual return that the dividend provides to the investor.

Dividend Yield as a Value Indicator

The dividend yield indicator, along with the price-to-book value ratio, is widely used by stock analysts. Historically, dividend yield has been the most consistent standard of value for investors. Dividend yields and P/E ratios are correlated as they both relate a measure of a company's performance to the same variable—the stock price. When a stock's dividend yield falls to very low levels, it indicates that the stock price may be too high.

The dividend percent yield of individual stocks is provided weekly in the *IBD* tables. The current and historical dividend yields for the DJIA are also reported every day in the *IBD* (Table 5.5). These include the five- and one-year high and low values.

---

[3]Ibid., February 11, 1997.

Historical Range

During the past 50 years, the dividend yield of the S&P 500 has fluctuated between a low of 1.58% and a high of 6.71%. Table 5.3 shows the range of values for the S&P 500 from 1977 to 1998. It has been observed that, typically, bull markets end with stocks yielding 2.8% to 3.3%. On the other hand, at bear market bottoms, the dividend yields are two to three times that range. A yield below 3% has historically indicated an overvalued market. Yields of 2.7% occurred at the market tops of 1929 and 1987. When the DJIA peaked on July 17, 1998, its dividend yield declined to 1.56—one of the lowest levels in history. The five-year high was 2.98, which was achieved in July 1993. The five-year low of 1.54 was reached on May 14, 1998.

Historically, though not in recent years, it has been considered a poor time to invest in the stock market whenever the yield on the DJIA fell below 3%. On the other hand, a high yield has been considered a good sign to jump in.

Usually, at or near a final bear market bottom, the DJIA's yield is greater than 6% while the P/E ratio is in the 6–8 range. When the market bottomed on September 1, 1998, the DJIA yield was still very low (1.88%) and the P/E ratio was 20.

The dividend yield should not be analyzed in isolation. Besides other variables, it also needs to be viewed in conjunction with inflation numbers. From 1967 to 1992, the average yield on the S&P was 3.8% while inflation averaged 6%. However, with the 1998 inflation rate being only 1.6%—far below the historic norm of 3%—a dividend yield in the 1.56% range did not indicate that the market was significantly overvalued in 1998.

Why Dividends Have Lost Their Importance

The dividend yield is no longer given the same importance as it was accorded a few years ago. In recent years, dividend payouts have been decreasing while free cash flow has been rising sharply. The reason for this is that companies are now using their free cash flow in other ways instead of increasing dividends. Their basic objective these days is to use free cash flow to make investments, which increase earnings, rather than to pay dividends, which are taxed twice—at both the company and the investor level.

Alternatives for using the cash available for dividend payouts include shares buyback and mergers/acquisitions, both of which boost EPS and the stock price (rather than dividends). Therefore, a low dividend yield can be quite misleading. In general, a low dividend yield becomes an important factor only if the company has inadequate cash to make its dividend payout. These days, with excellent cash flow, companies can double their current dividend payout and still have money available.[4]

Price-to-Dividend (P/D) Ratio

The price-to-dividend (P/D) ratio, another valuation indicator, is the reciprocal of the dividend yield. If a stock trades at $100 and it pays a $4 dividend, its dividend yield is 4% (i.e., $4/$100). The corresponding P/D ratio is 25 (i.e., $100/$4). Similarly, a P/D ratio of 20 is equivalent to a yield of 5%. The significance of this ratio is that it indicates the price, in dollars, that an investor has to pay to earn a one-dollar dividend. At the top of bull markets, when prices are high, the P/D ratio ranges between 28 and 38.

The price-to-dividend ratio should only be used as a general guide to determine the overvaluation and undervaluation of stocks. It should not be used as a tool to pick a market top or bottom. There are other more appropriate tools for that purpose.

Price-to-Cash Flow (P/CF) Ratio

This ratio is also used as a valuation tool. However, it is not used as widely as some of the other valuation tools. It is based on a company's cash flow (i.e., the amount of cash that can be distributed annually in the form of a dividend to the shareholders). The P/CF ratio is considered by many analysts to be a better reflection of a company's worth than other yardsticks such as dividend yield and price-to-dividend ratio. The P/CF ratio behaves in a manner similar to the P/E ratio except that it is lower. The reason for this is that the equation denominator, cash flow (CF), is larger because it includes net earnings plus tax-reducing *depreciation* and amortization charges. Table 5.6 shows the P/CF ratio of selected companies on December 31, 1998.

Price-to-Sales (P/S) Ratio

This ratio relates market valuation to total revenues (sales). The price-to-sales ratio is obtained by dividing the stock price by the prior 12 months' revenues per share. According to studies, stocks with the lowest P/S ratios have historically provided superior returns.[5]

Historically, the P/S ratio has ranged from 0.4 to 0.8 for most large

---

[4]*Wall Street Journal*, November 25, 1996, p. C1.
[5]*Money*, December 1996, p. 135.

Table 5.6   **Range of Price/Cash Flow Ratios**

	P/CF ratio	Industry average
S&P 500	22.74	
American Express	20.45	15.15
Bank One	13.64	17.70
Exxon Corp.	14.53	12.70
General Electric	24.64	20.72
General Motors	2.57	2.81
Intel Corp.	25.39	25.06
Life Financial Corp.	2.03	14.99
Lindsay Mfg.	7.74	6.15
McDonald's	21.17	17.80
Microsoft Corp.	57.49	44.08
Oracle Corp.	29.23	44.08
Papa John's Intl.	20.70	17.80
Sun Microsystems	25.45	18.34

Source: AOL/Market Guide, January 1, 1999. Reprinted with permission.

companies. If the ratio exceeded 0.8, it indicated a potentially overpriced stock. A ratio below 0.4 can be an indication that the company has a very high debt level, which should trigger further investigation. On December 31, 1998, the P/S ratio of the S&P 500 stood at 4.56. Table 5.7 shows the P/S ratios of some companies on that day.

The P/S ratio for emerging fast-growing companies can be much higher. Typically, such companies are not considered overpriced even if their P/S ratio is over 2. A number over 3 has generally indicated that the ratio may be too high. However, the P/S ratios of some winners clearly reveal the limitation of this ratio. On December 31, 1998, the P/S ratios of three excellent performers were far above this range: Microsoft (24.25), Cisco (16), and Oracle (4.88). In general, the P/S ratio is useful for analyzing companies with extremely volatile earnings.

Concluding Remarks

By far, the most important and widely used valuation tool is the P/E ratio. A stock's P/E ratio can indicate whether it is undervalued or overvalued. Also, P/E ratios can aid in identifying stocks capable of providing above-average returns. However, this tool is not foolproof. An investor should be very careful when using P/E ratios for selecting, valuing, or timing the pro-

Table 5.7   **Range of Price-to-Sales Ratios**

	Price-to-sales ratio	Industry average
S&P 500	4.56	
American Express	2.50	3.12
Bank One	3.74	4.54
Exxon Corp.	1.52	1.42
General Electric	3.33	2.75
General Motors	0.30	0.41
Intel Corp.	8.44	7.95
Life Financial Corp.	1.09	2.86
Lindsay Mfg.	1.42	0.71
McDonald's	4.34	2.99
Microsoft Corp.	24.25	17.00
Oracle Corp.	4.88	17.00
Papa John's Intl.	1.96	2.99
Sun Microsystems	3.21	2.77

Source: AOL/Market Guide, January 1, 1999. Reprinted with permission.

curement of stocks. In general, it is advisable to use the following guidelines:

▋ Use the P/E ratio only as a road sign.
▋ Analyze P/E ratios in conjunction with other fundamental factors.
▋ Price/earnings evaluation should include a comparison to other similar companies within the same industry.
▋ Use a P/E ratio based on estimated projected earnings for most analyses.

Usually, it makes good sense to favor a stock in an industry group having strong earnings growth even though its P/E may be high. The high P/E probably indicates that the stock is a leader and in demand by institutions.

It should be understood that book values are based on historical, rather than market, valuation. However, even if an adjustment is made to reflect the market value of a company's assets, book values should be used with care. In general, book value is a more appropriate tool when evaluating a company for breakup. Since price-to-book values have a serious limitation, in that they are affected by accounting decisions, the usefulness of comparing price-to-book values across companies is limited.

Chapter 6

Fundamental and Technical Analysis

There are two basic methods, or philosophies, for analyzing the stock market. These are:

▍ *Fundamental analysis*
▍ *Technical analysis*

Fundamental analysis involves the study of various factors that affect a company's earnings and dividends which, in turn, influence its stock price. About 90% of investors use fundamental analysis. This approach emphasizes the analysis of company fundamentals, financial statements, business and industry conditions, as well as general economic data. This research leads to estimates for important valuation criteria such as future earnings, book value per share, and other related measures.

Technical analysis attempts to analyze various forces affecting the prices of individual stocks and the overall stock market. It is primarily based on the study of stock market price movements and fluctuations, and is highly focused on a stock's price behavior, volume behavior, and pattern. Technical analysis is basically a short-term planning tool, and should not be used for long-term planning.

Fundamental Analysis

In fundamental analysis a company is researched in depth within its business environment. Included in this analysis are its competitors and the industry group, or sector, to which it belongs. It should be noted that no specific benchmarks are used for comparison purposes. Variables and ratios are analyzed in relation to industry norms, historical ranges, and the rest of the market.

Sources for Analyzing a Company

A number of sources can be tapped for conducting in-depth research on a company. The most commonly used sources are:

- Company literature and press releases.
- Company research and earnings estimate reports (authored by stock analysts following the company).
- Annual and quarterly reports (current and historical).
- 10K and 10Q reports (which contain more information than the annual and quarterly reports).
- Financial statements.
- Industry and trade journals.
- Newspapers.
- Shareholders' meetings.
- Online sources.

Factors to Be Analyzed in Fundamental Analysis

The basic objective of an investor is to pick companies with the best price appreciation potential in the long run. Such companies usually have a superior record of earnings and dividends. To identify such companies, the fundamentals of analyzing a company need to be learned. Factors that need to be identified and analyzed as part of this exercise are:

- Company's business.
- Corporate purpose and mission.
- Profitability (current and projected).
- Demand for products (current and future).
- Competition and pricing pressures.
- Performance track record and accomplishments.
- Relative performance compared to similar companies and the market (current and historical).
- Leadership status (whether the company is a leader or a follower).
- Management quality (strengths and weaknesses).

Basic Variables to Be Analyzed in Depth

There are many variables that affect a company's business, profitability, and stock price. Because an investor cannot analyze all these variables even in a cursory way, the practical approach is to pick a few important variables and analyze them in depth. These can be supplemented by a few additional variables, if needed. The most important and widely used variables are:

- Earnings per share
- Earnings growth rate
- Revenue (sales) growth
- Return on equity
- Cash flow
- Debt level and ratios
- Dividends

Analyzing Financial Statements

One of the basic requirements in fundamental analysis is the study of financial statements. Analysis of these statements allows an investor to determine a company's financial viability and profitability. The three financial statements most commonly analyzed are:

1. Balance sheet
2. *Income statement*
3. Statement of cash flows

Basic Approach

Analysis of any financial statement generally involves three types of comparisons:

1. Relative size of items within a set of statements.
2. Changes in each item and in the relative size of individual items.
3. Comparison of financial measures of the company to similar companies (or to industry averages); this can include single line item comparison or ratio analysis (Appendix F).

A serious stock market investor does not need to become a financial wizard. Keep in mind that only a few key items in these statements need to be analyzed. These items are usually provided in an easy-to-read format, after they have been extracted from financial statements, in company research reports that are readily available to all investors. These reports often provide additional valuable data not available in the original statements, such as comparison of various line items to the industry or group to which the company belongs (see various Appendixes).

Balance Sheet

This is a snapshot of a company's financial status that lists its assets and liabilities on a given date. It indicates a company's financial condition—what it owns, what it owes, and the stockholders' equity (net worth). Balance sheets list values for the company's assets, its liabilities (debt, long-term/short-term), and the stockholders' equity (assets/liabilities), with the basic equation being:

$$Equity = Assets - Liabilities$$

The Appendixes include a summarized balance sheet and other financial data for Oracle Corporation. The type of data contained in the Appendixes can be the basis for analysis—as will be shown in Chapter 16.

Income Statement

An income statement compares a company's total income to total expenses. The difference between the two is the profits earned or net earnings. An income statement reconciles revenues (sales), expenses, profits, and losses for a specific accounting period. It shows the annual business results, which include numbers for sales, costs, and earnings. It also includes a comparison of results against the previous year. Appendix G includes an example of Oracle Corporation's income statement.

Statement of Cash Flows

Cash flow is the net cash generated during the reporting period. It is generally defined as the net income before the deduction of charges such as depreciation and amortization. A statement of cash flow indicates how a company's financial position changed during the fiscal year. It shows where the funds came from and where they were spent, and is useful in the analysis of profit trends.

This type of analysis can be revealing. For example, while a company may have positive earnings, that does not necessarily mean that it is generating cash. Inventory and accounts receivable could be increasing, which, in turn, can cause cash to be consumed. Appendixes C and G include data on Oracle's cash flow over a multiyear period.

What to Look For in Financial Statements

An investor should determine whether this year's results were better or worse than the previous year. The cause(s) of positive and negative items as well as trends should be determined. Any management changes should be noted, which in some cases can materially affect the company. Where possible, performance should be compared to industry benchmarks and averages, because they comprise an important aspect of any analysis. When reviewing these statements, ensure that:

- The balance sheet is strong and allows the company flexibility to finance its growth.
- Revenues are growing at a healthy pace—indicating that ample demand exists for the company's products and/or services.
- Net income and earnings per share (net income divided by the number of outstanding shares) is rising.
- Margins are rising.
- If margins are not rising, they should remain steady; ideally, a company should have 15%+ pretax margins.
- Gross margin (revenues minus the direct cost of producing the product/service) is an excellent indicator of the efficiency with which the company produces goods; it is stated as a percentage of revenue.
- Research and development (R&D) expenditures are not decreasing as a percentage of annual revenues because:
  R&D is an investment in the company's future that indicates whether new products will continue to be introduced.
  Adequate R&D is a requirement for survival in a competitive environment.
- Number of outstanding shares is not increasing significantly.
- Cash reserves are ample; this can help a company to fund its growth, weather a downturn, pay dividends, buy back stock, or make an acquisition.
- Company has managed to generate cash rather than consume it.
- Any account receivable and inventory growth approximates growth in sales; too high receivable or inventory levels are warning signals.
- Profitability is not impacted by excessive debt levels.

A very important aspect of financial analysis is the study of a company's debt level and ratios, which can be obtained from company research reports (see Appendixes). These should be steady or improving. Small, successful companies usually have low debt. A company with low debt has flexibility. High debt ratios are highly undesirable, especially during poor business conditions. When analyzing the debt ratio of any company, compare it to the industry average and similar companies.

The debt ratio is often reported as a percentage of *long-term debt* to *capitalization* (capitalization ratio), which is equal to:

$$\frac{\text{Long-term debt}}{(\text{Long-term debt} + \text{Stockholders' equity})}$$

Financial statements include many footnotes that may contain significant information. These notes should be checked to ensure that there are no hidden surprises.

Analyzing the Industry

It is not sufficient to research a company without observing the environment in which it operates. An effective way to analyze a company is to study its performance, recent and historical, and then compare it to similar companies. Such companies should be in the same industry or have similar financial characteristics. Besides studying the performance of competing companies, the following need to be determined:

- Current condition of the industry to which the company belongs.
- Expected performance and prospects of the industry during the investor's investment horizon.

A method of tracking the current performance of any industry group is to note its group rank, which is reported by *IBD*—as shown in Table 6.1. It indicates how well the company's industry group has performed compared to all 197 groups. Industry group relative strength ratings, reported in *IBD*'s stock tables, are based on a scale from A (best) to E (worst). *IBD* also reports on groups with the greatest percentage of stocks making new highs as shown in Table 6.2. The *WSJ* also reports, in a limited manner, the performance of various industry groups. Industry rank is reported on the Yahoo! web site as well.

Technical Analysis

Technical analysis is based on observing a stock's behavior with the primary focus being on price and trading volume. It attempts to forecast stock price movements primarily through the use of:

- Stock price charts
- Some technical indicators

Table 6.1   *Investor's Business Daily* Industry Prices

This week	Last Friday	Three months ago	Industry	Number of stocks in group	% change since Jan. 1	Daily % change
			Rank			
1	1	18	Computer Software— Internet	62	+24.4	–2.8
2	2	25	Elec.— Semiconductor Mfg.	91	+6.4	–1.1
3	3	58	Computer— Memory Devices	46	+14.0	–0.9
195	196	190	Steel— Specialty Alloys	13	–3.7	–3.0
196	195	188	Oil & Gas— Machinery/Equip.	23	–1.0	–2.1
197	197	194	Oil & Gas— Drilling	20	+5.5	+0.2

Notes: Ranking is based on price performance. Only the three best and worst groups, out of a total of 197 industry groups, are shown in this table.
Source: Investor's Business Daily, January 15, 1999. Reprinted with permission.

Table 6.2   **Groups with the Greatest Percentage of Stocks Making New Highs**

Media—Cable TV	14%
Retail—Consumer Elect.	14%
Media—Radio/TV	7%
Media—Periodicals	7%
Transportation—Airline	7%
Utility—Water Supply	6%
Retail—Mail Order & Direct	6%
Computer Software—Security	6%
Computer—Mini/Micro	5%
Retail/Wholesale—Auto Parts	5%
Real Estate Development	5%
Commercial Svcs.—Printing	5%
Energy—Other	5%

Source: Investor's Business Daily, January 15, 1999. Reprinted with permission.

The cornerstones of technical analysis are the following principles:

■ Behavior of any stock, or the stock market, can be related to trends that develop over time; a trend refers to the main underlying direction of a stock (or the overall market).

■ Price movements are not random; they occur in patterns that can be analyzed to predict the future price movements of the stock (or the market).

In order to understand technical analysis, an investor needs to become familiar with a number of key technical analysis principles and terms. These are described, along with the typical stock price cycle, in the following sections.

Support

When a stock stabilizes after a big drop or a decline in price, technicians (technical analysts) say that it has found support or made a bottom. According to technical analysis, a stock's price should stop falling at the support level because supply will no longer exceed demand. A bottom can be recognized by a sharp sell-off (on heavy volume) or by successive price lows (on decreasing volume).

A line drawn across the low points, or bottoms, on a stock price chart is called a support line (Figure 6.1). Technicians view this as a level at which a stock will find support during a downward price move, which will prevent it from declining further. A stock may have several support levels. If a support level is breached to the downside, it is considered to be a bearish sign. When a support level is breached decisively, support is expected to be provided at the next support level.

A stock's underlying trend is represented by its moving average line, which effectively is its average price in the recent past. Typically, this period is 30, 50, or 200 days. Supply tends to diminish, and demand to rise, whenever a stock price decreases to the underlying trend (moving average line) or to levels located within a few percentage points, typically 3%, on each side of that trend. When a support level is reached, a large number of traders come in to buy, which causes the stock to rebound. In particular, buying at the support level is done by large institutional buyers. They use predetermined level(s) as their entry point.

A support line can be reached, and rebounded from, many times. A support level becomes more solid, acting like a floor, as the frequency with which support is provided by that level increases. Consequently, that level

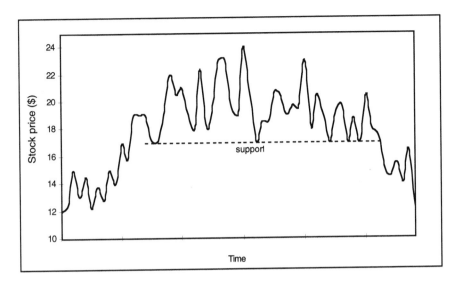

Figure 6.1 Support Line

becomes attractive as an entry point to more and more traders, as it is expected to provide a floor beneath which a stock will not slide easily, and from which a rebound can be expected. If the support line is broken, it may become a resistance level.

Resistance

A top, or resistance, is a mirror image of a bottom. According to technical analysis, it is the price at which a stock price should peak because supply will tend to rise while demand will fall off. A line drawn across the top points on a stock price chart is called a resistance line (Figure 6.2). In contrast to a floor for a support level, a resistance line provides a ceiling through which a stock cannot penetrate easily during its upward move. If it does, it is considered to be a bullish sign.

Resistance generally occurs when the price rises to the underlying trend (moving average) or to levels located within a few percentage points, typically 3%, on each side of that trend. Many investors use a resistance level as their exit point for that stock. When a resistance level is reached, a large number of sellers come in to unload their shares, which causes the stock to reverse direction. This can happen many times, with large numbers of investors dumping shares at the resistance level every time the stock price approaches that level.

A resistance level becomes more solid and important as the number of

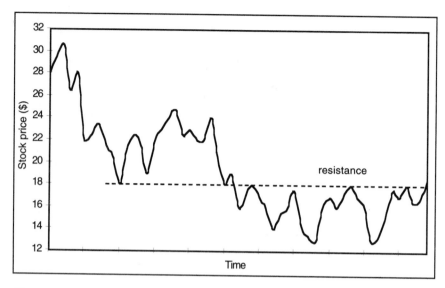

Figure 6.2   Resistance Line

approaches and failures to pierce it increase. Consequently, that level becomes attractive as a selling point to more and more traders, as it provides a ceiling above which a stock will not rise easily, and from which a reversal is expected. Therefore, technicians do not recommend buying near a resistance level. However, a powerful breakout through a resistance level on heavy volume is considered to be a very attractive point for getting into a stock. After a resistance level is breached, it usually becomes a support level.

Generally, stocks that have traded at a higher price for a long time, and with heavy volume, have the maximum resistance. Until selling dries up, a stock is unlikely to penetrate its resistance line. This can happen when some changes come into play—such as improved earnings or revenues, gain in market share, new product cycle, improving market or group, improving economy, and so on.

Basing

Basing Characteristics
When a stock trades within a narrow price range, often on low volume, it is said to be basing (Figure 6.3). During a basing period, resistance and support lines come close to each other. During this period, neither buyers nor sellers have an upper hand since they are more or less evenly matched. A basing pattern can occur for weeks, months, or even longer. During this phase, neither supply nor demand becomes one-sided. A basing period can occur:

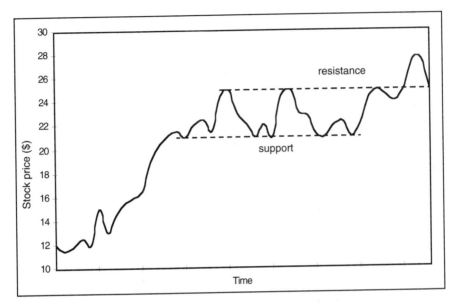

Figure 6.3   Basing Stock

- During an uptrend, when a stock pauses and rests, digesting prior gains.
- Quite often after a price decline, especially precipitous drops.

After a consolidation period, a stock will eventually move out of its trading range. This is known as a breakout, which can occur either to the upside or the downside. An upward breakout occurs when either there are few sellers left or new buyers start coming in. A downside breakout occurs when there are few buyers left and selling predominates. A guideline to confirm the validity of a breakout is for the stock to move over the top of its base by 3%.

Using the Breakout Strategy

Technicians use the breakout strategy to find strong stocks. However, buying a stock based on this strategy does not guarantee success. Many stocks have a breakout but still fail to make any significant upward move. Therefore, one should not use this strategy in isolation from other factors. When buying a breakout stock, make sure that it meets three criteria: is in a major uptrend, has based over seven weeks (preferably three to five months), and has strong earnings.

The following are some guidelines to determine the strength, or weakness, of a stock's breakout:

■ Basing duration: The longer the basing period, the more powerful is the expected breakout.
■ If most of the stock's basing has occurred above the 50-day moving average, it is the sign of a strong stock.
■ The larger the breakout (especially with heavy volume), the more bullish is the sign.
■ Higher the trading volume when breakout occurs, the more bullish is the sign; it is preferred that breakout volume be two to three times the average daily trading volume.
■ A stock breaking out of a base and quickly climbing 10% can be a very powerful mover.
■ A pullback of 3% from the top of the base is a failure indication (for example, from a 100 base top to 97).
■ Breakouts into new highs are less risky because they have less overhead resistance.
■ Relative strength should be higher than 70, preferably in the 90s (see Chapter 8).

Understanding the Stock Price Cycle

There are four major phases in a typical stock price life cycle. These are:

■ Phase 1: basing
■ Phase 2: rising
■ Phase 3: topping
■ Phase 4: declining

These four phases are shown in Figure 6.4. Technical analysts try their best to identify each phase as early as possible because of the potential for increasing, or protecting, profits through early recognition. However, in many cases these phases are not very obvious until after the fact to those viewing stock charts.

Phase 1

In this phase, the stock develops a basing area where buyers and sellers are more or less evenly matched. It trades sideways—up and down (in a range)—between the support and resistance levels. The following are important characteristics of this area:

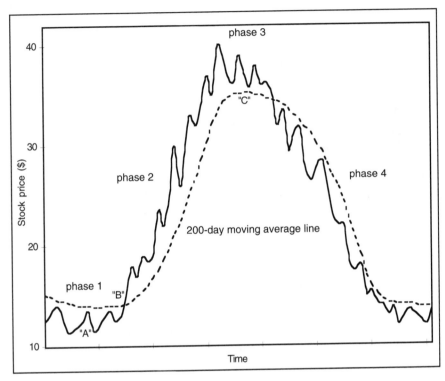

Figure 6.4   **Stock Price Life Cycle (Price versus 200-Day Moving Average)**

■ Basing can continue for weeks, months, or years.
■ Swings between the upper level (resistance) and lower level (support) are routine.
■ Buying at the low level (point A) can help ensure good trading profits.

A breakout over the top of the basing area and the 30-week or 200-day moving average, point B, signals the start of phase 2. If a stock is bought just when it starts basing, it entails the risk of tying up money for a lengthy period—without any expectation that there will be significant price appreciation until a breakout occurs.

Phase 2

In this phase, the stock starts to make higher highs. This is the most profitable phase in the stock price cycle and is considered to be the best time to buy a stock. In this phase, buyers are in control and maximum price appreciation occurs. The following are some characteristics of this phase:

- A breakout on heavy volume indicates a strong stock (even though fundamental news may not reflect that).
- The 30-week moving average starts moving up after the breakout.
- As the stock moves up, successive highs are higher.
- Lows on pullbacks are higher than the prior ones.
- If the stock drops below the 30-week moving average, it is a bearish sign.

At some point, months or years down the road, the stock price moves closer and closer to its moving average line, which starts to curve down. When this happens, it signals the end of phase 2.

Phase 3
In this phase, the stock begins to level out again. Buyers and sellers are more or less evenly matched, and the stock does not make any appreciable progress. A characteristic top (point C) starts to shape up, as in phase 1 basing, and the stock bounces up and down. While this action is mostly sideways, the stock may whipsaw across its moving average, which remains quite flat. This situation is a precursor to the start of phase 4. Hence, an investor needs to become more alert at this point and seriously evaluate exiting from the stock. No buying is recommended in this phase.

Phase 4
In this phase, the stock starts its decline, and selling, rather than buying, is recommended. This phase is characterized by the following:

- Moving averages move lower.
- Successive highs in any rally are lower than the prior one.
- Successive lows are lower than the prior ones.

Figure 6.5 shows two examples of a stock price cycle for Alliance Semiconductor and Central Sprinkler. For Alliance, one complete cycle is shown. However, the Central Sprinkler chart shows two cycles, with the second one being shorter than the first.

Trends

Trend Characteristics
Stocks do not move from one price level to another in a straight, unbroken line. Instead of moving in an uninterrupted manner to the next price

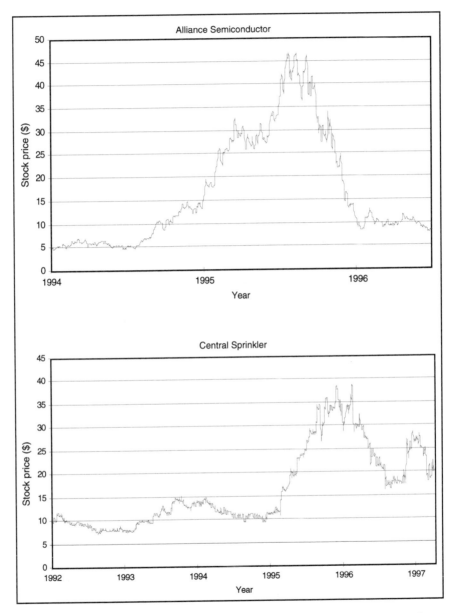

Figure 6.5 Examples of Stock Price Cycles (Alliance Semiconductor and Central Sprinkler)

level, they move in a characteristic jagged manner. A typical sequence of movements can be a slow rise up, down, up with a surge, sideways, and up again. These movements in different directions can occur during either an overall up or down price movement.

Over time, if the net price movement is up, the stock is said to be in an uptrend (Figure 6.6). If a stock's price is charted during an uptrend, it will be noticed that successive bottoms are higher than the preceding bottoms. Conversely, if the net movement is in the downward direction, the stock is said to be in a downtrend. In this case, successive bottoms will be lower than the preceding bottoms.

A trend can be either long-term or short-term. An established uptrend indicates that, for the time being, demand forces are stronger than supply forces. A major factor in establishing a trend is when institutions, which account for most trading activity in the stock market, take positions in a stock or get out of it. Once a trend is established, either up or down, it remains in place for some time due to momentum.

Identifying Trend Reversals

An investor's ability to identify an uptrend in an early stage provides an excellent opportunity to realize big gains. Usually, stocks in uptrends can be held until a reversal occurs. Trend reversal can occur after weeks, months, or even years. These trend reversals take place when there re-

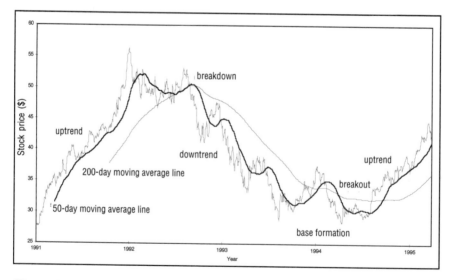

Figure 6.6   Analysis of a Stock's Price Chart (Merck)

main only a few buyers (during an uptrend) or sellers (during a down-trend). A trend can ultimately end in one of the following ways:

- A downward reversal following a rise
- An upward reversal following a decline
- Bottoming; a move into a basing pattern, especially after a decline
- Climactic rapid drop (after a decline)
- Climactic rapid rise (known as a blowoff)

Technical analysts consider an uptrend to have ended (i.e., the down-ward breakthrough to be valid) when the penetration of an uptrend line extends below the line by 5%. For example, a price decline to $95 from the uptrend line that is at $100, equivalent to a 5% drop, at the day's close is considered a valid breakthrough and a sell signal.

From a trading perspective, it is ideal to buy when trend reversal takes place at the bottom, or sell when trend reversal occurs during an upward move. For long-term investors, however, the ability to pinpoint trend re-versal points does not have the same importance. For those who plan to hold stocks for six months to many years, technical timing is not crucial. However, they can still benefit if they can determine when a trend rever-sal takes place—because they can sell or buy at more profitable exit/entry points. For this purpose, technical analysis can be a useful tool because it can help determine the points where an existing trend is likely to reverse or find support.

Tools for Identifying Trends

Investors use a number of tools to identify trends and trend reversals. The easiest and most widely used tools that an individual investor can use are described in detail in the following chapters. Sophisticated investors who want to get a handle on complicated indicators such as the moving aver-age convergence/divergence (MACD) and the stochastic index should re-fer to a number of excellent books that are available in most bookstores.

Investors can also use a number of software tools for identifying trends and trend reversals. These range from quite simple to very sophisticated and proprietary software packages. A number of these tools are listed in Chapter 3.

Concluding Remarks

There are two philosophies for investing in the stock market: fundamental and technical analysis. The vast majority of investors use fundamental analysis for investment evaluation of a company. Fundamental analysis is based on performing an in-depth analysis of the company and its environment. It includes analyzing the company's industry, financial statements, business prospects, and other related factors.

Technical analysis is based on the study of stock price movements and is favored by those with a short-term horizon—short-term traders. Investors using the fundamental analysis approach can use technical analysis as a tool to determine the appropriate time for buying a stock after a buy decision has already been made.

Stock market investors are always attempting to determine the current trend of a stock and the market, and any potential trend reversal. For those able to do this accurately, the gains can be magnified while any potential losses can be reduced appreciably. For identifying trends and trend reversals a number of tools are available to investors. A number of these are discussed in the following chapters.

Chapter 7

Stock Market Indicators

Understanding Indicators

A large number of forces, crosscurrents, and variables are at work in the stock market at all times. The effect of these variables, also called indicators, can vary significantly. The magnitude of the impact of any indicator depends on the time (recession, bull market, bear market, earnings season) as well as the presence or absence of other variables. The relative importance attached to various indicators varies according to an investor's investment philosophy, experience, and objectives. Most of these indicators, of which there are hundreds, are derived from the following main sources:

- Activity taking place in the stock market
- Actions and activities of market players (the investors)
- Economic and business data
- Coincidental factors (which may be unrelated)

Important Indicators

With hundreds of indicators to choose from, investors need to carefully pick and choose indicators. The indicators picked should be compatible with an investor's investment approach. Among the most widely monitored indicators are:

- Earnings per share (EPS)—quarterly and annual
- Earnings estimate revisions
- Earnings per share (EPS) rank
- Revenues (sales) growth

- P/E ratio
- Moving averages
- Trendlines, trend channels, and trading bands
- *Market breadth*
- Advance/decline (A/D) line
- Number of new daily lows and highs
- Relative strength (RS) rank
- Relative strength (RS) line
- Accumulation/distribution
- Trading volume
- Float—supply of stock
- Institutional ownership
- Number of analysts
- Buy/hold/sell recommendations
- Industry-specific indicators

With the exception of the P/E ratio indicator, all these indicators (as well as some related ones) are described in Chapters 7 and 8. The P/E ratio has been comprehensively discussed in Chapter 5.

Indicator Combinations

Many indicators are available to stock investors for analyzing the overall market and individual stocks. These indicators can be combined into hundreds of permutations and combinations. However, if the wrong indicators are combined, they can give very conflicting signals. The number and the types of indicators tracked by market professionals vary significantly. For example, one analyst closely tracks six indicators: *specialist short sales*, put-to-call ratios, *mutual funds cash*, technical pattern of Treasury bills and bond yields, advance/decline (A/D) line, and the bullish/bearish consensus numbers. Elaine Garzarelli, the stock market strategist who correctly predicted the DJIA crash of October 19, 1987, uses 14 indicators. She weighs monetary, economic, valuation, and sentiment indicators equally in her model.[1] The 14 fundamental factors used in her proprietary methodology for forecasting stock market movements are:

1. Earnings
2. Industrial production momentum
3. Coincident/lagging ratio

---

[1]*Garzarelli Edge*, 1996, pg. 3.

4. Free reserves
5. Three-month Treasury bill rate
6. Treasury bill rate versus *discount rate*
7. Interest rate momentum
8. *Yield curve*
9. Money supply
10. Money supply versus economy
11. Earnings yields to interest rates
12. P/E equations
13. Cash levels
14. Number of bullish advisers

As is obvious, analyzing so many indicators is beyond the capability of individual investors who have limited time and resources available to them. These investors should go for a simpler approach, which can be quite effective. Such investors should use only a few indicators that can be monitored and analyzed easily. Tracking too many indicators is not recommended because, besides being difficult to monitor and analyze, their effect is not cumulative.

Choosing Indicators

With many indicators to choose from, it is not easy to decide which ones to monitor and the relative importance to be assigned to each indicator. In general, an investor should use an assortment of indicators from different perspectives—monetary, psychological, and valuation. This combination gives greater depth than looking at one or two indicators only. Examples of indicator combinations for analyzing individual stocks are shown in Chapter 15.

Investors should realize that determining which indicator to use is an art rather than a science. Only over time, after making mistakes and gaining experience, do investors learn to pick and choose the right combination of indicators to meet their investment objectives and goals.

Earnings per Share (EPS)

One of the most important factors determining the success or failure of a stock is the company's ability to consistently earn profits. An analysis of past winners clearly shows that excellent profitability, or earnings, was a common factor in the success of most winners. Even companies whose earnings rose modestly but consistently, year after year, proved to be excellent investments.

To measure, compare, and analyze earnings, an indicator called earnings per share (EPS) is used. EPS is the net income earned by each share of common stock. Net income is equal to the after-tax income from continuing operations plus (or minus) discontinued operations and any extraordinary items.

Calculating EPS

The EPS number is calculated by dividing a company's net income by the total number of its outstanding shares. It is reported in two ways: annually and quarterly. Annual EPS is calculated by dividing the net annual income by the total number of outstanding shares. Quarterly EPS is calculated by dividing the net income for the quarter by the total number of outstanding shares.

Suppose a company's net annual earnings are $2 million and it has 4 million outstanding shares. Its annual earnings per share can be calculated as follows:

Annual EPS = $2 million/4 million shares = $0.50 per share

If the company earns $600,000 for the quarter, its quarterly EPS will be calculated as follows:

Quarterly EPS = $600,000/4 million shares = $0.15 per share

A company's annual EPS can also be calculated by adding its EPS for the prior four quarters. For example, if a company had EPS of $0.90, $1.00, $1.15, and $1.25 in the prior four quarters, its annual EPS will be:

$0.90 + $1.00 + $1.15 + $1.25 = $4.30 per share

EPS Growth Rate

To analyze a company's profitability, investors thoroughly analyze earnings because higher earnings translate into a higher EPS and a higher stock price. The two earnings components that receive the maximum attention from investors are:

1. Current quarterly earnings (EPS) and its rate of increase
2. Annual earnings (EPS) growth rate

The EPS growth rate is calculated as follows:

$$\text{EPS growth rate} = \frac{(\text{EPS in current year} - \text{EPS in prior year})}{\text{EPS in prior year}}$$

For example, if the annual EPS in the current year is $2.50, while it was $2.20 in the prior year, the annual EPS growth rate will be:

$$\frac{(\$2.50 - \$2.20)}{\$2.20} = 13.6\%$$

An important factor in the success of stocks is the acceleration in earnings growth. This refers to the rising percentage change in profit, as measured from one period to the next. Accelerating earnings growth is one of the most potent factors in the success of a stock. For example, starting in the third quarter of 1995, Ascend Communications increased its operating earnings in the following sequence: 133%, 300%, 325%, and 380%. During this period, the stock rose from 17 to over 70. Table 7.1 shows examples of some winners in recent years. It lists the characteristics of some leaders who had a phenomenal run-up despite poor market conditions at the time they made their big moves. As can be observed, all of them had high EPS rank (90+). Therefore, considering this potent factor, investors should monitor a company's EPS growth rate and earnings acceleration rate very closely.

EPS as a Comparison Tool

The EPS number helps in comparing companies of different sizes. It puts profits in perspective by comparing them by using the same yardstick. For example, a company earning $100 million annually, with 100 million outstanding shares, will have an EPS of $1 per share. However, if a smaller company earns $25 million per year, and it has 10 million outstanding shares, its EPS will be $2.50 per share—a far higher number. Obviously, the latter is a better value for the shareholders, even though company profits are $75 million less, since it provides them with a better rate of return.

Effect of Earnings on P/E Multiples

There are three important factors that can make a stock price rise:

Table 7.1 Characteristics of Winners

Company	Buy point	Percent increase	Period (weeks)	Five-year EPS growth % (at buy point)	Last quarter EPS change %	EPS rank %	RS rank %	P/E ratio	Industry
Cisco Systems	11/2/90	2,687	175	257	155	99	97	30	Computer—LANs
Micron Technology	1/20/95	294	33	312	132	99	94	10	Elec. Comp.—Semiconductors
International Game Technology	2/1/91	1,510	143	81	39	93	94	19	Leisure & Rec./Gaming
Home Depot	8/20/82	462	42	New issue	386	97	98	58	Bldg. Products—Retail/Wholesale
Amgen	3/16/90	658	94	Losses	700	94	90	281	Med.—Biomedical
Wal-Mart Stores	6/15/79	961	215	31	35	NA	74	12	Retail—Discount & Variety
Surgical Care Affiliates	2/24/89	1,410	146	Losses	267	92	89	28	Medical Products
Ascend Communications	7/29/94	3,223	93	New issue	100	91	94	49	Telecommunication Equipment
Microsoft	10/17/86	305	49	99	75	98	80	22	Computer—Software
Franklin Resources	9/7/84	1,294	126	102	115	99	96	13	Finance—Inv Mgmt

Source: *Investor's Business Daily*, August–Sept., 1996. Reprinted with permission.

1. Earnings increase; any rise in earnings gets translated into a higher price—assuming that the P/E remains steady.
2. Investors bid up the stock to a higher P/E, while earnings remain unchanged.
3. Both earnings and P/E rise.

Investors' changing perception of a company's future earnings potential can result in their awarding its stock a higher P/E than it currently commands. Any P/E increase over the current level combined with accelerating earnings can cause a stock price to increase tremendously. An example is Informix, which in May 1994 was trading at a P/E half that compared to other companies in its group. When investors realized that the company would release its products on time, and its earnings would most likely grow at a healthy pace, its price was bid up from $16.06 to $32.125 within seven months. Its P/E doubled during that period, rising to a level in line with other companies in its group.

If a company's earnings start to accelerate, as they did for Ascend Communications, they start beating earnings estimates. This causes analysts to start revising their earnings estimates, which fuels the price upward. This typically occurs at the start of a strong product cycle, when a company enters a strong and rapid growth phase.

How Earnings Are Reported

A stock's price rises or falls over the long term in tandem with the company's earnings, dividends, and financial health. Therefore, since investors are aware of how earnings influence a stock's price, they wait for a company's earnings announcements with anticipation. These earnings, accompanied with financial highlights, are released every quarter. The reporting months can vary from company to company; however, most companies follow the calendar year and report the quarterly earnings in April (1Q), July (2Q), October (3Q), and January (4Q).

Earnings are reported by the major newspapers, online services, and a number of Internet sites. The most comprehensive earnings data are reported by *IBD*, *WSJ*, and *Barron's*. These publications provide tables listing companies with the highest percentage change in earnings (up or down). Estimated earnings can also be obtained from the sources listed in Table 3.6.

Analyzing Earnings

Earnings releases from companies are accompanied by high-sounding and glowing descriptions of their performance. However, an astute investor will look closely at the results to discern the true picture. For example, while the reported earnings may be record ones, they may not show up favorably when compared year-to-year in percentage terms. The company's earnings growth rate could actually have decreased despite higher revenues.

An investor should study earnings reports closely and be on the lookout for write-offs and restructuring charges, which can distort earnings. Also to be noted are nonrecurring or extraordinary items because they too can distort earnings. One should always observe signs of acceleration or deceleration in earnings, a good indicator of potential gains or losses.

If it is observed that earnings decreased or failed to grow as expected, the cause(s) should be investigated. For example, earnings can be temporarily affected due to an acquisition which, while temporarily depressing the present earnings, has the potential to provide excellent growth and profits in the future. An example is the acquisition of a number of companies by Platinum Technology in 1995 and 1996, which depressed its earnings and stock price. However, the acquisitions positioned Platinum strategically for the future and, as expected, it rebounded strongly and the share price more than doubled in 1997.

Quarterly EPS (Current Quarterly Earnings per Share)

The earnings per share reported for the latest quarter is a very good indicator of the current profitability of a company. It shows the magnitude and trend of its recent earnings, which is the fundamental basis for stock valuation.

What to Look For

Analysts look for a company's EPS to be increasing consistently. The EPS chart in Appendix D shows the consistent stock price rise for Oracle Corporation in tandem with the rise in its quarterly and annual EPS. More than seeing a simple increase in EPS, investors prefer to see an accelerating rate of increase in EPS (i.e., the percentage increase). For example, if a company's earnings have been growing at 20% per year and accelerate to 35% or even higher, it is a sure sign that its stock is poised to make a significant upward price move.

The greater the rate of increase in EPS, the greater is the price appreciation potential for the stock. This is borne out by the behavior of past winners whose profits increased 60% to 90% prior to their significant and rapid price advance. Consequently, one of the most important factors in stock selection is the percentage increase in EPS compared to the same quarter of the previous year. In general, the current quarterly EPS should have a high percentage increase (20% to 30% over the previous year's comparable quarter). Examples of winning stocks rising in tandem with accelerating quarterly EPS are shown in Table 7.1.

Periods to Analyze

When analyzing EPS, both the quarterly and six- to nine-month periods should be analyzed separately. Analyzing EPS for only a combined six- or nine-month period can cause an important trend to be missed. Suppose that the total EPS for the last nine-month period (current fiscal year) was higher than the corresponding period of the previous fiscal year. The limitation of this combined nine-month EPS number is that it will be unable to show whether the last quarter was worse compared to both the prior quarter (of this year) and the comparable quarter (of last year).

Specifically, a combined EPS for the first nine months of 1999 would be unable to show that the EPS for the third quarter (3Q) of 1999 was lower than both the EPS of the second quarter (2Q) of 1999 and the EPS of the third quarter (3Q) of 1998.

Such a situation is considered bearish because it indicates decelerating earnings and, hence, it would definitely need to be investigated.

Guidelines and Tips for Analyzing Quarterly EPS

▪ Analyze EPS for at least two or three prior quarters; analyze the quarterly trend, not a consolidated period.

▪ EPS in the last quarter should be compared to the same quarter of the previous year. For example:
  EPS for the first quarter of 1999 should be compared to the first quarter of 1998.
  EPS for the first quarter of 1999 should not be compared to the fourth quarter of 1998.

▪ The current quarterly earnings increase, in percentage terms, should be compared to the same quarter a year ago.

▪ The higher the percentage increase in EPS, the better it is.

▪ Select stocks with accelerating quarterly earnings growth.

▪ Favor companies with 20% to 30% increase in earnings in the last reported quarter (versus the comparable quarter of the previous year).

▪ Winning stocks with accelerating earnings usually see a very heavy increase in trading volume prior to their price breakout to the upside.

▮ Comparison can be misleading if earnings in the previous year were low or there was a loss; in such a case, a poor current EPS can appear good compared to the previous year's earnings.

▮ Notice any unusual factors, extraordinary charges, onetime items, or an increase/decrease in number of outstanding shares, which can distort earnings.

▮ Compare earnings to other stocks in the same group/industry; if earnings at similar companies are growing at 30%, and the company being analyzed is growing at 20%, it is not a positive sign and should be investigated.

▮ Analyze current earnings in conjunction with anticipated future prospects (based on fundamentals and news).

Annual Earnings per Share

An Indicator of Consistent Profitability

Investors should analyze both the quarterly and annual earnings per share. While recent quarterly earnings results are a good indicator of a company's current profitability and momentum, its annual earnings provide another useful perspective. It enables investors to confirm a consistent and healthy earnings history, which is the sign of a winning stock. As mentioned, the EPS chart in Appendix D shows Oracle's consistent price rise in tandem with the rise in its quarterly and annual EPS.

Investors want to see a company's annual EPS show an increasing trend for the past five years. A down year can be ignored if a quick earnings recovery was made in the following year, and the upward earnings trend continued. This five-year growth criterion is used by many analysts as a screening criterion in the stock selection process. When used as a screening method, the five-year earnings growth criterion can easily screen out 75% of stocks.

Use Projected Annual Earnings

A widely used valuation method employed by investors to determine if a stock is overvalued or undervalued is based on analyzing its P/E ratio. These investors consider a stock to be undervalued if its P/E is low and overvalued if its P/E is high. Typically, using the under/overvalued criteria, such investors decide whether a stock should be bought or sold.

As is quite obvious, the magnitude of the P/E ratio is directly dependent on the annual earnings number used in the P/E calculation. Typically, this ratio is calculated using the trailing earnings figure. However, using this backward-looking number does not make much sense. Instead, it is more appropriate to use projected future earnings, which are more relevant to a stock's future price movement and achievable level.

How to Forecast Earnings

Estimating future earnings, which depend on a company's future earnings growth, is not an easy or simple task. Investors who are able to forecast future earnings growth of companies manage to get a head start in predicting stock price appreciation. Consequently, they are able to reap excellent financial gains. One way to predict this growth rate is to analyze the growth prospects of the industry group to which the company belongs, as well as the company itself. There are a number of sources from which estimated earnings growth rates for the company and the industry can be obtained. These include Value Line (Appendix A), First Call (Appendix B), Standard & Poor's (Appendix C), Zacks (Appendix D), S&P industry surveys, Yahoo! (Appendix I), and various other Internet sites.

Guidelines and Tips for Analyzing Annual Earnings

- The annual compounded earnings growth rate should be 20% to 50% or higher for the prior three-to-five-year period.
- If growth rate decreases, say from 35% to 20%, evaluate selling the stock even if it has been a leader.
- The faster the earnings growth, the greater are future earnings and stock price to be expected.
- Both annual and quarterly EPS should be growing at a healthy pace.
- Consistent earnings growth in the past few years combined with strong current earnings in recent quarters are the ingredients of an outstanding stock.
- P/E ratios reported in newspapers are typically based on trailing (past) earnings, which have little bearing on future performance; use projected earnings.

Earnings Estimate Revisions and Earnings Surprises

Earnings Estimates

The level of earnings affects stock prices significantly. Therefore, analysts try to forecast a company's earnings for the current quarter and year. These forecasted earnings are called earnings estimates. Some analysts conduct their own research, while others publish the average of what has been estimated by stock analysts tracking the company. The earnings estimates published by

S&P Corporation and Value Line are based on the research each conducts as a single organization.

Other estimates reported by First Call, Zacks, and the Yahoo! web site are based on data provided by a large number of analysts working for different organizations. These earnings estimates are called consensus earnings estimates. Besides the average estimate, First Call, Zacks, and Yahoo! also report the high and low range of earnings estimates. The consensus earnings estimates generate more confidence than estimates from single sources. The reason is that a single wrong estimate in a large number of estimates cannot distort the average (consensus) estimate significantly.

When analyzing earnings estimates, the range of earnings estimates should be checked. Suppose two companies have the same mean earnings estimate of $1.50 per share—with the first company's earnings in the $1.40 to $1.60 range and the second company's earnings in the $1 to $2 range. The reaction by investors to an earnings surprise of the same magnitude from these two companies will be different. A 10-cent shortfall or positive surprise will have a greater impact on the company with the narrower band ($1.40–$1.60) than on the company with the wide earnings estimate spread ($1–$2).

Earnings estimate reports can be purchased for a small fee through a broker or from several Internet and online investment sites. A number of these are listed in Chapter 3. Many web sites, including Yahoo!, provide free earnings estimates.

Understanding Earnings Estimates

The market usually prices a stock based on its expected future earnings. Since the market is quite knowledgeable and efficient, earnings estimates are generally already reflected in a stock's price. Simply stated, current expectations are already reflected in a stock's price and any change in expectations brings swift market reaction. For example, if the market is used to a company beating earnings estimates, and it announces earnings that do not beat Wall Street expectations, its stock price will drop in most cases. Also, if a company does not meet estimates, its stock will invariably be punished.

Earnings estimates should be used with care. The following are some important factors to keep in mind when using earnings estimates:

- One-time gains/losses can distort earnings estimates.
- Only operating earnings should be considered.
- Many five-year growth projections for relatively young firms can be completely unrealistic due to excessive bullishness—this results in higher P/E ratios.

▮ Estimates for companies made by only a few analysts should be viewed with extreme caution.

▮ Analysts typically underestimate earnings when they are rising and overestimate them when they are falling.

Earnings Estimate Revisions

What Revisions Indicate

Usually, estimates revised upward indicate that something positive is happening in the company or its industry. The positive factors could be accelerating revenues, introduction of successful new product(s), gain in market share, cost cutting, and so on. All these tend to increase the bottom line profitability. Consequently, the upward revision of an earnings estimate is one of the best indicators for predicting a rising stock price. Therefore, investors should seek stocks whose earnings estimates are being revised upward rather than downward.

Investors should watch earnings estimate revisions very closely. When a company's earnings estimates are being lowered, the probability of the stock outperforming the market is considered slim.

Effect of Revisions

While the earnings estimate figures are important for analyzing stocks, the key is earnings revision rather than the estimates themselves. As earnings expectations change based on the changing prospects for the company or the economy, analysts following the company translate the information and news they collect into numbers. These are used to revise the current earnings estimates upward or downward to reflect the positive or negative developments. Any upward earnings revision is considered positive, which causes the stock price to rise. Any downward revision is considered negative, which tends to drive the stock down.

Investors use revisions in earnings estimates to gauge the direction and magnitude of the improving or deteriorating fundamental health of a company. Based on the new estimates, their expectations for price appreciation or decrease change proportionately.

How Revisions Are Reported

Upward and downward earnings revisions, which indicate the average revision in each estimate, are typically reported for the past 7, 30, and 60 days. The higher the one-month change in earnings estimate, the better it is. A significant upward revision in earnings estimate can occur if several analysts raise the estimate simultaneously or if a single analyst raises the estimate by a large amount. Appendix B shows the earnings estimate revisions made for Oracle Corporation.

The effect of revisions can be gauged from the case of Project Software and Development Company. In its July 1996 earnings estimate report, issued by First Call, the following revisions were made for fiscal years 1996 and 1997:

▮ Five upward revisions, with no downward revision, in the past 7 days.
▮ Six upward revisions, with one downward revision, in the past 30 days.
▮ Six upward revisions, with one downward revision, in the past 60 days.

After these revisions were made, the stock rose from $29.75 on July 30, 1996, to $42.375 by December 31, 1996.

Earnings Surprises

Effect of Earnings Surprises

A company's earnings results are viewed positively if its quarterly result compares favorably against the previous year's comparable quarter. A stock is viewed even more favorably if it exceeds earnings expectations. When a company reports better than expected earnings figures, it is known as an earnings surprise. Any earnings surprises reported on a particular day are highlighted by the WSJ, Barron's, and IBD as shown in Table 7.2.

Companies beating estimates are well rewarded with price appreciation. However, those failing to meet investor expectations are severely punished. Even small disappointments can cause big price drops. If the leading stock in a group (such as Intel in the semiconductor group) reports better than expected earnings, it almost invariably moves the whole group positively. The converse also holds true. Sometimes beating estimates is not considered good enough by the market because such an increase may have resulted from cost cutting, aimed at boosting profits, rather than from increased revenues.

Effect on Smaller Companies

Small growth companies are affected more dramatically than large cap companies by earnings surprises. The reason is that fewer analysts cover them and, therefore, any unexpected positive earnings news attracts other analysts and investors—creating additional buying. Conversely, any nega-

Table 7.2   **Earnings News: Best Ups and Most Downs**

Company	Symbol	Last quarter change	Last quarter earnings ($/sh)	Last quarter sales	After-tax margin
Best Ups					
Wachovia Corp.	WB	+5850%	1.19 vs. 0.02	+0%	+0.0%
Genesys Telecomm Lab Inc.	GCTI	+183%	0.17 vs. 0.06	+68%	−32.5%
ATI Technologies Inc.	ATYTF	+100%	0.26 vs. 0.13	+95%	+15.3%
Cree Research	CREE	+91%	0.21 vs. 0.11	+39%	+20.3%
Unisys Corp.	US	+76%	0.44 vs. 0.25	+8%	+6.8%
Community Banks Inc.	CTY	+74%	0.40 vs. 0.23	+0%	+0.0%
Most Downs					
Motorola Inc.	MOT	−52%	0.25 vs. 0.54	+1%	+1.9%
Raychem	RYC	−39%	0.40 vs. 0.66	−3%	+7.0%
Premisys Communications	PRMS	−37%	0.10 vs. 0.16	+3%	+10.0%

Source: Investor's Business Daily, January 15, 1999. Reprinted with permission.

tive earnings surprise initiates heavy selling, which usually causes small, low-trading-volume stocks to decline considerably due to the disproportionately large selling volume.

A reason for the disproportionate price effect relative to positive or negative surprises is communications. For investors who want it, earnings information is available the moment it is released. So when they see a disappointing result, they react and exit from the stock immediately. These days, when a bad report comes out, selling takes place instantaneously, rather than slowly. This availability of instant information amplifies the price change due to earnings surprises both ways, though more so on the downside.

Company executives know how a stock can be affected due to any failure to meet earnings expectations. Therefore, they typically try to downplay their earnings prospects so that, later on, they can beat analysts' estimates and give their stock a boost.

How Investors Should React to Earnings Disappointments

Short-term traders are significantly influenced by earnings results and surprises. They react accordingly—selling at the first sign of any weakness. A long-term investor should not buy or sell stocks based solely on quarterly results. Serious investors should perform fundamental research and be confident with the long-term prospects of the company. The focus should be on analyzing how well the company will perform in the next 12 to 18 months.

A long-term investor should stick with his or her investment style and not be overly swayed by short-term trading fluctuations and the opinion or actions of other investors or traders. If an investor's stock falls due to a temporary earnings shortfall, but the fundamentals remain solid, the investor should buy more. The price decline should be viewed as a buying opportunity. However, in such a case, an investor should buy more shares only if he or she knows the company very well. If an earnings disappointment comes in and the company's outlook is not bright, it should be sold without hesitation.

Earnings per Share (EPS) Rank

Calculating the EPS Rank

EPS rank is a yardstick for comparing a company's profit growth with all other companies in the stock market. It measures a company's earnings growth and the stability of that growth over the past five years with emphasis being placed on the last two quarters.

To calculate EPS rank, the percentage earnings change in the two most recent quarters (compared to the same quarters of the previous year) are combined and averaged with the five-year figure.[2] The number thus obtained is compared to the results of all other companies and ranked on a scale from 1 to 99. An EPS rank of 99 indicates that the company's profits have been better than 99% of the companies in the stock market. An EPS rank of 75 means that the company's earnings growth place it in the top 25% of all companies. EPS rank is reported daily in *IBD*'s stock tables; *IBD* is the only daily newspaper reporting this data.

Relating EPS Rank to Stock and Market Performance

Stocks with high EPS rank tend to perform better than other stocks. Cisco Systems and International Game Technology are examples of companies with high EPS ranks that had superior price appreciation. Cisco, with an EPS rank of 99, had quarterly profit gains averaging 150% during its first three years as a public company starting in 1990. During the same period, its stock made a 12-fold move. International Game Technology, with an

---

[2]*Investor's Business Daily*, February 27, 1998.

EPS of 99, made a 10-fold move from 1991 to 1992. In the previous five years, its annual profit growth had been 112%.

An *IBD* survey in 1997 covering 6,000 stocks also provides confirmation that stocks with the best price performance in the prior 12 months (i.e., with an RS rank over 95) have had superior earnings.[3] The survey found that 54% of these stocks had EPS rank greater than 70. Only 32% of the stocks had an EPS rank below 50.

When the market is trending higher, companies with high EPS rank tend to outperform. For example, one study of the market revealed that there were 75 stocks with an EPS rank of 99 priced above $4 per share, out of 7,000 stocks that were analyzed. Three months later, after the market improved, 57 of these stocks had moved higher for an average gain of 29%. Even after including stocks that had moved lower, the 75 companies with 99 EPS rank had moved up for a 19% gain. During the same period, the S&P 500 rose a meager 1.5%.

Using EPS Rank for Stock Selection

Many investors use EPS rank for stock picking. They realize that companies with high EPS rank have strong momentum. They also tend to produce fewer earnings disappointments, which can decimate a stock. An investor can realize tremendous gains by picking low-EPS-rank stocks that will ultimately rise to a 90+ EPS rank. However, this requires sound fundamental analysis in order to ensure that a basis exists for the selected company's earnings to rise in the future. This is imperative because only rising earnings can make the EPS rank rise.

Investors should not focus only on the EPS rank when evaluating a company as a buy candidate. A better approach may be to buy a company whose EPS rank is trending higher. Such companies are also favored by trend-following momentum investors.

Risk of EPS Rank

High EPS rank does not guarantee profits and safety. Since such companies generate high valuations and expectations, any sign of a disappointment is enough to decimate their stock. A good example is Micron Technology. In November 1995, after a fantastic run-up that took it to a high of $94^3/_4$ from its January low of 22, Micron was trading

---

[3]Ibid., January 29, 1997.

with an EPS of 99 and RS of 90. However, when investors realized that a slowdown was occurring in the semiconductor industry that would impact earnings, Micron started to decline rapidly and give up almost all its gains. By January 1996 it had declined to 29, and by mid-1996 its shares had reached a low of $16.625 (Figure 7.1). To avoid such disasters, investors should closely monitor such stocks. They should always be alert so that they can pick up signs or any subtle hints of a slowing earnings momentum.

A Word of Caution

It should be noted that EPS rank has its limitations. It is calculated with earnings that have already been reported. It does not indicate any potential earnings slowdown in the future. Also, it cannot be a substitute for sound fundamental analysis. An investor should never buy a stock based only on its EPS rank. The EPS rank should be just one of many tools in an investor's arsenal.

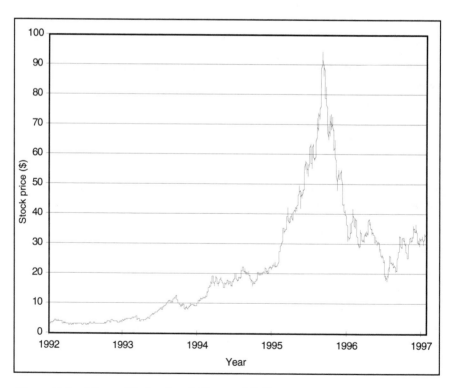

Figure 7.1   Micron Technology's Rise and Fall

Revenue (Sales) Growth

One of the most important items that an investor needs to analyze is a company's revenues. Revenue or sales is the dollar value of goods and services that a company brings in, by selling its products or services, during a quarter or the year. Revenues along with net income are a very good barometer of a company's health. For a company to increase profitability consistently, revenues should show consistent growth. Revenue growth indicates a growing demand for products and services that customers want or need. Rising sales also mean that the product(s) can be produced at a lower cost per unit, which can improve profit margins.

Analyzing Sales

Sales growth drives everything on the income statement and balance sheet. Every analysis should determine whether sales increased or decreased, since focusing on the gross sales number alone is inadequate. The reason(s) for any decrease or increase in sales should be determined. For example, analysis can reveal that gross sales changed due to a decrease/increase in the number of units sold, unit prices, or currency fluctuations. Since sales are less volatile than earnings, an investor should closely analyze sales trends. If it is noticed that the rate of increase in sales is declining, a warning flag should go up.

Sales growth must translate into earnings at the bottom line. If sales are increasing but earnings are not keeping pace, the reasons should be determined. For example, costs and expenses may be rising faster, which could be a temporary phenomenon. As part of the analysis, one should look closely at margins (operating profit, pretax profit, and net profit). Improving operating margins indicate that the company is becoming more dominant in its industry. Net margins are reported in company research reports (see various Appendixes).

Return on Sales

Another indicator that is analyzed by investors is return on sales. It is the percentage of sales that a company converts into profits. It is equal to net income divided by sales. The higher the return on sales, the more efficiently the company is converting sales into net income and managing its business.

Comparing Sales

To put sales numbers in perspective, they should be compared where possible to those of other companies in the same group or industry. A number of benchmarks are available for this purpose. For example, the retailing industry uses the "same store sales" number for comparison. This is the percentage increase in sales generated by stores that have been in business for at least one year. The price-to-sales (P/S) ratio relates market valuation to total revenues (sales). It is a useful ratio that is also used for comparison purposes (Appendixes D and F).

Company research reports can be used for comparing performance data and ratios with other companies in the same industry. Financial statements also contain valuable revenue information. Some useful information can be gleaned with a simple comparison to other companies. For example, analysis of a software company's sales showed that when its far larger but less efficient competitor had comparable revenues a few years earlier, it had four times as many employees. The competitor had maintained poor control of its expenses and sales force and, not surprisingly, it ran into serious financial problems. Therefore, in this case, it was quite obvious that the company being analyzed was operating quite efficiently.

Moving Averages

Besides fundamentals and psychological indicators (market sentiment indicators), investors use mechanical technical tools to analyze the stock market and individual stocks. Among the widely used tools in this category are the various moving averages, which determine trends.

A moving average is essentially the average price of a stock for a specified period. The objective of a moving average is to get a smooth directional trend by eliminating random, irregular fluctuations and noise. A moving average is an important tool because it helps determine whether a stock is in an uptrend or downtrend.

Moving averages can be plotted for any time period. However, the most widely used ones are the 30-day, 50-day, and 200-day moving averages. Some analysts use a 60-day instead of the 50-day moving average. Moving averages can be plotted for individual stocks or for any stock market index. The same basic interpretation principles and analysis guidelines apply in both cases. However, differences do exist, which are listed and explained in the following sections.

What a Moving Average Indicates

The use of a moving average is based on the assumption that if a stock pushes through its moving average line, such as the 30-day or 50-day moving average line, it will continue moving in the same direction for some time due to momentum. If penetration is to the upside, momentum will make the stock continue its upward move, rather than let it move in the downward direction (Figure 7.2). Similarly, if penetration through the moving average line is to the downside, it is expected that the stock will continue to move downward, rather than reverse direction upward. Therefore, when a stock trades above its moving average line or pushes through it, investors view it bullishly and consider it a buy signal. On the other hand, selling is indicated when a stock trades below or slides below its moving average line.

The explanation for this behavior is investor sentiment and psychology. Consider a stock that is trading above its 50-day moving average line. The majority of its recent buyers will have bought their shares at a lower price. Therefore, they will view their investment positively. Conversely, if a stock is trading below its 50-day moving average, most of its recent buyers will have bought it at a higher price. Therefore, they will view their investment bearishly, which will become a further drag on the stock. This helps explain the basic technical analysis rule of investing: Buy stocks in uptrends and sell them in downtrends.

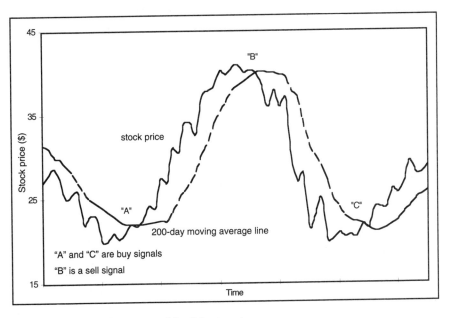

Figure 7.2   **Stock Price and Its Moving Average**

Calculating a Moving Average

A 50-day moving average is the average price of a stock over the past 50 days. It is calculated in two steps:

1. Add a stock's closing price of the day to the closing prices of the previous 49 days.
2. Divide the resulting sum by 50.

This number is plotted daily, generating a line that becomes a moving average that shows a smoothed trend of past prices. Typically, a moving average line is plotted against the stock price with the aim being to clearly show their relationship.

Once created, a moving average line is maintained, or made to "move," by using a simple procedure. Every day, the newest closing stock price is added to the 50-day sum after the oldest value (the stock price 50 days ago) is dropped (subtracted) from the 50-day sum. The new sum is then divided by 50 to get the current moving average. This procedure ensures that the 50 most recent days are always used in the calculations.

The 50-day moving average is shown in most stock and market charts provided by various sources. For individual stocks, the Yahoo! web site is a good source for determining a stock's current price relative to its 50-day moving average.

Which Moving Average to Use

A study of a stock's pattern can be revealing when deciding which moving average to use. In general, the time span to be used for a moving average depends on the investment time frame. A long-term investor uses a moving average based on a longer period, typically 50 or 200 days, while a short-term trader uses a shorter period. The 21-day moving average is commonly used by short- and intermediate-term players. Day traders use the five-day moving average.

The 30-day moving average is very often followed. Since it is so widely used and monitored, any price move below this line causes a rather severe negative sentiment and reaction.

The time period for a moving average also varies according to a stock's volatility (*beta*). Since a stock with a high beta can have wide and sharp price swings, it is analyzed with a moving average based on a longer time period.

Moving Averages and Buy/Sell Timing

The main objective of using a moving average is to determine its position relative to the stock or market index price, as well as its direction. When a stock or an index (like the DJIA or the S&P 500) is above its moving average line, it is viewed bullishly. On the other hand, if it is below its moving average line, this is considered to be a bearish sign. If an index or a stock is moving decisively above or below its 200-day moving average, this is usually considered to be a buy or sell signal, respectively. However, one should be very careful in using the 30-day moving average line as a buy or sell indicator, because a stock can move back and forth across this line quite frequently.

Moving averages are lagging indicators. If used as tools to generate buy and sell signals, they can be rather late—with associated consequences. It should be realized that a moving average is just one of many tools that technical analysts use for analyzing trends. This indicator must not be used in isolation while ignoring other factors. It is preferable to use it as a signal that something has changed, rather than using it purely as a timing device (i.e., a sell or buy signal for getting out of, or into, a stock or the market).

Moving Average as a Forecasting Indicator

A downward breach of a moving average line is a bearish sign that often precipitates massive selling. Perhaps one of the best-known instances of the stock market plunging after a moving average line was breached occurred in October 1987. Until then, for the prior three years, the S&P 500 had been trading above its 200-day moving average line. On October 15, 1987, the index cut below its moving average line, sending a warning signal. On October 19, Black Monday, the stock market crashed 22.6%.

In April 1997, the Nasdaq's 200-day moving average line was breached. After trading below this line for approximately a month, the Nasdaq rebounded and continued to climb strongly. By early October, the index had risen to 1,700 from its April low of 1,194—a gain of 42%.

In August 1998, the DJIA's 200-day moving average line, as well as the Nasdaq's 200-day moving average line, were breached. It signaled the start of the bear market that caused the DJIA to decline 21.56% and the Nasdaq to lose 33.09%.

An investor should realize that penetration of the 200-day moving average does not guarantee a change in the market's direction. In January 1998, the Nasdaq slipped below its 200-day moving average line. However, it stayed below the line for only two days and then started a powerful move upward. From a low level of 1,465 on January 12, it climbed to a level of 1,770 by the end of February.

An index can crisscross its moving average line for months without any meaningful change in direction. For example, from October 1997 through January 1998, the DJIA moved below its 200-day moving average line four times. However, the long-term upward trend remained intact. In recent years, due to the instant availability of information, the number and impact of momentum players have increased considerably. Since so many investors are simultaneously monitoring the stock market, and taking almost collective action when a technical sell signal is generated, a strategy based on moving averages tends to end up being self-fulfilling.

Rules and Tips for Using Moving Averages

Though all moving averages help determine the price trend, their interpretation can be somewhat different depending on the moving average period. However, some common rules do exist for using moving averages for both individual stocks and the market. These rules are:

- Like all indicators, moving averages are not infallible.
- No definitive way exists to interpret the violation of a moving average line.
- Technical patterns should be analyzed in conjunction with fundamentals.

Rules and Tips for Stocks

- Stock is in an uptrend if it has been trading above its moving average line for some time.
- Stock is in a downtrend if it has been trading below its moving average line for some time.
- If a stock is moving decisively above or below its 200-day moving average line, it is considered a strong buy or sell signal respectively.
- Stock is vulnerable to a correction if it is overextended above its moving average line.
- Stock that breaks below its moving average line:
  May be headed lower.
  Is viewed bearishly if accompanied with heavy volume.
- Stock breaking out above its moving average line is expected to make good price gains.
- If a moving average line is breached to the upside on heavy volume, and:
  Fundamentals are positive, it is considered a buy signal.

Fundamentals are negative, do not rush to buy; if penetration of the moving average line is significant, a comprehensive review and analysis is in order.

∎ If a stock moves above its 30-day moving average line when it is trading above its 200-day moving average line, it is considered bullish; a move in the opposite direction is considered bearish.

Rules and Tips for the Market

∎ If major market indexes (such as the DJIA or the S&P 500) remain above their 200-day moving average, an upward trend is indicated.

∎ Note divergences between important market indexes and their moving averages:

If major market indexes are above their 200-day moving average and one suddenly drops below it, the other market averages will often follow.

If an index is moving decisively above or below its 200-day moving average line, it is considered a strong buy or sell signal respectively.

∎ If an index moves above its moving average line, it is a bullish sign.

∎ If an index moves above its moving average line after staying below it for a long time, it indicates an upward change in direction.

∎ If an index cuts below its moving average, it is a:

Bearish sign.

Sell signal if you are bearish.

Sign to be cautious if you are bullish.

∎ If an index cuts below its moving average after staying above it for a long time, it indicates a downward changing trend for the market.

∎ Observe the slope of the moving average line:

If the average is rising sharply and the index is well above it, it is considered bullish.

If an index is below a sharply declining moving average, it is considered bearish.

Using Moving Averages in Conjunction with Trendlines

Some analysts use a moving average line in conjunction with a trendline to interpret stock charts. They use an uptrend line and a rising moving average to provide dual confirmation that an uptrend is in progress. The following are the basic points for using this technique:

∎ An uptrend continues to be valid even after the uptrend line is penetrated to the downside if the moving average line has not been penetrated to the downside.

- An uptrend continues to be valid even after the moving average line is penetrated to the downside if the uptrend line has not been penetrated to the downside.
- An uptrend is considered to have ended if both the uptrend and moving average lines have been penetrated to the downside.

Monitoring Moving Averages

Moving averages of the major market averages as well as a number of individual stocks are provided daily by the *IBD*. Among the market averages shown every day to monitor the overall market trend are the 200-day moving averages of the DJIA, S&P 500, and the Nasdaq Composite. The 50-day moving average is plotted in the charts of companies shown in *IBD*'s NYSE and Nasdaq stocks in the news sections. The 10-week moving average is shown for 28 stocks exhibiting strong characteristics, which are displayed in the "Your Weekend Graphic Review" graphs on Fridays.

The moving averages of individual stocks are also shown in the stock charts provided by a number of Internet and online sources. Typically, the 30-day, 50-day, and 200-day moving average lines are shown. A large number of sources that provide investment research, including moving averages, are listed in Chapter 3. Two excellent sites for this purpose are Yahoo! and Tradingday.com.

The 200-Day Moving Average

Long-Term Trend Indicator

The 200-day moving average is an excellent long-term trend indicator. It is calculated by averaging the closing prices of the past 200 trading days. This average smooths out daily price fluctuations and erratic gyrations to give a better view of the long-term trend of a stock or the overall market.

A stock trading above its 200-day moving average is considered to be in an uptrend and, therefore, in bullish mode. A stock trading below its 200-day moving average is considered to be in a downtrend and has bearish implications. In contrast to short-term averages, which are favored by short-term traders, the 200-day moving average is closely monitored by long-term investors.

Stocks and the 200-Day Moving Average

Guidelines and Tips

- If a stock trades above its 200-day moving average line, it is in an uptrend.

- If a stock holds above its 200-day moving average line, it is a bullish sign.
- If a stock trades below its 200-day moving average line, it is in a downtrend.
- If a stock breaks below its 200-day moving average, it is a bearish sign.
- A stock trading 50%, or more, above its moving average line is considered overextended; *profit taking* is suggested if it is overextended by 70% to 100%.
- Most professional investors want to:
  Buy a stock trading above a rising 200-day moving average line.
  Sell a stock before it goes under the 200-day moving average line (because it is usually a late signal).

Understanding Gaps across the 200-Day Moving Average

A gap occurs when a stock skips a price, either up or down from the previous day's close, at the start of a trading day. This jump or drop can be significant and can extend to many dollars per share. If a stock gaps below its 200-day moving average, it is considered by many market players to be a reliable sell signal.

When a stock gaps, its trading range is either above or below the trading range of the previous day. A gap is usually triggered by some unexpected news, which significantly affects the stock positively or negatively. A gap to the upside indicates strong demand, especially for a liquid stock that has a large supply. Some analysts view a gap as a sell signal only if a stock cuts below its 200-day moving average and does not rally within two to three days. If the rebound does not position it above the 200-day moving average line, then they sell the stock.

Market and the 200-Day Moving Average

The 200-day moving average, shown for the DJIA in Figure 7.3, is one of the most closely monitored market indicators. During bullish periods, the 200-day moving average acts as a floor under the market averages. However, when the market is under pressure and the DJIA is trading below its 200-day moving average, this line acts as a resistance.

Analyzing the 200-day moving average lines for the DJIA, S&P 500, and Nasdaq can indicate where the current action and price momentum are centered. For example, if the DJIA is below its 200-day moving average line, with the S&P 500 just above its 200-day moving average line and the Nasdaq way above its 200-day moving average line, it clearly indicates that

Figure 7.3 Dow Jones Industrial Average (Price versus Moving Averages)

the action is at Nasdaq—the home of small cap growth stocks—and that small cap stocks are outperforming the large cap stocks.

Relating the 200-Day Moving Average to Market Health

Market analysts closely observe the percentage of stocks trading over their 200-day moving average line. This number indicates the overall health and trend of the market. The higher the percentage of stocks trading over their 200-day moving average, the healthier the market.

In 1995, when the stock market had a tremendous run-up, the percentage of stocks trading over their 200-day moving average line peaked at 79% in mid-September, when the rally in most stocks ended. By late October, the percentage had fallen to 61%. By December, the percentage had risen to 69% following a rebound in the market.

In April 1997, when the market was in a correction, the percentage of NYSE stocks trading over their 200-day moving average line was 50%. This meant that half of the NYSE stocks were in a price decline. By October, when the correction was over and the market was rising strongly, the situation had reversed and 85% of NYSE issues were trading above their 200-day moving average line.

For a bullish scenario, the percentage of stocks trading over their 200-day moving average line should be trending higher. The number of NYSE stocks trading over their 200-day moving average is reported daily by *IBD*. The percentage of NYSE stocks trading above the 200-day moving average has historically ranged from a high of 80% to 90% (at the peak) to a low of 10% to 20% (at the market bottom). This percentage fell below 20% at market bottoms in 1998, 1990, December 1987, late 1981, and late 1974. At the market low on September 1, 1998, only 15% of NYSE stocks were trading above their 200-day moving average. Just a few weeks earlier, at the market high in July 1998, 50% of NYSE stocks had been trading above their 200-day moving average.

As a Market Direction Change Indicator

The 200-day moving average line has been known to signal important changes in the market's direction. When the DJIA declines below its 200-day moving average line, it is a bearish sign for the market. In August 1998 and August 1990, when the market experienced bear markets, both the DJIA and the S&P 500 dropped below their 200-day moving average lines. In 1987, both these averages dropped through their 200-day moving average lines two days prior to the October crash.

A drop through the 200-day moving average line does not necessarily indicate a trend change. In July 1996, both the DJIA and the S&P 500 cut through their 200-day moving average lines. However, they rebounded quickly within a few days. In the following months, both the indexes rose to new record highs. In January 1998, the Nasdaq and the DJIA 200-day moving average lines were breached. However, both the indexes rebounded quickly and continued their climb to new highs.

Guidelines for Interpreting the Number of Stocks Trading above Their 200-Day Moving Average Line

- If the majority of stocks are:
  Above their 200-day moving average line, the market is in an uptrend.
  Below their 200-day moving average line, the market is in a downtrend.
- If the percentage of stocks trading over their 200-day moving average:
  Is trending higher, it is a bullish sign.
  Is trending lower, it is a bearish sign.
  Is over 80% and starts to decrease, it may indicate that the market is correcting.
  Drops below 20%, it is almost certain that a market bottom has been reached.
  Moves over 90% and remains there, it indicates a powerful market with the potential to generate more gains.

Shortcoming

A criticism of the 200-day moving average is that it is a lagging indicator. Typically, by the time it indicates a change in direction, most investors already have reached the obvious conclusion. Besides, according to these critics, there is nothing special about the 200-day average. After all, it is valid to ask: "Why not use a different period such as a 210-day or 170-day moving average?"

In response, it can be said that the 200-day moving average is the one almost invariably chosen by investors using long-term moving averages. This group of investors is very large. Consequently, a lot of the market action and event triggers are determined by the 200-day moving average. By ignoring this and using a different period such as 180 days, an investor can miss the advance warning that this important market trigger can provide.

Trendlines, Trend Channels, and Trading Bands

Trendlines

Trendline analysis is a very important foundation of technical analysis. It is used to analyze and forecast the future direction of a stock based on its behavior in relation to its trendlines. The basic concept is that once a trend is established, it remains in effect for some time. Trend analysis primarily aims to determine if there are signs of a weakening, or change, in the established trend.

A trendline (Figure 7.4) is a line drawn by connecting the low (bottom) points on a stock chart for a rising trendline, or the high (top) points on a stock chart for a falling trendline.

Technicians believe that a rising trendline acts as a support to a stock during its upward move, while a falling trendline acts as a resistance to any attempt to move up through it. The following are two key signs that analysts look for when analyzing trendlines:

1. Frequency with which a stock touches a rising trendline: The more frequently a rising trendline is touched, the greater is the support and trend validity considered.
2. Change in trading volume on a trend break: A break with heavy volume is considered more significant.

The following are some guidelines and tips suggested by technical analysts when using a trendline as a buying indicator:

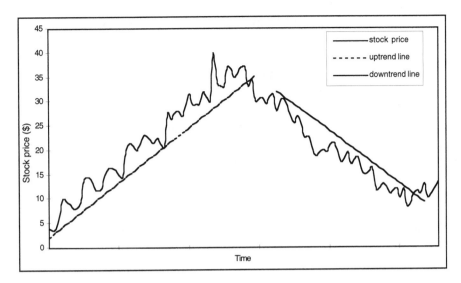

Figure 7.4   **Trendlines**

▪ Never use a trendline in isolation; use it in conjunction with other indicators and fundamental analysis, and buy a stock only if other indicators confirm the buy signal.
▪ During a rising trend:
  A trend change can take place; a support can fail.
  After a support line is hit (tested) and rebound has started (in the upward direction), buying may be done.
  Avoid buying if a stock is too far above the rising trendline.
▪ A falling trendline decisively penetrated to the upside is viewed as a buy signal; buy only if other indicators are in confirmation.

The following are two points that should be kept in mind when using a trendline as a selling indicator:

1. Never use a trendline in isolation; use it in conjunction with other indicators and fundamental analysis.
2. A drop below a rising trendline signals an end to the upward trend and, therefore, is bearish.

Trend Channels

Some technicians analyze stocks by studying their trend channels. A trend channel is created by drawing a straight line connecting the stock's price lows, which can be rather tricky, along with a parallel line for its price highs (Figure 7.5). Trend channel followers expect that a stock will remain within a channel—bouncing up and down between the top and bottom of the rising or falling channel. It is important to understand that a trend does not mean going from a trough to a peak; rather, it means going from peak to peak and trough to trough.

If a stock is in an uptrend, it will move back and forth within the extremes of its rising trend channel. This action will continue until the stock breaks below the bottom of the trend channel, which is a sign that the trend may be ending. If a stock breaks out of the top of a channel, the expectation is that it can move significantly higher. Trend channel followers buy a stock when it is in the lower area of a rising trend channel. They sell if it breaks below the channel. Short-term traders sell when a stock moves to the top of a trend channel.

About three out of every four stocks move within trend channels. However, many market players do not use trend channels. Instead, they prefer to use trendlines.

Trading Bands

It has been observed that stocks tend to trade in the short term within a fairly narrow and predictable range around their moving average line. This range is called a trading band (Figure 7.6). When a stock moves to

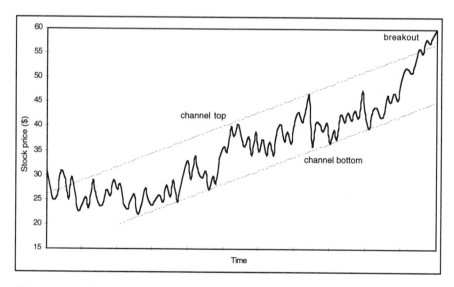

Figure 7.5   **Trend Channel**

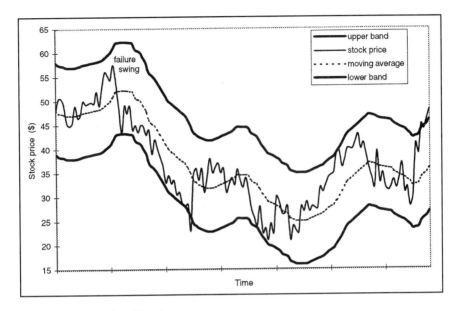

Figure 7.6 Trading Band

either end of its trading band, it unleashes forces pulling in opposite directions. These forces are created by the short-term traders and long-
term investors. When a stock reaches the top of its trading band,
short-term traders start selling for profit taking, which pressures the
stock and slows its upward move. Typically, the stock will reverse direction without touching the top band. This is known as a failure swing. A
failure swing can occur at the bottom also—when reversal takes place
without touching the bottom band. This happens when buyers step in
and the stock rebounds. A failure swing at the bottom is considered to
be a positive sign.

If a stock's rebound continues until it pushes through its 30-day moving average line, continued strength is indicated. When a stock pene-
trates its top band with sufficient strength, this indicates that buyers have
the upper hand over sellers and, therefore, the stock has strong momentum to the upside. This is considered a good buying point by momentum
investors.

In general, technicians consider the following to be positive signs:
failure swing at the bottom band, penetration of the top band, and rebound off the 30-day moving average line after the top band has been
penetrated.

Concluding Remarks

There are literally hundreds of variables, or indicators, that influence the stock market and individual stocks. The influence of each indicator varies, depending on:

■ Company
■ Industry
■ State of the economy
■ Health of the stock market
■ Presence or absence of other indicators
■ Combination of indicators existing at any given moment
■ Investor psychology

It is not possible for any investor to monitor more than a limited number of indicators. Besides being difficult to monitor, too many indicators can give conflicting signals. Therefore, only a few indicators reflecting the philosophy, approach, and risk level of the investor should be picked. Important indicators that should be monitored closely include earnings per share (quarterly and annual), EPS rank, P/E ratio, and the 200-day moving average (which indicates the long-term trend of the stock).

Chapter 8

More Stock Market Indicators

Market Breadth

Calculating Breadth

To determine the overall market trend, investors track market breadth—a comparison of the total number of stocks that decline and advance each day. If the number of advancing stocks outnumbers declining stocks by a big margin, the market is said to have good breadth. If advancers outnumber decliners by a slim margin, breadth is said to be weak. During a correction, breadth is very weak because declining stocks outnumber advancing stocks by a wide margin. For example, when the DJIA declined 4.8% during the week of January 5, 1998, decliners swamped advancers (Table 8.1).

Analyzing Breadth

If the market breadth is negative for many straight sessions, typically 10 or more, it usually signals an end to upside momentum. This occurred in July 1996, when the market had over 10 days of negative breadth and was followed by a market correction. In 1998, starting on July 17, decliners swamped advancing stocks for eight consecutive days. This was followed by the bear market—which caused the DJIA to decline to 7,379 (by September 1) from a high of 9,337 reached just six weeks earlier.

If the DJIA moves higher, analysts like to see market breadth improve simultaneously. Such an improvement indicates that most stocks are participating in the upward trending market. They also like the other indexes to be moving in the same direction as the DJIA. The term "confirmation" is often used to describe the market phenomenon of various indexes being in sync.

A technical tool for measuring breadth, which is very widely used by

Table 8.1 Advancing/Declining Stocks, Week of
January 5, 1998

	Advancing stocks	Declining stocks
January 5, 1998	1,659	1,417
January 6, 1998	1,039	1,997
January 7, 1998	1,213	1,800
January 8, 1998	1,120	1,892
January 9, 1998	552	2,540

market analysts, is the advance/decline (A/D) line for the NYSE. It is the simplest of all breadth measures.

Advance/Decline (A/D) Line

Plotting the A/D Line

The A/D line is produced using a simple procedure. Every day, the total number of stocks falling in price (daily decliners) are subtracted from the total number of stocks rising in price (daily advancers). The positive difference, of daily advancers minus daily decliners, is added to a cumulative total. If the difference is negative (i.e., if decliners outnumber advancers), this number is subtracted from the cumulative total. Stocks that remain unchanged in price are not included. This cumulative A/D number is then plotted. Over time, this yields a trend line.

A weekly A/D line is also widely used by analysts. It is based on a weekly, rather than a daily, price change. The weekly A/D line has an advantage in that it eliminates some of the volatility and noise associated with daily trading.

What the A/D Line Indicates

The A/D line gives a broader view of the market's condition than the well-known averages (DJIA and S&P 500). If more stocks advance than decline, the A/D line moves upward. When more stocks decline than advance, the A/D line moves downward. The basic idea for using the A/D line is quite simple. If the number of stocks rising in price is more than the number of declining stocks, the market is improving and, consequently, this is bullish. If more stocks are declining, it portrays a weakening or bearish market.

The A/D line for the market is shown in most major newspapers.

While the A/D line for the NYSE is the one most widely used, some analysts use the A/D lines for the Nasdaq and the American Stock Exchange (AMEX) to get a broader view of the stock market.

Divergence

What Divergence Indicates

The DJIA and the broader market, as represented by the A/D line, do not always move simultaneously in the same direction. If both are moving upward, it is considered to be a bullish sign. If the DJIA is making new highs (or moving up), while most stocks are declining as indicated by the A/D line, it is a bearish sign. It is analogous to the generals advancing while the troops are retreating. When the DJIA and the overall market move in opposite directions, or move in the same direction (up or down) at different rates, a divergence is said to occur.

Divergence can exist between any pair of indexes. For example, if the utilities index is headed lower, the Dow Jones transportation index could be moving up in the opposite direction. Divergence indicates that most stocks (or some major sectors at least) are deteriorating while the DJIA is rising or vice versa. An explanation for this phenomenon is that some sectors are forward-looking and, therefore, are often the first to react to forthcoming negative news such as a weakening economy or rising interest rates.

Divergence and Trend Change

Divergence between the DJIA and the broader market signals a potentially important change in the trend of the stock market. Therefore, analysts try to forecast whether the overall market or the DJIA will change course and move in the other direction. Generally, if the NYSE A/D line is headed lower, the DJIA is expected to follow suit. If the A/D line is moving up while the DJIA is declining, it is considered to be a better situation than the other way around. This is based on the expectation that the DJIA will more likely play catch-up with the A/D line, to the upside, than the other way around.

A divergence near the end of a bull market can be caused by:

▪ Some sectors starting to head lower in anticipation of a weaker economy six to nine months prior to its actual occurrence.
▪ Rising interest rates that cause utilities, which are very interest sensitive, to start heading lower.
▪ Firmness in the DJIA components, which typically are the last ones to be sold because they are considered more stable.

Investors should note that divergences are not necessarily good indicators when it comes to timing. They can emerge weeks and months before the major averages react.

Warning Signs Associated with Divergence

- Declining issues outnumber advancing stocks.
- A new market high is not accompanied by heavier volume.
- Stocks rally on declining volume.
- The number of stocks setting new highs drops off; there are fewer and fewer highs.
- The number of stocks trading above their 200-day moving average line declines.

A/D Line: An Early Warning System

The Record

The A/D line indicates the performance of the broader market. Therefore, it is considered a better indicator than the DJIA of where the market is headed. In the past 18 years, the A/D line has turned significantly lower prior to major market peaks. This happened in 1980, 1983, 1987, 1990, and 1996. In 1987, the A/D line peaked in August. However, the DJIA continued to move upward, by another 10%, for two more months before it underwent a massive plunge in October. The A/D line also flashed warnings prior to the severe bear market of 1973–1974.

In 1994, the A/D line started to deteriorate sharply after the Federal Reserve started to hike interest rates. It started to turn up only at the end of the year. Even though the S&P 500 earnings rose 40% that year, the market's poor performance, when the DJIA and S&P 500 respectively gained 1.2% and 2.1% for the year, can be classified as a stealth bear market. Normally, in a year when the earnings rose so much, the stock market would have risen considerably. In 1996, the A/D line started declining at the end of May. This was followed by the market correction in July.

The A/D line does not always act as a leading indicator. For example, it failed to act as an early warning signal for the DJIA's decline that occurred in April 1997. The A/D line, rather than act as a leading indicator, started to decline simultaneously with the DJIA in mid-March 1997. It followed the Nasdaq, which had started declining earlier after peaking at 1,400 in late January. Both the A/D line and the DJIA reversed direction at the same time, in mid-April, after the market corrected in the first two weeks of April. Again, in October 1997, January 1998, and July 1998, the A/D line did not act as a leading indicator. Instead, it started its decline simultaneously with the DJIA.

Do Not Be Misled by the DJIA

Investors should be wary if the DJIA and/or the S&P 500 are making new highs while the A/D line is not improving. When the overall market turns south at the end of a bull market, blue chip stocks are typically the last ones to be sold off by bearish investors. At such times, a steady or higher-trending DJIA or S&P 500 can mask the deterioration in certain market sectors. These sectors may already be discounting deteriorating business conditions six to nine months down the road. A typical example is the interest-sensitive utility stocks, which can weaken earlier due to an anticipated rise in interest rates.

Lead Time

In the past, the lead time indicated by the A/D line has varied from 10 to 49 weeks, with an average of 24 weeks. However, as has happened many times since 1980, it is not necessary for every divergence to lead to a major market decline. The A/D line can actually reverse direction and follow the upward trending DJIA. In 1986 and 1988, investors using the declining A/D line as a sell signal missed an S&P 500 rise of 13% and 16% respectively. Therefore, any divergence should not be used as a precise timing tool for leaving the market.

Using the A/D Line

The A/D line can be used as an early warning system since it is a good, though not an infallible, leading indicator of a market top. However, it should not be used in isolation. Instead, it should be used in conjunction with other indicators. When market turning points are suspected, several averages should be checked to see if any significant divergences (different averages moving in different directions) exist. Additionally, other trend indicators should be analyzed in order to get a better picture of the overall market health and trend.

Guidelines and Tips for Analyzing an A/D Line

■ If divergence continues for several weeks, it is bearish.
■ If the A/D line makes a significant new low, it is bearish.

▌ The A/D line is not a good indicator of a market bottom since it reacts very slowly compared to the DJIA, which can reverse direction faster because it represents only 30 stocks.

▌ The A/D line is more accurate at forecasting market tops.

▌ When analyzing an A/D line, the following need to be observed:

An upward or downward trend of the A/D line.

The pattern of the highs and lows; if each high is higher than the last one, it is bullish; if a high does not exceed the last high and/or a low is lower than the last low, it is bearish.

Divergence from the market averages; a tenet of technical analysis is that market divergence precedes weakness.

Number of New Daily Lows and Highs

If a stock trades at a price that is its lowest trading level in the past 52 weeks, a new daily low is said to have been made. If it reaches its highest level in a year, a new daily high occurs. The total number of stocks reaching new highs during a day, as well as the total number of stocks reaching new lows, is an indicator that is tracked by stock market analysts. While these numbers are reported for the three major exchanges, the NYSE numbers are the ones most closely analyzed by market watchers.

A Market Health Barometer

The new daily low and high numbers, especially the number of daily new lows on the NYSE, indicate the health of the market. While these numbers have limited use on a day-to-day basis, they are important for discerning trends. For example, if more stocks are making new price highs than new lows, the market is considered to be in an uptrend. In such a positive environment, the market is expected to rise further. Conversely, the outlook is bearish if there are more new daily lows being made compared to new daily highs.

On April 13, 1997, when the market was correcting, the number of new highs was 32 and the number of new lows was 215. At that time, only 50% of stocks were trading above their moving average line. On October 3, 1997, when the market was rising, the number of new highs was 1,035 and the number of new lows was only 15. At that time, 85% of stocks were trading above their moving average line.

On February 27, 1998, when the market was rising strongly to new highs after having undergone a correction, the number of new highs was 461, while the number of new lows was only 33. On November 27, 1998, when the DJIA was rebounding from a bear market, the number of new highs was 169 versus only 22 new lows.

Forecasting Market Declines

A rise in the number of new daily lows has been a good indicator of a market decline in the past. This indicator signaled market declines starting in October 1994, February 1994, August 1990, and October 1987.

In November 1995, while the DJIA had been climbing to new highs, the NYSE A/D line had been lagging. This indicated bearish divergence. Actually, the rise in new lows began in September 1995, when the market leading group, semiconductors, started falling apart. Reinforcing this divergence was the rising number of NYSE stocks making 52-week lows. This indicated a market with an undercurrent of problems beneath the surface.

In the first half of October 1997, the number of new lows ranged between 15 and 33. However, during the second half of October, the number of new lows increased sharply and ranged from 50 to 311. This increase in the number of new lows preceded, by only a few days, the DJIA's decline from 7,938 (on October 16) to 7,161 (on October 27).

When the DJIA peaked on July 17, 1998, the new high/low indicator did not flash any advance warning. New highs had consistently, except for one day, been exceeding the number of new lows for three weeks. The number of new highs had ranged from 150 to 293, while the number of new lows had ranged from 130 to 207—not an excessive difference that this indicator is capable of showing.

Analysis Guidelines

The following are some guidelines for analyzing this indicator:

- In a healthy market, the number of daily new lows on the NYSE will not exceed 40.
- Exceeding 40 new lows should not be a serious cause for concern if it occurs for only a day or two.
- It is bearish if the NYSE new daily lows exceed 40 for five consecutive days.
- During uncertain times, a rise in new daily lows can result due to a flight from low-priced speculative stocks to quality issues.

Where to Find These Numbers

Every day, *IBD* provides price charts of 28 stocks each on the NYSE and Nasdaq. These stocks are highlighted because they met one, or more, of the following criteria:

- ▊ Hit new price highs
- ▊ Are near new highs
- ▊ Had greatest percent increase in volume

Many newspapers report the number of new highs and lows on each of the major exchanges. For example, Table 8.2 shows the numbers that were reported by *IBD* on November 26, 1998—when the DJIA had rebounded strongly to 9,314 after declining to 7,379 on September 1, 1998.

Just four months earlier, on July 28, after the DJIA had started its major decline, the market tone was very different. Table 8.3 shows the numbers that were reported then.

Relative Strength (RS) Rank

Relative strength (RS) rank is a technical indicator that measures a stock's price performance relative to all other stocks. It measures a stock's price change during the past year compared to other stocks. More weight is given to the most recent three-month period when determining the rank. The ranking ranges from 99 (highest) to 1 (lowest). A 99 rank for a stock means that it outperformed 99% of all other stocks in price appreciation. Figure 8.1 shows the RS rank as marked by the pointer "Relative Price Strength Rank and line."

If a stock's relative strength rank is below 70, it shows that the stock is lagging the better-performing stocks in the overall market. An RS of 75 means that a stock outperformed 75% of all stocks, or three out of every

Table 8.2   New Highs/New Lows,
November 26, 1998

	New highs	New lows
NYSE	58	19
Nasdaq	83	22
AMEX	9	10
Total	150	51

Table 8.3   New Highs/New Lows,
July 28, 1998

	New highs	New lows
NYSE	9	294
Nasdaq	21	216
AMEX	3	51
Total	33	561

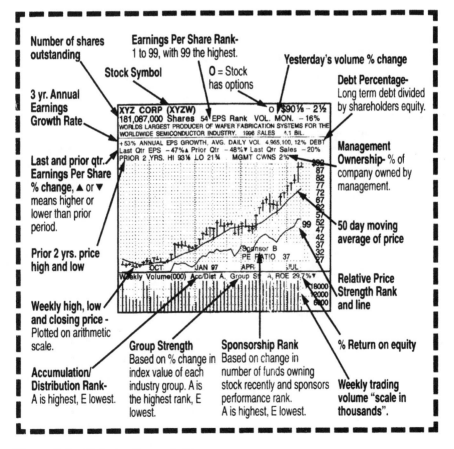

Figure 8.1   Relative Strength Line

Source: Investor's Business Daily, January 15, 1999. Reprinted with permission.

four stocks, during the same period. Looking at it from another angle, it means that 25% of all stocks performed better than the stock being analyzed. In other words, such a stock is definitely not a leader.

Basic Principle

The basic principle underlying RS is momentum. It is based on the belief that a stock that has performed strongly compared to other stocks will continue to do so in the near future. On the other hand, a relatively weak stock will continue to be weak. Analysts using RS believe that the probability of a high-RS stock continuing to outperform is very high. The logic is that a trend once begun is very likely to continue. Consequently, they believe that the likelihood of finding winners from among stocks with high RS rank is greater. This is backed by a study that found that many top-performing stocks in the past 40 years began their big moves with an average RS of 87.[1] Examples of big winners in the past couple of decades include Microsoft, Wal-Mart, and Amgen. All of them showed high RS prior to their big price moves.

The Risk

The RS technique of finding a winner is in direct contrast to the value-based technique of buying a stock when it is down in price. The risk with the value-based technique is that a stock may remain out of favor for a long period, with consequential associated risks. The RS rank method also has its critics who point out that buying a high-RS stock is a step too late. A preferable technique might be to buy when RS is in the high 80s, prior to a stock making its most meaningful move. Also, one can avoid buying when a stock is at the very top, in the 98–99% rank, when most of the price appreciation may already have occurred.

RS and Stock Picking

RS rank is one of the basic selection criteria for momentum investors. For stock picking, they try to confine their buying to companies with an RS rank of 80 or higher. This is based on the belief that leaders will have an RS rank greater than 80. This ensures that laggards are rejected.

If a stock is picked based on its RS rank, its earnings projections

---

[1]*Investor's Business Daily*, June 20, 1995.

should also be checked. If the earnings forecast is not positive, such a stock should be avoided. Buying a stock with a high RS rank but a poor earnings outlook is very risky. If a stock has strong earnings momentum, but low RS in the 50s or 60s, it can be considered as a buy candidate.

It is important that RS rank should not be used in isolation. Instead, it should be used as a final check after a company's earnings have passed the evaluation process.

Using RS with Other Criteria

The RS rank can be combined with EPS rank to create a potent combination. A company whose EPS and RS ranks are greater than 80 demonstrates strong performance. While one is a fundamental measurement, the other indicates market valuation. Such a company is indicated to be a superior one and a potential winner. However, keep in mind that strong historical performance does not necessarily guarantee similar results in the future. An indicator like RS rank should only be taken as a sign, which should be followed by further research prior to buying a stock.

Monitoring RS

If RS rank decreases while a stock is moving sideways, or even while it is moving up, this indicates that the market is rising faster than the stock. This is a warning that the stock may soon start to decline. In a declining market, the RS ranks of leading stocks drop sharply. If a stock's RS rank holds up well in such a scenario, a potential winner is indicated. When the market rallies, such a stock has a greater probability of performing very well.

Other factors to note when analyzing RS are:

■ Relative strength rank often starts to go down after a stock price starts declining; it can be an early warning of a potential larger drop in the near future.
■ RS can decrease due to many reasons including weakening company, or industry, fundamentals.
■ Stocks with RS declining for a couple of months should be watched carefully; the cause of the decline should be determined.
■ Stocks with RS rising for a couple of months are performing more strongly than the overall market and should be viewed bullishly.
■ Check a stock's price pattern to ensure that it has a solid base and is not extended more than 5% to 10% above this base.

Relative Strength (RS) Line

What the Tool Indicates

The RS line is another tool used to indicate a stock's price trend. It is based on comparing a stock's price to the S&P 500 index. Figure 8.1 shows the RS line as marked by the pointer "Relative Price Strength Rank and line." The comparison can also be made for an index or average. The RS line of the Nasdaq versus the S&P 500 is shown in Figure 11.1 (Chapter 11).

As with any trendline, it is expected that once an RS trendline gets established, it will continue for some time. Analysts also use a moving average line, in conjunction with the RS line, to confirm a stock's uptrend. When evaluating a stock for buying, it is preferred to pick a stock whose RS line is trending higher. Some analysts recommend buying stocks with strong earnings growth, with an RS above 80, when they emerge from a price consolidation area after at least seven weeks. In general, if a stock's price breaks out of a base, its RS line should also do the same.

Guidelines for Analyzing RS Lines

Bullish Signs

If a stock's RS line:

- Breaks out before the price, it is bullish and may lead to a price breakout.
- Does not pull back much even though the price corrects, it is a bullish sign.
- Remains in an uptrend, it is bullish.

Bearish Signs

If a stock's RS line:

- Fails to make a new high and undercuts a prior low, it is bearish.
- Fails to confirm a new high in price, it is bearish.
- Has been rising and the trend is broken, it is bearish.

Accumulation and Distribution

What the Tool Indicates

This is a proprietary tool used to analyze a stock's supply and demand by trying to determine the direction of money flow. This indicator is based on a stock's daily trading volume and price change, with volume being measured on up days (when price rises) and down days (when price decreases). The basic idea is that money is flowing into a stock if its trading volume, during the specified period, is heavier on up days than on down days. This phenomenon, which is referred to as accumulation, indicates positive momentum. Distribution is the opposite of accumulation.

Accumulation indicates professional buying by institutions or that buyers outnumber sellers. Distribution indicates the opposite. Accumulation indicates that there is good demand for the stock. Therefore, the probability is high that it will make further progress to the upside. On the other hand, distribution indicates poor demand for the stock. It occurs when a stock or market index drops in price or closes at the low end of its daily range despite heavy trading volume. Distribution often precedes a stock, or a market, price decline.

Accumulation and distribution are reported in a range, from A through E, as follows:

A & B   Stock is undergoing accumulation
C   Neutral
D & E   Stock is undergoing distribution

Recognizing Accumulation and Distribution

A stock is considered to be undergoing accumulation if:

- Its price rises when it trades on heavy volume.
- It closes at the high end of its daily trading range when it trades on heavy volume.

A stock undergoes distribution if:

- Its price drops on heavy volume.
- It closes at the low end of its daily trading range when it trades on heavy volume.
- No price increase occurs despite heavy trading volume.
- After an advance, there is no further upside price progress despite heavy volume.

Guidelines and Tips for Analyzing Accumulation/Distribution

- Do not use this tool alone; it must be used in conjunction with other tools.

- When evaluating a stock for buying, favor stocks with an A or B rating.
- A continuous rating of A is more reliable than one that occasionally slips to a B rating; the same applies for E changing to D occasionally.
- If a stock moves up and starts forming a base, it should retain a rating of C or better.
- Do not expect the market to advance if leaders start showing distribution (C, D, or E).
- If a stock shows distribution (D or E) and even if it has not suffered a big price drop (which usually comes later), technicians recommend that you evaluate your sell options.
- Distribution is often covered by a misleading slight price rise.
- Sell-off on heavy volume followed by rallies on low volume is a bearish sign.

Trading Volume

Relating Volume to Trend

A very important indicator, for both individual stocks and the overall market, is trading volume. Savvy investors closely monitor trading volume levels because heavy trading often precedes major price moves. They know quite well that simultaneously rising volume and price often precede further price appreciation. Typically, rising volume and increasing price momentum indicate the potential start of a trend.

Focusing on Percentage Change

For analysis, monitoring daily trading volume alone is not enough. One should also monitor the percentage change in trading volume. The reason is that the daily trading volume for different stocks varies considerably. Therefore, if the trading volume of only the most active stocks is monitored, it can prevent stocks with meaningful volume changes from being noticed. For example, it is more meaningful to pinpoint a stock whose trading volume swelled to 1 million shares from an average daily trading volume of 250,000 shares than a stock whose trading volume increased to 1.8 million shares from an average daily trading volume of 1.5 million shares. The 400% increase for the first company is more meaningful than the 20% increase for the second company. The massive volume rise of 400% can alert an investor to some potential news or development. Therefore, if only the daily trading volume criterion is used, the first company may not be noticed despite its more meaningful change.

Guidelines and Tips for Interpreting Trading Volume

∎ During an uptrend, trading volume usually increases and remains higher than average.

∎ During a downtrend, trading volume is usually lower than average.

∎ Trading volume increases:

Whenever a stock breaks out of its trading range (either up or down); this indicates high interest.

When a breakout occurs to the upside; a large volume increase is a strong buy signal.

∎ Price increase on:

Above-average (heavy) volume indicates professional buying by institutions.

Increasing volume is bullish.

Lower volume is not considered bullish.

∎ Price breakout to the downside is considered a sell signal—whether trading volume increases or not.

∎ Falling price on heavy volume is bearish:

In a weak market.

Especially in a rising market.

∎ Falling price on lower volume indicates a bottom (selling almost, or fully, completed).

∎ Lower price on massive volume indicates a bottom (selling climax).

∎ Heavy volume with no upward progress is bearish.

∎ Trading volume should be compared to the average trading volume; traders compare the daily volume to the average of the prior 5 or 10 trading days.

Monitoring Abnormal Trading Volume

Most daily newspapers list the most active stocks on the three main exchanges. This information is of limited use because the typical list usually contains the names of very big companies with large trading volumes. A more useful reporting format is provided by the *IBD*. It lists stocks that have the largest percentage increase in volume above their average daily trading volume. The *IBD* tables list such stocks in the three major exchanges: NYSE, Nasdaq, and AMEX. Each list is separated into two parts—stocks making price moves to the upside and downside, respectively. These lists include only stocks that are priced over $18 per share for the NYSE, $16 per share for the Nasdaq, and $12 per share for the AMEX.

To aid investors, these lists also provide the EPS and RS ranks of each stock. Consequently, if the winners list includes many stocks with EPS and RS rank greater than 90, this indicates that the leaders are the movers. This could signify the start of a major move. On the other hand, if these leaders are on the losers list, they might be losing steam and a market decline may have begun.

Unusual volume as indicated by these lists can steer an investor to a potential investment. The basic idea is that heavy volume is caused by unusual interest. Therefore, the chances are good that such a list may contain winners if their EPS and RS ranks are above 80%. Since such stocks have the potential for a major upward move, the best among these should be investigated.

Float—Supply of Stock

Supply and Demand Balance

A very important factor affecting a stock's price and the extent to which it will appreciate is the balance between supply and demand. The greater the number of outstanding shares, the more difficult it is to move such a stock in either direction—because a greater amount of supply will be required to create any downward or upward price pressure.

Companies like GE and AT&T have a large number of outstanding shares. Therefore, it is very difficult to make their price change appreciably. Consider the case when the *Exxon Valdez* was grounded off the coast of Alaska in 1988. Exxon's stock, which has 2.43 billion outstanding shares and a daily trading volume of 3.96 million shares, barely moved despite the very bad news. To appreciably move such a stock, a massive amount of buying or selling far above its normal trading volume is required. In contrast, the price of a smaller company, with only 50 million shares and a daily trading volume of 200,000 shares, can change significantly even if there is a small change in trading volume.

A company's float, the number of shares available for trading, is a factor analyzed by investors when they evaluate a stock for procurement. Besides the available supply, the percentage of outstanding stock held by a company's management is also a factor that they analyze. The reason is that it can effectively reduce the number of shares available for trading.

Institutional Factor

Large institutional buyers use somewhat different stock procurement criteria than individual investors, which makes them favor large cap companies. Consequently, they overlook the best growth companies, which typically have small floats. Individual investors are not constrained by the limitations imposed on institutional investors. Therefore, they can favor a smaller company over a larger one (with a bigger float) when selecting a stock. Hence, they can achieve higher returns due to their exposure to smaller companies—which usually achieve far superior returns.

Effect of Share Buybacks

The supply of stock can also be reduced, especially in small and medium cap companies, due to stock buybacks. This refers to a company buying back its own shares in the open market. Usually, buyback is initiated if a company believes that its stock price does not reflect its true value or it needs to acquire shares for its employee stock option plan. When the number of shares is reduced, the earnings number in the EPS calculations gets divided by a smaller number of shares, which causes the EPS to increase. Therefore, if a company buys back its shares, it is viewed by investors as a positive development and, consequently, they boost the share price.

Institutional Ownership

Role of Institutions

A large percentage of trading in the stock market is done by institutions such as pension funds, mutual funds, insurance companies, and others. If a small company starts attracting their attention due to its performance, this can become the catalyst for moving its stock to great heights. On the other hand, when a company with institutional shareholders does not perform well and they start dumping its stock, the share price can be severely depressed.

There are thousands of companies available for investment. Yet, most of them are out of bounds to institutional investors. The reason is that they have very restrictive investing criteria. These include minimum trading volume, market capitalization, and positive earnings history for five years. Many companies, especially smaller ones, are unable to meet these minimum requirements. However, those companies able to get institutions' attention and investment by meeting their rigorous screening criteria are reasonably assured of a good price boost.

Level of Desired Institutional Ownership

While it is a positive sign to have institutional ownership, the level of such ownership should be limited. In companies that have a high percentage of institutional presence, the potential for upward price appreciation is quite limited. The reason is that probably additional institutional buying will be unavailable to provide the thrust that can make a stock move to new heights. Therefore, when selecting a company for investment, favor a company with a low percentage of institutional ownership, preferably in the 25% to 50% range. If institutional presence is over this range, the company is already discovered, and, hence, its price appreciation will be limited. The problem with selecting an undiscovered company is that good companies with low institutional ownership are difficult to find.

A disadvantage for companies having large institutional ownership is that it makes them very vulnerable to wild price swings if they fall out of favor. If there is some negative news, mass institutional exit can cause a small company stock to drop 25% to 50% in a single day. Despite this risk, it is more desirable to have some degree of institutional participation than to have none at all.

Number of Analysts

Brokerage and investment companies periodically issue investment recommendations for individual stocks for their clients. These recommendations include buy, sell, hold, and other slightly different variations. These recommendations are made after intensive research conducted by analysts who are employed by these companies.

Analysts' Function

An analyst's job is to study a company and its industry in depth—understand the business, interview company officials, and analyze business conditions that have the potential to impact the company. Therefore, if an analyst is astute and conducts satisfactory research, he or she will become an expert on the company. Consequently, any recommendation made by such an analyst will carry weight. When a well-informed analyst makes a statement regarding the company, the market listens. Stocks can rocket up or nose-dive when an influential analyst changes a recommendation for the better or issues a downgrade.

Typically, an analyst will follow only a few companies. For each company that is being studied, an analyst will issue a comprehensive company research and/or earnings report. Typically, this report will include detailed information such as earnings estimates for each quarter (and the following year), forecast for the company's five-year annualized earnings growth rate, business prospects, evaluation of competition, and so on. Details contained in typical company research and earning reports are shown in the Appendixes.

Desired Coverage

Usually, small and emerging companies have few analysts or, in many cases, no analyst following them. A large, well-established company may have 25 to 30 analysts following it. It is desired that at least four analysts be covering a company. This ensures that the company has been analyzed thoroughly by a minimum number of professionals. It also creates a higher level of confidence in the consensus earnings forecasts made by these analysts, because a single wrong estimate will not significantly distort the reported average estimate.

Buy/Hold/Sell Recommendations

Understanding Recommendations

Stock recommendations made by analysts are typically categorized into buy, sell, or hold. A "buy" recommendation means that the stock is recommended to be bought because it is expected to have good price appreciation. A "sell" means a recommendation to get rid of the stock because the company is expected to have poor price performance. A "hold" means to let the current status remain—maintain any existing positions in the stock, but no additional buying should be done.

There are many variations of stock recommendation categories used by brokerage companies. Examples are strong buy, accumulate, moderate buy, and trading buy (for short-term trading). An investor should clearly determine what each recommendation term means, if he or she plans to follow an analyst's recommendations, because each term can indicate something different at various brokerage companies.

Obtaining Current Status of Recommendations on a Company

Some research reports issued by companies such as Zacks and First Call, besides reporting buy/hold/sell recommendations, also provide the mean of all analysts' recommendations (Appendixes B and D). These typically range from 1 (buy) to 5 (sell). Changes in these recommendations, better known as upgrades and downgrades, are reported by many Internet sites and by various publications including the *IBD*, *WSJ*, and *Barron's*.

Industry-Specific Indicators

Which Indicators to Monitor

There are a number of indicators that are applicable to specific industries. Investors track these indicators with the aim of monitoring a particular industry. For example, new car sales and new home sales are good indicators of the health of the automobile and housing industries. Similarly, chain store sales, which are a barometer of the health of retailers, also indicate the potential impact of consumer spending on the economy. Therefore, investors should determine which available indicator is the most appropriate for the industry they are analyzing and monitor it closely.

Benefiting from Industry-Specific Indicators

Investors who followed the semiconductor book-to-bill ratio in 1995, and acted on it, were handsomely rewarded. The ratio, which is obtained by dividing the month's bookings number by the billings number, rose sharply in 1994 and continued to trend higher. The higher-trending ratio indicated a booming semiconductor business. Therefore, it was no surprise that the semiconductor companies had a huge stock price run-up in 1995. This is exemplified by Micron Technology, which went up from 22 in January 1995 to $94^3/_4$ by September 1995. However, as the semiconductor chip sales slackened, as indicated by the book-to-bill ratio, the semiconductor stocks started slipping and Micron declined dramatically to 29 by January 1996. Micron investors tracking this ratio managed to avoid disaster.

Concluding Remarks

Stock market investors track a very large number of indicators. Some of the most important indicators were described in Chapter 7. They are supplemented by other important indicators described in this chapter. Of these, the most important ones are the advance/decline line, trading volume, and the level of institutional ownership.

It should be realized that no indicator can be analyzed in isolation. Each indicator's influence and importance can vary—depending on a number of other factors such as the industry/group to which the company belongs, state of the economy and the stock market, presence or absence of other indicators, combination of indicators existing at any given moment, and investor psychology.

Chapter 9

Sentiment Indicators

Role of Psychological Indicators

The stock market is a place where economics and psychology are intertwined. Investors need to understand both in order to achieve success. For this purpose, stock market investors use a number of sentiment, or psychological, indicators to monitor the pulse of the market and gauge investor sentiment. These indicators are regularly reported in many newsletters, periodicals, and newspapers. The most commonly monitored sentiment indicators, reported daily in the *IBD*, are listed in Table 5.5 (Chapter 5).

Basis for Using Psychological Indicators

Psychological indicators are based on supply and demand. The premise is that if there is more investor bullishness, less demand for stocks can be expected—because it can be assumed that the bulls have already invested their available cash. Conversely, if there is widespread bearishness, it means that a lot of cash is available for buying stocks. Therefore, the potential exists for stocks to be pushed higher.

As a Leading Indicator

When investor sentiment becomes one-sided—too bullish or optimistic, for instance—it becomes an early warning signal of trouble ahead for the market. Due to their leading indicator status and ability to give signals before market tops and bottoms, psychological indicators are widely used as investment tools. These indicators track the bullish/bearish sentiment of those who can influence the market—market specialists in the NYSE, corporate *insiders*, and professional investment advisers.

Limitations

While psychological indicators are readily available to those who want to use them, their signals are often ignored by investors at market bottoms. This happens because most investors do not have the courage to buy when everything looks so bleak—a decimated market, poor economy, and so forth. Generally, the market turns positive two to three months after the psychological indicators turn positive. Analyzed as a group, psychological indicators rarely fail.

Investors should note two factors when dealing with these indicators:

1. Sentiment indicators work best at extremes.
2. A significant gap may lie between data collection and reporting times.

Bullish/Bearish Readings

Savvy market players try to gauge the level of optimism and pessimism permeating the market. For this, they use a variety of tools including bullish/bearish numbers and consumer confidence levels. These are reported in surveys that measure the degree of bullishness/bearishness (of investors, investment advisers, and market professionals) and consumer confidence. Three of the most closely followed surveys are:

▌ Investors' Intelligence Survey.
▌ Conference Board's consumer confidence index.
▌ University of Michigan index of consumer sentiment.

Investors' Intelligence Survey

This is a survey of 130 investment advisory firms that publish market newsletters. It reports the percentage of bullish versus bearish advisers (Figure 9.1). *IBD* reports these numbers daily even though they change only once a week (Wednesday).

Bullish Numbers

If the bullishness number exceeds 55%, it is a bearish warning signal. The reason is that these numbers are viewed in a contrarian way by market watchers. They assume that if a vast majority of investors are bullish, it is highly probable that buyers have already made their investments. Therefore, few buyers and little cash is left to move the market higher. Also, in-

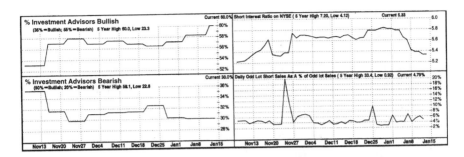

Figure 9.1   **Graphic Display of Psychological Indicators**
Source: Investor's Business Daily, January 15, 1999. Reprinted with permission.

vestment letter writers, who mostly are trend followers, have a poor track record in forecasting the market's direction.

In the past, market tops have been preceded by excessive bullishness, while bottoms have been preceded by pessimism. For example, in the third week of June 1996, 49.1% of advisers, a high number, were bullish. Three weeks later, the market suffered a sharp correction. In the last week of July 1997, when the DJIA was trading at 8,116, 46.3% of advisers were bullish. By September 1, 1997, the DJIA had declined sharply to 7,622—causing only 37.6% of advisers to remain bullish by mid-September. However, by mid-October, bullishness had risen to 48.8%, which coincided with the market peak. On October 16, 1997, the DJIA started a sharp decline, which culminated in a massive drop of 554 points on October 27.

On July 23, 1998, a week after the market peaked, bullishness reached 54.3%. This preceded the painful bear market decline in the following weeks.

Bearish Numbers

The other side of the coin is the bearishness number. A well-known cliché is that the stock market climbs a wall of worry. In line with that view, a high bearish number is considered positive for the market. For example, 59.1% of advisers were bearish in mid-December 1994. However, they completely misread the market, which at that time started its explosive upward move that resulted in tremendous gains for the market in 1995. Again, in late 1990, 55% of advisers were bearish. However, contrary to their expectation, the market turned upward for a sizable gain.

Generally, a bearish number below 20% is very bearish and a loud warning sign. It indicates that very few advisers are negative on the market. In a contrarian way, that is bearish for the market. This situation preceded the big crash in October 1987—when only 19% of advisers were bearish and 61% were bullish. On July 23, 1998, only 23.3% of advisers were bearish. This contrarian indicator proved correct as the market slid into a bear market in the following weeks.

A high bearish number, while considered bullish, is not always bullish. Investors should remember 1974 when the market dropped even though the bearish figure was 59%.

Analyzing Bullish/Bearish Numbers

Both bullish and bearish numbers should be analyzed in conjunction. When both are in dual confirmation, the signal should be viewed very seriously. A combination of 55% bulls with bears dropping below 20% is dangerous, with very bearish implications for the market.

After the market has been going down, if a high percentage of advisers are bearish and there is only a low percentage of bullish advisers it is a good indication of a turning point. In general, if bearish advisers are in the 55% to 60% range during a bear market, it can be concluded that a bottom has been reached.

It is also advisable to use the bullish/bearish sentiment numbers in conjunction with other sentiment indicators such as mutual fund cash, put-call ratio, short interest, insider selling, and so on.

Conference Board's Consumer Confidence Index

This index, reported monthly, measures the confidence level of consumers (Figure 9.2). It is a monthly survey of 5,000 households. Since consumer

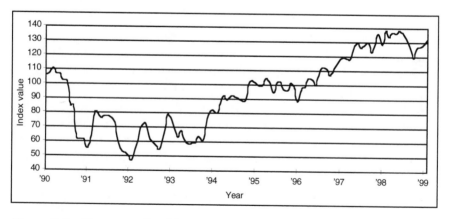

Figure 9.2   Consumer Confidence Index

spending is such a big component of the overall economic activity in the country, the level of consumer confidence is a good indicator of future consumer spending. The consumer confidence index includes two main components: current conditions and expectations for future conditions six months later.

Investors monitor the consumer confidence index closely because it indicates future consumer spending and can influence both the stock and bond markets. In September 1996, the consumer confidence index fell to 106.2 from the October level of 111.8. This indicated a potential slowing down of consumer spending and, consequently, it led to the expectation of lower inflationary pressures in the economy. This was viewed positively by the bond market, which rose on this news.

In December 1997, the consumer confidence index rose to 136.2 from 121.8 in November. This was a 28-year high and reflected consumers' positive outlook for the economy. The index continued to rise to a 30-year high by February 1998. With confident consumers providing fuel for the economy, the effect on the stock market was positive; it continued to trend higher—reaching an all-time high by early March 1998.

In June 1998, the index peaked at 138.2. It then went into a slump for four months which, combined with the bear market, raised serious concerns about consumer spending and future economic growth.

In general, higher consumer confidence is positive for stocks but negative for bonds. The reason is that bond traders fear that strong consumer spending can lay the seeds for future inflationary pressures.

University of Michigan Index of Consumer Sentiment

The University of Michigan survey also measures the confidence level of consumers (Figure 9.3). This is a very good indicator of how consumers, whose spending has a very powerful effect on the economy, view current economic conditions and their own personal financial situation. It also reports consumer expectations.

A report indicating that consumers view their future positively is a bullish sign because it indicates potentially strong consumer spending in the near future. This means that the economy will have one powerful engine of growth in its favor. If consumer confidence numbers decline over a period of months, this indicates a potentially slowing economy, which is a negative for stocks. It has been observed over the years that extreme consumer pessimism usually occurs in tandem with stock market bottoms.

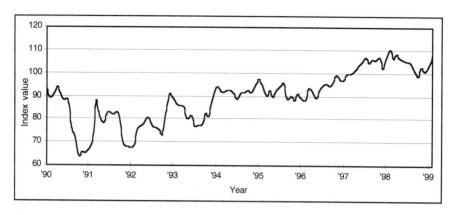

Figure 9.3 Consumer Sentiment Index

Mutual Funds Cash

Growth of Mutual Funds

The importance of mutual funds can be gauged from the fact that their assets were $5.53 trillion at the end of 1998—up 24% from $4.46 trillion at the end of 1997.[1] In comparison, $4.9 trillion were held by commercial banks at the end of September 1997.[2] At the end of December 1998, total stock fund assets were $2.98 trillion.[3]

In 1998, stock funds brought in $158 billion—down 30% from the $227 billion inflow in 1997.[4] In 1996, $221 billion had been pumped into these funds. Compared to bonds, stock funds have been gaining in importance over the years. In 1987, bonds accounted for 36% of all fund assets compared to 23% for stock funds. In 1997, the situation was the opposite, with 53% of fund assets being held in stocks compared to 23% in bonds.[5] The bear market of 1998 caused stock fund inflows to decrease due to investor nervousness. In the flight to safety, flow to bond funds more than doubled—from $28.43 billion to $74.38 billion.[6] However, after the bear market was over, flows to stock funds again started to increase.

---

[1]*Investor's Business Daily*, February 1, 1999.
[2]Ibid., March 5, 1998.
[3]Ibid., February 1, 1999.
[4]Ibid., February 1, 1999.
[5]Ibid., March 11, 1998.
[6]Ibid., February 1, 1999.

Role of Mutual Funds Cash

When there is a large cash inflow into mutual funds, most of it gets invested in stocks, which helps propel stock prices higher. However, not all the cash received from investors is invested by mutual funds. They always keep aside a certain amount, which is a percentage of their total funds, in cash. This is required for meeting obligations due to potential redemptions, which can be heavy during a rapidly falling market. If mutual funds have inadequate cash and they get hit by heavy redemptions, especially during a weak or panicky market, they can be forced to sell some of their stock holdings in order to raise cash. This can worsen the market decline.

Low Cash Level—A Bearish Signal

A 10% mutual funds cash position is considered bullish. A 7% cash level is considered to be a fully invested and, consequently, bearish position because mutual funds need cash reserves for redemptions. The lowest mutual funds cash level in recent years was 4.5% in October 1976. In December 1998, the mutual funds cash position was only 4.6%. Mutual funds cash level, which is reported by newsletters and newspapers, is a widely monitored indicator.

Low cash levels indicate excessive bullishness. As a contrarian sign, this might indicate a market top. The reasoning is that if mutual funds are fully invested, a very important engine for moving the market up is missing. Low cash levels combined with record money inflow into funds is an indication of extreme bullishness—or euphoria. This is a good indication of a market top.

Low mutual funds cash levels have often preceded market tops. For example, in January 1973, prior to the 1973–1974 bear market, cash levels were only 4.5%. In 1996, mutual funds cash levels declined to 6.6% in June from the January level of 8%. This was followed by a sharp correction in mid-July. Again, by October 1996, mutual funds cash levels declined to a bearish 5.9%. This was followed by a market decline of 4.2% in mid-December.

The forecasting record of this indicator has been somewhat mixed since 1973. In the recent past, the level of mutual funds cash has been very low by historic standards and yet the market has continued to rise higher and higher. In the 12-month period ending January 1998, the average monthly level of mutual funds cash was 5.66%, while the average for the prior 18 months was 5.82%. From January through October 1998, the average mutual funds cash position was only 5.03%, with the low point being reached in April (4.3%). The low point preceded the start of the bear market by three months. In January 1999, the Nasdaq rose 14% and the DJIA rose 1.9%—despite the cash level being only 4.6% in December 1998.

High Cash Level—A Bullish Signal

When mutual funds get bearish and start increasing their cash percentage, it is an indication that the market is ready to turn upward. When these funds start deploying their cash, it propels the market upward. However, if the cash levels drop too much, it is a bearish signal. To some market analysts, mutual funds cash level is one of the most important psychological indicators.

In October 1990, mutual funds cash levels were at 12.9%, an extremely bullish number, which coincided with the bear market bottom. However, this indicator is not infallible. For example, cash levels were quite high prior to the bear markets of the 1980s. Prior to the October 1987 crash, the cash level was 9.5% (in September). When the market hit bottom in September 1998, mutual funds cash levels were only 5.8%—not a high percentage by historical standards.

Limitations of This Indicator

Some analysts point out that low cash levels do not always portend a problem. For example, the market rocketed up in 1995, as well as in the past couple of years, despite decreasing cash levels. The belief is that so long as investors keep pumping money into mutual funds, low cash levels can be safe. In recent years, a flood of cash has been poured into mutual funds. We can expect this cash inflow to continue due to changing demographics—such as the aging of the boomers. Therefore, this indicator may not be the danger signal that it used to be. Also, keep in mind that mutual funds are not the only sources of large-scale investment in the stock market. Others include corporations, pension funds, and insurance companies.

Insider Trading

Insider Advantage

An insider is a person who has access to important corporate information that is not available to the general public. Typically, such persons include officers, directors, and major shareholders of the company. These insiders are well-informed investors. They have a distinct edge over analysts and individual investors because they are more informed about the day-to-day operations of their companies. Hence, they can use their positions to buy or sell their own company shares in a more timely fashion—before any good or bad news becomes common knowledge.

To keep the playing field level, the Securities and Exchange Commission (SEC) prohibits insiders from trading secretly on the basis of their access to confidential company information. All *insider trading* has to be reported to the SEC. Some newsletters keep close tabs on insider trading. The *Vickers Weekly Insider Report* publishes a weekly ratio of insider sales to purchases. Also, many newspapers and Internet sites, including Yahoo!, report insider trading activity. Insider trading reporting by local newspapers is often limited to transactions taking place in local companies.

Insider Selling

There can be a number of reasons for insider selling other than the belief that the company's future prospects are bleak. These can be transactions related to the exercise of stock options, personal expenses, children's education, need to diversify, and so on. Therefore, analyzing insider selling is more complex than analyzing insider buying. In general, if insider selling is taking place it is either bearish or neutral. It does not always indicate that the company will underperform or that it will go down in price.

Both insider buying and selling patterns should be studied before any conclusions are drawn. Also, any unusual inside activity should be investigated. If insider selling has been taking place, the following should be taken as serious warning signs:

■ Unusually heavy insider selling
■ Abnormal insider selling pattern for the company
■ No insider buying—only insider selling taking place
■ Selling after quick price appreciation

Historically, insiders sell stock about twice as much as they buy. So if they are selling at a lower rate than that number, it is a bullish sign. Conversely, if they are selling at a higher rate, it is considered to be bearish. When analyzing insider selling, two points need to be noted:

1. Historically, insider selling has tended to be a leading rather than a coincident indicator of market tops.
2. Selling information is available to the public only after a time lag.

Insider Buying

If insiders are buying their own company's stock, it is considered to be a bullish signal. It indicates their belief that the open market price of their company's stock is too low or that the fundamental outlook for the company is very good. In October 1990, insiders were buying at the market lows because they realized that their companies' stocks were undervalued based on anticipated corporate profits.

Compared to selling, insider buying is a more reliable indicator of a stock's future price direction. The explanation is that there exists only one very strong reason for insider buying—believing that the stock is going to perform very well, which typically is due to one of the following:

- High earnings expectations
- Upcoming new product(s)/cycle
- Belief that stock is undervalued
- Access to confidential information

Sometimes, though not too often, a new executive may buy a company's shares to signal faith in the company or to indicate a team player attitude.

Guidelines and Tips for Analyzing Insider Trading

The number of buyers and sellers is more informative than the size of the transactions because less chance exists that the collective judgment of insiders will be wrong. Therefore, one should be on the lookout for any sign that key officers of a company are trading in tandem. Consider the case of Telular Corporation, whose executives were buying heavily in March 1996—three months before the stock took off in June.

The following are some guidelines and tips for evaluating insider trading:

- Insider selling is not particularly meaningful; it is significant only if there is an unusual or significant amount of selling.
- Buying is more meaningful than selling; however, large sells or multiple sells are a warning sign.
- Buy close to insider prices.
- Companies with more than one insider buying should be favored.
- Open market purchases are more significant than company-sponsored stock option purchases.

■ Do not be influenced by insiders exercising options to purchase stock.

■ Look for patterns—number of shares and number of insiders who are trading.

■ A stock that has experienced recent selling by a number of insiders should not be bought.

Put/Call Ratio

Understanding Options

A *call option* conveys to its buyer the right, but not an obligation, to buy the underlying stock at a specific exercise or *strike price* by the *expiration date* of the contract for the *option*. A *put option* conveys the right, but not an obligation, to sell the underlying stock at a specific (exercise) price by the expiration date of the contract. A call buyer is bullish and expects the price to rise. A put buyer is bearish and expects a price decline.

Analyzing the Put/Call Ratio

The volume of puts and calls traded in the market is used to calculate the put/call ratio. This ratio, which is reported in various newspapers, measures the sentiment of option traders who are basically *speculators*. This ratio is shown graphically in Figure 11.1 (see Chapter 11). When the put/call ratio is high, it indicates that option buyers are favoring puts because they are bearish. However, they have historically been wrong, and contrary to their expectations the market has usually headed higher. The opposite also holds true: When the ratio is low, the market usually declines. Analysts also monitor the "ratio of price premiums in puts versus calls" for gauging market sentiment (Table 5.5).

On December 9, 1994, the put/call ratio hit a five-year high of 1.23. However, option traders were wrong as the market emerged from a sideways pattern to begin a new bull market phase. On August 6, 1997, the put/call ratio hit a five-year low of 0.38, indicating that option traders were bullish. However, they were wrong and the market topped the very next day.

The put/call ratio works best at extremes. A high put/call ratio indicates that most, if not all, selling has taken place. At this point, fear is at its peak and the market is ready to rebound.

Short Interest (Short Selling)

Most investors buy stocks with the objective of selling at a higher price. However, there also exists a very small group of investors, called short sellers, who buy a stock based on the belief that it will decline in price. Their technique is called *short selling* or shorting.

Understanding Short Selling

A short seller borrows stock from a broker, sells it, and then waits—hoping to buy back the same stock when it trades at a lower price. When the stock price actually declines, the short seller buys the stock (at the lower price), and then returns the newly bought stock to the broker-lender. In other words, a short seller sells first (at a higher price) and buys later (at a lower price). The difference in the sell and buy prices is pocketed by the short seller as profit. However, if the stock price rises against a short seller's expectations, after having borrowed and sold the stock, the short seller will be forced to buy back the stock at a higher price. When *covering* in such a case, the short seller suffers a loss.

Potential Loss through Short Selling

The maximum profit in shorting a stock is 100%—if the stock declines to nil value. However, the loss potential is infinite. The reason is that there is no limit to which a stock price can rise before a short sale is covered. Short sales can be profitable in many cases. However, the odds and the system favor those who are stock investors rather than short sellers.

Analyzing Short Interest

The number of shares that have been sold short on the NYSE as well as the Nasdaq are periodically reported by the major newspapers and on the Internet. Also reported are the total number of shares that have been shorted for each company. Rising short interest is viewed as a growing sign of skepticism.

A useful indicator for monitoring short interest is the "short interest ratio" on the NYSE. This is the ratio of NYSE short interest to average daily volume for the prior 30 days. A ratio above 2.5% is considered bullish, while a number below 1.5% is considered bearish.

High short interest numbers can give conflicting signals: bearish in indicating that many investors believe that the stock price will decline, but bullish because the shorted stock must be repurchased some time in the future and, therefore, represents potential buying power. The effect of short selling has been somewhat diminished in recent years by the expanded use of options trading.

Public/NYSE Specialist Short Sales

What the Smart Money Thinks

New York Stock Exchange (NYSE) *specialists* are responsible for maintaining an orderly market for specific securities traded on the exchange. They have access to both buy and sell orders and are very knowledgeable. Therefore, their actions can give a good indication of where the market is headed. Some of their actions, such as the level of shorting that they perform, can indicate market turning points. When the smart money turns bullish, analysts view it as a signal to start buying. This is in contrast to mutual funds, speculators, and investment advisers who typically are wrong and get excited at the wrong time.

Analyzing Public/NYSE Specialist Short Sales

The specialists' opinion can be gauged from the "ratio of public/NYSE specialist short sales" (Table 5.5). This ratio shows the ratio of short positions held by specialists compared to the general investing public. In general, when specialists become more confident and start shorting less than the public, it indicates an improving market. A public/NYSE specialist short sale number above 0.6 is considered bullish, while a number below 0.35 is considered bearish.

Nasdaq/NYSE Volume

While a certain amount of speculation in the stock market is normal, an excessive amount raises a warning flag for investors. Being aware of this danger, investors are always watching for signs of excessive speculation, which generally precedes a market top. In contrast, very low speculation occurs at market bottoms, when pessimism is widespread.

Analyzing Nasdaq/NYSE Volume

A number of tools are available to investors for determining whether speculation is excessive or minimal. One such indicator is based on a comparison of the volume of shares traded on the Nasdaq to that on the NYSE (Table 5.5). If this number is high, it indicates increased trading volume on the Nasdaq. Since the Nasdaq is home to small cap, speculative, and *initial public offering (IPO)* issues, a high Nasdaq/NYSE ratio indicates more speculation. The reasons why Nasdaq volume increases include:

▮ Rally chasing by institutions who feel they may be missing a powerful upward move.
▮ Risk-averse individuals getting into the market very late in the cycle.

A sharp increase in the Nasdaq/NYSE volume ratio has coincided with several market tops. Examples are spikes that occurred prior to the October 1987 crash and the 1990 bear market. This ratio also spiked when the small cap stocks topped in mid-1983. A decrease in the Nasdaq/NYSE ratio to very low levels often indicates a market bottom. This occurred in late 1990 (at the end of the bear market) and in mid-1982 (just prior to the start of the super bull market).

When the bear market bottomed on September 1, 1998, Nasdaq volume was 103% of NYSE volume—declining to 85.4% by September 3. By November 26, when the market was in a powerful rebound, this figure had spiked to 139%.

Effect of a Changing Stock Market

In 1983, Nasdaq volume exceeded the NYSE volume for the first time. Since then, Nasdaq volume has increased as a percentage of the NYSE volume. A reason is that many large Nasdaq stocks that in the past would have moved to the NYSE—such as Cisco, Microsoft, and Intel—have opted to remain on the Nasdaq. This has caused its trading volume to swell. Therefore, due to the distortion caused by the presence of these heavily traded stocks, the Nasdaq/NYSE ratio has lost some significance in recent years.

Using the Nasdaq/NYSE Ratio

When trading becomes speculative, an investor should become wary, rather than follow the frenzied crowd who often are wrong at critical junctures. While the Nasdaq/NYSE trading volume ratio should be monitored, it should not be used in isolation. It should be used in conjunction with other sentiment indicators. The Nasdaq/NYSE volume ratio is reported by the *IBD*, a number of newsletters, and many Internet sites.

Concluding Remarks

Psychology is a very important component in the stock market, where greed, fear, and hope are in ample supply. Their influence on the behavior of individual stocks, and the overall stock market, cannot be ignored by an investor without taking a high risk. Psychological indicators are very important tools because they help to analyze stock market behavior, which cannot be explained through numbers alone.

Psychological indicators are based on a contrarian idea—if investors are bullish, it actually means the reverse. The logic is that it is highly probable that bullish investors have already invested their cash and, therefore, a fuel source for pushing the market higher does not exist. Extreme sentiment readings indicate a market top (too bullish readings) or market bottom (too bearish readings). An extremely bullish sentiment indicates problems for the market and should be taken as a warning sign. The most valid confirmation of bullishness or bearishness occurs when both bullish and bearish numbers are in sync.

Chapter 10

Economic Indicators

Monitoring Economic Indicators

The state of the economy and the business cycle have an important bearing on the earnings prospects and the price trend of individual companies and the overall stock market. Therefore, variables affecting the business cycle should be closely monitored by stock market investors. These include general economic conditions, interest rates, local and international developments, currency rates, labor rates, and so forth.

Key Indicator Reports to Be Monitored

The most important economic indicators that can help stock market investors gauge the performance and health of the economy are:

- Inflation
- Employment
- Gross domestic product (GDP)
- National Association of Purchasing Management (NAPM) index
- Factory orders
- Housing and construction spending
- Retail sales
- Personal income and consumption expenditures
- Industrial production and capacity utilization
- *Leading economic indicators*
- Money supply

Every month, the government and associated agencies like the Federal Reserve Board issue economic reports. Each of these reports, based on the status of various economic indicators, indicates the performance and health of some sector(s) of the economy. Therefore, investors review these reports very closely in order to pick up signs of an accelerating or slowing economy, inflationary pressures, or changes in consumer spending or manufacturing activity.

These reports are very eagerly awaited and quite often are the catalysts that move the market—up or down. This typically happens if the contents of a very important report, such as inflation or employment, are not in line with investor expectations. The highlights of these reports, along with their comprehensive analysis, are reported by the *WSJ*, *IBD*, and many Internet sites. These reports are also the topics of discussion with experts on CNBC as soon as they are released. These analyses can be very informative and revealing.

Other Important Indicators to Be Monitored

Besides the monthly economic reports and the quarterly GDP report, investors should also keep themselves informed regarding the following important factors, which can significantly affect the investment climate for stocks:

▪ Federal Reserve actions on interest rates.
▪ Interest rate trends—the most important indicators being the 30-year bond rate and the prime lending rate.
▪ Changes in the tax rates.
▪ Level of government spending and the deficit, which has a significant effect on interest rates due to the level of government borrowing.

Effect of Economic Indicators on the Markets

The February 1996 employment report, released on March 8, 1996, is a good example of the importance that investors attach to economic reports. The report indicated that 705,000 new jobs had been created in a single month, which was more than double the expected rise of approximately 317,000 jobs.

The surprisingly strong job number made investors fear that an explosively growing economy would ignite inflation and cause interest rates to rise, which would make stocks less competitive with bonds. Higher interest rates also have the potential to eventually slow the economy—hurting corporate profits. Therefore, investors dumped inflation-sensitive stocks, causing the DJIA to lose 171 points, or 3.04%. The Nasdaq Composite index plunged 2.7%. This also turned out to be the worst day for bonds in nearly six years. The 30-year Treasury bond's yield, a gauge of expectations for economic growth and inflation, shot up to 6.72% from 6.47%. It lost 3 points (or $30 per $1,000 bond)—a very significant loss.

Understanding Economic Indicators
That Can Influence the Market

Inflation

Inflation decreases the value of money due to rising prices. It influences the business cycle and, in turn, is affected by the business cycle. The inflation rate has a direct impact on the investment environment. Any rise in the inflation rate makes interest rates rise and negatively impacts stocks. Rising interest rates also influence the way investors allocate their investments in bonds, stocks, and other investment vehicles. The two most important inflation indicators are the producer price index (PPI) and the consumer price index (CPI).

Producer Price Index (PPI)

The PPI is an index of commodity prices (Figure 10.1). No services are included in this index, which is a gauge of prices paid to factories, farms, and other producers. The PPI measures price changes at three production levels: crude goods like raw crops, intermediate goods like lumber and paperboard, and finished goods like clothing and furniture. The PPI measures inflation at the wholesale (producer) level. It is the first inflation report of the month and can considerably affect the stock market because the infla-

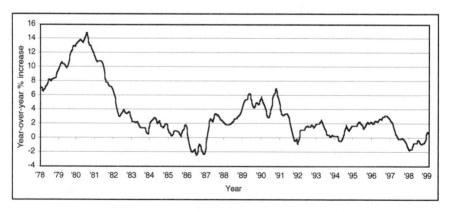

Figure 10.1   Producer Price Index (PPI)—Year-over-Year Change

tion rate, whether measured by the PPI or the CPI (consumer price index), influences everything from Federal Reserve policy to consumer and auto loans. Any change in the inflation rate as indicated by the PPI should be investigated to determine its cause.

Two PPI numbers are reported each month—the overall rate and the core rate. The core rate is calculated after excluding the PPI's two volatile components: food and energy. The core rate is the one investors usually focus on. In general, an annualized PPI rate below 3% is desired. In 1997, the overall PPI declined 1.2%, the biggest annual decline since 1986 when oil prices dropped. The core PPI rate rose only 0.1% during 1997. This indicated that inflation was under control—a positive for the stock market, which loves a benign inflation scenario. The 1997 trend continued in 1998, when the PPI declined 0.1%.

If the PPI rate increases, it negatively affects bonds and stocks. On the other hand, if it decreases or is maintained at a low level, it boosts the market. For example, in September 1996, the PPI was reported to have risen 0.2%, which was slightly below the forecasts. This caused the bond and stock markets to move higher since the report confirmed the view that inflation would remain low.

Consumer Price Index (CPI)

The CPI is widely regarded as the most important measure of inflation at the retail level (Figure 10.2). It measures the prices of both consumer commodities and services for a fixed basket of goods and services. Again, two CPI numbers are reported—the overall rate and the core rate (exclud-

Figure 10.2   Consumer Price Index (CPI)—Year-over-Year Change by Month

ing food and energy). As with the producer price index, investors focus on the core rate. It is advisable that the CPI average of several months be analyzed to get a better idea of the price trend.

Over time, the CPI is closely correlated to the PPI. On a monthly basis, however, they can vary measurably. In 1998, the CPI rose at a 1.6% rate—the lowest in 12 years. This followed increases of 1.7% in 1997 and 3.3% in 1996. Most investors believe that inflation has been tamed and, therefore, the CPI is not causing Wall Street the concern that it used to in the past. In fact, the decreasing CPI trend, coupled with the economic crises in Asia, Russia, and Brazil, has led economists to consider the possibility that deflation might be around the corner.

If the CPI rate rises, it negatively affects bonds and stocks. If it decreases or is maintained at a low level, the market benefits. For example, it was reported that the overall CPI rate, as well as the core rate, increased by 0.3% in September 1996 after a 0.1% rise in August. The numbers were still considered positive because the year-to-date core CPI was 2.8% compared to 3.0% for the comparable period in 1995. This caused the bond market to move higher, lowering the yield, which was positive for the stock market.

Commodity Research Bureau (CRB) Index

The CRB index, which indicates the commodities price trend, is another indicator tracked by investors (Figure 10.3). It represents an unweighted average of 17 prices grouped into energy, grains, industrials, livestock/meats, precious metals, and softs. Since 1996, the CRB has been in a downtrend. On January 26, 1999, the CRB index fell to 187.5—its lowest level in more than 21 years.

Declining commodity prices are a positive for the economy, consumers, and the stock market. Low commodity prices help keep inflation and interest rates low. Changes in the CRB index can affect the stock and bond markets. For example, when the CRB index of raw material prices fell in September 1996, bonds surged because it reinforced expectations that inflation would not increase in the near future. Although the CRB index does not affect the market like the CPI or the PPI, it is monitored by stock analysts because it can indicate potential inflationary pressures in commodities, which ultimately can work their way into the PPI and the CPI.

Employment Report

What It Includes and Indicates

The employment report is the most important and closely monitored report pertaining to the health of the economy. The GDP report provides

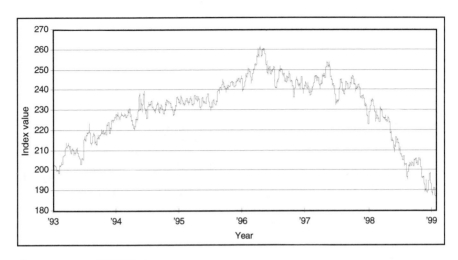

Figure 10.3   CRB Index

better insight than the monthly employment report. However, since the GDP report is published only quarterly, investors look to the employment report to fill the two-month gap when the GDP report is not published. The employment report includes both the goods- and service-producing sectors. It provides useful data about various sectors of the economy and is a very good measure of the economy's health and future direction. The report's various components are closely scrutinized by economists and investors.

The employment report contains numbers for nonfarm jobs created in the goods-producing, services, and government sectors (Figure 10.4), jobless rate, weekly hours, and hourly earnings (in manufacturing). Each of these is analyzed to gauge the health of the economy in a particular area. The two numbers most closely watched in this report, which is reported by most newspapers, are:

∎ Nonfarm jobs growth (number of new jobs created)
∎ Unemployment rate

In general, if payroll employment increases at a healthy pace, the stock market considers it to be positive, while the bond market views it negatively due to its potential inflationary effect. While investors desire steady growth, any sign of excessive jobs growth creates jitters in the markets—because investors fear that the economy may overheat and consequently cause inflationary pressures. However, a weak jobs growth number

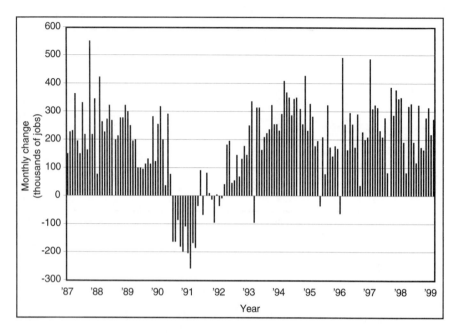

Figure 10.4   Nonfarm Payroll Employment

indicates that the economy is slowing and, therefore, is viewed positively by the bond market.

The Labor Department also reports the employment cost index (ECI) every month. Employment costs include wage and salary costs as well as the cost of providing employee benefits. The ECI is considered to be a leading inflation indicator because labor compensation is the single biggest cost of production. Therefore, analysts like to see the ECI trend remain steady.

Jobs Growth: An Important Number to Analyze
A monthly jobs growth of 200,000 to 300,000 is generally considered good since it indicates a steadily growing economy. Any number above, or below, this range indicates an economy growing strongly, or slowly, respectively. The overall jobs growth number can vary depending on the state of the business cycle—whether the economy is coming out of a recession, is in a recession, or has been expanding for a while.

The main driving force for any reaction by the market to the jobs report is expectations. The reported numbers have to be within the range of estimates made by economists, which usually are in tune with the state of the economic cycle. The jobs growth numbers estimated by economists are reported by major publications (including the *WSJ*, *IBD*, and *Barron's*), prior to the release of the employment report.

Care should be used in analyzing these reports. Besides being on the lookout for onetime factors skewing results, one should not read too much into a single report. Instead, one should look at a few reports before jumping to any conclusion regarding the direction of the economy.

Market Reaction to the Employment Report
On July 5, 1996, it was reported that 239,000 new jobs were created in June—about 50% more than economists had expected. The result was that the DJIA dropped 114.88 points. Both the DJIA and the Nasdaq lost about 2% of their value that day. On the other hand, the September 1996 report showed a surprising drop of 40,000 nonfarm jobs. Economists had been expecting a gain of 170,000 jobs. This indicated that the Federal Reserve would not raise interest rates in the near future since the economy appeared to be slowing rather than overheating. Therefore, the benchmark 30-year bond gained $1^1/_8$ points—or $11.25 per $1,000 bond. The yield fell 9 basis points to 6.74%. The stock market moved up 60 points, or 1.01%, to a new high of 5,992.

In October 1996, 210,000 new nonfarm jobs were created—in line with most estimates. The market hardly yawned. Compare this to the similar job growth number in June 1996, which had so negatively affected the market. The different reactions to the two reports were due to different expectations. In October, higher job growth had been expected because 35,000 jobs were lost rather than created in September. When analyzed in conjunction with the 35,000-job loss in September, the average for the two months (September/October 1996) showed anemic jobs growth. The three-month average growth slowed to 152,000 jobs. Hence, the market did not react.

Recently, strong job growth numbers have not spooked the stock market as they did in the past. In February 1998, 310,000 new jobs were created after an increase of 375,000 jobs in January. The February report indicated that the economy was healthy and growing. Therefore, continued growth in corporate profits could be expected. The release of this report caused the DJIA to rise 125 points (1.5%). The positive reaction, in contrast to the reaction to a similar report in June 1996, was due to the different inflation scenario expected in 1998. During 1997, inflation as measured by the CPI was only 1.7% and, consequently, investors were not worried about the inflationary effects of a tightening labor market in 1998.

Again, in November 1998, nonfarm payrolls surged 267,000—far more than the 175,000 expected by analysts. Since the economy had been weakening during 1998, the DJIA reacted positively—rising 1.5% while the Nasdaq gained 2.5%. The bond market reaction was negative—but not to the same extent as would have been the case if the economy had been growing robustly. Most of the bond reaction could be attributed to the dashed expectations of a Federal Reserve interest rate cut at its forthcoming December 1998 meeting.

Gross Domestic Product

The gross domestic product (GDP) is the total value of goods and services produced in the country during the year (Figure 10.5). It is reported every quarter and is a good indicator of how fast the economy grew during that quarter. The GDP is the broadest measure of aggregate economic activity in the country. This report also contains the GDP deflator, which is believed to be a more precise inflation measure than the CPI.

If the GDP increases at a healthy pace, stocks tend to rise due to the potential for higher profits resulting from a healthy business climate. On the other hand, anemic or negative GDP growth affects the stock market negatively. In both 1997 and 1998, GDP growth was 3.9%. This healthy economic growth translated into healthy corporate profits and a rising stock market.

The release of the GDP report does not impact the stock market significantly. Most of the components used to calculate the GDP are already known when it is released and, therefore, major surprises are rare. The

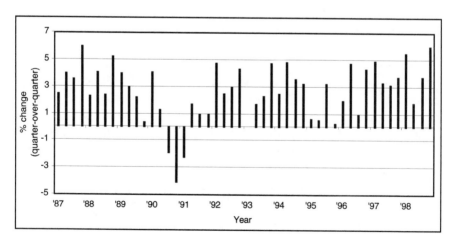

Figure 10.5   **Real Gross Domestic Product (GDP) Growth**

stock market reacts strongly to the GDP number only if it is significantly above or below the advance estimates made by economists.

National Association of Purchasing Management (NAPM) Index

What It Includes and Indicates

The NAPM index provides an indication of economic growth (Figure 10.6). If the overall NAPM index is above 50, it indicates that the manufacturing sector is expanding, while a reading below 50 indicates that it is contracting. This index, which provides a comprehensive view of the manufacturing sector, tracks the economy's ups and downs fairly well. For example, the NAPM index declined for six straight months till November 1998. This was consistent with a slowing economy and reduced overseas demand due to the deepening international economic crisis. In December 1998, the NAPM dropped to 45.1—the lowest level since May 1991. This raised a serious concern that factory weakness could spread to the rest of the economy in the coming months. In general, if the NAPM rises, it tends to move the stock market up while pushing bonds down. If the NAPM decreases, especially below 50, the effect is the opposite.

The overall NAPM index includes many components with each providing valuable insight into a specific area. These components are new orders, order backlog, production, supplier deliveries, inventories, prices paid, employment, new export orders, and import orders. Each component indicates what is going on in a particular sector. For example, the supplier deliveries component is considered to be a barometer for inventory

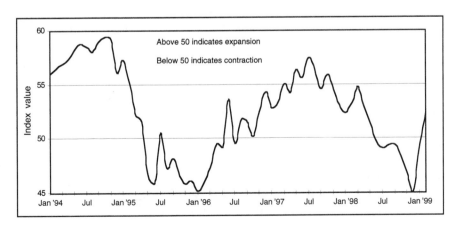

Figure 10.6 **National Association of Purchasing Management (NAPM) Index**

investment and capacity utilization. It is one of the numbers monitored by the Federal Reserve for making a decision on whether to tighten the money supply, which can affect economic growth.

Effect on the Market and Economy

In September 1996, the NAPM index decreased to 51.7, down from 52.6 in August, which was lower than had been expected. This indication of a slower pace for manufacturing was viewed positively by the bond market, which rallied. The December 1996 report showed that the index rose to 54 from 52.7 in November, reversing the declines in the previous two months. The prices paid component also surged to 51.5 in December from 45.9 in November. This triggered inflation fears, and the DJIA dropped 100 points in early trading. The 30-year bond lost $1^3/_{16}$ points or $11.875 for a $1,000 face value. The bond yield, which moves in the reverse direction compared to the price, rose from 6.64% to 6.74%.

Bonds and stocks do not always react in the same way to the NAPM report. For example, in February 1998, the NAPM index rose to 53.3 from 52.4 in January—ending a three-month decline. This was higher than expected and indicated that the economy was stronger than expected. The DJIA did not react to this news and rose 4 points for the day. However, the reaction of the bond market was very negative. The 30-year bond fell $1^1/_4$ point or $12.50 per $1,000 face amount.

Investors and economists pay more attention to the direction and steadiness of the numbers than to the actual NAPM index number itself. For example, after ranging around 50 for most of 1993, in 1994 the index climbed 10 points within a few months, which indicated increasing bottlenecks and cost pressures. At the same time, the NAPM prices paid component rose significantly—from the 50s into the low 60s. This indicated a strong and potentially overheating economy—which became a factor in the Federal Reserve's decision to raise interest rates. In the past, the Federal Reserve has hiked interest rates when the NAPM index was around 56 and the vendor performance index was about 57.[1] Vendor performance indicates how fast companies fill their orders.

Factory Orders

What It Includes and Indicates

Each month, the Commerce Department releases the "Factory Orders" report. This report is another indicator of how certain sectors of the econ-

---

[1]*Investor's Business Daily*, January 3, 1997.

omy are performing. The components of this report include new factory orders (durable and nondurable goods), inventories, factory shipments (measure of current demand), and unfilled orders (measure of longer-term pent-up demand and backlogs). A positive factory orders number indicates growth, while a decline in factory orders indicates a slowing or contracting economy. In 1998, when the economy started to slow down, factory orders rose only 2.1%, down from 5.4% in 1997.

Monthly factory orders are volatile and need to be analyzed as such. For example, in September 1996, factory orders rose 2.7%, the largest increase in more than two years. This was followed by declines in November and December. In January 1997, factory orders rose a robust 2.5%, which was followed by an increase of just 0.8% in February.

Durable Goods

The durable goods component indicates the new orders placed for big-ticket items expected to last three years or more (Figure 10.7). Tracking these orders helps investors anticipate changes in production activity in the country. Typically, orders tend to decline 8 to 12 months ahead of a cyclical downturn and rise about a month ahead of the trough of a recession.

A strong rise in orders is expected to spur manufacturing activity in order to meet rising demand, and indicates a stronger economy in the months ahead. At the end of 1998, orders were strong after a weak year. This indicated a healthy start for the economy in 1999. A drop in orders indicates a weakening in the manufacturing sector in the following

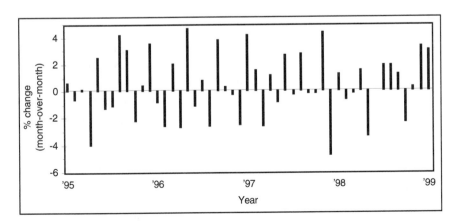

Figure 10.7   Durable Goods—New Orders

months. In general, if the durable goods orders are up, bonds tend to go down while stocks tend to rise.

Durable Goods Report Volatility

This component tends to be volatile from month to month. In August 1996, orders for durable goods fell a surprising 3.1%, the biggest drop in more than a year. This indicated an economic slowdown, which raised questions about future corporate earnings. The result was that investors started to sell economically sensitive stocks. Stocks less tied to swings in the economy fared better. Bond traders also liked the news and its implications of a weaker economy. They pushed the 30-year Treasury up $^{17}/_{32}$—bringing down the yield from 6.92% to 6.88%.

The volatility range of this indicator can be gauged from the reports issued in the last four months of 1996. In September, durable goods orders rose a very strong 4.6%, followed by a meager rise of 0.1% in October. Then, orders declined by 1.7% in both November and December 1996, only to be followed by a robust rise of 3.6% in January 1997.

Inventories

Any increase or decrease in inventories has a direct effect on orders placed, which can affect the production of goods and, in turn, the economy. Hence, the buildup or depletion of inventories is tracked by investors. These numbers are analyzed in conjunction with other indicators. For example, wholesalers' inventories, which are reported monthly, are tracked in conjunction with sales. If sales of autos, lumber, and metal products decrease, while inventories increase, the combination might indicate that businesses could have more problems further down the road.

Housing and Construction Spending

The housing sector, one of the biggest sectors of the economy, is a leading indicator of economic activity. Investors view it as an extremely important indicator because it helps forecast the direction of the economy. It is one of the first indicators to turn down when the economy goes into a recession and subsequently rise when the economy rebounds. Changes in the housing sector are primarily triggered by changes in mortgage rates, which in turn are affected by inflation and interest rates. Historically, changes in consumer spending patterns have first appeared in the housing and auto sectors.

Housing Starts

A gauge for measuring the health of the housing market is the housing starts number (Figure 10.8). An increase in this number is considered pos-

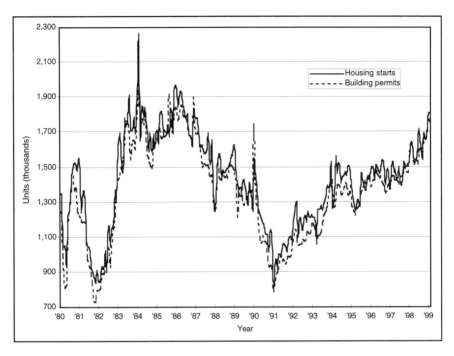

Figure 10.8   **Housing Starts and Building Permits**

itive for the economy. This is due to the large effect that the housing industry has on construction spending, building activity, and associated sectors of the economy. When housing starts increase, stocks tend to rise
while bonds tend to go down—and vice versa. Housing starts figures can
be volatile from month to month. For example, in December 1997 they
declined 0.7% following a 0.3% rise in November. In October 1998, housing starts soared 7.3%—the biggest one-month rise in over a year. Month-
to-month volatility is also influenced by the weather due to its effect on
construction activities.

An associated number monitored by investors is the number of
building permits issued, which is a gauge of future construction spending (Figure 10.8). Building permits and housing starts are leading indicators of future spending in the housing sector—usually by many
months.

Sales of New and Existing Homes
Also reported and closely monitored are monthly sales of new and existing
homes (Figures 10.9 and 10.10). New home sales affect sales of furniture,

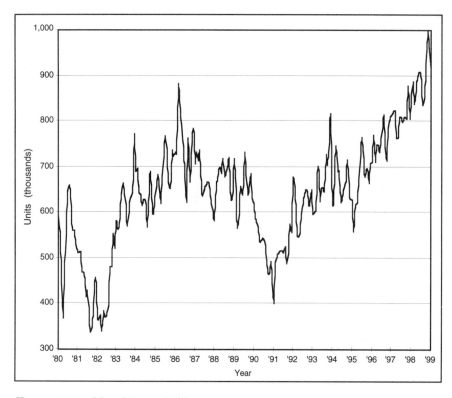

Figure 10.9   New Homes Sold

appliances, and other durable goods. Strong new home sales indicate strength in the key housing sector. Sales of new homes, as well as existing homes, are negatively impacted by higher mortgage rates. Therefore, rising interest rates tend to slow down an important sector of the economy. A rule of thumb is that a one-point drop in interest rates adds 100,000 existing home sales and 50,000 new homes.[2]

In general, when new home sales increase, stocks rise and bonds decline. Existing home sales, which account for 80% of the total housing market, are considered a more accurate indicator of the housing market than housing starts. The reason is that they measure actual rather than expected closings (which the housing starts number indicates).

---

[2]Ibid., January 8, 1998.

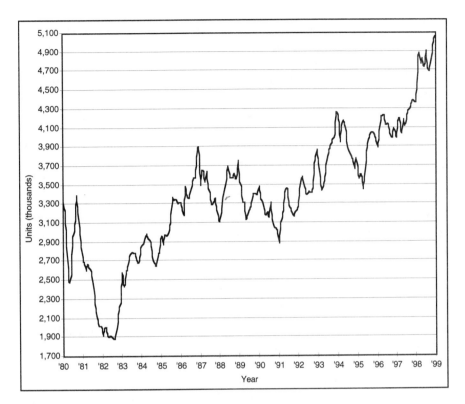

Figure 10.10   **Existing Homes Sold**

Construction Spending

This is another report that reflects housing activity. It includes residential and nonresidential new construction spending, as well as public construction spending. The level of construction spending is influenced by mortgage rates, which impact both home sales and construction. The monthly construction spending report typically does not have any significant effect on the stock market or the bond market. Since these numbers can be volatile from month to month, it is advisable to consider three months of data in order to determine the trend.

Retail Sales

Retail sales are reported every month by the Commerce Department. An increase in retail sales indicates good consumer spending. Since consumer spending makes up two-thirds of the overall economy, it is closely monitored by analysts. In December 1998, retail sales rose 0.9% following a

0.6% gain in November. This increased confidence that overall consumer spending was going to remain healthy through early 1999—allaying a concern due to the international economic crisis of 1998.

A good indicator of consumer spending is monthly sales at the nation's major retailers. Comparable store sales, for stores open a year or more, are reported as "chain-store" sales. These sales—which do not include the effects of recent store openings, closings, and expansions—indicate the level at which consumers are spending their money. A component of retail sales is auto sales, which can be volatile from month to month.

Retail sales are the first good indication of the strength or weakness of consumer spending in a given month. These figures can affect the market. If retail sales rise, it is a positive for retailers because it indicates good business. This tends to cause bonds to decline and stocks to rise.

Personal Income and Consumption Expenditures

Personal income represents the compensation individuals receive from all sources. An increase in personal income provides fuel for consumer spending. Therefore, if personal income increases, stocks tend to rise and bonds tend to decline.

Consumption expenditures represent the market value of all goods and services purchased by individuals. Tracking these expenditures is important because consumer spending makes up a very large component of overall economic activity.

Industrial Production and Capacity Utilization

The industrial production index is a measure of the physical volume of output of the nation's factories, mines, and utilities (Figure 10.11). A healthy rise in industrial production indicates a growing economy. Therefore, when this index rises, stocks tend to rise and bonds tend to decline. A slackening in this indicator is viewed as a sign of a potential slowdown in the economy. This occurred in February 1998, when industrial production remained unchanged from a month earlier—the first time this happened in over a year. This was attributed to the effect of the Asian economic crisis, which was expected to slow down the U.S. economy.

Capacity utilization indicates the extent of usage, or the "employment rate," of the nation's manufacturing capacity (Figure 10.12). It is an indicator of potential bottlenecks and, consequently, inflationary pressures building up in the manufacturing sector. The reason is that high utiliza-

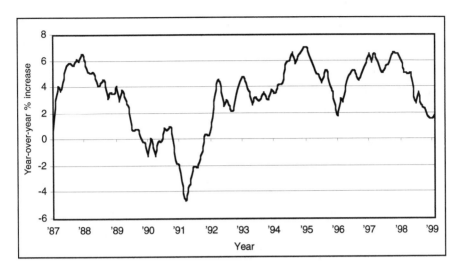

Figure 10.11 Industrial Production

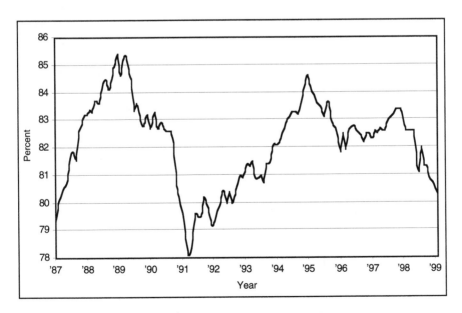

Figure 10.12 Capacity Utilization

tion rates can be inflationary. At the end of the expansion peak in 1989, capacity utilization rate was 85.3%. In late 1994, it stood at 84.5%, which was among the factors that led the Fed to increase the federal funds rate through early 1995. In November 1998, capacity utilization was 80.6%—the lowest rate since August 1993. This reading was consistent with the economy slowing during 1998.

An 85% rate is viewed by some economists to be the point when inflationary pressures tend to start. When capacity utilization is down to about 80%, concerns arise about excess capacity. Then, less investment in capital equipment and new plants is needed—which affects the economy.

If capacity utilization rises, stocks tend to go up and bonds decline. However, if capacity utilization is very high, it becomes a negative for stocks as well. The reason is that the stock market starts anticipating inflationary pressures, which can impact the stock market negatively. However, if capacity increases faster than production, it is expected that inflation will remain in check.

Index of Leading Economic Indicators (LEI)

The LEI, reported monthly by the Conference Board, is a composite of 10 different indicators (Figure 10.13). It is used to predict future aggregate economic activity. The LEI indicates the direction of the economy six to nine months down the road through the use of a group of leading economic indicators. It is designed to give advance warning of turning points in the business cycle. Three consecutive monthly changes in the LEI in the same direction signal turning points in the economy. The 10 components of the LEI, each of which has its own predictive value, are:

1. Average workweek
2. Consumer orders
3. Equipment orders
4. Stock prices
5. Consumer expectations
6. New jobless claims
7. Vendor performance
8. Building permits
9. Money supply
10. Yield spread

In November 1996, the yield spread replaced the material prices and unfilled factory orders components—to better measure changes in the

Figure 10.13   Index of Leading Economic Indicators (LEI)

business cycle. The yield spread measures the difference between the yield on the 10-year Treasury note and the federal funds rate and is often called the yield curve. When this spread narrows, the expectation is that the Federal Reserve will either keep interest rates unchanged or reduce them in the not too distant future.

The LEI peaks and troughs about six to nine months earlier than the economy. Consequently, it is widely used as a forecasting and planning tool. While the LEI is a good indicator of the future direction of the economy, it is not infallible. Since 1952, the LEI predicted 10 recessions out of which only seven occurred. Since the individual components of the LEI are released prior to the monthly release of the overall index, it does not affect the stock market in any significant way.

Money Supply

Money supply is the total of all money held by the public. It includes total cash and checking account balances at commercial banks held by everyone in the country except the government and other banks. Many investment professionals believe that a correlation exists between the nation's money supply and stock prices. When money supply is expanding at a steady rate, with low inflation, stock prices tend to rise. However, when money supply contracts or inflation increases, stock prices are negatively affected.

The growth and size of money supply are influenced by the reserves at member banks and the discount rate—which are controlled by the Federal Reserve. In the 1970s, money supply grew at an average of 10% annually while inflation averaged 7% per year.[3] As the negative effects of inflation became apparent, a tighter monetary policy was applied by the Federal Reserve. The result was that from 1986 to 1996—a period when inflation averaged only 3.5%—money supply increased at an annual rate of 4%. With low inflation, the stock market prospered during this period. Recently, U.S. money supply has grown faster than the economy—10% annually[4] (Figure 10.14). However, foreigners have soaked up the excess, since dollars are in high demand overseas.

Concluding Remarks

The price appreciation of a stock depends on its profitability, which to a large extent depends on the business cycle and the health of the economy. Therefore, it is very important that an investor continuously monitor the state of the economy, discern trends, and identify forces that may affect

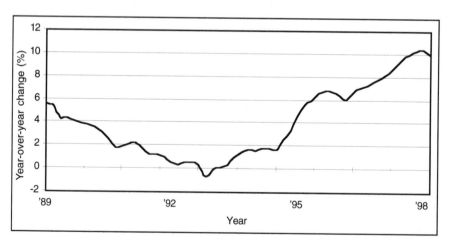

Figure 10.14   **Money Supply**

[3]*Individual Investor*, November 1996, p. 34.
[4]*Investor's Business Daily*, February 1, 1999.

the profitability of individual stocks and the overall market. For this purpose, the periodic reports issued by the various government departments
and agencies are very useful.

The best sources for the timely monitoring of various economic reports and statistics, which are usually released monthly, are the *Wall Street
Journal, Investor's Business Daily*, and CNBC. The *WSJ* and *IBD* provide
analysis and comprehensive comments on the various economic reports
the day after they are released. On CNBC, the highlights of these reports
are reported as soon as they are released, along with analysis and comments from experts in the field.

Chapter 11

Understanding Stock Market Behavior

Determining Market Trend

Need to Determine Market Direction

Long-term, the stock market rises about 75% of the time, which sets a positive tone for most individual stocks. Similarly, when the market declines in a correction or a bear market, it takes down with it three out of every four stocks. During a declining market, an excellent stock may either hold its own or rise modestly. In a bull market, such a stock will outperform admirably. However, practically no stock can be assured of remaining unaffected when the market is declining during a correction or a bear market.

In view of this effect on individual stocks, it is important that an investor learns to determine the overall market's direction and trend. An investor needs to understand the state of the market (bear market, bull market, choppy market trading in a narrow range—with or without appreciable volatility) because each one of these factors can affect any stock.

What Needs to Be Monitored

Market behavior and trends can be monitored through the major stock market averages and indexes. These indexes are groupings of individual stocks, ranging from 30 to almost 7,000, which track market and sector behavior. Their primary purpose is to highlight the underlying trend. Investors also use them as a benchmark against which they measure the performance of their stock or portfolio.

To keep abreast of what is happening in the stock market, an investor should monitor and observe, as applicable, the following:

■ Market averages—DJIA, S&P 500, Nasdaq, AMEX, Russell 2000
■ Trading volume levels
■ Trend reversals
■ Market tops and bottoms

Various daily newspapers reporting daily stock prices also provide data on some selected indexes and averages. However, the most comprehensive data on these indexes and averages are reported by *Investor's Business Daily* and the *Wall Street Journal*.

What Needs to Be Done: Follow-Up Action

The level to which an individual stock ultimately rises depends on the company's fundamentals. However, it pays to study the behavior of the market and the forces that impact it such as the inflation trend, economic cycle, investor confidence, and alternative investments. To realize maximum benefit, serious investors should master the art of recognizing market extremes and changes in market direction. For example, when a market peak or a downturn is recognized, an investor can begin to:

■ Decrease holdings (25% to 50%)
■ Sell the weakest stocks first

Conversely, when plenty of bargains are available at a market bottom, investors can start increasing their investments in stocks.

Market Averages and Indexes

Each of the three big exchanges (NYSE, Nasdaq, and AMEX) has a primary index for indicating the collective price movement of its stocks. Figure 11.1 shows three major averages (Nasdaq Composite, S&P 500, and the DJIA). The most widely quoted and monitored stock market index is the Dow Jones Industrial Average (DJIA), which was created more than a century ago.

Dow Jones Industrial Average (DJIA)

Many investors incorrectly think that the DJIA, also called the Dow, is the stock market. The DJIA's daily movements are reported in the media

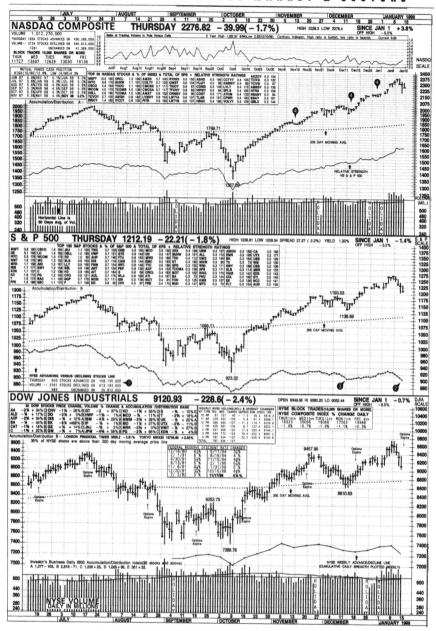

Figure 11.1 **Major Market Averages**

Source: *Investor's Business Daily*, January 15, 1999. Reprinted with permission.

to reflect the performance of the market as a whole. This is quite misleading because even though the DJIA includes the largest American companies, it contains only 30 stocks. Therefore, it does not reflect the action of the overwhelming majority of stocks in the stock market.

The DJIA price moves are reported in points, rather than dollars, in terms such as "the Dow went up 20 points." The DJIA moves are calculated in such a way that for each one-dollar rise in an individual DJIA stock, the overall DJIA moves up approximately two points.

Each Dow Jones average (industrial, transportation, and utility) reflects the performance of a specific market sector. While the industrials are a blend of growth and cyclical stocks, which tend to respond to prevailing moods of the market, the transportation average is composed of cyclical stocks that respond to economic and earnings forecasts. The utilities average is driven by interest rates and dividend yields, while the financial average also is interest-sensitive.

DJIA Components

The 30 DJIA stocks are AlliedSignal, Alcoa, American Express, AT&T, Boeing, Caterpillar, Chevron, Coca-Cola, Disney, DuPont, Eastman Kodak, Exxon, General Electric, General Motors, Goodyear, Hewlett-Packard, IBM, International Paper, Johnson & Johnson, McDonald's, Merck, 3M, J.P. Morgan, Philip Morris, Procter & Gamble, Sears Roebuck, Travelers Group, Union Carbide, United Technologies, and Wal-Mart.

Indicator of Market Health

The DJIA is closely monitored due to the belief that the performance of the country's largest companies reflects the state of the overall stock market. However, while this is correct to some extent, it does not adequately reflect the performance of the entire market, which includes thousands of small and medium-sized companies. Because of this inadequacy, investors use other indexes to get a better overall view of the stock market's health. These indexes give investors a feel for underlying currents that the more widely followed DJIA index may miss.

Other Important Market Indexes

The DJIA is very good at reflecting the market's behavior over the long term. However, on a short-term basis, it can often be misleading. Among the most important indexes tracked by market watchers to get a comprehensive view of the overall market are the following indexes:

- NYSE indexes (Composite, Industrial, Transportation, Utilities and Finance)
- S&P 500
- Nasdaq
- Russell 2000
- Wilshire 5000
- *IBD* Mutual Fund index

NYSE Indexes

The NYSE Composite indicates the aggregate market value of all stocks listed on the NYSE. The sum of the individual market values is expressed relative to the market value, 50, of the base period year (1966). The market value is calculated by multiplying the price per share by the number of outstanding shares. Other NYSE indexes (Industrial, Transportation, Utilities, and Finance) enable the monitoring of specific market sectors.

S&P 500 Index

The S&P 500 index, which measures the performance of the 500 largest companies in the United States, gives a broader view of the market than the DJIA. It includes stocks traded on the NYSE and AMEX, as well as *over-the-counter* (OTC). The index includes 400 industrial, 40 financial, 40 utility, and 20 transportation companies. The S&P 500 index was introduced in 1957. It is a benchmark against which the performance of mutual funds and portfolios is compared. The median market capitalization of companies in the S&P 500 is $4.5 billion, with the largest being $332 billion (GE).

Nasdaq Index

The Nasdaq index primarily consists of smaller, lesser known companies. However, some big names like Microsoft and Intel are also included in this index. The Nasdaq index is weighted according to market capitalization. Because of their larger market capitalization, bigger companies have a disproportionately large effect on this index. Any big movement in such a stock causes a large change in the Nasdaq index.

Russell 2000 Index

The Russell 2000 index is a good gauge for monitoring the performance of small company stocks. Small stocks are also tracked by a relatively new index—the S&P 600.

Wilshire 5000 Index

Another broad-based index is the Wilshire 5000. It tracks about 7,200 stocks and is considered a good measure of the total value of wealth contained in the stock market.

IBD *Mutual Fund Index*

Investor's Business Daily's mutual fund index is a useful measure for tracking the overall performance of mutual funds. It is a benchmark against which money managers and many individual investors measure the performance of their portfolios.

Industry and Sector Indexes

A number of industry and sector indexes, some of which are shown in Table 11.1, are available to investors for monitoring specific stock sectors

Table 11.1   Market Sector Indexes, January 14, 1999

Change since Jan. 1, 1999	Three-month change	Index	Index value	Change	Yesterday's change
+8.46%	+74.37%	Junior Growth Index	679.75	−27.55	−3.90%
+4.39%	+62.81%	High-Tech Index	554.10	−11.75	−2.06%
+3.06%	+58.56%	New Issues Index	412.16	−12.58	−2.96%
+3.84%	+47.75%	Nasdaq OTC Composite	2,276.82	−39.99	−1.73%
−1.97%	+31.44%	Consumer Index	571.18	−8.61	−1.49%
−3.67%	+28.88%	S&P Midcap 400	377.93	−4.96	−1.30%
−0.60%	+24.49%	IBD 6000 Index	775.85	−11.93	−1.51%
−2.19%	+23.62%	Dow Jones Transportation	3,080.28	−89.14	−2.81%
−1.12%	+22.83%	Value Line Index	917.42	−12.82	−1.38%
+1.33%	+19.75%	AMEX Composite	698.16	−1.23	−0.18%
−4.78%	+19.33%	Medical/Healthcare	2,694.59	−45.62	−1.66%
−3.57%	+18.78%	Bank Index	732.12	−25.22	−3.33%
−2.39%	+17.99%	NYSE Finance	508.95	−12.66	−2.43%
−2.47%	+16.92%	NYSE Composite	581.07	−9.65	−1.63%
−2.24%	+14.43%	Senior Growth Index	789.88	−21.67	−2.67%
−2.70%	+8.77%	Insurance Index	525.17	−9.39	−1.76%
−4.91%	+4.63%	Defensive Index	1,103.76	−21.23	−1.89%
−3.91%	+0.96%	U.S. Defense Index	275.25	−2.58	−0.93%
−2.84%	−2.25%	Dow Jones Utility	303.43	−4.64	−1.51%
+8.99%	−16.44%	Gold Index	32.01	−0.21	−0.65%

Source: Investor's Business Daily, January 15, 1999. Reprinted with permission.

and groups. These indexes can be analyzed to check the relative performance of individual sectors. Before buying a stock, many investors use these indexes to determine the performance of the industry to which it belongs. A good source for analyzing these indexes is the *IBD*—which ranks them according to their performance.

Practical Application of Averages/Indexes

Using Indexes for Comparison

Indexes can be used to compare the market or sector's rise and fall with prior years. For example, on October 12, 1989, the DJIA dropped 190 points. While this was a pretty bad day, it was not as disastrous when compared to the October 19, 1987, drop of 508 points. Another advantage of indexes is that the performance of a portfolio can be compared to an appropriate index or average. If the comparison is unfavorable, the investment strategy or tactic(s) being followed may need to be changed.

The best source of information for tracking various market indexes is *IBD*. Besides comprehensive data, *IBD* also provides charts for individual stocks and selected stock sectors for key sectors of the U.S. economy. These include the high-tech, junior growth, consumer, and defensive sectors. These price charts also include RS lines that compare the performance of these sectors against the overall market represented by the S&P 500.

Which Average/Index to Use

With so many averages and indexes to choose from, one needs to be careful in selecting the right one. An investor should pick the correct index— for comparing its performance against one's own stocks—or the results will be misleading. For example, the performance of a small growth company should not be compared to the DJIA or the S&P 500. Similarly, investors who want to monitor the overall market should not focus only on the DJIA. By doing so, they will miss major movements in the overall stock market. Instead, they should also monitor broader measures like the S&P 500 and the Nasdaq.

In 1996, for example, an investor who monitored only the DJIA would have missed the significant underperformance of the small cap stocks. They had a very poor year while the DJIA was making new highs. Again, the Nasdaq Composite fell by more than 10% in 1992, 1994, and 1996, while the DJIA did not have a correction of any major significance until July 1996, when it declined 7.47%.

It should be realized that even if different sectors are moving in the same direction, the magnitude of their moves can be significantly different. In early 1997, the Russell 2000, a small cap benchmark, lagged the S&P 500 appreciably. Starting in July, it exploded on positive earnings news while the S&P 500 and many blue chip stocks lagged. In 1998, from November 23 to December 14, the DJIA declined 8.6%. During the same period, the Nasdaq declined only 0.55%. Therefore, one should not monitor only one or two sectors or indexes and assume that they represent the overall behavior of the stock market.

Bull and Bear Markets

Bull and Bear Market Characteristics

The stock market is a very dynamic place characterized by perpetual price movements. The direction of these movements can be up, down, or sideways. Like the economy, the stock market climbs steadily upward in its characteristic jagged manner for a few years. This period is known as a bull market. This is followed by a period in which the market moves steadily downward, interspersed with small rallies, for an extended period. This period, typically less than a year, is known as a bear market.

The state of the stock market, bull or bear, directly impacts the profitability of companies. Therefore, market analysts are continuously engaged in the exercise of trying to forecast the market's future direction. During bull markets, investors try to be fully invested. During bear markets, they reduce exposure to stocks.

Defining Bull and Bear Markets

Market players use different definitions for bull and bear markets. A bull market is commonly defined as a market in which there is a 20%, or greater, rise in stock prices. Another defines a bull market being characterized by a 30% price rise. In this century, there have been 20 bull markets with an average duration of 3.1 years. The previous bull market run started in October 1990 and ended in August 1998. During this period, the DJIA rose from 2,365 to 9,412.

A bear market is defined as one in which the stock market declines 20%. Some of the recent market lows were made in 1998, 1990, 1982, 1978, 1974, 1970, 1966, and 1962. A market low also occurred in 1987, which missed the pattern by one year. In 1990, the Nasdaq fell 31%, and it declined 33.09% during the 1998 bear market.

Bull and Bear Cycle

When the stock market undergoes a significant price decline, it generates a climate of fear. When a market bottom is reached, extreme pessimism reigns. At that time, a bull market starts. As price gains are made, fear starts to recede. As further gains are made, caution sets in. However, as significant price appreciation takes place with the bull market continuing, investors tend to forget the pessimistic bear market days. At that time investor attitude can be described as confident and euphoric.

By the time a top is reached, most investors remain convinced that the market will keep going up indefinitely. At that point, the bear market starts. As the market starts declining, the same emotions characterize the market but in the reverse direction—confidence, caution, and fear. Finally, when the bottom is reached, the feeling is widespread that prices will continue to decline even further. At that time, the next bull market is ready to start.

Bull and Bear Statistics

If we consider an *IBD* survey in which a bull market was defined as any upward move greater than 22% that lasted longer than one year, there have been 25 bull markets in this century. Their average duration was two years and three months, with an average gain of 84.4% in each. Of these 25 bull markets, only three were less than 30%, while seven bull markets soared more than 100%.

IBD's survey, which was conducted prior to the 1998 bear market, also reported that there have been 26 bear markets during this century. The average bear market lasted 17 months with an average drop of 30.8%. The market declined more than 40% eight times, including 1968, 1973, and 1987. The worst bear market, which followed the market collapse of October 1929, lasted 35 months. During that debacle, the DJIA declined almost 90%, to 40 from a peak of 390. In 1973–1974, the DJIA dropped 45%, with many high-flying stocks plunging as much as 80%.

The 1998 sharp decline barely lasted a month, which made it the shortest bear market on record. During this period, the average stock fell 37% from peak to trough—the same loss as was experienced in the 1990 and 1987 bear markets.[1]

Table 11.2, reported by the *WSJ*, shows the frequency and severity of stock market declines in this century.[2] Compared to the *IBD* survey,

---

[1]*Investor's Business Daily*, January 4, 1999.
[2]*Wall Street Journal*, July 19, 1996, p. C1.

Table 11.2   **Stock Market Declines since 1900**

	Routine declines (5% or more)	Moderate correction (10% or more)	Severe correction (15% or more)	Bear market (20% or more)
Number of times since 1900	318	106	50	29
Frequency	About three times a year	About once a year	About once every two years	About every three years
Last occurrence	July 1996	August 1990	August 1990	October 1990
Average loss before decline ends	11%	19%	27%	35%
Average length	40 days	109 days	217 days	364 days

Source: Ned Davis Research Inc. (*WSJ*, July 19, 1996).
Note: This table does not include statistics for the corrections and bear market that took place in 1997 and 1998.

which indicated 26 bear markets, Table 11.2 shows that 29 bear markets took place this century. These differences can be attributed to different criteria being used for defining a bear market. Table 11.4 lists the major bull markets of this century, along with their duration in days and their percentage gains. The longest bull market started in October 1990 and ended in August 1998.

According to the data provided by Ned Davis Research in 1998,[3] the mean decline for bear markets is 31.2%—with a duration of 418 days (Table 11.3). The median drop is 26%—with a 374-day duration.

Table 11.4 lists the major prolonged bull markets of this century.

Understanding Bull Markets

Birth of a Bull Market

Great Bull Markets
Many bull markets start during recessions. In fact, one of the greatest bull markets started during the Great Depression in July 1932. In just 20 months, it rocketed the DJIA from 40 to 110, a gain of 175%. Another roaring bull market, which realized a gain of 160%, took place during the

---

[3]*Investor's Business Daily*, September 2, 1998.

Table 11.3   **Magnitude of Bear Markets**

Starting DJIA	Ending DJIA	Start date	End date	Duration—days	% decline
78	42	06/17/01	11/09/03	875	46.1
103	53	01/19/06	11/15/07	665	48.5
100	72	11/19/09	09/25/11	675	27.4
94	71	09/30/12	07/30/14	668	24.1
110	65	11/21/16	12/19/17	393	40.1
119	63	11/03/19	08/24/21	660	46.6
105	85	03/20/23	10/27/23	221	18.6
381	198	09/03/29	11/13/29	71	47.9
294	41	04/17/30	07/08/32	813	86.0
79	50	09/07/32	02/27/33	173	37.2
110	85	02/05/34	07/26/34	171	22.8
194	98	03/10/37	03/31/38	386	49.1
158	121	11/12/38	04/08/39	147	23.3
155	92	09/12/39	04/28/42	959	40.4
212	163	05/29/46	05/17/47	353	23.2
193	161	06/15/48	06/13/49	363	16.3
521	419	04/06/56	10/22/57	564	19.4
685	566	01/05/60	10/25/60	294	17.4
734	535	12/13/61	06/26/62	195	27.1
995	744	02/09/66	10/07/66	240	25.2
985	631	12/03/68	05/26/70	539	35.9
950	797	04/28/71	11/23/71	209	16.1
1,051	577	01/11/73	12/06/74	694	45.1
1,014	742	09/21/76	02/28/78	525	26.9
907	759	09/08/78	04/21/80	591	16.4
1,024	776	04/27/81	08/12/82	472	24.1
1,287	1,086	11/29/83	07/24/84	238	15.6
2,722	1,738	08/25/87	10/19/87	55	36.1
2,999	2,365	07/16/90	10/11/90	87	21.2

Source: Ned Davis Research Inc. (*Investor's Business Daily*, September 2, 1998).

1920s before the October 1929 crash. One of the greatest bull markets ever started in 1990 with the DJIA at 2,365 and reached a high of 9,412 in July 1998—when a bear market set in.

What Starts a Bull Market

The explanation for a bull market starting in a recession is fairly simple. When the economy contracts, the Federal Reserve attempts to stimulate it by reducing interest rates. This has a very powerful effect on the market

Table 11.4   **Top Bull Markets**

Period	% gain by DJIA	Duration in days
10/11/90–07/17/98	297	2,837
06/13/49–04/06/56	222	2,489
10/27/23–09/03/29	344	2,138
04/28/42–05/29/46	128	1,492
07/24/84–08/25/87	150	1,127
10/19/87–07/16/89	72	1,001
07/26/34–03/10/37	127	958
10/22/57–01/05/60	63	805
11/09/03–01/19/06	144	802
10/07/66–12/03/68	32	788

Source: Ned Davis Research Inc. (*IBD*, January 20, 1998).

as it eases credit and improves liquidity in the system. This helps corporations and businesses, whose borrowing costs decrease, which helps their bottom line—net profits. With the prospects for corporate profits improving, investors start bidding up stock prices, which start moving up sharply.

Federal Reserve's Tools
Among the two most powerful tools that the Federal Reserve uses to stimulate the economy—and sow the seeds of a bull market—are the discount rate and bank reserve requirements. Reducing either one strongly affects the market. This happened during 1990–1991, when the economy was in a recession and a bear market had set in. The discount rate was reduced to $3^1/_2$% by December 1991—from a $6^1/_2$% level in December 1990—in a series of cuts that powered the bull market.

End of Bull Markets
When the reasons for high valuations no longer remain intact, bull markets end. Typically, the stock market starts having trouble when recession worries disappear and get replaced by inflation concerns. When short-term interest rates start rising, stocks start getting competition for investment dollars and they start to be negatively impacted.

Bull Market Phases

Typically, bull markets can be divided into two phases. The first phase begins when the economy is in a recession and corporate profits are falling. As interest rates decline and liquidity is increased, stocks start rebounding in anticipation of improved corporate profits. In this initial bull market phase, when the economic recovery and expansion have just begun, stocks show the largest price appreciation.

During the second phase, when the economy is in full gear, expanding corporate profits drive the price appreciation of stocks—even though interest rates either remain steady or start moving up. An analysis of 11 bull markets since 1953 indicates that the following gains were realized for the S&P 500 in the two bull market phases:

- Phase I: Prices rose an average of 28.2% while profits fell 1.1%.
- Phase II: Prices rose an average of 31.1% while profits rose 26.2%.[4]

The following are points to keep in mind when analyzing bull markets:

- A typical bull market lasts more than two years, with gains exceeding 80%.
- Buy and hold until signs appear that the bull market is nearing its end.

Riding the Bull Market

To get the maximum benefit from a bull market, an investor should have the courage to buy stocks when the economic picture looks very bleak. This occurs during the latter part of a recession, when the gloom and doom mood is pervasive. An investor should be fully invested when a bull market starts—which is its strongest phase that generates huge gains for those who are invested at that time. For example, after bottoming in October 1990, the DJIA climbed 650 points to 3,000, a gain of 28%, in only five months. In 1998, after bottoming on September 1 at 7,379, the DJIA rose to 9,425 by November 23. This rise of 27.72% was achieved in just 12 weeks.

Stocks should not be bought indiscriminately during the early stage of a bull market. Instead, one should try to identify its potential leaders—those who will be its big winners. One should try to identify and buy leaders because they are the first ones to rise when the bull market makes its powerful move. They are also the first ones to make new price highs.

---

[4]*Argus Update*, January 1993.

Recognizing Bullish Signs

▌ Favorable interest rates; lower interest rate trend.

▌ Low inflation.

▌ Moderate economic growth coupled with low inflation and a low, or falling, discount rate.

▌ Fiscal responsibility.

▌ Excessive pessimism.

▌ Market moving to new highs without widespread bullishness (such a market contains a lot of power).

▌ High level of mutual funds cash.

▌ Very small number of stocks on the NYSE making new lows.

▌ NYSE A/D line improving—trending upward.

▌ Decreasing flow of new stock issues (new issues can adversely affect the market's supply/demand balance).

▌ More buyers than sellers.

▌ Accumulation taking place (as indicated by high volume on up days and low volume on down days).

Understanding Bear Markets

Birth of a Bear Market

A bear market is every investor's nightmare. Many bear markets begin when the economy is steaming ahead and catch investors by surprise. When it does arrive, a bear market creates panic and pessimism. However, for those who are able to forecast the onset of a bear market and lighten stock investments in time, it presents a great opportunity. Such investors can pick up bargains and reap significant profits.

Ignoring Bear Market Signs

There are many signs of a bear market. However, many investors ignore them. These signs typically are at market tops—when there is a tendency to ignore bad news and warning signs. Investors start believing that the market will continue to go up and up. A very good example is what happened in 1987 when, between January and August, the DJIA rose an astounding 40% and the S&P 500 rose 30%. During this period, bond yields rose from 7.5% to 9%, which by any standard were very high. By October, when the crash occurred, bond yields had risen to 10%. In 1987, the DJIA crashed because while stocks rose to lofty levels, the Federal Reserve tightened money supply and interest rates increased. In just two months of the 1987 bear market, the DJIA fell 41%.

Every investor fears a repeat of the 1929 and 1987 crashes. Any such decline can wipe away all profits made even in the best bull market. Therefore, investors need to recognize bear market characteristics and remain prepared for such events. This is not too difficult as bear markets do not arrive overnight. When signs point to a market top and an impending bear market, it is advisable to take appropriate action such as reducing exposure to stocks.

Recognizing Bearish Signs

- Similarities with prior market rises: Both 1987 and 1929 markets had parabolic price rises.
- Rising long-term interest rates plus an economic recession: This is one of the worst-case scenarios.
- Markets rising when interest rates are rising.
- Excessive economic growth coupled with rising inflation and a rising discount rate.
- More corporate earnings reports coming in below expectations.
- Overvalued P/E multiples which, historically, have traded in the 12–15 times earnings range; market rises too much from normal "valuation" levels, such as the P/E of the S&P 500 rising above 20.
- Excessive enthusiasm and euphoria, especially by professionals, which typically occur near the end of a bull market and the start of a bear market.
- Individual investors not shorting since they turn bullish.
- Excessive speculation; signs include:
  Increased trading volume on the Nasdaq versus the NYSE.
  More new issues and secondary offerings (from existing public companies) which can adversely affect the market's supply/demand balance.
  High-flying IPOs (in price and volume).
  Increasing number of stock splits.
  Low-quality and low-priced stocks start to appreciate in price.
- Investors seeking shelter in blue chips (either DJIA stocks or Nasdaq blue chips such as Microsoft and Intel).
- Leadership warning signs:
  Market leadership changes to speculative issues.
  New leadership emerges from the defensive group, which performs well.
  Leading stocks falter; distribution in the bull market leaders.

Original bull market leaders undergo distribution for days, or even weeks, prior to the market break.

■ NYSE A/D line deterioration; starts trending lower.

■ Greater number of new lows versus new highs; the number of stocks on the NYSE making new lows is 40 or more.

■ Advancing market unable to make further progress while volume is heavy (called churning).

■ Distribution as indicated by high volume on down days and low volume on up days.

■ Rallies failing and on lighter volume.

Understanding Corrections

Correction Characteristics

An individual stock or the stock market does not rise in an uninterrupted manner when it is in an uptrend or a bull market. While the overall upward trendline is jagged, which indicates minor price pullbacks along the rising path, it is not unusual for a correction to occur during the overall upward movement (Figure 11.2). A correction is a price drop during a bull market whose magnitude is typically only a few percent. However, it can be as high as 10%.

Market declines and corrections tend to come unexpectedly—just when most investors least expect them. When investors decide they can no longer afford to hold cash and miss any more gains in a rising market, the market surprises them with a correction.

During the life of a bull market, there can be many minor corrections of 5% to 8%. In some cases, there can be an intermediate-term correction of 15%. However, after each correction, the market reverses direction and resumes its rise.

Reasons for Corrections

There are a number of reasons for corrections, including:

■ Asset allocation by investors (from stocks to bonds and/or cash)
■ Increasing interest rates
■ Higher than normal stock valuations
■ Change in the state of the economy and business cycle
■ Stock group rotation
■ External factors (news, political events, etc.)

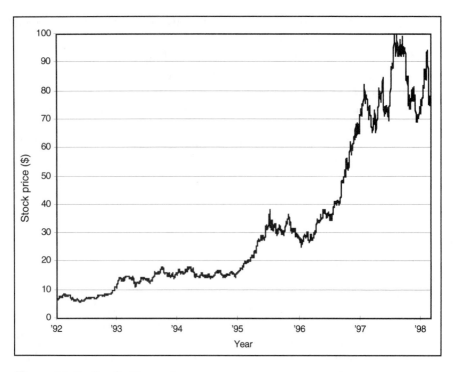

Figure 11.2   Intel's Corrections

Examples of Corrections

The most recent market correction occurred in November 1998, when the DJIA declined 8.6%. Another correction occurred in January 1998—when the DJIA declined 8.4% (Figure 7.3) and the Nasdaq declined 8.55% (Figure 11.3). In 1997, there were three corrections—in April, August, and October. In April 1997, the DJIA declined 10.7%, while the Nasdaq lost 14.2%. From August to September, the DJIA lost 9.4%. This decline was followed by a rally that propelled the DJIA 8.76% higher by October 7. However, this was followed by another correction in October when the DJIA lost 12.8% in just three weeks.

While corrections occurred periodically between July 1996 and November 1998, there had been a dearth of corrections between 1990 and 1996. In a sharp correction in July 1996, the Nasdaq lost 16.5% of its value on an end-of-the-day basis, while the DJIA lost 7.47%. On an intraday basis, the DJIA declined 10.59%. When it finally underwent the July 1996 correction, the DJIA had gone more than five years without a 10% correction. The previous longest stretch was three and a half years. How-

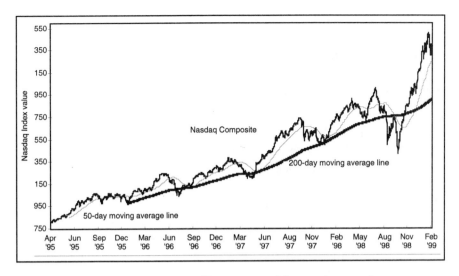

Figure 11.3   Nasdaq Composite (Price versus Moving Averages)

ever, while the DJIA did not correct during this very long period, individ-ual stocks as well as many sectors (such as technology) suffered significant corrections. Some groups were decimated and underwent a bear market rather than a correction. During this period, the Nasdaq suffered only one correction, which caused it to decline 13.7% in 1994.

While corrections and price declines are typically spread out over weeks or months, they can also occur in a shorter period. For example, on November 15, 1991, the DJIA dropped 120 points—a 3.92% fall. On March 8, 1996, the DJIA dropped 171 points, equivalent to a 3% decline, while the Nasdaq plunged 2.7%. Again, on August 31, 1998, the Nasdaq plunged 8.6% while the DJIA dropped 6.4%.

Corrections: A Healthy Phenomenon

A correction should be viewed as a healthy phenomenon that allows the market to get on solid footing and reduce investor expectations. A price correction of several percentage points helps put a damper on excessive speculation that can increase stock prices beyond reasonable valuation levels, especially during a quickly rising market.

Even the best individual stocks suffer corrections. Typically, such stocks rebound and rise to new highs. For example, Intel declined 33% from July 1995 to January 1996 (Figure 11.2). However, it rebounded and more than tripled between March 1996 and January 1997. In 1994, it declined 24%, while in 1993 it suffered two corrections—a 26% decline (between March and April 1993) followed by a 23% decline (from September through November 1993).

Timing to Avoid Corrections

Long-term investors should not try to time the market in order to avoid a market correction. By the time most investors realize that a correction is under way, it is often too late to bail out. Also, if one exits the market, it is difficult to know when exactly to move back in. By moving in and out of the market, one increases the risk of missing the short powerful moves characterizing the market—which are very difficult to predict.

In late 1994, many leading market watchers predicted a mediocre, or even worse, market performance in 1995. By sitting on the sidelines, they missed the extremely powerful move that the market made in 1995. Again, in 1997, the DJIA rose 29% between April and July. In just one month, between April 11 and May 11, the DJIA gained 883 points—a gain of 13.8%. Investors who bailed out due to the April correction missed a very powerful market move. Those who bailed out when the bear market bottomed in September 1998 missed the powerful upside move that resulted in the DJIA rising 27.7% in just under three months.

What a long-term investor should do is to look beyond these corrections and avoid being preoccupied with short-term uncertainties. There is no doubt that some years will be good and some mediocre—or worse. However, using a horizon of five years or more, and by remaining invested using the buy and hold strategy, investors can expect to post fairly healthy gains in the long run.

Sector Rotation

Rolling Correction Phenomenon

Sometimes, corrections taking place in certain market sectors or groups can be masked by the major market indexes, which may be trading normally within a narrow range or even rising. This phenomenon of rolling corrections when only a group or sector corrects, rather than the entire market, is called sector rotation.

In 1994, the market averages barely moved. Yet, this was a rotating bear market. The market experienced a rolling sector-by-sector correction. The major averages hid extensive damage among individual stocks. Also, since earnings during this period increased by 30%, the effect was that P/E ratios decreased because prices remained steady. This drastic reduction in multiples was, in effect, a silent correction.

Reason for Sector Rotation

In the 1990s, sector rotation has been quite pronounced. The reason is that investors have been reluctant to pull out of stocks completely. The explanation for this is their realization that stocks are the best investment choice coupled with their fear of missing major market moves. However, at the slightest sign of reduced expectations, or trouble with a group, they have had no hesitation in moving on to more attractive sectors.

In the past three years or so, approximately every six months, investors have been stampeding with a herd mentality into one or more stock groups. After bidding up their prices to high valuation levels, they stampede off to greener pastures. This has typically occurred when the sector/industry fell out of favor with institutional investors—who account for almost 75% of all trading activity.

Recent Sector Rotations

One of the most severe sector corrections occurred during the latter part of 1995. While the DJIA was rising 10.6% from 4,630 to 5,182, from August to December, high-technology stocks were being decimated. During this period, the high-technology index declined 7.8% from 229 to 211. Due to worries caused by the peaking of technology companies' earnings, slowing computer sales, and fears of a slowing economy, investors fled to defensive stocks. The largest U.S. mutual fund, Fidelity Magellan, reduced its technology stock holdings from 43% in October to 24.5% by November 1995. To the casual observer, no correction was taking place. However, the "stealth" correction was camouflaged by the sector rotational action of the market, which was not reflected in the DJIA.

The following are some more examples of sector corrections in the past few years:

■ January 1999: Internet sector lost 24% in a one-week period
■ 1994 to early 1996: Retail apparel sector lost 26%
■ Early 1992 to the end of 1994: Biotech sector lost half its value
■ *IBD*'s chip (semiconductor) index lost 50% in a 10-month period starting in September 1995[5]

Opportunities in the Ruins

Two central emotions drive the stock market—greed and fear. During corrections and bear markets, fear is pervasive, but these are also times of

---

[5]*Investor's Business Daily*, February 7, 1997.

opportunity for investors who will be severely tested. Savvy investors who are able to understand the stock market cycles can pick up bargains while others are dumping stocks. Also, during market tops, such investors can sell while others are still buying.

During corrections, try to pick the potential leaders of the next upside move. Typically, these leaders make the most significant moves when the market rebounds. Besides conventional methods for picking winning stocks and leaders (based on fundamentals), investors should focus on stocks with an EPS rank over 90. These stocks have a greater probability of outperforming when the upside move finally takes place.

Care should be taken in picking up stocks that have fallen sharply during a correction. Stocks that fall sharply during a bull market correction reveal their inherent weakness. Many investors mistakenly believe that if a stock falls more than others, it will rebound more, which usually does not happen.

Recognizing a Market Top or Bottom

Importance of Recognizing a Top or Bottom

It is very important for investors to learn how to select stocks and, after buying, monitor their performance. They should also develop the ability to read the status of the overall market. This is important because the health and performance of the market influences the performance of individual stocks in the short term. It is well known that when the market is in trouble, due to a bear market or correction, about 75% of stocks drop in price. At such times, even good stocks suffer declines. Therefore, an investor should learn to recognize a market top or bottom, which can lead to making more profitable decisions in one of two ways—by delaying buying to a more favorable time or by selling before investors start dumping en masse.

The following sections enumerate signs associated with market tops and bottoms. However, it needs to be recognized that some conventional signs of a market top have had a poor forecasting record in recent years.

Market Top Signs

In the 1990s, a period characterized by low interest rates, a continuous flood of cash poured into mutual funds. An important factor causing this phenomenon has been a shift in the attitude of the population at large, which has made stocks the investment vehicle of choice. They realize that in the current low inflation and low interest rate environment, stocks can provide reasonable and higher returns compared to money market funds, CDs, and bonds. So while, by many conventional criteria, this attitude would have indicated speculation and a market top in the past, the paradigm has shifted. This attitude shift has been a factor in the market moving a lot higher this decade. Those who recognized this shift and invested in the stock market participated in the great bull market that started in 1990.

In general, the following signs can be recognized as indicators of a market top:

- High valuation levels
- Dividend yield on the DJIA and S&P 500 falling below 3% (this has been a poor indicator in recent years)
- Widespread bullishness:
  Belief that the present scenario is different and history will not repeat this time
  Making heroes of money managers
  Trumpeting enormous gains to be made in the stock market (by the media)
- Rising interest rates:
  Especially short-term rates (as indicated by the discount rate)
  Long-term interest rates (as indicated by the 30-year Treasury bond)
- Stocks no longer reacting positively to strong earnings
- Nasdaq volume expanding significantly
- DJIA:
  Rallies but on contracting volume
  Stalls but trading remains heavy
  Declines on expanding volume
- Excessive speculation, especially among low-priced stocks
- Distribution and topping among the market leaders
- Breakdown of a large number of secondary stocks—even as the DJIA and S&P 500 make new highs
- Market unable to move higher despite increasing volume; typically, the total market volume will increase over the previous day's high volume with little or no upward progress
- Downward trending A/D line

Market Bottom Signs

When the market declines either in a correction or a bear market, an investor should be able to recognize the bottom. This is the level where all sellers have dumped their shares and the market finds support. It is at this level that the market stabilizes before starting its rebound. This first phase of the rebound is the most profitable and, therefore, it pays to learn to recognize a market bottom. Signs of a bottom include:

■ Intense selling on heavy volume
■ Successive lows on decreasing volume
■ Increase in market price, with increasing heavy volume on successive days of a rally
■ Extreme pessimism; very high bearish numbers and low bullish numbers

Forecasting Market Direction

Forecasting Record

The track record of most money managers, newsletter writers, and Wall Street market strategists in forecasting market gains has been fairly mediocre. A study of the market's performance in 1995 will show how far off the mark they can be. At the end of 1994, a year when the bond market had a miserable performance, the DJIA closed at 3,834. At the start of 1995, the bulls had an optimistic DJIA target of 4,300 for the year—with a high forecast in the 4,500 range. The bears were forecasting that the DJIA could retest the April 1994 low of 3,539, and perhaps decline even further.

The actual result was quite different. The DJIA gained 33.5% and rose to 5,117. What went wrong? After the battering the bonds received in 1994, most market analysts did not believe that interest rates would decrease. Therefore, they based their valuation forecasts on higher interest rates. Other reasons put forward by the various strategists for expecting a mediocre performance were the following:

■ Divergence of stocks and bonds
■ Poor market internals
■ Mutual fund speculation
■ Political gridlock
■ Overvalued stocks
■ Low dividend yield

However, contrary to expectations and forecasts, interest rates decreased in 1995, companies were able to sustain profit growth, and inflation remained in check. Since the basic assumptions were wrong, the forecasts were inaccurate.

In 1995, according to *Timer's Digest*, 36 market timers made forecasts on where the DJIA was headed by the end of 1996. Their forecasts ranged from 3,550 to 6,600. In 1996, the DJIA actually closed the year at 6,448 after reaching an intraday high of 6,606 in November. However, only seven timers had predicted a DJIA of 6,000 or higher. Only two had forecast a DJIA greater than or equal to 6,200. However, only one predicted the DJIA reaching 6,600. This should be an eye-opener for those who overemphasize the forecasting ability of professionals.

The Investor's Intelligence Survey, which measures the bullishness and bearishness of market newsletter writers, is another example of how incorrectly professionals can read the market. Often, when they are bullish, the market turns south and vice versa. Therefore, investors should not be overly swayed by their opinions and forecasts, which are often shown to be quite inaccurate.

Forecasts Can Change

Forecasts are based on many assumptions. Over time, as more economic and market data becomes available, they are refined and changed. Usually, this happens gradually because the economy and the market rarely change overnight. Typically, the magnitude of the forecast changes is minor. However, at times, these changes can be drastic. This happened in 1994 when the Federal Reserve started increasing interest rates—after years of easing them and having an accommodative policy. As a result of the change in the interest rate trend, the basis for valuations and market forecasts changed immediately. Consequently, new forecasts had to be made.

Overall, market strategists have a mixed forecasting record at best. Adding to the confusion caused by inaccurate forecasts are the sudden and drastic changes in forecasts that analysts sometimes make. Take the case of a Garzarelli forecast. In July 1996, Elaine Garzarelli forecast that the DJIA would rise to 6,400. Two days later, she reversed her forecast and predicted that both the DJIA and the S&P 500 would fall 15% to 25% from their highs. For the Nasdaq, she predicted a fall of 35%. The reason for her changed forecast was a bearish change in one of the indicators that she tracked, which indicated that cash flow was not keeping up with reported earnings. The actual market performance was quite different. The DJIA managed a 6,547 closing high for the year, which was reached on November 25, 1996. For the year, the DJIA gained 26%.

Groups to Watch for Market Direction

Investors use a wide range of indicators and groups to forecast market direction. Among those monitored for this purpose are the NYSE A/D line, utilities index and the brokerage index. The A/D line and the brokerage index top out six months before the overall market. The utilities have also led the market in both directions. For example, in 1987, the utilities plunged just prior to, and with, the 1987 crash. They also led the market by six months in 1990, when the market underwent a bear market.

A group to watch for market direction is the technology sector. This sector is a good indicator for the health of the market. Stocks in this group are relatively volatile and have a high beta. Therefore, when the technology sector is performing well, it means that institutions are investing in this sector. The fact that they have confidence in a relatively risky sector sets a positive tone for the market. An investor should closely watch this sector, even if one's investments are in other sectors.

Seasonal Factors

A number of seasonal factors have a bearing on the behavior of the stock market and industry groups. For example, it is well known that semiconductor companies have a slow summer season. Typically, just before the start of summer, these stocks get dumped somewhat indiscriminately. By fall, they are back in favor. Therefore, if a purchase decision is reached in spring, a knowledgeable investor tends to put off a planned purchase of a semiconductor stock to a more favorable time—a few months later. On the flip side, many investors holding semiconductor stocks tend to lighten their holdings at the start of the summer season.

January Effect

Stock prices have been observed to surge in January. In particular, small stocks have shown a tendency to outperform large cap stocks during this period. This phenomenon is known as the "January effect." Historically, small cap stocks have outperformed the large cap stocks by 5.5% during January.[6] From 1953 to 1997, the S&P beat small cap stocks in January only five times.[7]

From 1980 to 1998, January has been the best-performing month for

---

[6]Ibid., January 14, 1998.
[7]Ibid., November 17, 1997.

the DJIA. During this period, it has shown an average monthly gain of 2.63% (Table 11.5). For a longer period, from 1950 through 1998, January has been the third best month with an average monthly gain of 1.70%—which compares favorably with the best month (1.72% in April).

The seeds for the January effect are sown in the previous months. At year-end, usually from October through December, investors sell their poorly performing stocks for the purpose of taking a tax loss. Institutional investors, such as mutual funds, also sell their laggards in order to make their portfolios look better. Additionally, there is large money inflow into IRAs and company retirement plans. Therefore, when the cash generated from these sources, plus year-end bonuses, pours into the stock market at the beginning of the year, it boosts stock prices. In recent years, this effect has been missing. In the three years from 1996 to 1998, the January effect was noticeably absent. In 1999, small stocks again outperformed in January, when the Nasdaq rose 14.3% while the DJIA rose only 1.9%.

October Jitters

As October gets closer, investors start getting nervous for good reason. For the DJIA, it has been the most frightening month due to the great stock market crashes of October 1929 and October 1987. Six of the 12 largest daily percentage drops of the DJIA, including the three largest, have occurred in October. The average October rise for the DJIA has been 0.36% since 1980. However, if the 1987 October plunge is ignored, the DJIA gained an average of 1.67% during this month. For the 1950–1998 period, the DJIA gained 0.15% during October. But if the 1987 decline is ignored, the DJIA shows an average gain of 0.63% for the month of October.

Contrary to common wisdom, September has been the worst month for the DJIA's average performance since 1950, with an average decline of 0.46%. Since 1980, the average monthly decline during September has been 0.28%. Also, since 1980, the DJIA has been up only seven times in September. In the 1980–1998 period, August has been the worst month, with an average loss of 0.34%.

An explanation for the market's volatility during September and October is the decrease in expectations among investors. At the beginning of the year, investors are optimistic about earnings and performance. However, by September, these expectations get tempered as realization sets in that only a few months remain for earnings forecasts to be met. This causes analysts to accelerate reductions in earnings estimates in September—just before the companies start reporting their third-quarter results. This causes share prices to start declining.

Table 11.5   Average Monthly Gain/Loss for the DJIA

	Jan.	Feb.	March	April	May	June	July	Aug.	Sep.	Oct.	Nov.	Dec.
1980–1998	+2.63	+1.53	+0.36	+1.84	+1.65	+0.69	+1.59	–0.34	–0.28	+0.36	+2.33	+1.52
1950–1998	+1.70	+0.40	+0.90	+1.72	+0.03	+0.00	+1.30	–0.14	–0.46	+0.15	+1.57	+1.71

Quarter End Fluctuations

At the end of each quarter, the market sees above-average volatility due to window dressing by portfolio managers. This is the time when fund managers are required to file their quarterly reports, which have to list the stocks that the fund is holding. To look good, fund managers sell their poorly performing stocks and dress up their portfolio with stocks that have outperformed recently and have had good press coverage. The utility of this technique is questionable because publicity gain does not generate any profits for the fund.

Monthly Performance

Since 1950, the best month for the DJIA has been April, with an average gain of 1.72%. December has been the second best month with an average gain of 1.71%. For a shorter period, from 1980 through 1998, January has been the best month with an average gain of 2.63%. The second best month is November—when the DJIA gained an average of 2.33%. Since 1980, the DJIA has declined only six times during December and five times each during January and November. The good performance in December and January is attributed to large money inflows into mutual funds as well as pension and profit sharing plans.

The average gain by the DJIA from June through October during the 1980–1998 period has been 0.41%. During the November to May period, the average monthly gain has been 1.69%. Looking at a longer period, from 1950 to 1998, the results are similar. From June through October, the average monthly gain was 0.17%. For the November through May period, the gain was 1.15%.

For some investors, this has been a very compelling argument for moving in and out of the market. However, rather than focus on probabilities, investors should be driven more by individual stock picking and valuations than the expected performance of market averages in the next 6 to 12 months.

Other Seasonal Factors

Market gains or losses in any given year are to some extent dependent on the market's performance in the previous year. Usually, a very good year will be followed by a year in which gains are lower. Some coincidental factors have also been observed. For example, it has been observed that presidential election years have been winning years for stocks. Other observations include:

- In the 25 U.S. presidential election years this century, 20 years ended with gains.
- In the past 10 presidential elections (i.e., since 1960), there was only one down year for the market.
- Since 1832, stocks have fallen in the first year of every reelected president's second term with one exception (Ronald Reagan).

How to Play the Seasonal Observations

While an investor should be aware of seasonal factors, buy or sell decisions should not be based primarily or solely on seasonal factors. While it would be a mistake to ignore seasonal factors, they should not be given undue importance. Investors should be knowledgeable about the seasonal effects on stocks in order to better understand price movements caused by this phenomenon. However, to make informed investing decisions, other criteria for evaluating, selecting, and selling stocks should be used. In general, to take advantage of seasonal effects, the following two guidelines can be used:

1. Planned stock purchases should be done near the beginning of the favorable seasonal period.
2. Planned sales should be deferred till the end of the favorable period.

Market Volatility and Drops

Market Volatility

Volatility is measured as the spread between the highest highs and the lowest lows on the S&P 500. According to the Investment Research Institute, the average volatility has been 33% during the 28-year period starting in 1970.[8] A long-term volatility chart is shown in Figure 11.4. For the DJIA, the average annual volatility has been approximately 28% in the past two decades. In 1992, it was only 7.5%—the lowest in a century. See Table 11.6 for data on recent volatility.

Aftereffects of a Low-Volatility Period

The lack of volatility, characterized by flat behavior, indicates the potential for an explosive price movement. A drop in volatility usually follows an explosive year for the market. A low-volatility year is typically (about 85% of

---

[8]Ibid., January 29, 1998.

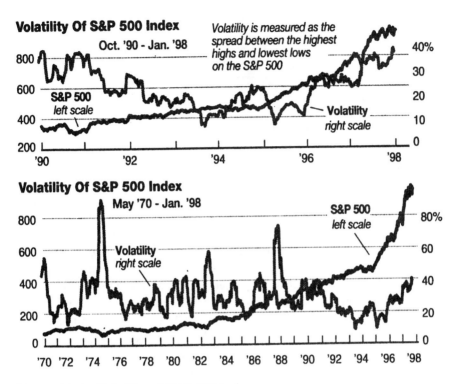

Figure 11.4 Volatility of S&P 500 Index
Source: Investor's Business Daily, January 29, 1998. Reprinted with permission.

the time) followed by a high-volatility year. The movement can either be upward or downward. However, the initial move out of the trading range can
often be misleading. When the market roars out of a narrow trading range, it
can be a short-term move prior to a longer-term move in the opposite direction. For example, on October 5, 1992, the market initially dropped 100
points, then recovered 82 points before finally closing 22 points down. This
move was followed by a significant S&P gain of 9% in the next two months.

Guidelines for Analyzing Volatility

- The market may be flat and hide high volatility among individual
  issues; big down moves can cancel big up moves.
- Some groups may be canceling the effect of other groups (technology sector rising with biotechnology declining).
- Nasdaq volatility can be twice that of the S&P 500 in a typical year.
- Low volatility may reflect the use of derivative products—options
  and futures—for hedging.

Table 11.6   DJIA 100-Point Gains

	100-point gains Jan. 2, 1998–Jan. 6, 1999	Number of days up/down 1% or more
Up	39	54
Down	25	34

Source: Wall Street Journal, January 7, 1999.

Daily Volatility

The market periodically experiences extremely volatile days. For example, on October 28, 1997, the DJIA dropped 554 points, equivalent to a 7.2% loss. A day later, it recovered 337 points, a gain of 4.7%, on a volume of 1.2 billion shares. The Nasdaq gained 4.4% on a volume of 1.38 billion shares.

Daily gyrations, when the market moves up and down rather than in just one direction, are routine. For example, on March 8, 1996, the DJIA dropped 171 points. It started off dropping 120 points in the first 20 minutes of trading. After the initial selling, the DJIA rallied to cut the loss to 64 points within 90 minutes of trading. It then traded sideways for three hours until it collapsed further. At its worst point, it was down 217 points.

In the past couple of years, 100+ point gains/declines have become quite frequent. Sometimes volatility can extend for many days in a row. For example, at the end of August 1997, the DJIA rose or fell at least 1% on seven of 10 consecutive trading days.[9]

In terms of the size of price drop, the largest declines of the DJIA are shown in Table 11.7. The largest declines for the Nasdaq have been as follows:

- October 19, 1987—11.35%
- October 20, 1987—9%
- October 26, 1987—9%
- August 31, 1998—8.6%
- October 27, 1997—7.02%

The largest point gains ever for the Nasdaq were on:

- September 1, 1998—when it rose 75.84 points, equivalent to a 5.1% gain
- September 8, 1998—when it rose 94.34 points, equivalent to a 6.02% gain

---

[9]*Time*, September 22, 1997.

Table 11.7   **Largest Declines for the DJIA**

DJIA *(largest point drops)*			DJIA *(largest percentage drops)*		
October 27, 1997	554 points	7.18%	October 19, 1987	508 points	22.61%
August 31, 1998	512	6.40%	October 28, 1929	38	12.82%
October 19, 1987	508	22.61%	October 29, 1929	30	11.73%
August 15, 1997	247	3.11%	November 6, 1929	25	9.92%
June 23, 1997	192	2.47%	December 18, 1899	5	8.72%
October 13, 1989	190	6.91%	August 12, 1932	5	8.40%
October 23, 1997	186	2.32%	March 14, 1907	6	8.29%
March 8, 1996	171	3.04%	October 26, 1987	156	8.04%
July 15, 1996	161	2.90%	July 21, 1933	7	7.84%
March 13, 1997	160	2.28%	October 18, 1937	10	7.75%
March 31, 1997	157	2.33%	February 1, 1917	6	7.24%
November 12, 1997	157	2.07%	October 27, 1997	554	7.18%

Concluding Remarks

A number of stock market indexes and averages are available to investors for monitoring the health of the market. While some give a very broad view of the market's performance, others focus on specific market sectors. An investor should monitor the broader averages as well as an appropriate index or average against which the performance of a stock or portfolio can be compared.

The stock market moves alternately in bull (rising price) and bear (declining price) cycles. While buying winning stocks is the key to reaping profits, the ability to understand market extremes, as represented by bull market tops and bear market bottoms, can enhance these profits significantly. These market extremes do not occur suddenly. They give investors ample advance signs that every investor should learn to recognize.

Investors should not view bear markets as disasters. Instead, bear markets should be viewed as opportunities when stocks can be picked up at bargain prices. It is recommended that investors remain invested at all times. However, when market extremes are recognized, investors can either lighten up or increase their exposure to stocks. Also, they can use these cycles to invest in the sectors/groups most likely to benefit from the cycle in the next year or so. Investors should also be aware of seasonal patterns.

Chapter 12

Understanding Stock Behavior

Monitoring a Basing Stock

Recognizing Forces at Work

No stock moves straight up in price. Even the strongest stock will pause at times in its relentless run-up to digest and consolidate gains before continuing its upward move. These pauses can last several weeks or months. During this consolidation or basing period, also known as backing and filling, the following forces are at work:

▮ Profit taking by short-term traders
▮ Continued accumulation by long-term investors
▮ Some selling by nervous long-term investors aimed at locking in profits already made

When a stock is correcting or consolidating recent gains, investors try to determine the direction in which it will make its next big move—up or down. An investor who is able to correctly recognize a bullish or bearish basing pattern can reap handsome profits or avoid losses. Such an investor can remain invested when the indicated pattern is bullish and reduce exposure if the pattern is bearish.

Signs of a Stabilized Basing Pattern

After heavy selling, even a strong stock may break its long-term trendline and decrease in relative strength. Before such a stock can begin a sustained move back to the upside, it typically needs to go through a basing period. The following are some positive signs of a stock having stabilized in a basing pattern:

- Stock that has been falling stops making lower lows.
- The 50-day moving average line flattens out.
- Stock's price begins to go sideways.
- Accumulation starts taking place (volume increases on up days and decreases on down days).

Overhead Supply

This refers to the higher price level at which a stock traded for some time before it declined. When a stock rises to a level where overhead supply exists, investors who previously bought at that level tend to sell. This happens because these investors attempt to break even and dump a stock in which they had losses. Usually, this occurs when a stock recovers from a correction or a sharp pullback.

If a stock has traded at an overhead supply level for a long period prior to its decline, its overhead supply will be large. Therefore, it becomes harder to push through such a level due to stiff resistance.

Monitoring Guidelines and Tips

A stock will ultimately move out of its basing pattern—either to the upside or downside. Therefore, an investor needs to be alert to any potential moves out of the basing pattern. This requires regular monitoring of the stock's basing pattern and behavior. Factors that should be monitored to determine whether a basing pattern is bearish or bullish include:

- Volume to price relationship
- Trend of the prior advance
- Basing pattern
- Market and industry group behavior

While each basing pattern is different in that price fluctuations are unique, there are some common characteristics for basing stocks. The following are some useful tips that can be used to monitor a basing stock:

- Stocks tend to be supported at the top of previous bases.
- Stocks often retrace about 50% of their prior gain.
- If a stock tries to advance off a base after soaring over 100% and not correcting much, be careful.
- If a stock's price holds above its 200-day moving average line, it is a positive sign.

- A declining stock does not always find support at support levels; if it does, it is a positive sign.
- The strongest stocks usually hold during a correction, then rally, retest their lows, and then turn higher.
- Tremendous profits can be realized if a leading stock is held for a year or two—while it goes through several basing patterns.

Recognizing a Weakening Stock

Signs of a Weakening Stock

Even if a stock has performed admirably in the past and has high EPS rank and RS rank, an investor should always be alert to its behavior, because past performance is no guarantee of future performance. Any stock, including a winner, can weaken at any time for a number of reasons. The following are typical warning signs for a weakening stock:

- Volume is heavy on down days and light on up days (sign of distribution).
- Stock that declined recently rallies back on below-average volume.
- Stock does not move in tandem with the market.

Breakout Failure

A sign of a weakening stock is when it tries to move higher after a consolidation period and then fails to do so a few times. Such action can signal a breakdown, or price failure, even though there may be no fundamental reasons for this behavior. A common explanation is that a stock that has reaped substantial profits by rising sharply higher presents an opportunity to a large number of shareholders to bail out. This happens even as momentum players are still piling up without being able to make the stock achieve a breakout. When momentum players start realizing that the stock is unable to make any upward progress, they also start bailing out—sending the stock into a tailspin. If the stock cuts the lower end of its price base or an important trendline, it initiates even more heavy selling from investors who previously placed stop sell orders.

Unexpected Breakdown

Even if a stock has performed well and its behavior is normal, it can be hit by massive selling for a number of reasons. Typically, massive sell-offs are precipitated by negative announcements that concern earnings or some development with the potential to impact business prospects. Sometimes, even a good earnings report can trigger a sell-off. This can often be attributed to an earnings report containing some negative item, such as slowing revenue growth, even though the overall report may look good.

Another common reason for a stock to be hit by massive selling is an unexpected change in the competitive environment, such as the introduction of a killer product by a competitor, entry of a formidable competitor into the industry or niche, or loss of market share.

How to Avoid Getting Trapped

To avoid being trapped, investors should closely monitor their stock and note if any distribution is taking place. Distribution occurs when a stock trades on heavy volume but fails to make any upward price movement. When a stock closes lower or remains unchanged in price despite a heavy increase in volume, it is a good indication that distribution is taking place. After a major decline, if a stock rises on lower volume on the following day, it is a bearish sign.

Investors should monitor the stock's industry group leaders. Their behavior can be a leading indicator of what is in store for the stock. If a group leader starts undergoing distribution, it may not be long before the other stocks follow. Therefore, an astute investor will monitor his or her own stocks as well as their group leaders.

Finally, one should be an informed investor and constantly monitor the company's fundamentals. Usually, surprises are rare for those who keep on top and stay informed. Signs of deterioration in fundamentals are visible to most investors who keep a close eye on their investments.

Handling Sizzling Stocks

Periodically, the attention of investors becomes riveted on a stock that seems to go only higher and higher, defying all predictions for its fall. A question many investors ask when they see such a hot and sizzling stock is, "Should I buy this stock?" The answer to this question from seasoned investors will be quite obvious: "Look before you leap."

A sizzling stock has far greater risk and reward potential. Therefore, prior to its purchase, it should be analyzed far more thoroughly than a normal stock. Unfortunately, many investors get carried away by their emotions and do not perform any meaningful investigation before buying such a stock.

Understand the Reasons

A number of reasons can cause a stock to exhibit sizzling behavior. For example, a potential winner could just have been discovered and achieved legitimacy because an important institution started buying its stock or an influential analyst recommended it. Other common factors include the introduction of a new product, new technology, control of a niche market (with a unique product), a very small float, or a short squeeze that forces short sellers to cover their positions.

A potential winning stock typically shows great strength. It is not unusual for such a stock to rise while others in the same group may be stumbling. In many cases, rather than rise steadily, such a stock shoots straight up. Prior to investing in such a company, an investor should determine whether the stock's price move is sustainable or is just a passing stage with the potential to burn investors.

What Needs to Be Investigated

Before investing in a sizzling stock, it should be thoroughly analyzed and subjected to fundamental analysis. Factors that need to be investigated include:

- Reason for the price behavior
- Projected earnings
- Business conditions: Can they permit earnings to be sustained (or achieved)?
- P/E ratios
- Competing products and companies
- Barriers to the entry of competition
- Management strength and quality
- Strengths and weaknesses of the company

Blowoff Move

Signs of a Blowoff Move

The phenomenon of an advancing stock suddenly shooting straight up in price, as shown in Figure 12.1, is called a blowoff move. When the stock market makes a very powerful move, like the one which started in December 1994, it can put many stocks in positions that can make them go into a blowoff stage. For those able to recognize such stocks, the profit potential is tremendous.

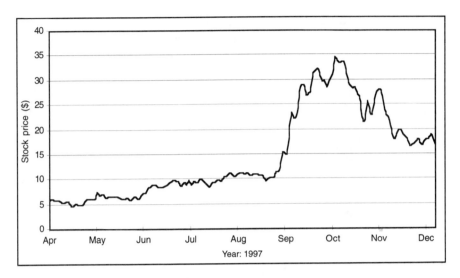

Figure 12.1 Onsale's Blowoff

Among the signs of a potential blowoff move are:

▮ Needle-like price formation with heavy volume; if this pattern shows up on a weekly price chart, it is an even stronger indicator.
▮ Stock price 80% or more above its 200-day moving average.

Among the warning signs that investors should be aware of when monitoring a blowoff situation are:

▮ Climactic top: This can occur if a stock that has been advancing rapidly gaps up at the start of the trading day.
▮ Reliable sign of a top: After trading with a wide spread, the stock price closes near its low for the day.
▮ Ultimate top: This may take place on the heaviest-volume day since the move began.
▮ No price gain despite heavy volume: This indicates that the move is near its end.
▮ New price highs on significantly lower volume: a bearish sign.

Dealing with a Blowoff Situation

Traders have some choices available for dealing with stocks after recognizing a blowoff pattern or after the blowoff move actually takes place. These include:

■ Selling a portion of the holding; selling too early misses additional gains, while a delay in selling results in lost profits.

■ Using trailing *stop orders* based on the stock's chart pattern.

Investors, while scaling back, can continue to maintain positions because such a stock may still be in an uptrend and, therefore, can continue its upward move after a consolidation period. An example is Micron Technology, which was trading at 22 in January 1995. It then experienced a blowoff move that caused it to rise $8^1/_2$, from $34^1/_8$, in just over a week. It consolidated for six weeks and then continued rising to a high of 94 by September 1995. It then reversed direction and declined to 29 by January 1996. Micron ultimately declined to a 1996 low of $16^5/_8$ (refer to Figure 7.1). This decline occurred while the DJIA was making major gains.

Investing in a Superhot Stock

Irrational Behavior

At times, a stock suddenly takes off like a rocket, defies all logic, and continues to move higher for a while. For example, Comparator Systems leaped 32-fold in only five trading days in May 1996. On just a single day, May 6, its price rose 400%. When momentum players see such a streaking stock, they jump on it no matter what its price or valuation. They expect such a stock's momentum to realize quick profits for them. However, serious investors should maintain a different attitude and never buy a stock based only on its price momentum.

Ultimately, superhot stocks run out of gas. When this happens, rather than base like ordinary stocks, they fall very rapidly and with devastating effect. For example, Presstek, a developer of digital-imaging technology, soared 74% in a month to a high of 200 on May 21, 1996. It then dropped to a low of 60 by June 1996, a fall triggered in part by news that the SEC had started an investigation of Presstek.

Netscape Communications Corporation, which develops Internet products including the Navigator web browser, has been another recent superhot stock. It went public in August 9, 1995. It was priced at $28 a share, opened at 71, and closed that day at $58^1/_4$. It continued to rise to 174 before ending 1995 at 139. By the summer of 1996, it had traded as low as 69 (split-adjusted). While this company had an excellent product, its lofty stock price had no relationship with its current or projected earnings for years to come. As was to be expected, after the initial euphoria died down, the stock declined precipitously. On December 27, 1998, buoyed by a takeover offer from AOL, the stock was trading at $58^{11}/_{16}$—higher than it had traded in the past year.

Dealing with a Superhot Stock

An investor cannot easily determine a superhot stock's future direction. However, it is quite obvious that high risk is associated with such a stock; therefore, it needs to be handled with caution. Using some guidelines, the risk from such a stock can be minimized. For example, an investor can determine:

■ The cause of the move; this should be fundamental rather than speculative—do not buy a stock rising on speculation.

■ Whether the story makes sense.

■ Whether the effect of the news or rumor propelling the stock (new products, turnaround, etc.) has already been *discounted* (through a price increase) and to what extent.

■ What the company's competitors are doing.

■ If a short squeeze (when short sellers are forced to cover their positions) is driving up the price; once short sellers have covered, the stock can be expected to quickly run out of gas.

■ If the fast rising stock is extended; it should not be purchased when it is trading:

10% above its 50-day moving average.

10% beyond the breakout point from its base, which is the trading range where the stock traded for at least seven weeks on relatively low volume.

■ Available float; a company with a small float can be very volatile and difficult to sell during a decline.

Factors Boosting Share Price

Share Buybacks

There are a number of ways in which companies try to boost the share price of their stocks. A common way is to buy back their own company shares in the open market. This reduces the total number of outstanding shares. Since EPS is calculated by dividing net income by the total number of shares, any decrease in the total number of outstanding shares boosts the EPS. A company announcement that it will buy back its shares usually causes an upward push in its stock price.

Manipulation

Investors should realize that stock prices can be manipulated in a number of ways. Self-serving changes in brokerage analyst recommendations do occur, though not frequently. Sometimes an analyst will issue a negative rating on a stock in order to make its price drop intentionally. The usual reason, in such a case, is to give the analyst's brokerage company the opportunity to buy the stock for its own clients at a lower price.

A few years ago, a well-known analyst issued a buy rating on a start-up biotechnology company that had no products in production or in the pipeline. Since the company had just started its R&D effort, it had no expectations for having a product in production for at least five to seven years—the time typically required to bring a drug to the market. The analyst's buy recommendation made the stock rise from 12 to 18 within a few weeks. When the stock reached 18, the analyst downgraded the stock to a "hold" because of "high valuation." The stock dropped to 14 within a few days. At 14, the analyst again issued a buy recommendation based on its "current reasonable valuation"! Obviously, no one can value such a company, with no products except hype, so precisely and accurately within a $14 to $18 range. This was a classic case of manipulation.

Sometimes, a company will issue press releases to shore up its stock price—to counter negative news on the company. At times, short sellers start rumors in order to put pressure on the stock. In short, investors should realize that stock prices are subject to some degree of manipulation. However, in the long run, what ultimately matters is the company's earnings. What investors should do is be careful, focus on the fundamentals, and remain informed about developments that have the potential to affect the company's fundamentals.

Stock Splits

Stock splits are primarily carried out to reduce the price of each share in order to make it more attractive to individual investors who prefer to buy lower-priced shares. Suppose an investor has 500 shares of a $50 stock. After a two-for-one split, the price of each share will decrease to $25, while the number of shares will double to 1,000. Therefore, the stock split will result in no change in the total value of the shares held by the investor.

Advantages

An advantage of a split is that it increases the float, which makes the company's shares more liquid. If a company has a total of 50 million outstanding shares, a two-for-one split will increase the total number of outstanding shares to 100 million shares. As a consequence of the split, the stock's daily trading volume will increase. Sometimes, an increase in a stock's daily trading volume makes it eligible for investment by some institutions. The reason for this is that many institutions are restricted from investing in stocks whose daily trading volume is below a certain limit.

Long-Term Effect
The effect of a stock split on a stock's price is debatable. In many cases, a split increases the stock price prior to the actual split due to increased interest. After the split, a sell-off often occurs due to profit taking. In the long term, the effect of a split is negligible because, ultimately, a stock's price is dependent on the company's fundamentals. A disadvantage of a stock split is that trading commissions increase since they are usually based on the number of shares traded—which increase when a stock split occurs.

Influence of a Stock's Industry Group/Sector

To understand the behavior of any stock, an investor needs to study more than just the company. Also to be understood and monitored is the behavior of other stocks in the same industry group.

What Is an Industry Group?

To monitor, compare, and analyze groups of stocks, usually with similar characteristics, many sector and industry groups have been created. The reason for creating such groups is that stocks within a group act together. Hence, if a stock's group is underperforming, the stock cannot be expected to outperform. Usually, stocks in the same group, with some exceptions, follow the same trend. Therefore, knowledgeable investors monitor and compare the performance of their stocks to other stocks in the same industry sector or group.

It is important that investors determine which groups/sectors their stocks belong to. Then, as part of monitoring activities, they should regularly compare the behavior of their stocks to that of the relevant group.

A useful source for conducting industry research is the S&P industry surveys, which examine the prospects for the industry in question. The S&P surveys analyze trends and problems. These are examined with reference to historical data and behavior. Also, within an industry, important sectors are highlighted in these surveys. Another valuable source is Market Guide's Ratio Comparison Report (Appendix F), which compares companies to their respective industries and sectors.

Monitoring Industry-Specific Indicators

A number of indicators are used by investors to monitor the health of various industries. For example, the retail industry uses the same store sales figures to compare sales. The semiconductor industry used to follow the book-to-bill ratio—which has now been discarded.

Investors should become familiar with the relevant industry-specific indicators, if they exist, for their stocks and understand the importance and implications of such indicators for their investments.

Monitoring an Industry Group Rank

Investors should note the group that a stock belongs to and its rank. *Investor's Business Daily* provides the relative rank of 197 industry groups, which is based on the price performance of all stocks in the industry in the prior six months (Table 6.1). Also indicated are the positions held a week ago, as well as three months ago, for comparison purpose. Comparison of industry group ranks can provide useful information. For example, if a group has a high rank or it is rising, it is a positive sign. On the other hand, if its rank is low or decreasing, it is a warning sign. When the signs based on an industry rank are negative, an investor can lighten up by selling part of the position.

Picking the Leaders

The action in a group can be a tip-off to the movement of institutions into that group. When institutions move into a group, P/E ratios and prices of stocks in the group invariably start to rise. An astute investor can jump on the bandwagon and be rewarded, provided the fundamentals of the company are sound. Therefore, to take advantage of the performance ranking of industry groups, an investor should:

- Note the industry groups showing an increase in stocks making new highs.
- Focus on stocks with an EPS rank above 90 in such a group (potential leaders will typically be found here).
- Predict industry groups having the best growth prospects in the next two to three years (because institutions pick the best companies in such groups).

Failing to Monitor Industry Groups

For those who fail to monitor their stock's group, the consequences can be disastrous. Consider the case of investors who owned semiconductor stocks in 1995. The technology sector, including the semiconductor group, had a banner year until September when the semiconductor group started falling apart. Those who did not monitor the semiconductor group failed to see it deteriorate in the last quarter. They got badly burned because the technology sector, and the semiconductor group in particular, had a massive downturn. Remember that the stock market is a very dynamic place and no one can afford to be complacent.

Monitoring Other Groups and Sectors

Tool for Forecasting Market Direction
Even if an investor owns stocks in only one industry or sector, he or she needs to monitor other sectors also because they can provide clues to the future direction of the market. For example, cyclical stocks (automobile manufacturers, home builders, paper products, and basic chemicals) tend to advance when a recession appears to be ending because the profits of such companies tend to rise and fall with the state of the economy. An investor who waits for a recession to end and an economic upturn to become fully apparent before jumping in will miss most of the profits that can be generated by anticipating such a move. Typically, by the time the economy is growing at a healthy pace, cyclical stocks have already made their most significant move.

On the other hand, defensive stocks (such as Procter & Gamble and ADM, the largest food processor) and utilities grow steadily. Therefore, the earnings of such companies are fairly predictable. These companies find favor when the economic growth starts slowing at the end of an economic cycle. Since these companies are only slightly affected by a slowing economy and any downturn is relatively mild, investors flock to them for parking their money. If this sector starts improving during a bull market, it is a sign that the market may have trouble ahead because investors usually start moving their money defensively into this sector in anticipation.

Limitations of Using Sector Behavior as a Forecasting Tool
Sector behavior does not always correctly forecast future market moves because assumptions of investors and market participants can be wrong and the market has a way of its own. For example, when it appeared that the economy was slowing fast during mid-1995, investors flocked to defensive companies after getting rid of cyclical companies. However, the economy grew much stronger than these investors expected.

Riding with Winning Groups and Market Leaders

Recognizing Leadership Signs

A very successful way to recognize a winning stock is to identify an industry, or a group, that is poised to take over market leadership. A group in an uptrend will typically have many stocks making new highs. This is a sign of current leadership. Such a group can be expected to continue its leadership role in the near future. An example is the technology sector, which led the market during its powerful rise during most of 1995. Within the technology sector, the semiconductor group was the leader. An analysis of this group, for that period, reveals many winners including Intel, C-Cube Microsystems, Applied Materials, and Motorola.

Avoiding Suspect Leadership

Do not invest in a sector or group even if it is in an uptrend with many new highs if its fundamentals are suspect or the future is cloudy. A group with healthy and rapidly improving earnings, with potential to beat estimates handily, should be the ideal one for investment. An example is the technology sector and its semiconductor component whose exploding earnings rocketed the sector in the first half of 1995.

Be wary of investing in a group that has been a leader for some time, because the best move may already be behind it. A safer approach involves taking the following three steps:

1. Pick the industry group moving up or showing a big percentage of new highs.
2. Observe which stocks in the group are making new highs.
3. Pick the stock(s) with the best fundamentals.

Sources to Scan for Group Leadership

Industry leaders can be identified from the data for various sectors, groups, and industries provided in various publications. The most comprehensive data is provided by IBD, which tracks 197 industry groups. It provides the following important data:

- IBD industry prices showing top industry groups (Table 6.1)
- Groups with the greatest percentage of stocks making new highs (Table 6.2)
- Performance of market sector indexes (Table 11.1)

The performance of various sectors and groups can be easily obtained these days. While some newspapers and magazines publish this information, the Internet and *IBD* are the best sources for comprehensive and timely data. The Market Guide web site is an excellent source for obtaining sector and industry rankings. On a daily basis, the *IBD* provides charts for some market sectors, including high tech, junior growth, and consumer indexes. Weekly data is provided for some sectors such as banks, health care, and defense.

Concluding Remarks

The price movement pattern of every stock is unique. However, there are some common characteristics among individual stocks, such as basing (after a rise or fall from its prior level), weakening, and breakdown. Developing the ability to recognize signs of danger, and opportunity, for a stock can aid an investor in making an informed and profitable decision—avoiding a stock when it is about to collapse or riding a winner as it takes off.

In general, stocks in a group rise and fall together. Therefore, the performance of a stock is also influenced by the state of health and performance of its industry group. Hence, it is important that a stock's industry/group be monitored as part of an investor's monitoring activities. A serious investor should also monitor the performance of other industries/groups because their performance can often provide early indication of trend changes.

It should be realized that stock prices can be boosted or manipulated in a number of ways. However, keep in mind that the effect of any such attempt is temporary because the ultimate level of a stock's price is dependent on its earnings.

Chapter 13

Investment Principles and Strategies

Investing Requirements

Investors use a number of investment strategies and techniques because a prerequisite for success in the stock market is the use of a strategy. Investing without a strategy is an invitation to disaster. Therefore, an investor must choose a strategy, fine-tune it according to his or her own needs and experience, and then stick with it. A strategy need not be sophisticated. What is important is the need to follow a strategy—no matter how simple it is.

Some strategies work in specific investment environments but will fail under certain unfavorably changed circumstances or a paradigm shift. Even very successful Wall Street investors, such as Benjamin Graham, have had to modify their strategies with changing times. Therefore, periodic strategy and techniques review should be done and, depending on the results achieved to date, appropriate changes should be made.

In general, there are five basic requirements for achieving success in the stock market, which are described in the following sections.

1. Method
2. Discipline
3. Experience
4. Positive attitude
5. Long-term horizon

Method

Before investing in the stock market, an investor should establish objectives, assess his or her risk tolerance, determine the length of time for investing, and decide on the investment plan and strategy to be followed. What should never be done is to randomly buy a stock based on the hope that it will go higher. Instead, expectations for success in the stock market should be based on a method or system.

A method should clearly spell out the decision-making process for buying and selling stocks, which can be based on simple rules. For example, an investor can have the following basic rules that will be followed strictly:

For Buying
- Company's earnings growth rate must be at least 25%
- P/E ratio must be less than 15

For Selling
- Stock does not meet earnings expectations
- Stock price appreciates 30% or declines 12%
- Earnings growth rate declines
- The reason(s) for buying no longer exist

A method should be followed consistently. While a method can be changed or improved based on experience gained, it must not be changed frequently.

Discipline to Follow Your Method

An investor should not follow a method only from year to year, from season to season, or from trade to trade. For success, the discipline to follow a method consistently is required. A decision to use or discard a method should never be based on an isolated experience—such as incurring a loss on a stock that suddenly collapsed.

Experience

Before starting to trade in the stock market, a potential investor can gain some experience by simulating trades. Such trading is useful for testing a methodology. However, it has practically no value in the real world because it cannot simulate emotions involving real gains and losses. For an inexperienced investor, it is advisable to start with a strategy that has been proven over the years. Some well-known strategies are described later on in this chapter.

Positive Attitude

To be successful in the stock market, an investor requires patience and the discipline to hold on, or add, to investments through both declining and rising markets. Making a fast buck should not be an investment goal. An investor must have the mental fortitude to accept the fact that losses are a part of the investing game. Instead of blaming professional traders, program trading, insiders, and others for losses, an investor should try one's best to improve and outperform most of the competition.

Long-Term Horizon

Investment in the stock market should be made for the long term. One should not be a trader and try to time entry into and exit from the stock market. Timing is a far less important factor for those with a long-term horizon than it is for short-term traders. Timing is something that only very knowledgeable and experienced investors should attempt. Average investors should remain invested in the best-performing stocks and let their profits run.

Investment Principles and Strategies of Some Pros

There are many investment principles and strategies espoused by stock market professionals. Some confine their strategy to a few basic principles while others follow a fairly extensive list. This section lists the principles and rules followed by a highly successful individual investor and some well-known and successful investment professionals, as well as rules followed by the authors.

Anne Scheiber's Rules

Anne Scheiber has been one of the most successful stock market investors in recent times. Her $5,000 investment, made in 1944, grew astronomically into a $22 million portfolio by 1995. This works out to a 22.1% annual return,[1] which compares very favorably against the 12.4% annual gain of the S&P 500. It even bettered Benjamin Graham's 17.4% return.

---

[1]*Money*, January 1996, p. 64.

However, it was just shy of the returns generated by the best investors the stock market has known: Warren Buffett (22.7%) and Peter Lynch (29.2%). The following were Scheiber's basic investing tips:

- Favor firms with growing earnings
- Capitalize on your interests (convert what you like into investment themes)
- Invest in leading brands
- Invest in small bites (dollar cost averaging)
- Reinvest your dividends
- Never sell
- Keep informed

Warren Buffett's Principles

- Buy a business—not a stock; focus on four tenets:
  Business tenets
  Management tenets
  Financial tenets
  Market tenets
- Don't worry about the economy
- Turn off the stock market (don't pay attention to the overall market fluctuations and movements)
- Manage a portfolio of businesses

A Money Manager's Basic Investment Philosophy

- Don't be an extremist (on the upside or downside)
- Let your profits run
- Be humble and admit your mistakes (and learn from them)
- Combine technical analysis with fundamentals
- Rely on industry group movements

John Templeton's Investment Factors

- P/E ratio
- Present and anticipated growth rate in earnings per share
- "Perfect blend" consisting of the highest possible growth rate for the lowest possible P/E
- Rising pretax profit margins
- Consistency of earning rates (consistent earnings growth is a plus; however, too-high growth rates often signal trouble ahead)

- Validity of a company's long-range planning
- Level of effectiveness of the company's competitors
- Major company challenges other than competition
- Maintaining a degree of flexibility
- As everyone makes investment mistakes, knowing when to acknowledge them and cut your losses (sell)
- Keeping a diversified portfolio

Cyber-Investing Process
(David L. Brown and Kassandra Bentley)

- Find a list of stocks that most closely match your major investment goals
- Narrow the list to a few top stocks
- Maximize your profit potential with technical buy signals
- Implement good portfolio management procedures
- Reduce risk and enhance profits by a continual assessment of a stock's risk/reward relationship

The Authors' Rules

- Invest for the long term; don't be a trader (don't try to time the market) unless you are a professional
- Use a simple investing approach (use a minimum number of indicators)
- Use the growth investing approach (focus on companies whose earnings are growing at an above-average rate); favor small/mid cap stocks
- Thoroughly research a stock prior to buying it
- Ride your winners (do not sell early)
- Analyze your past trades and mistakes
- Do not follow the crowd
- Stay informed (note anything that might materially affect your stocks)

Three Basic Approaches to Stock Investing

There are many approaches that are being followed for stock investing. However, over the years, only three have proved to be consistently successful. They are:

1. Growth investing
2. Value investing
3. Momentum investing

Growth Investing

Objective and Approach

This is the most widely used investing approach. The basic objective is to buy fast growing companies based on the expectation that large capital gains will be realized over time. Such companies have above-average sales and EPS growth compared to the market as a whole. Investors expect a successful growth company's earnings to continue growing steadily at a good pace. Consequently, their expectation is that its higher earnings will be followed by a higher stock price.

Growth Criterion

The primary criterion for those using this approach is the company's growth rate. The rate of growth acceptable to growth investors varies, depending on:

- Type of growth company: aggressive or established
- Investor's profile: conservative, moderate, or high-risk

Aggressive Growth Companies
These are new and fast growing companies, which are usually low priced. They have a shorter performance track record and are quite volatile. The risk and reward associated with these companies is much higher compared to the better-established growth companies. It is not unusual for such companies to be growing at a 25% to 50% annual rate.

Established Growth Companies
These are relatively large companies that have been in business for a number of years. These companies, while still growing at a healthy pace, have lower growth rates compared to aggressive growth companies. Their share prices are less volatile. The risk and reward associated with such companies is lower compared to aggressive companies. Typically, such companies grow at a 15% to 20% annual rate.

Characteristics of Promising Growth Companies

With the primary objective being to pick a growth stock, investors should learn how to recognize the characteristics of growth stocks. This will increase the probability that a winning stock with the potential for good price appreciation will be selected for procurement. In general, the following are the characteristics of good growth stocks:

- Revenues and earnings are growing at an above-average rate.
- Profitability is based on revenue growth (not through cost controls, restructuring, disposal of assets, etc.).
- Earnings growth rate is higher than P/E ratio.
- Belongs to a growing industry, which will permit the company's growth rate to be maintained or increased.
- Has some unique advantage(s) over its competitors (product/service, technology, market niche, etc.).
- Is able to grow without requiring heavy debt financing.
- Has minimum or no debt.
- Cash reserves and lines of credit are adequate (provides flexibility).
- Return on equity is high (usually over 15%).
- Company is early in a theme—is a leader.

Potential Reward and Expectations

The growth investing approach has the potential to achieve high returns for investors prepared to take higher risks. For growth stocks, the market has high expectations. Any positive surprise over expectations results in a stock getting handsomely rewarded through exceptional price appreciation. However, stocks failing to meet growth and earnings expectations get severely punished.

Value Investing

A stock's true worth is derived from its earnings and the value of its assets. Therefore, these criteria are used by value investors to determine if a stock is overvalued or undervalued. An undervalued stock currently trades at a price substantially below the company's true (or liquidating) value. To a value investor, such a stock is a bargain that can be bought at a substantial discount. Such an investor sees little risk in buying something for 70 cents, or even substantially lower, when its true value is $1.

Objective and Approach

The primary objective of investors following the value investing approach is to buy undervalued stocks. Value investors seek above-average returns by acquiring a stock that is underpriced relative to the underlying value of its earnings and yield potential. In other words, the aim is to acquire a stock at considerably less than its real worth. The logic is that if a stock is bought at a price less than its true worth, risk is minimized while the potential for gain is maximized.

The value investing approach is based on a two-step process:

1. Determine the intrinsic value of a stock in terms of its earnings, dividend, and yield.
2. Compare the value, determined in the first step, to the current share price.

If the stock price is lower than its intrinsic value, it is considered to be undervalued and, therefore, attractive for investment.

Value Criteria

To determine if a stock is trading below its intrinsic value, a number of criteria such as P/E and price-to-sales ratios are used. Typically, value investors focus on buying stocks with low P/E ratios. The belief is that such a stock protects them from a steep decline because the P/E, due to its already low value, can fall only a limited distance. However, it should be realized that a very low P/E is a reflection of the market's concern about the company's business in addition to expectations of reduced earnings. Therefore, such a company clearly has weak prospects for growth. Hence, there always exists the danger that such a stock can languish and tie up valuable capital for a long period.

Potential Reward and Expectations

Stocks with relatively low P/E ratios that are expected to increase can be very rewarding to investors. Typically, these companies are those that have been out of favor for some time but are expected to turn around. Indications of a potential turnaround, and consequently rising P/E, include buying by insiders, improving margins, earnings estimates being raised, and expanding volume.

For an undervalued stock, the market expects very little or nothing. Therefore, any positive surprise results in the stock being rewarded with exceptional gains. However, before investing, an investor should determine the reasons for a company being undervalued. Typically, reasons for this include economy slowdown, business cycle, product cycle, management change, unappreciated assets, or fundamental problems. An undervalued stock with fundamental problems and a deteriorating business outlook should not be bought.

Momentum Investing

Objective and Approach

The term "momentum" refers to the rapid price movement of a stock or a market index. Momentum investing has been described as "buying because others are buying." Momentum investors are those who primarily base their buy and sell decisions on a stock's pattern and price momentum. Typically, momentum stocks are characterized by rapidly growing earnings and/or price appreciation. However, if either one of these start slowing, momentum players sell the stock immediately.

Momentum Criteria

Momentum players do not pay much attention to high P/E ratios, insider trading, or other fundamental indicators. Instead, they only try to identify stocks with the greatest price, earnings, and industry group momentum. Once a stock with these characteristics is recognized, they jump on it. They continue riding it until its momentum slows down or they find a faster-moving stock.

Momentum investors do not agree with the logic "buy low and sell high." Their argument is that no one knows precisely when the market or a stock is at its low point. They point out that too often a high-flying stock comes crashing down, loses 50% or more of its value, looks "cheap" and "close to the bottom"—only to fall another 50% shortly. An example is Borland, which went down from $87 to $8 in less than one year. In this case, cheap became cheaper every few days.

In contrast to the "buy low and sell high" principle, momentum investing is based on the principle "buy high and sell higher." Momentum investors believe that if a stock starts rising rapidly, the probability is very high that it will continue to rise for some time to come. They do not believe in buying value stocks. Their investment approach does not allow them to hold a problem stock and wait for it to turn around. Instead, they prefer to board a rising stock with upward earnings and/or price momentum. This approach involves waiting until after a stock hits bottom, forms a base, and then breaks out as it starts a major new advance. Buying is done only after a breakout. Before boarding a stock, momentum players like to see the stock having earnings and/or price momentum. They also prefer to see high relative strength rank (over 80), which indicates that the stock has been outperforming in price.

Risk of Momentum Investing

Momentum investing can expose an investor to big risks. At the first sign of trouble for a stock, momentum players bail out en masse, magnifying any normal decline. In 1991, momentum players hitched onto biotechnology stocks, causing them to rise to very lofty levels. When they started to exit, the biotech stocks suffered tremendous price declines, from which they took years to recover. The declines were magnified because many stocks in this group had risen to stratospheric levels, without the support of any tangible earnings. Again, in late 1995, momentum players bailed out of semiconductor stocks when the group started to lose momentum. For those who failed to jump ship in time, the losses were tremendous.

The most dangerous period for momentum investing is at market tops in a bull market. This is the period when trend following reaches a climax. However, if an investment has been made in a fundamentally strong growth company that is part of a strong group, the damage during a declining market will be limited.

Concluding Remarks

There are a few basic points that every investor should understand. First, stock market investing should be done for the long term. Second, it is imperative that an investment strategy be used, which need not be sophisticated. Even successful professional investors use only a few simple rules to their advantage. Once selected, it is important that investors follow a method with consistency and discipline.

There are three basic approaches to investing in the stock market: growth, value, and momentum. Growth investing, which is the most widely used approach, aims to invest in companies that are growing at an above-average rate. Value investing is based on investing in stocks that are undervalued. Such stocks currently trade at a price substantially below the company's true (or liquidating) value. Momentum investing primarily focuses on price momentum. It is not based on fundamentals and, therefore, exposes an investor to relatively higher risk.

Growth investing is the most viable approach for the vast majority of investors who do not have the patience to sit and watch a stock for years before it makes a profitable upward move. While growth investing rewards are not inferior to those of momentum investing, growth investing is inherently safe because it is based on sound fundamentals.

Chapter 14

Screening and Selecting Stocks: An Overview

Basic Requirements

Understanding the Investing Environment and Challenge

The stock market has always been characterized by a dynamic environment. However, in recent years, it has become even more dynamic and challenging due to:

- Massive corporate structural changes forced by an increasingly competitive environment (global and domestic).
- Availability of instant information to investors.

Due to the changing nature of business, rapid changes in conditions, and ever shortening cycles, very few companies find their business environment stable for any length of time. This impacts the profits that can be earned which, in turn, affects stock prices. Consequently, a serious challenge is created for investors who have to deal with the shifting fortunes of a company.

In the current environment, an investor cannot afford to invest in a good stock and then take it easy. No one can afford to stop monitoring a company in the belief that its price will appreciate in the years to come, just because it is a good company. Gone are the days when an investor could buy a stock and just hold it forever. However, this also presents an opportunity. If an investor researches diligently and picks stocks that are going to perform well, excellent profits can be reaped in a shorter time span.

Objective

The basic objective for achieving long-term success in the stock market is to buy the shares of a company in which financial success is expected. Such a company will be characterized by revenues and profit margins that are currently increasing at a healthy pace or expected to do so in the near future. Typically, a winner will have some positive fundamentals such as new products (or services), is riding a recently established trend, has an improved business outlook for its industry, or has new management.

Prerequisites

Picking winning stocks when investing in the stock market requires discipline and diligence. Any investor can have a hot year or so. However, to get consistently high returns, especially in a market that changes quite rapidly, investors need to:

- Have a methodology for selecting stocks that meets their investment goals.
- Use selected indicators for monitoring the health of individual stocks and the market.
- Have a selling strategy.

Every investor should be prepared to conduct self-analysis periodically. If the results are consistently below expectations, the investment objectives and strategy need to be reviewed to determine if they need to be changed or modified. However, this should not be done frequently. Finally, it should be realized that no investment yardstick remains successful forever. Over time, investment selection formulas become obsolete and need to be replaced by more successful ones.

Selecting the Investment Strategy

Most investors follow one of three commonly used investment strategies: growth, momentum, and value. Before starting to invest, an investor should determine which strategy and risk level is appropriate based on one's own investment objectives. Once a strategy has been selected, it should be adhered to. All successful investors, even though they may have different strategies and techniques, use a disciplined and methodical approach to investing that they follow rigorously. Those who are not disciplined enough to develop or follow a strategy and lack dedication are the ones who frequently lose in the stock market.

An investor need not pick stocks based on only one strategy. For example, a stock investor who picks all stocks based on the growth strategy can make an exception by picking one or two stocks based on the momentum strategy. Another investor may plan to invest 80% of his money in growth stocks and use the value-based strategy for the remaining 20%. However, the rules defining any such deviations should be specific.

Recognizing and Picking Winning Indicators

Widely Used Indicators

There are many indicators that an investor can use. Therefore, one needs to be selective and choose only a few—but powerful—indicators. These should be based on the investment approach that has been selected. While indicators used by the various approaches are usually different, a few indicators are used by all three approaches. However, the acceptable value for each indicator, for the three investing approaches, may be quite different. The most widely used indicators are:

- Projected long-term earnings growth rate
- Annual and quarterly earnings increase
- Revision in earnings estimates
- P/E ratio
- P/E-to-growth ratio
- Relative P/E ratio
- Insider buying
- Number of analysts following company
- Stock price
- Market capitalization
- Institutional ownership
- EPS rank
- Relative strength rank (RS)
- 200-day moving average
- Accumulation and distribution
- Return on equity (ROE)
- Debt/equity ratio
- Cash flow growth rate
- Company management

Assigning Weights to Picked Indicators

Winning indicators are not equal in terms of their ability to help select a stock or to forecast its future price level. Also, the relative importance given to each indicator by investors following the different investment approaches can vary significantly. Therefore, to reflect the relative importance of each indicator for ranking stocks in the screening and selection process, a weighting system can be used. This means assigning a weight to each indicator based on its relative importance. The higher the weight, the more important the indicator. Weights are assigned arbitrarily, based on the investor's experience and preference. For example, an investor can assign weights as follows:

- Indicator #1 = 100%
- Indicator #2 = 75%
- Indicator #3 = 50%

In this example, indicator #3 has only half as much weight or importance as indicator #1. Indicator #2, too, is less important than indicator #1. These weights can be assigned using different scaling methods. For example, another method assigns weights on a scale ranging from 1 (lowest) to 10 (highest). The method of using a scale from 1 to 10 is explained in depth in Chapter 15 (Tables 15.4 and 15.7).

The advantage of using weights is that an indicator assigned the highest weight will become the most important indicator and, therefore, will bias the selection process in favor of stocks scoring high on this indicator. However, it should be noted that while assigning weights has its advantages, it is not a requirement for stock selection.

Recognizing Characteristics of Winning Stocks and Leaders

The leaders of one bull market are not necessarily the stars of the next. Latching onto a former highflier just because it has reentered the atmosphere is not a winning technique that should be followed by serious investors. The danger exists that even after a drastic price drop, a stock may still be overvalued and its best gains may already be history.

A better way to succeed is to find potential new winners. To achieve this, investors need to recognize the characteristics of winning stocks and leaders. Once they are able to do this, they can independently pick stocks with the best attributes.

Common Characteristics of Winners

Table 7.1 showed some important characteristics of some very successful stocks of recent years. In general, the following are the common characteristics of winning stocks and leaders:

- Accelerating earnings (quarterly and annual)
- Growth better than its industry, sector, and the S&P
- Excellent sales and EPS growth over the past three to five years
- Small cap company
- Low, but increasing, institutional ownership
- Insider buying with no insider selling
- High relative strength
- New price highs
- Positive technical indicators such as relative price, moving averages, and so on
- Financial ratios better than its industry or sector: key ratios include margins, ROE, debt level, and inventory turns
- High R&D expenditure

Characteristics of Winning Small Cap Stocks

An analysis of successful small stocks shows many common characteristics, which include the following attributes:

- Good steady growth
- Control of a niche area
- Product(s) that large numbers of people will buy
- New product or service that represents a breakthrough
- Low labor costs and minimum government regulation
- Benefit from high industry entry barriers
- Diversified customer base

Other positive signs are:

- The company is following the trend of the industry into new technology.
- It is a user of technology.
- Institutions either do not own the stock or have only a small presence in the stock.
- Few, or no, analysts follow the company.
- Insiders have a heavy stake in the company or are buying the stock.
- Company is a spin-off.
- Company is buying back shares.

Characteristics of Leaders Emerging from Corrections

It can be very profitable to pick a leader as it emerges from a correction and is poised to make a significant move up. The important factors that indicate emerging new leadership include new highs, high relative strength, and improving fundamentals. Generally, in a bull market correction, growth stocks decline one and a half to two times the market averages. Those that do not correct much, or even rise, are the potential leaders when the rebound occurs. A stock maintaining a high relative strength (RS) rank stands out as a potential winner because the RS of leading stocks usually tends to drop sharply during a falling market. When the market rebounds, such a stock has a greater probability of rising significantly higher.

Stock Selection Process

After the basic requirements have been met, an investor can proceed to screen and select stocks in a five-step process that includes:

1. Identifying stocks for investing
2. Screening
3. Ranking
4. Fundamental analysis
5. Timing the purchase—technical analysis

Figures 14.1, 14.2, and 14.3 show the processes used to screen stocks manually or with software tools. Each screening process, and the individual steps involved in each method, are described in the following sections.

Step 1: Identifying Stocks for Investing

Common Sources
In this step, a number of stocks are initially identified for potential investment. Usually, these investments can be identified through one of the following conventional methods:

- Investment sources such as Market Guide, Zacks, Value Line, S&P, and others.
- Investment newsletters, newspapers, magazines, Internet, online services, and so on.
- Personal network (colleagues, friends, business partners, and others).
- Hot tips from colleagues, friends, neighbors, unsolicited investment literature, and so forth.
- *IBD*: companies featured in "The New America" section, active lists, and mutual fund lists.
- Recommended lists.

Stocks identified in this step can be handled in two different ways:

1. Subject the stock to the full screening and analysis process; this means starting the process from step 2a.
2. Subject the stock to fundamental analysis without going through the screening process; this means starting the process at step 4—fundamental analysis.

Computerized Databases

These are huge databases that contain historical and current investment data on all publicly traded stocks. These databases can be tapped only by using a computer and investment software. Investors using this source for identifying stocks for potential investment will proceed directly to step 2b.

Best Sources

The authors' experience shows that for the average investor, the following sources can be quite useful for the initial identification of stocks:

- S&P Outlook
- Zacks Analyst Watch
- Value Line Investment Survey
- Investor's Business Daily
- OTC Insight
- Investor's Digest
- Individual Investor
- California Technology Stock Letter

These sources, which are not listed in any particular sequence, contain recommended lists, company profiles, performance tables, screening lists, and so on. This list of sources should be used only as a starting point for research and analysis. Using such a list can help investors who do not use computerized tools save considerable time and effort in their research efforts.

Step 2: Screening

a. Manual Screening without Software Tools

Stocks identified in step 1 are put through a manual screening test using indicators such as earnings, growth rate, P/E, and moving averages. The limitation of this manual method is that only a few stocks can be screened due to the time and effort involved. However, this is not a problem for most individual investors because, typically, they will be screening only a few stocks for potential investment at this stage.

Screening Process for a Single Stock
This process is shown in Figure 14.1. Screening for a single stock can be done in one or two passes. In the first pass, only a few indicators are used. If the stock passes this screening, it is subjected to the second pass screening, which is performed using more stringent criteria and additional indicators. Stocks surviving the second pass can be directly subjected to fundamental analysis in step 4—because no ranking (step 3) is required for a single stock.

Screening Process for Multiple Stocks
This process is shown in Figure 14.2. Screening for multiple stocks can be performed in one or two passes. If too many stocks survive the first pass, a second pass can be made in order to reduce the number of passing stocks. This elimination is required for limiting the number of stocks to be processed in the subsequent steps—especially for the time-consuming fundamental analysis process described in step 4. The second pass is performed by either using more stringent criteria (for the indicators used in the first pass) or using additional indicators.

If only a few stocks pass the screening step, they can skip the ranking process—step 3. Such stocks can be directly subjected to fundamental analysis—step 4.

b. Screening with Software Tools
If a brand-new search needs to be performed, with all stocks in the major exchanges to be considered for potential investment, then a rigorous method for identifying, screening, and selecting stocks is needed. Such a method is shown in Figure 14.3. For all practical purposes, this cannot be done manually. However, a software tool running against a database, containing data on thousands of stocks, can efficiently narrow down the number of stocks using specific screening criteria. Some well-known software tools are TC2000, TradeStation, Stock Investor Pro, and Window on Wall Street. A number of other tools are listed in Tables 3.9 and 3.10.

Using specific search/screen criteria, software tools can eliminate undesirable stocks and narrow down prospects to a manageable number. Typically, the screening criteria are based on one of the three main investment approaches: growth, momentum, and value investing. The actual combination of indicators used for specifying the screening criteria reflects the investment philosophy and risk tolerance of the investor.

Some indicators, like market capitalization and stock price range, can

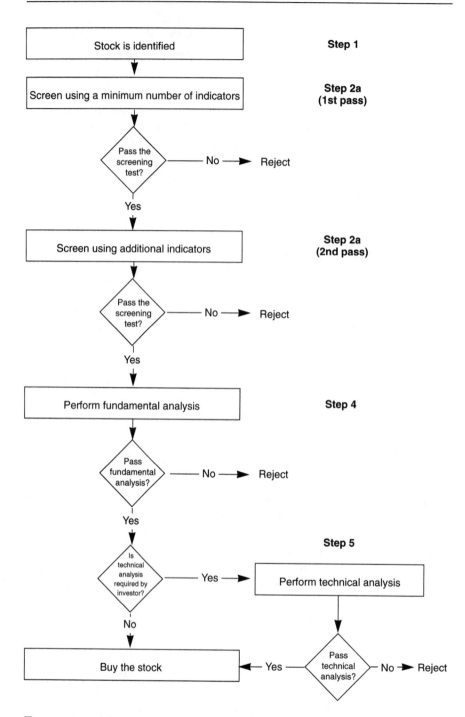

Figure 14.1   Manual Screening Process for a Single Stock

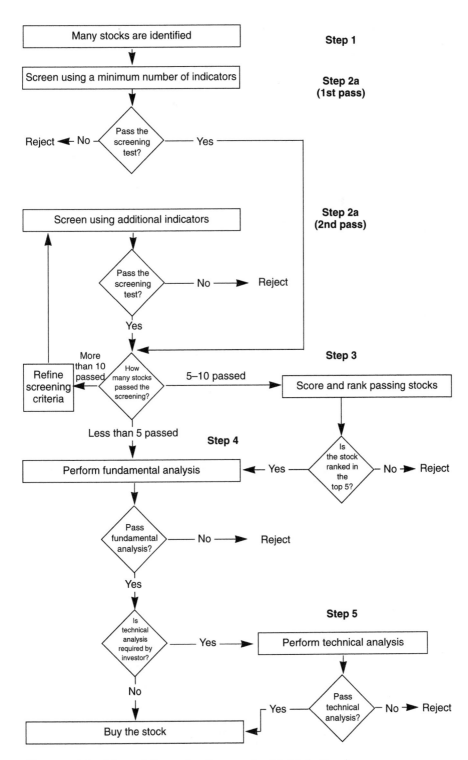

Figure 14.2 Manual Screening Process for Multiple Stocks

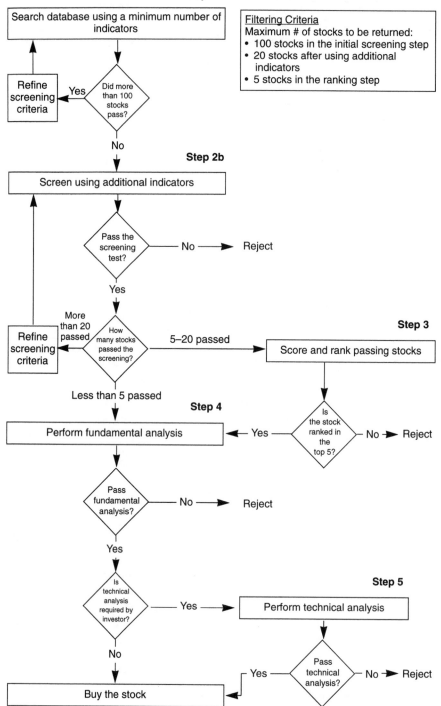

Figure 14.3 **Screening Process with Software Tools**

appear in all three investment approaches (growth, value, and momentum). For example, the P/E ratio can be used in both the growth and value strategies. However, the values selected for this indicator will be quite different for each strategy. For example, a value investor will make sure that a stock with a P/E ratio greater than 15 is screened out, while a growth investor might use a screening value of 30 for the same indicator.

Depending on the search criteria specified, a search can return a few or even hundreds of stocks. If too many stocks pass the screening test in this step, the screening process can be repeated after specifying more stringent search criteria. Depending on the number of stocks surviving the screening process, the next step in the process can be either ranking (step 3) or fundamental analysis (step 4).

Step 3: Ranking

The ranking process is used to eliminate stocks with the lowest rank. It is usually required when more than the required number of stocks survive the screening test (step 2). Ranking may be required if more than five to six stocks pass the screening test in steps 2a or 2b. This step is optional and some investors do not use this step. For the ranking exercise, stocks can be scored and ranked based on:

- Indicators used in step 2.
- All indicators used in step 2 supplemented by additional indicators.
- Some indicators used in step 2 supplemented by additional indicators.
- A completely different set of indicators compared to those used in step 2.

The scoring and ranking methodology is shown in a step-by-step process in Chapter 15 (Tables 15.3–15.8).

Step 4: Fundamental Analysis

In this step, every company that passes the screening and, where applicable, ranking process is analyzed thoroughly. This analysis includes in-depth research on the company. As part of this effort, an investor studies company research and earnings reports. These reports include a review of the company's earnings history and estimates, financial statements, news articles, and other fundamental data.

It is possible that further ranking may be required after fundamental analysis—if more than the desired number of stocks survive in-depth fundamental analysis. The new ranking process will be similar to the procedure in step 3—with the difference being that more stringent, and possibly different, screening and elimination criteria may be used.

Step 5: Timing the Purchase—Technical Analysis

If a company passes the fundamental analysis evaluation, an investor can buy its stock confidently. However, technical analysis may be used in conjunction with other factors to determine a more beneficial entry point. This can increase the long-term profitability of the investment. Such a step will require technical analysis of both the company and the overall market. For a long-term investor, with a three- to five-year horizon, this step has less significance than for a trader who has an investment horizon of one year or less. Many long-term investors, including very successful ones, ignore technical analysis completely.

Concluding Remarks

An investor's ability to pick winning stocks depends on his or her skills in selecting winning indicators and recognizing the characteristics of winning stocks. If these skills are mastered, such an investor's stock screening and selection process will ensure that only superior stocks, which can be expected to outperform significantly, get picked.

After identifying stocks, the next step in the stock selection process is screening. It enables the filtering out of stocks that fail to meet specified screening criteria. The indicators used for the screening criteria, as well as their values, are specified by the investor based on investment approach, experience, and risk tolerance. This screening can be performed either manually or with software tools.

In the next step, stocks passing the screening test are ranked in order to narrow down the list of stocks passing the screening test. However, if only a few stocks survive the screening process, they can be directly subjected to fundamental analysis—which involves in-depth company research and analysis—without going through the ranking step. Companies passing the fundamental analysis test can be subjected to technical analysis, which can help determine a more appropriate time for buying the stock.

Chapter 15

Screening and Ranking Stocks: The Details

Screening Process

Basic Objective

The objective of the stock screening and selection process is to find promising growth stocks, especially those in their fastest growth period. The reason why investors desire to select such stocks is because they are aware that the top 1% of growth stocks will consistently beat the market averages by 50% to 100%.

The Process

The basic process for screening stocks involves the following two steps:

1. Eliminate stocks using preliminary screening criteria matching the investor's objective and investment philosophy in order to narrow the search universe. Initially, only a limited number of indicators are used. If required, more stringent criteria or additional indicators can be used to further narrow the search.
2. Stocks passing the screening test are scored and ranked using a number of indicators (usually the same ones that were used for screening). If required, scoring and ranking can be done using these indicators supplemented with additional indicators. The purpose of these additional indicators is to enhance the screening criteria and, if needed, to bias the selection process to stocks with specific characteristics. The result is that stocks with preferred characteristics get pushed to the top of the list.

Screening

Manual Screening

Investors who are limited by their ability to use computers need not worry that they will be unable to screen and select stocks without using software tools. This limitation is a real handicap for professional investors and traders because they need to select stocks from gigantic databases on a continuous basis. An individual investor, on the other hand, typically analyzes only a small number of stocks—which can be done without a computer. However, the manual process is slower and requires additional effort.

Ordinary investors, especially those who cannot use computers, can quickly screen and analyze an individual stock using the "Express" method shown in Chapter 20. This is an easy and fast method for screening individual stocks. To complete the "Express" table, which even unsophisticated investors can use, only a calculator and 5 to 15 minutes of simple data entry and calculations are required.

It is strongly recommended that every investor, including those who are not computer-savvy, review the next section, "Screening with Software Tools," because it contains fundamental concepts and basic screening/selection criteria that every investor should be familiar with.

Screening with Software Tools

A number of software search tools can be used for screening stocks' databases. Their cost ranges from a few hundred to thousands of dollars. These tools have very sophisticated features. They can access online databases that contain a wealth of investment data, current and historical, about every exchange-listed stock. A number of these tools are listed in Tables 3.9 and 3.10.

Screening Process

The screening process is fairly simple. To start with, an investor specifies the screening criteria on easy-to-use screens. In the next step, the search tool extracts and lists all stocks meeting the specified criteria—after eliminating all companies failing to pass the screening test. If too many stocks are returned, the search criteria list is modified using more stringent criteria and/or additional indicators—so that fewer stocks pass the screening test in the next pass. Most investors prefer to end up with 10 to 20 stocks in this step.

Screening Criteria

Software search tools contain scores, some even hundreds, of indicators that can be combined in various permutations to create different search strategies. The combination used should reflect the investment philosophy being followed: growth, value, or momentum. The following is an example of a search based on four screening criteria:

1. P/E ratio less than 45 but greater than 5
2. Highest historical earnings
3. Highest estimated earnings over next three years
4. Stock price above $5 and below $75

A single indicator is very rarely used for screening. However, neither should too many indicators be used because they will eliminate too many good stocks. Typically, three to five indicators are used.

Backtesting

The most important test of a search is to see how it performs over time—during different business cycles as well as in up, down, and sideways markets. Such an exercise can help refine an investor's search technique. Therefore, users of software screening tools should perform backtesting. This means conducting a search using historical data, and then observing how search criteria performed over time. Such a test evaluates stocks on the basis of their values at the time of the search rather than their current values.

Screening on the Internet

Investors can use easy-to-use software available on the Internet, as well as the online services, to perform custom screening of stocks. An Internet site that individual investors can use is Zacks' Analyst Watch on the Internet (http://aw.zacks.com or http://www.reswizard.com). Its "custom equity screening" function allows an investor to interactively screen Zacks' 5,000-plus equity database using any combination of 81 investment criteria. For example, it can search for companies that have experienced significant changes, such as:

- Earnings surprises
- Price movements
- Changes in analysts' buy/hold/sell recommendations
- Changes in analysts' earnings per share estimates

Some of the specific criteria that can be used for screening, using Analyst Watch on the Internet, include the following:

- Best EPS surprise
- Best change in:
  Current quarter consensus EPS estimate
  Next quarter consensus EPS estimate
  Current fiscal year consensus EPS estimate
  Next fiscal year consensus EPS estimate
  Long-term growth estimate
- Best average recommendation
- Largest increase in average recommendation.
- Best industry recommendation rank
- Best change in industry recommendation
- Highest dividend yield

Zacks' system is flexible enough for an investor to design, build, back-test, and operate virtually any fundamentally or technically based stock selection system. More information on Analyst Watch on the Internet can be obtained from (800) 399-6659.

An online source that can be used for screening and selecting stocks is the Strategic Investor. It is a versatile tool that can use stock selection models such as CANSLIM and the Graham-Dodd model. This service can be accessed through Prodigy.

Screening Criteria for the Four Approaches

The indicators to be specified for screening stocks depend on an investor's investment approach and risk tolerance. In the following sections, search indicators and screening criteria based on four approaches, three well known and one uncommon, are described. The four approaches are:

- Growth
- Momentum
- Value
- Combination (based on criteria picked from the other approaches)

Growth Investing Search Indicators

Objective
The objective of this search is to pick companies with superior growth prospects. In general, the following requirements are desired for selecting winning growth stocks:

▌ Strong earnings growth and momentum
▌ Insider buying with no insider selling
▌ Strongly performing industry group
▌ Small capitalization company
▌ Low level of institutional ownership

Indicators Commonly Used

There are many indicators used to search for growth companies with winning characteristics. The most important and widely used screening criteria used by growth investors are:

▌ Earnings growth rate (the higher, the better)
▌ Earnings that are rising (higher than a specified rate)
▌ Upward changes in earnings estimates by analysts (the higher the upward revision, the better)
▌ Positive annual earnings history for the prior five years
▌ Absolute P/E (should be in line with its industry/group range)
▌ Relative P/E (preferred below 50%—must not be near the high end of its range)
▌ Insider buying (the greater, the better)
▌ Stock price range (between $5 and $75)
▌ Market capitalization (preference for small cap)
▌ Bullish technical situation:
  Preferably above 200-day moving average line
  Not more than 5% to 10% below its 200-day moving average line

Screening Criteria: An Example

Specific screening criteria for growth stocks could be based on the following three indicators:

▌ Earnings growth rate greater than 20%
▌ One-month change in analysts' earnings estimates—upward revision
▌ Stock price in the $5 to $50 range

Secondary Screening

After the first-step elimination has been performed with these three indicators, additional indicators can be used to screen the surviving stocks. For example, the following secondary indicators can be used:

- Relative P/E ratio less than 60%
- Stock trading over its 200-day moving average line

Scoring and Ranking

The following is a typical grouping of indicators used to score and rank stocks passing the screening test in the previous step:

- Earnings growth rate (the higher, the better)
- Insider buying (the higher, the better)
- One-month change in analysts' earnings estimates—upward revision (the higher, the better)
- Relative P/E (the lower, the better)
- Market cap (bias toward small caps)

Indicator Weighting

To reflect the investor's bias and/or experience, each indicator can be assigned a different weight. This will cause some indicators to be favored at the expense of others. The advantage is that it permits the tailoring of a search to a particular goal or objective. For example, screening criteria favoring insider trading can be weighted as follows:

- Insider buying: 100%
- Earnings growth rate: 90%
- One-month change in earnings estimate: 75%
- Relative P/E ratio: 10%

Similarly, if an investor wanted to favor projected earnings, the following weights could be used:

- Projected earnings: 100%
- Historical earnings: 80%
- P/E ratio: 40%

Momentum Investing Search Indicators

Objective

The objective of this search is to pick companies with good price and earnings momentum. This search is not concerned with indicators like insider selling, high P/E ratios, and other fundamental yardsticks. The overriding criterion is momentum—with everything else being secondary.

Indicators Commonly Used

- Price momentum (RS rank)
- Earnings momentum (EPS rank)
- Industry group momentum (group rank)
- Accumulation/distribution

Screening Criteria: An Example

There are many indicators that momentum investors can use for their screening criteria. The following is an example of primary screening criteria that a momentum investor might use to eliminate unwanted stocks:

- RS rank (at least 70%, preferably over 80%)
- EPS rank over 80%
- Accumulation/distribution indicator (A or B)

Scoring and Ranking

The scoring and ranking done by a momentum investor on stocks passing the screening test can be based either on the indicators used earlier (in the screening step) or on a different set of indicators. For example, the following indicators can be used to score and rank stocks that passed the screening test in the previous step:

- RS rank change in recent one-week, four-week, and eight-week periods
- EPS rank change in recent three-month, six-month, and nine-month periods
- Accumulation/distribution indicator (A or B)

Value Investing Search Indicators

Objective

The objective of a search for undervalued growth companies is to pick stocks that:

- Are trading below their true value
- Have had high historical growth
- Have good projected growth

Indicators Commonly Used

Value investors use a number of indicators for valuing and screening stocks. The following are some important criteria used by these investors for picking value stocks:

▮ Lowest P/E ratio
▮ Very low price-to-book ratio (stock price currently trading below book value)
▮ Yield above an absolute value or high compared to its historical yield
▮ Minimum 10-year growth rate (the higher, the better)
▮ Low price compared to its long-term price trend (the lower, the better)
▮ High long-term price trend (the higher, the better)
▮ High projected EPS growth rate for the next five years (the higher, the better)
▮ Projected earnings comparable to the historical growth rate

An interesting value-based selection method is the "Dow 10 yield" criterion. This concept is based on investing in the 10 stocks with the highest yield among the 30 DJIA stocks. It involves listing the DJIA stocks in the order of their current dividend return and then selecting the 10 stocks with the highest yield. This strategy has been quite consistent in its returns. Almost every year, these stocks return more than the DJIA itself. Between 1973 and 1995, this method yielded a 17.7% annual compounded return. An even better result is achieved by buying the five lowest-priced stocks from among the 10 highest yielders. The low-priced yield system beat the DJIA in 18 out of 23 years—usually by a substantial margin.[1]

Screening Criteria: An Example
The following is an example of a set of screening criteria that value investors might use to search for value stocks:

▮ P/E ratio below 10
▮ Rising earnings in the past five years
▮ Stock price below book value

Scoring and Ranking
The scoring and ranking done by a value investor on stocks passing the screening test could be based on a different set of indicators such as:

▮ Relative P/E ratio
▮ Lowest price/sales ratio
▮ Dividend yield

---

[1]*Individual Investor*, March 1996, p. 10.

Combination Searches

It is possible to combine elements from the different investment approaches to create a combined set of search criteria. However, this must be done with extreme care. Suppose that an investor wants to combine the undervalued and momentum search criteria. The preliminary search can usually be conducted without a major problem. However, tricky problems arise when the indicator results need to be scored and ranked. Due to their bias, the different investment approaches may require a particular indicator to be scored differently. For example, the value investor will tend to assign a high score to indicators such as dividend yield and P/E ratio, while the momentum investor will tend to assign them a low score.

To get around this problem, two independent searches based on the two investment approaches can be run initially. This will create two lists: one each for momentum and value criteria. If the same stock appears on both lists, though it is going to happen rarely, it is reasonably certain that a winner has been identified.

Screening/Selection Criteria Used by Some Professionals

Range of Indicators Used for Screening

Successful stock pickers are able to generate above-average returns because their stock selection methods are superior. The portfolios of such pros consist of unique stocks, which have distinct characteristics pertaining to earnings growth rate, historical earnings, P/E ratios, and other indicators. Investors can learn from these market pros by analyzing their screening and selection criteria.

When the selection criteria used by professional and successful investors are compiled, a vast array of indicators get listed. Some indicators appear in the selection criteria used by most professionals. However, the combination of indicators used by each of these investors is somewhat distinctive.

Table 15.1 lists the basic screening criteria of some investment professionals and money managers. A review of this table shows the wide range of selection criteria being used in the stock market. As expected, some indicators appear in most lists. However, no two identical sets of indicators are used by these professionals. Guidelines for using screening indicators, based on Table 15.1 and the authors' own experience, are listed in Table 15.2 on page 277.

Table 15.1   Screening/Selection Criteria Used by Stock Market Professionals

No.	*Indicators*
1.	▪ Earnings outperforming the S&P 500 by 10% ▪ Volatility within 20% of the S&P 500 ▪ RS greater than 80 ▪ EPS greater than 80
2.	▪ P/E ratio less than the five-year earnings growth rate ▪ P/E ratio below the latest ROE ▪ Five straight years of profitability ▪ Price greater than $5 but less than $25 ▪ Price at least 20% below the stock's 52-week high
3.	▪ Price above $5 ▪ Market capitalization greater than $150 million ▪ Three years annual earnings growth exceeding 12% ▪ Three years revenue growth over 8% ▪ ROE greater than 11% ▪ Long-term debt to capitalization ratio less than 55%
4.	▪ Market cap between $100 and $500 million ▪ Profits growing at least 15% per year ▪ P/E ratio less than the growth rate
5.	▪ Growth rate (sales and earnings) at least 20% ▪ Growth rate at least twice that of the S&P 500 ▪ High ROE (three to ten times the money market rates) ▪ Low debt (below industry average) ▪ Good cash flow ▪ Price momentum especially in the past few quarters (high RS)
6.	▪ Revenues growing at least 30% a year ▪ Earnings growth keeping up with sales (greater than 30%) ▪ P/E ratio no more than half the growth rate ▪ Earnings acceleration ▪ High sales-to-price ratio ▪ RS 75 or higher (preferably 90–95)
7.	▪ Earnings growth at least 30% ▪ P/E ratio (based on current year's estimated earnings) less than the growth rate
8.	▪ Earnings growth greater than 25% ▪ Earnings growing at a faster rate than the P/E ratio ▪ Sales growth greater than 25% ▪ Historical growth greater than 10% ▪ Low debt ▪ High ROE (16% or higher) ▪ Management ownership over 20% ▪ Institutional ownership

Table 15.1   **Continued**

No.	Indicators
9.	■ Accelerating quarterly revenue growth ■ Earnings estimates being raised ■ Earnings growth rate (for the next year) to be greater than the P/E ratio.
10.	■ Sales $200 million or less ■ Daily trading dollar value: $3 million or less (ideally between $50,000 and $3 million) ■ Price between $5 and $20 ■ Net profit margin 10% or more ■ RS 90 or higher ■ Earnings and sales growth 25% or greater ■ Insider holdings at least 15% ■ Cash flow from operations: a positive number
11.	■ EPS rank 90+ ■ RS rank less than 20
12.	■ Sales growth greater than 15% ■ Pretax margin greater than 15% ■ ROE greater than 15% ■ R&D expenditure greater than 7% of sales

Additional factors that were listed as being important by some of these investors:
■ Sustainable growth
■ Growth from existing operations—not any acquisitions
■ Among top two companies in a niche market
■ High industry ranking (in top three)
■ Barriers preventing new competition
■ Superior product line—no dependence on a single product
■ Strong upcoming product cycle
■ Excellent management team
■ Conservative accounting, with a minimum of deferred expenses.

Indicator Combinations Used for Screening

Table 15.1 shows that investment professionals use different combinations and a varying number of indicators for their screening process. Even when the same indicator is used by different professionals, a different screening value for the indicator may be used due to two reasons. Firstly, they may have a different investment approach (growth, momentum, or value). Secondly, their acceptable risk levels may be different despite having the same investment approach. For example, one could be an aggressive growth investor while the other could be a conservative growth investor.

If Table 15.1 is analyzed, it will be observed that both #6 and #7 use the growth investing approach. However, they use the following criteria, which are quite different, for the same indicator:

- #6: P/E ratio no more than half the growth rate
- #7: P/E ratio less than the growth rate

Unusual Combinations Used for Screening

The range, variety, and combination of indicators that can be used are only limited by an investor's imagination. However, it is advisable that investors, especially inexperienced ones, use well-known and proven indicators.

An interesting combination is shown in Table 15.1, item #11, which searches for stocks with an EPS rank higher than 90 and an RS rank less than 20. Such a search will find companies that have had excellent earnings. However, while such companies obviously have performed well on the earnings front, they have failed to appreciate in price. The reasons for a depressed share price could be many—such as litigation, actual/perceived competition, unsubstantiated rumors, poor marketing (not getting the story out), and so forth.

Using the screening criteria in item #11, hundreds of small stocks can be picked up at any time. However, any stock passing this set of screening criteria would need to be subjected to thorough investigation. This would require confirmation that the company is fundamentally sound—with solid product(s) and good future potential. If nothing fundamentally wrong turns up in an investigation, a company picked up in this search might turn out to be a good investment.

More Rigorous Screening: An Example

Table 15.1 showed examples of preliminary screening, using some basic criteria, which are used as a springboard for launching in-depth analysis. The following is an example of how a company can be subjected to rigorous analysis—based on a number of indicators and criteria that evaluate both the stock and the market. The overall selection process involves a three-step approach:

1. Basic screening
2. Absolute value
3. Relative value

In the first step, basic screening is done, using the following criteria:

- Projected revenue growth in the next five years: greater than 25%
- Projected earnings growth in the next five years: greater than 25%
- Market capitalization less than 1 billion
- Total debt less than 40% of market cap
- ROE approximately 20%

In the next step, the absolute value of the stock is determined. This requires discounting projected earnings with reference to long-term interest rates. Additionally, the P/E-to-projected growth ratio is analyzed. For this analysis, a stock is considered attractive if this ratio is less than 0.75 and overpriced when it is greater than 1.25.

In the last step, relative value is established. This is done by comparing the P/E of a well-known diversified growth fund to that of the S&P 500. Such a comparison helps determine whether growth stocks are currently overvalued or undervalued compared to the S&P 500. This helps avoid growth stocks during their period of underperformance relative to large caps, which occurs in cycles lasting a few years. Other indicators (market, sentiment, and economic) are then analyzed in order to determine the overall market health and investment climate.

CANSLIM Method for Selecting Winners

William O'Neil, author of the best-selling book *How to Make Money in Stocks* (New York: McGraw-Hill, 1991) and founder of *Investor's Business Daily*, has developed the CANSLIM method for picking stocks. Mr. O'Neil conducted a comprehensive study of the top-performing equities just before they began their major price moves. He analyzed virtually every big winner during seven or eight market cycles dating back to 1953.

The analysis covered most fundamental and technical variables for each company, including sales, earnings, products, profit margins, P/E ratios, relative strength, and so on. It was observed that there were seven common variables in almost all the top-performing companies. He assigned a letter to each of these seven characteristics and created the acronym CANSLIM. These seven characteristics are:

C	Current quarterly earnings per share
A	Annual earnings per share increase
N	New products, new management, new highs

S   Shares outstanding
L   Leader or laggard
I   Institutional sponsorship
M   Market direction

According to this stock picking methodology, the following are the basic requirements that a stock should meet before it can be selected for investment:

"C"   Current quarterly earnings per share for the most recent quarter should be higher by a significant percentage compared to the same quarter of the previous year. This desired increase is at least 18% to 20%.

"A"   The annual EPS should have increased at a meaningful rate compared to the previous year's earnings for each of the prior five years.

"N"   This refers to the company having either a significant new product (or service), new management, or a change in industry conditions. It also means that one should buy a stock when it is close to, or has made, a new high in price after having had a correction and spent time in a base-building phase.

"S"   Evaluate the supply and demand for a stock. A stock should have a small number of outstanding shares. A stock with small capitalization and with fewer shares available for trading is expected to have a better chance of moving significantly higher than a large cap stock—if all other factors are equal.

"L"   This is the price performance of a stock. This method recommends buying a leader, with high RS, rather than a laggard (even though it looks very cheap). The stock's relative price strength should be very high. Only stocks having an RS rank of 80 or higher are considered for investment.

"I"   Do institutions own the stock? The presence of three to 10 institutions is considered reasonable. Ownership by too many institutions is not desired.

"M"   Determine the state of the general market. An investor should understand market behavior and be able to interpret general market indexes. This will enable an investor to determine the overall market direction—up or down. This requirement is based on the fact that during declining markets, even good stocks lose value.

Summarizing the Screening Criteria

A wide array and combination of indicators are used by professional investors; the value used for each of these indicators can be quite different—depending on the investor's approach and risk tolerance. This can be very confusing for most ordinary investors, who do not have easy access to indicator guidelines available in an easy-to-use format. Therefore, it is very difficult for individual investors to pick the right indicators and choose their acceptable values.

To help investors select values for the most commonly used indicators, Table 15.2, "Guidelines for Screening Indicators," has been compiled. These guidelines are based on data compiled in Table 15.1 and the authors' own experience.

Ranking Process

The technique of scoring and ranking stocks will be demonstrated through examples in this section. The objective of these exercises is to score and rank two stocks, A and B, using a number of indicators. The assumption is that only stocks A and B have survived the screening process. The exercise will be conducted in two parts:

Table 15.2 **Guidelines for Screening Indicators**

No.	Indicator	Preferred value
1.	Projected long-term earnings growth rate	> 20%
2.	Annual and quarterly earnings increase	> 25%
3.	Revision in earnings estimates (one-month change)	Positive
4.	P/E ratio	< growth rate
5.	Relative P/E ratio (ignore for young companies)	< 70% for established companies
6.	P/E-to-projected growth (PEG) ratio	< 0.75; not more than 1.0
7.	Insider buying	At least one buyer
8.	Number of analysts following company	Four or more
9.	Stock price	Between $5 and $75
10.	Market capitalization	Small cap
11.	Institutional ownership	> 20% and < 50%
12.	EPS rank	> 80%
13.	RS rank	> 80%
14.	200-day moving average	Within +/– 10% of stock price—trending up
15.	Accumulation/distribution	A or B
16.	Return on equity (ROE)	15% (minimum); prefer > 20%
17.	Debt/equity ratio	Below industry average
18.	Cash flow growth rate (historical)	> earnings growth rate
19.	Profitability	3+ years

■ Case 1: Using indicators based on the growth investing strategy.
■ Case 2: Using indicators based on the momentum investing strategy.

The results, not surprisingly, are different for the two cases. Stock B is favored using the growth strategy indicators, while stock A is favored when the momentum strategy indicators are used. The reasons are obvious: different indicators and weighting factors are used in the two cases.

Case 1: Growth Investing Strategy

Table 15.3 lists the five indicators that will be used to score and rank stocks A and B. These indicators are based on the growth investing philosophy. Table 15.4 lists the scores to be used for different values of each indicator. For example, if the projected long-term growth rate of the company is 24%, its score will be 7—because it falls in the indicator value range 20–24%. The actual scores to be used will, in the real world, be provided by the investor based on his or her own experience. For the inexperienced investor, the values shown in Table 15.4 can be used to start with.

The Data

For the ranking exercise for stocks A and B, the following three tables will be required:

■ Table 15.3: Contains the actual values of five indicators for both stocks (A and B).
■ Table 15.4: Contains the score for each possible indicator value based on the growth investing approach.
■ Table 15.5: Worksheet for calculating the total scores required to rank stocks A and B. Indicator values and corresponding scores—required to be plugged into this table—are extracted from Tables 15.3 and 15.4 respectively.

Table 15.3   Actual Values of Indicators (Growth)

No.	Indicator	Stock A	Stock B
1.	Projected long-term growth rate	30%	24%
2.	P/E-to-projected growth ratio	1.0	0.7
3.	Number of analysts following company	3	7
4.	Insider buying	0	2
5.	EPS rank	90%	80%

Table 15.4   Growth Investing Indicators and Scores

No.	Indicator	Indicator value	Score
1.	Projected long-term growth rate	35% or higher	10
		30–34%	9
		25–29%	8
		20–24%	7
		15–19%	6
		< 15%	5
2.	P/E-to-projected growth ratio	< 0.5	10
		0.5–0.59	9
		0.6–0.69	8
		0.7–0.79	7
		0.8–0.89	6
		0.9–0.99	5
		1.0–1.09	4
		1.1–1.19	3
		> 1.19	2
3.	Number of analysts following company	> 10	10
		7–10	9
		3–6	8
		1–2	7
		None	0
4.	Insider buying	3 or more buyers	10
		2	9
		1	8
		None	0
5.	EPS rank	90% or higher	10
		80–89%	9
		70–79%	8
		< 70%	5

The Calculations

Table 15.5 can be completed as follows:

Assign a weight for each of the five indicators in the "weight" column (W)—to reflect the indicator's relative importance.

For stock A:

■ Enter the "Value" column data (X1) for each of the five indicators. This data is extracted from Table 15.3.

Table 15.5 **Ranking Based on Growth Investing Approach**

		Stock A			Stock B		
No.	Indicator	Weight (W)	Value* (X1)	Score** (Y1)	Total score (Z1=W×Y1)	Value* (X2)	Score** (Y2)	Total score (Z2=W×Y2)
1.	Projected long-term growth rate	10	30%	9	90	24%	7	70
2.	P/E-to-projected growth ratio	10	1.0	4	40	0.7	7	70
3.	Number of analysts following company	7	3	8	56	7	9	63
4.	Insider buying	6	0	0	0	2	9	54
5.	EPS rank	5	90%	10	50	80%	9	45
	Grand total				236			302

*Values obtained from Table 15.3.
**Scores obtained from Table 15.4.

■ Enter the "Score" column data (Y1), corresponding to the (X1) column value, for each of the five indicators. This data is extracted from Table 15.4.

■ Calculate "Total score" (Z1), for each of the five indicators, by multiplying columns W and Y1.

■ Obtain the "Grand total" by adding the five calculated values in the "Total score" column (Z1).

For stock B:

■ Enter the "Value" column data (X2) for each of the five indicators. This data is extracted from Table 15.3.

■ Enter the "Score" column data (Y2), corresponding to the (X2) column value, for each of the five indicators. This data is extracted from Table 15.4.

■ Calculate "Total score" (Z2), for each of the five indicators, by multiplying columns W and Y2.

■ Obtain the "Grand total" by adding the five calculated values in the "Total score" column (Z2).

The Result
The result of the ranking exercise, as shown in Table 15.5, is:

■ Stock A = 236 points
■ Stock B = 302 points

Hence, based on this analysis, it is indicated that stock B should be favored over stock A due to its higher overall score.

Case 2: Momentum Investing Strategy

Table 15.6 lists the four indicators that will be used to score and rank stocks A and B. These indicators are based on the momentum investing philosophy. Table 15.7 lists the scores to be used for different values of each indicator. For example, if the EPS rank of the company is 85%, its score will be 9—because it falls in the indicator value range 80–89%. Again, the scores to be used will, in the real world, be provided by the investor based on his or her own experience. For the inexperienced investor, the values shown in Table 15.7 can be used to start with.

Table 15.6   **Actual Values of Indicators (Momentum)**

No.	Indicator	Stock A	Stock B
1.	EPS rank	90%	80%
2.	RS rank	85%	90%
3.	Accumulation/distribution	B	A
4.	200-day moving average: % extended	+1%	+6%

The Data

For the ranking exercise for stocks A and B, the following three tables will be required:

- Table 15.6: Contains the actual values of four indicators for both stocks (A and B).
- Table 15.7: Contains the score for each possible indicator value based on the momentum investing approach.
- Table 15.8: Worksheet for calculating the total scores required to rank stocks A and B. Indicator values and corresponding scores—required to be plugged into this table—are extracted from Tables 15.6 and 15.7 respectively.

The Calculations

Table 15.8 can be completed as follows:

Assign a weight for each of the four indicators in the "weight" column (W)—to reflect the indicator's relative importance.

For stock A:

- Enter the "Value" column data (X1) for each of the four indicators. This data is extracted from Table 15.6.
- Enter the "Score" column data (Y1), corresponding to the (X1) column value, for each of the four indicators. This data is extracted from Table 15.7.
- Calculate "Total score" (Z1), for each of the four indicators, by multiplying columns W and Y1.
- Obtain the "Grand total" by adding the four calculated values in the "Total score" column (Z1).

For stock B:

- Enter the "Value" column data (X2) for each of the four indicators. This data is extracted from Table 15.6.

Table 15.7   **Momentum Investing Indicators and Scores**

No.	Indicator	Indicator value	Score
1.	EPS rank	90% or higher	10
		80–89%	9
		70–79%	8
		< 70%	5
2.	RS rank	90% or higher	10
		80–89%	9
		70–79%	8
		< 70%	5
3.	Accumulation/distribution	A	10
		B	9
		C	6
		D	3
		E	2
4.	200-day moving average: % extended	1–1.9%	10
		2–3.9%	8
		4–5.9%	6
		6–7.9%	4
		8–9.9%	2
		> 9.9%	0

■ Enter the "Score" column data (Y2) corresponding to the (X2) column value, for each of the four indicators. This data is extracted from Table 15.7.
■ Calculate "Total score" (Z2), for each of the four indicators, by multiplying columns W and Y2.
■ Obtain the "Grand total" by adding the four calculated values in the "Total score" column (Z2).

The Result
The result of the ranking exercise, as shown in Table 15.8, is:

■ Stock A = 323 points
■ Stock B = 288 points

Hence, based on this analysis, it is indicated that stock A should be favored over stock B due to its higher overall score.

Table 15.8 Ranking Based on Momentum Investing Approach

		Stock A			Stock B		
No.	Indicator	Weight (W)	Value* (X1)	Score** (Y1)	Total score (Z1=W×Y1)	Value* (X2)	Score** (Y2)	Total score (Z2=W×Y2)
1.	EPS rank	10	90%	10	100	80%	9	90
2.	RS rank	10	85%	9	90	90%	10	100
3.	Accumulation/ distribution	7	B	9	63	A	10	70
4.	200-day moving average: % extended	7	+1%	10	70	+6%	4	28
	Grand total				323			288

*Values obtained from Table 15.6.
**Scores obtained from Table 15.7.

Concluding Remarks

Successful stock pickers are able to achieve above-average returns because their stock selection methods, based on winning indicators, are superior. Their portfolios consist of unique stocks with distinct characteristics pertaining to earnings growth rate, historical earnings, P/E ratios, and other indicators. Investors can learn from these market pros by analyzing their screening and selection criteria—which are summarized in this chapter.

Stocks are screened by specifying screening criteria using a combination of indicators. The selection of these indicators depends on the investment approach being used: growth, momentum, and value. The number of indicators used by investors for screening and selecting stocks is very large—spanning the broad spectrum of variables available to stock market investors. However, only some indicators appear in the selection criteria of most professionals and successful individual investors. Also, while some indicators appear frequently in their selection criteria, the combination of indicators used by each of these investors is somewhat distinctive.

Screening can be done in a couple of passes. In the first pass, a few indicators are typically used to conduct preliminary screening. This is followed by secondary screening, which can be done with the same indicators (but with different values) or with the original indicators supplemented by additional ones. Screening is followed by scoring and ranking, which aim to narrow the selection to the top stocks with the best characteristics. In this step, weighting factors can be used to give more importance, based on the investor's bias and experience, to specific indicators.

Chapter 16

Analyzing Stocks

Fundamental Analysis

Basic Requirements

Every stock identified as a potential investment during the initial screening and selection process must be thoroughly analyzed using fundamental analysis prior to buying. In this step, a company's health and business prospects are evaluated. This complete process involves quantitative as well as qualitative analysis.

Choosing the Right Indicators and Criteria

Many criteria and indicators can be used to subject a company to fundamental analysis. However, one must not use too many indicators for evaluating stocks. Besides requiring too much effort, it has the potential to cause confusion and lead to the wrong conclusions due to conflicting signals. Therefore, only a few indicators should be chosen that conform to the investor's investment strategy, goals, and risk tolerance. Where possible, indicators should be prioritized and ranked in the order of importance. This can typically be done by using weighting factors.

Indicators should be analyzed with care. When working with many indicators, flexibility is also needed. For example, if a few relatively unimportant indicators get a low score during analysis, they can be ignored safely. However, if a single important indicator is negative, it must never be ignored.

Basic Indicators for Evaluating a Company's Fundamentals

In fundamental analysis, a number of indicators are used to analyze the health and business prospects of a company. In this section, only the most important indicators used in fundamental analysis, described in depth in earlier chapters, are presented in a summarized form. These indicators, it may be noted, are also used for preliminary stock screening and selection as shown in the previous chapter.

Earnings per Share (EPS)

Investors analyze two types of EPS numbers: quarterly EPS and annual EPS. More than the dollar per share number (EPS), investors focus on the percentage change in quarterly EPS—in comparison to the previous year's comparable quarter. Investors want the current quarterly EPS growth rate to be higher by a significant percentage compared to the same quarter of the previous year. A company with accelerating earnings growth, such as growing from 20% to 25% to 30%, is highly favored by investors. Also, the annual EPS should have been increasing consistently for a number of years.

Projected Earnings per Share (Quarterly and Annual)

This is the consensus annual earnings estimate for the following year, which is provided by analysts monitoring the company. Quarterly earnings estimates for the next quarter, and in some cases for each quarter of the next fiscal year, are also provided. The higher the projected earnings, relative to a company's current earnings, the better it is.

Projected Five-Year Earnings Growth Rate

This is a very important indicator. Successful growth stocks should have a historical earnings growth rate of over 20%. Generally, a company with a forecasted three- to five-year growth rate of 20% to 30% is a very good investment. Unless there are exceptional circumstances, avoid companies with historical annual earnings growth rates below 15%.

Earnings Estimate Revisions

Periodically, analysts revise their earnings estimates for a company. Usually, this is triggered by an earnings release, news item, or an improving/deteriorating business outlook for the company. An upward revision is considered positive and pushes the stock price up. On the other hand, a downward revision tends to make the stock price decline. The number of changes in projected EPS are reported for one-week, one-month, and two-month periods. However, the most closely watched number is the one-month change in projected EPS.

Revenue (Sales) Growth

Revenues are reported by companies every quarter and annually. These should be growing at a healthy pace. Without revenue growth, the earnings growth of a company will be limited. A useful number to track is "quarter sales percent change." This is the percentage change in quarterly sales compared to the same quarter of the previous year.

P/E Ratio

This valuation tool, obtained by dividing the current stock price ($) by the earnings per share ($/sh), is used very widely. For this indicator, extreme values are undesirable. Typically, very low (P/E under 5) or very high (P/E over 35) ratios are undesirable. A high P/E ratio needs to be justified by the company's revenue and earnings growth rate. In general, fast growing growth stocks may have a P/E ratio ranging from 20 to 40 without being considered overvalued by growth investors.

Relative P/E ratio

This indicates the current value of a company's P/E ratio when compared to its own historical P/E range—with 100 being the highest historical value. Value and growth investors want this number to be low, or within accepted norms, depending on the growth rate of the company. Momentum investors do not place any emphasis on this number.

P/E-to-Projected Growth Ratio

This ratio is obtained by dividing the P/E ratio by the expected annual earnings growth rate. If the P/E ratio is 30 and the annual earnings growth rate is 40%, the P/E-to-projected-growth ratio is equal to 0.75 (i.e., 30/40). Generally, a stock is considered attractive if this ratio is less than 0.75 and overpriced when it is over 1.25.

Insider Trading

Investors view it as a very positive sign if insider buying is taking place in a company. The greater the number of insider buyers, the more positive is the sign. Insider selling should be noted even though it does not have the same significance as insider buying.

Number of Analysts Following the Company

This is not a direct indicator of a company's health. However, it is an important number because it indicates the degree of importance that can be given to earnings projections. The more analysts that follow a company, the higher is the confidence generated in the accuracy of the forecasts. The greater the number of analysts, the lower the chance that a single wrong estimate will distort the average estimate figure being reported.

Cash Flow

This is the net cash generated during the reporting period. Good cash flow is vital for growth companies. Poor cash flow can force borrowing (which affects overall earnings) or the issuance of more stock (which affects earnings per share). Both of these are a negative for the stock price. Cash flow per share is used for analyzing a company's cash flow. It is equal to the cash provided by operations divided by the total number of outstanding common shares.

Five-Year Cash Flow Growth Rate

The more cash generated by a company, the better it is. Positive cash flow helps a company to finance its growth and weather business downturns. It is a positive sign if the company's cash flow growth rate is significantly higher than its earnings growth rate.

Debt-to-Equity Ratio

A company's debt burden is analyzed by investors because it can affect profitability. Obviously, the lower the debt-to-equity ratio, the lower is the risk and, consequently, the safer it is for the company and the investment. Therefore, avoid buying a company with a high debt-to-equity ratio. If the debt/equity ratio has been decreasing in the past two to three years, or even in recent quarters, it can be viewed positively. A company's debt/equity ratio should be compared to other companies in its industry. It should be in line with, or less than, the industry average.

Return on Equity

Return on equity is a measure of how effectively a shareholder's investment is being used. It is calculated by dividing net income (after taxes) by the common stockholders' equity. The higher a company's ROE, the better it is as a prospective investment.

Return on Sales

This is a measure indicating the percentage of sales that a company converts into profits. The higher the return on sales, the more efficiently the company is converting sales into net income and managing its business.

Performance Indicators

A number of indicators are used to gauge the performance of a stock. The most popular of these performance indicators, which are particularly favored by momentum investors, are:

Relative Strength (RS) rank

This measures and compares a stock's price performance over the past year, with the last quarter being given greater weight, against all other stocks. In general, a company having an RS rank greater than 80 is preferred. Such a stock has the potential to be a leader or a winner—rather than a laggard.

Earnings per Share (EPS) Rank

This is a measure of a company's EPS growth over the past five years and the stability of that growth. It measures, and compares, a stock's earnings momentum against all other stocks. Since the best stocks, the leaders, have the highest EPS rank, stocks with an EPS rank over 80 are preferred.

Accumulation/Distribution

Accumulation indicates professional buying by institutions, while distribution indicates selling. Stocks with an A or B rating indicate accumulation and positive momentum. D and E ratings indicate distribution while C indicates a neutral rating.

Understanding the Company

The stock market heavily favors informed investors. For such investors, consistent success is quite common. While success is also achieved by casual investors who invest without conducting any meaningful research, it comes their way only occasionally. In the long run, the odds do not favor those who venture into the stock market depending only on hunches and hopes. It should be realized that for success to be achieved, the stock market requires investors to:

■ Conduct adequate research prior to investing in any company.
■ Remain informed by constantly monitoring their stock investments.

Research Requirements

For initial research prior to procurement and for subsequent monitoring, investors need to review the quantitative and qualitative aspects of an investment. The quantitative aspect includes review of earnings projections and trend, dividends, financial statements, and operating performance. The qualitative aspects include company profile, competition, business prospects, and management quality. For analysis, neither the quantitative nor qualitative aspects should be ignored because both provide important perspectives and information.

Investment Information Sources

Company Research Report

Investment information can be obtained from many sources. The best source of investment data and news on a particular company is a company research report, which is typically issued by a brokerage company or an investment firm. Such a report, which is readily available to investors, typically includes financial and performance data as well as important news affecting the company in the prior 12 to 18 months. Important sources of company research reports include Market Guide, S&P, Zacks, Value Line, and many Internet sites. Sample company reports are included in the Appendixes.

All company research reports contain earnings data. However, only some reports contain comprehensive historical, current, and projected earnings data. To supplement information contained in the company research reports, investors can use the more focused earnings reports from First Call Corporation or Zacks Investment Research.

The Company Being Researched

A very good source of information is the company itself. Upon request, companies will provide their own investment literature free of charge. Besides the annual and quarterly reports, they typically provide other reports (10K and 10Q), copies of news articles concerning the company, and press releases. Some companies also provide complimentary copies of company research reports issued by analysts following the company. To obtain any report or other pertinent information, contact the company's investor relations department, which every publicly traded company is expected to have.

Other Sources

There is no dearth of sources for an investor prepared to spend the time and effort required to conduct investment research. The most useful sources are listed in Chapter 3.

Where to Get Company Research Reports

Brokers provide a complete company research report package for their clients. This package, generically called a company research report or a stock report, is usually a collection of reports and data from multiple sources. Such reports may include data sheets from Market Guide, S&P, Zacks, First Call, and other research information providers. Instead of collecting this information from multiple sources, it is better for an investor to obtain it from a broker, which will save considerable time and effort. The Internet is also an excellent source for getting company research reports.

Company Research Reports: What They Contain

A company research report is extremely valuable in that it can reveal material information, which can be positive or negative, such as:

- Company-related news
- Press releases and announcements by the company
- Consensus earnings estimates (from analysts)
- Comments on earnings estimates
- Changes in competition and environment
- Product cycle and any delays
- Fundamental and performance data

Typically, a detailed company research report will include the following general, performance, and financial data pertaining to a particular company:

General Information

- Company business summary, comments on performance and earnings trend, important developments, and news items referencing the company.
- Industry outlook.
- Ratings:
  S&P issues five stars to a company recommended as a buy; one star is issued to a company with a sell recommendation.
  Zacks rates companies from 1 (best) to 5 (worst).
  Value Line issues ratings from 1 (highest) to 5 (lowest) for both "Timeliness" and "Safety."
- Risk associated with the stock (beta).
- Price chart and average daily volume.

■ Shareholder's data (outstanding shares, insider ownership, percentage of institutional ownership).
■ Market capitalization.
■ Number of analysts following the company.
■ Breakdown of analysts' buy/hold/sell recommendations and the mean value of recommendations.

Performance Indicators

■ EPS (quarterly and annual): current and historical.
■ EPS projection: for the next two quarters as well as the next two years.
■ EPS projected growth rate: for the next two years; average for the next three to five years.
■ EPS growth rate comparison (versus the industry and the S&P 500).
■ Earnings revisions: average revision in each estimate, upward or downward, over the past 7, 30, and 60 days.
■ Earnings surprises: comparison of actual earnings to the analysts' earnings estimates.
■ P/E ratio (current and five-year average).
■ Relative P/E.
■ Comparison of current versus projected P/E ratio.
■ Sales (revenues): quarterly and annual (current and historical).

Financial Data and Information

■ Summarized financial data
■ Income statement
■ Balance sheet and other financial data
■ Net margin (current and five-year average)
■ Return on equity (current and five-year average)
■ Debt levels and ratios
■ Analysis of key financial data

Historical and Comparison Data

■ Five- to ten-year historical per share data including:
  Book value, cash flow, earnings, dividends.
  Stock price: high and low.
  P/E ratio: high and low.
■ Comparison with the industry average (and the S&P 500) of various indicators including current P/E, estimated five-year EPS growth, price/book ratio, price/sales ratio, dividend yield, net margin, ROE, and debt/capitalization ratio.

Examples of News Items in Company Research Reports

A company research report lists major news items relating to that company, which were reported in the prior 12 to 18 months. This information can be very useful for relating the company's performance and price gyrations to specific news items. The following are examples of news items from two stock reports from Standard & Poor's:

April 25, 1997: "Qualcomm shares up 8% today on news that Motorola's motion for preliminary injunction and restraining order against Qualcomm has been denied. Motorola claims that Qualcomm's 'Q' phone infringes Motorola's patents related to its StarTAC phone."

April 2, 1997: "Informix down $7/8 to $9. Robertson Stephens & Gruntal, Inc., reportedly downgraded stock. Yesterday, company forecast substantial 1st quarter operating loss, net loss due to weakness in all regions."

Tips for Analyzing a Company

General Tips

Many factors need to be evaluated when analyzing a company. Besides the guidelines listed in Table 15.2, which can be used for analyzing a company, investors can use the following tips:

▮ Institutional ownership of 10% to 20% is a sign that institutions have started buying—and that plenty of institutional buying remains to be done.
▮ Does company have solid products or services (no fad products)?
▮ Evaluate status of product cycle and upgrades.
▮ Study quarterly and annual sales results; check for seasonal distortions.
▮ Break down sales categories—which can be helpful in pinpointing strong and weak areas.
▮ Analyze international sales as a percentage of revenues.
▮ Determine company's market share.
▮ Is the company a leading player or established in a niche market?
▮ Compare to competition; identifying a better competitor might indicate a superior investment prospect.

Performance Tips

▮ Sales growth is insufficient by itself—it must be accompanied by expanding profit margins.
▮ Simultaneously expanding sales and margins can fuel exceptional growth.

■ Sales growth combined with margin expansion and P/E expansion will rocket a stock price.

■ Profit margins are useful in comparing profitability of companies within the same industry.

■ Analyze net profit margins (measures a company's margins after taxes).

■ Realize that margins will eventually level off.

■ Rapidly contracting margins can be disastrous.

■ Determine positive trends.

Analyzing Company Management

The ability of a company to perform successfully or continue doing so is dependent to a large extent on its management. A company's management should have the ability to lead and execute its strategic plans. Therefore, an investor should try to determine the quality, experience, and aggressiveness of the management team. Any changes that might improve or diminish the team's effectiveness should be noted. If management makes excuses for poor results, this should serve as a warning sign. However, if management has a large stake in the company, but not large salaries, it is a positive sign.

The impact of quality management on the performance of a company cannot be minimized. This is understood by Wall Street, which places high value on company management. For example, the president of Project Software & Development left the company in late July 1996. He had been most closely associated with Maximo, the software product that accounted for most of the company's revenues. Following his departure, the stock slid from $49^3/_4$ in early July to a low of $27^1/_2$ in the second week of August. The reason was investors' concern that a visionary had left the company and that his leadership would be missed.

Investors can obtain the name of a company's chairman, chief executive officer (CEO), and chief financial officer (CFO) from its annual report, the Internet, or the Market Guide Snapshot report. This can be a starting point to work backward—to determine how successfully the executive(s) performed at the last company they worked for. Usually, the performance of that company can be a good indicator of the executive's prior performance.

Analyzing the Industry Group/Sector

A company should never be analyzed, purchased, or monitored in isolation. Instead, its environment should be studied and analyzed at every stage. An investor should never ignore the bigger picture because picking winners involves more than just selecting good companies. In other words, this means observing the behavior of the market as well as the industry group/sector to which the company belongs.

Why Analyze the Industry Group/Sector

It is well known that the long-term performance of a company rests on its ability to earn profits and grow at a healthy rate. However, the short-term performance quite frequently depends on two important external factors:

1. Outlook for the industry or group to which the company belongs
2. The state of the economy

Therefore, it becomes imperative for investors to understand which industry group/sector their stocks belong to—such as technology, financial services, and so on. This will enable them to understand and compare the behavior and performance of their stocks to similar stocks.

Industry analysis should be an integral part of a solid investment strategy. Being able to understand the future prospects for the industry, and where the stock being analyzed fits in the bigger picture, can be crucial for enhancing the profits to be made.

What to Do

As an investor, you should determine the group/sector to which your stock belongs. Sometimes this is not very obvious. For example, technology stocks are considered by some to be cyclical stocks even though they are growth companies. However, their cycles are quite different from those of conventional cyclical companies.

After a company's industry group/sector has been determined, an investor should understand, monitor, and forecast, if possible, its expected performance relative to other groups and the market. This will enable you to forecast, to a reasonable degree, the expected performance of your own stocks. When it appears that the group/industry performance is going to deteriorate, you can lighten up. When the future performance of the group is forecast to be positive, you can increase your exposure to the group by adding to existing holdings or by taking up new positions.

Technical Analysis

After a company has passed the fundamental analysis exercise, an investor can confidently buy its stock. However, it can be worthwhile to subject the stock to technical analysis, at least a limited one, in order to determine a more profitable entry point.

Entry Point Determination

A basic technical analysis test is to determine if a stock is trading over its 200-day moving average. A stock trading over this line is considered to be in a long-term uptrend and, consequently, this is considered bullish. If a stock pushes above its 200-day moving average line, many investors consider this to be a buy signal. On the other hand, if a stock slides below its 200-day moving average, these investors consider this to be a bearish signal and, therefore, they sell the stock. Similarly, if a stock trades over its 50-day moving average line, it is considered to be a bullish sign by short-term traders. These players use the 50-day moving average line as both an entry and an exit point.

A profitable time to buy a stock occurs after it has had a price correction and undergone consolidation (i.e., experienced a 2-to-15-month basing period). According to technicians, a stock should be bought after it has emerged from a base building period and when it is close to or actually making a new high in price. Horizontal support and resistance lines are also used by some investors as entry/exit points. A support line is used as an entry point if the stock has reversed direction and other indicators are also positive.

Limitation

Technical analysis is no substitute for fundamental analysis. It should be used only for a limited purpose. For example, by determining resistance and support levels, an investor can have a better understanding of a stock's price swings and behavior. In general, the following guidelines should be used when using technical analysis:

- Use it to confirm fundamentals.
- Do not buy a stock even if technical analysis provides confirmation, if little or no research material is available.
- If market analysis shows that the market is making a top, reduce overall stock holdings.

Analyzing a Company in Depth: An Example

In this section, a company will be analyzed in depth. The objective is to introduce the reader to fundamental analysis principles using a specific real-world case. The basic procedure involves:

■ Extracting important statistical, performance, and financial data from company research reports.

■ Collecting business information, industry data, and performance prospects from various sources including company annual reports, company research reports, and trade publications.

■ Forecasting the potential price appreciation.

■ Highlighting specific parameters in support of, or against, the case for buying the stock.

The Company

The company to be analyzed is Oracle Corporation—an enterprise software and information management services company. The company develops, markets, and supports computer software products used for database management, network communications, applications development, and end-user applications. The company's core product is the Oracle relational database management system (RDBMS). The company offers its products—along with consulting, education, support, and systems integration—throughout the world.

Statistical and Shareholder Data

An analysis of the shareholder data, presented in Table 16.1, indicates that most of the factors analyzed are positive. The company has a very large number of outstanding shares—which usually is a negative factor. The reason is that a large float tends to make it difficult for a stock to make a major upward move. However, this is balanced by the very high percentage of insider holdings—which is a very positive factor.

Data Sources Being Used for Analysis

The primary data sources used in the analysis are Oracle's 1996 earnings and company research reports. Data from 1996 has been used because it will permit the comparison of Oracle's forecasted performance, based on its fundamental analysis using these reports, with its actual performance in 1997 and 1998. The reports used in this analysis are:

■ Appendix B: First Call earnings estimate report for Table 16.5
■ Appendix C: S&P stock report for Tables 16.2 and 16.3
■ Appendix D: Zacks company report for Table 16.4

Table 16.1   **Analysis of Oracle's Basic Statistical and Shareholder Data**

	Miscellaneous data and values	Observations and analysis	Investment perspective
Industry Group	Data processing Computer software	High forecasted growth Above-average growth	Positive Positive
Shares outstanding	654 million	Very large float	Negative
Average daily volume	3.89 million	High	Neutral
Insider holdings	40%	Very high	Very positive
Institutional holdings	54%	High	Negative
Beta	0.83	Near S&P average	Positive
Risk	Average		Positive
Current stock price ($)	$37^1/_2$	10% below recent high	Positive
52-week range ($)	$23^3/_8 - 42^1/_8$		
Insider activity	Neutral		Neutral
12-month P/E	41.7	Five-year average = 41.2	Positive
P/E on 1997 estimate	29.3	Below estimated 35% growth rate	Positive

It may be noted that it is not necessary to use all three sources for analysis. These reports contain a considerable amount of duplicate data. For most practical purposes, one or two reports are adequate. It should also be noted that reports from different sources can contain minor data discrepancies—which can usually be ignored. The reason is that, occasionally, the data included in these reports is preliminary and subject to minor revisions.

For example, the S&P report shows Oracle's 1996 earnings equal to $0.90 per share (Appendix C), while the number reported by Zacks' report is $0.95 per share (Appendix D). The $0.05 difference is attributed to the $0.05 per share charge that Oracle took, in the first quarter of 1996, to reflect costs associated with an acquisition. So depending on when the data is updated, reports issued by different sources may contain slightly different numbers. If the difference is material, the data should not be used prior to an investigation being made.

Table 16.2   **Oracle's Revenues (Million $)**

Fiscal year ending May 31	1996	1995	1994	1993	1992	1991
1st quarter	771.8	556.5	398.0	307.0	245.0	215.0
2nd quarter	967.2	670.3	452.2	353.0	284.0	257.0
3rd quarter	1,020	722.3	482.8	370.0	290.0	269.0
4th quarter	1,464	1,018	668.1	472.6	235.0	287.0
Year	4,223	2,967	2,001	1,503	1,178	1,028

Source: Standard & Poor's. Reprinted by permission of Standard & Poor's, one of the McGraw-Hill Companies.

Table 16.3   **Oracle's Earnings ($/Share)**

Fiscal year ending May 31	1996	1995	1994	1993	1992	1991
1st quarter	0.08	0.09	0.06	0.02	0.00	–0.05
2nd quarter	0.21	0.14	0.09	0.05	0.02	0.00
3rd quarter	0.22	0.16	0.11	0.04	0.03	0.02
4th quarter	0.40	0.27	0.17	0.10	0.04	0.01
Year	0.90	0.66	0.43	0.21	0.10	–0.02

Note: Due to rounding numbers, some column totals do not add up exactly.
Source: Standard & Poor's. Reprinted by permission of Standard & Poor's, one of the McGraw-Hill Companies.

Table 16.4   **Oracle's Performance and Financial Data**

- Current ROE = 41%; compares favorably with:
    - 12% for industry average
    - 20% for the S&P 500
    - 33.9% for Oracle's five-year average
- Net margin: 14.3% vs. average 10% for the last five years
- Net margin: 14.3% vs. average 3.3% for the industry
- Long-term debt/capitalization:
    - Current = 0%
    - Five-year average = 11%
- EPS growth rate for last 12 months: 42%
- Price/book ratio: 13.1 vs. 3.5 for the industry average
- Price/sales: 5.8
- Price/CF: 29.8 vs. 19.9 for the industry average

Source: Zacks Investment Research, Inc. Reprinted with permission.

Performance and Financial Data

■ Revenues: 4.22 billion for fiscal year ending May 1996.
■ Total revenues in the fourth quarter of fiscal year 1996, ending May, grew 44% year-to-year.
■ Growth in business areas:
Core database licenses: +49%
Applications: +73%
Tools: +13%
Services: +44%

Broker Recommendations

■ From Zacks (Appendix D):
Strong buy: 12
Moderate buy: 10
Hold: 4
Sell and strong sell: nil
■ From First Call (Appendix B):
Mean of recommendations based on 20 brokers (analysts): 1.4
where 1 = buy, 2 = buy/hold, 3 = hold, 4 = sell/hold, 5 = sell

Stock Price Forecast

Earnings Assumptions and Estimates

The primary source for this analysis are the earnings data and estimates from First Call's earnings estimate report (Table 16.5). Where required, data from Zacks' company report and S&P's stock report have been used to supplement the primary data provided by First Call.

Table 16.5 **Oracle's Earnings Estimate ($ per Share)**

Fiscal year end is May 31	1996 (actual)	1997 (estimated)	1998 (estimated)
Mean estimate (EPS)	$0.90	$1.28	$1.69
No. of analysts making estimate		25	20
Estimate range		$1.22–$1.34	$1.55–$1.79

Source: First Call Corporation. Reprinted with permission.

Forecast Calculations for Fiscal Year 1997

▌ EPS growth in the last fiscal year (1996): 35%
▌ Estimated EPS: $1.28
▌ Earnings growth estimates (short-term: one year):
   S&P report estimates that earnings will grow over 35% during fiscal
   year 1997.
   Zacks' report also estimates a 35% EPS growth for fiscal year 1997.
▌ Report date: September 7, 1996
▌ Months remaining till the end of the current fiscal year (May
   1997): 9

Forecasted price at the end of the current fiscal year (May 1997):

   = Annual earnings growth rate × Estimated EPS
   = 35% × $1.28
   = $44.80

Forecasted price rise:

   = $44.80 – $37.50 = $7.30

Percent price increase:

$$= \left(\frac{\$7.30}{\$37.50} \right) = 19.47\%$$

This means that the stock is forecasted to rise 19.47% in the next
nine months (ending current fiscal year, May 1997). On an annualized basis, this equals:

$$19.47\% \times \left(\frac{12}{9} \right) = 25.96\%$$

Forecast Calculations for Fiscal Year 1998

▌ Estimated EPS: $1.69
▌ Earnings growth estimate (long-term):
   First Call estimate from analysts: 29.6% (average annual long-term
   growth rate)
   Zacks estimate: 33%/year (fiscal year 1998)
   For this analysis, we will be conservative and use the lower EPS an-
   nual growth rate (29.6%) for fiscal year 1998.

■ Report date: September 7, 1996
■ Months remaining till the end of fiscal year (May 1998): 21

Estimated price at the end of fiscal year ending May 1998:

$$= \text{Annual earnings growth rate} \times \text{Estimated EPS}$$
$$= 29.6\% \times \$1.69$$
$$= \$50$$

Forecasted price rise:

$$= \$50 - \$37.5 = \$12.50$$

Percent price increase:

$$= \left(\frac{\$12.5}{\$37.5}\right) = 33.33\%$$

This means that the stock is forecasted to rise 33.33% in the next 21 months (ending fiscal year, May 1998). On an annualized basis, this equals:

$$33.33\% \times \left(\frac{12}{21}\right) = 19\%$$

Overall Analysis

The Big Picture

Corporate America is competing in a very competitive global market. Efficiency (lean and mean) and increased productivity are some of the traits of successful companies competing in this environment. To either become or remain competitive, companies need many tools, including robust enterprise software. Companies providing these tools will benefit from the efficiency and productivity improvement trend—which is expected to continue for many years. Oracle is a leader in this group and stands to benefit tremendously from this continued push for efficiency.

Positive Business Factors

■ Oracle is a well-established company growing at a very rapid pace; such growth is usually associated with smaller companies.
■ Software industry is growing rapidly; database sector is also growing very fast and Oracle is expected to grow in tandem.

- Overall business growth is excellent; revenues grew 44% in the last quarter (ending fiscal year May 1996).
- Core database business is strong; secondary businesses are also healthy with the exception of tools.
- It is difficult for new companies to enter business.
- Market share: 37.9% of the relational database software market.
- Diversified product line: core product supplemented by tools, education, and consulting.
- Strong balance sheet.
- International presence.
- Very high percentage of management ownership.
- Excellent management team.

Positive Technology Factors

- Technical leader: products dominate the market.
- Software available on all hardware platforms: enables customers to easily migrate from other platforms.
- Well positioned to take advantage of two of the hottest trends in the computing world—Internet and data warehousing.
- Internet and data warehousing products being introduced rapidly.

Negative Factors

- Potential of price war, with severe impact on earnings, if Microsoft enters the enterprise database market.
- A company as large as Oracle may be unable to maintain its current high growth rate for a long time.

Price Appreciation Potential

Oracle's current price (year: 1996) is $37.5. As calculated earlier, Oracle's stock has very good price appreciation potential in the next two years as tabulated in Table 16.6.

Table 16.6   Oracle's Forecasted Price Appreciation Potential

Current price $37.50	Forecasted price	Rise over current price	Annualized return
Ending fiscal year, May 1997	$44.80	19.47%	25.96%
Ending fiscal year, May 1998	$50.00	33.33%	19.00%

Financial Data Analysis

An analysis of Oracle's financial tables (Appendix C) shows that it is in a very strong financial position—with most ratios and debt status improving year after year. Its balance sheet is very strong. The following is a summary of the financial data analysis:

■ Cash balance has increased consistently since 1990
■ Cash flow has increased every year since 1991
■ Long-term debt has decreased every year since 1991
■ Debt ratios have decreased every year since 1992
■ Return on assets increased in four out of the last five years
■ Return on equity increased in four out of the last five years

Performance Data Analysis

The performance indicators, shown in Table 16.7, are very positive with the exception of the price/book ratio, which is high compared to the industry.

Technical Indicator Analysis

Most of the technical indicators shown in Table 16.8 are positive. Both the short-term and long-term trend indicators are positive. The accumulation/

Table 16.7   **Analysis of Oracle's Performance Data**

	Value	Comparison	Investment perspective
ROE—current	41%	12% for industry average 20% for S&P	Very positive
ROE—five-year average	33.9%		Very positive
Net margin	14.3%	10% for last five years 3.3% for the industry	Very positive
Long-term debt/ capitalization	0	11% average last five years	Very positive
EPS growth rate last 12 months	42%		Very positive
Price/book ratio	13.1	3.5 for the industry	Negative
P/E (current)	41.7	41.2 average last five years	Positive

Table 16.8   **Analysis of Oracle's Technical Indicators**

Indicator	Value	Investment perspective
Accumulation/distribution	C	Neutral
RS rank	79	Neutral/positive
EPS rank	98	Very positive
% above 10-week moving average	12%	Positive
Trading above 200-day moving average line	Yes	Positive

Source: Investor's Business Daily.

distribution indicator is neutral because Oracle, along with other members of the technology sector, had suffered a correction during the summer—which decreased the value of this indicator to a neutral C.

Confirmation Signals

The fundamental analysis of Oracle Corporation reached a positive conclusion. As a final check, we can compare our conclusion to the recommendations being made by the professional analysts (Appendixes B and D). Not surprisingly, they are also very positive:

- No sells
- Very high percentage of buy recommendations (22 out of 26)
- High mean of recommendations (1.4)

Recommendation and Logic

It is quite clear that Oracle's fundamental health is good. Fundamental, technical, performance, and financial analysis indicate a positive investment climate. Current fiscal year's estimated profit potential is excellent (25.96%). In the following year, the rate of return is expected to decrease to 19%. With such a positive forecast, this analysis clearly indicates that Oracle's stock is a very good buy.

Monitoring after Procurement

An investor should continuously monitor a company—even if everything looks good. Oracle is no exception. Even after procurement, it should be monitored regularly. At the first sign of slowdown in its earnings or revenue growth rate, the company should be thoroughly reevaluated to determine if it should remain in the portfolio.

If Oracle maintains its growth rate, analysts will periodically increase its earnings estimates. In tandem with the revised earnings forecasts, reruns of the calculations should be done—with the new earnings and growth figures. Such an exercise will enable an investor to determine if the expected return on investment (ROI) remains acceptable and also help determine the new target price.

Actual Performance in 1997 and 1998

The performance of Oracle Corporation was in line with expectations derived from its fundamental analysis. The company continued to grow at an excellent pace during fiscal year 1997. Not surprisingly, its stock price appreciated in tandem with the growth in its revenues and earnings. Compared to a forecasted price of $44.80, Oracle was trading at $46.62 at the end of the 1997 fiscal year (May 1997).

It had been forecast that the stock would appreciate to $50 by the end of the 1998 fiscal year (May 1998). This price level was reached in June 1997—much earlier than expected. The stock continued to appreciate—reaching a high of $63 before starting to decline. This decline came as no surprise because the stock had appreciated far more than its estimated earnings warranted. By January 1998, Oracle had declined to a low of $27.09 (after adjusting for a three-for-two stock split that took place on August 15, 1997). A strong rebound followed and the stock had recovered to $47.82 by April 1, 1998—which placed it within a shade of its May 1998 forecast price of $50.

Results of a Periodic Evaluation

Following a correction that started in April 1998 and ended with the bear market bottom in September, the stock again rebounded strongly. By December 28, 1998, Oracle had reached an all-time high of $65.81. Assuming that First Call's long-term earnings growth estimate of 29.6% was still valid in December 1998, we can forecast Oracle to reach a price target of $64.80 by May 1999—a price level already achieved. Hence, at this level, even though the company is fundamentally very sound, Oracle's stock will be considered overpriced.

Concluding Remarks

Every company passing the screening test must be subjected to fundamental analysis, which helps determine its health and future business prospects. For performing in-depth company analysis, investors use a number of indicators.

The relative importance of these indicators depends on the investing approach, philosophy, and risk tolerance of the investor.

The most important indicator is earnings, which is analyzed in many different ways such as annual and quarterly earnings, EPS rank, and earnings history. Other commonly used indicators include revenue (sales) growth, P/E ratio, cash flow, and debt level. A number of performance indicators, such as relative strength rank, are also used. As part of fundamental analysis, a company's management and its industry/group/sector are also analyzed.

Finally, after passing the fundamental analysis test, a company can be subjected to technical analysis. This can help determine a more appropriate time for buying the stock. However, most investors do not use technical analysis for timing their procurement.

Chapter 17

Selling Strategies

Common Problems

Poor Selling Performance

Any investor, despite thorough research and analysis, can make a mistake and pick a loser that will need to be sold. In fact, not even the best and most savvy investors are immune to making mistakes. Also, even though it is recommended that profits run, every winner needs to be sold ultimately. Therefore, every investor has to deal with selling issues at some time or other. However, it has been observed that while many investors are good stock pickers, their performance in selling stocks leaves much to be desired. The disinclination to sell, in many cases, can be attributed to:

- Belief that a sound, long-term investment has been made that precludes selling.
- Refusal to acknowledge that a mistake has been made.

Lack of Selling Strategy

Generally, investors focus their attention only on buying stocks and, in many cases, do not have any selling strategy. However, to be a successful player, an investor must have both buying and selling strategies. Therefore, it is imperative that every investor pick and follow a selling strategy—no matter how simple. Otherwise, selling will be based on emotional factors, hunches, and reaction to events.

Plan Your Selling

Avoid Forced Selling

Deciding when to sell a stock is as important as making a buy decision. Therefore, every investor must have a strategy, or a rules list, for determining when to sell a stock. An investor must not let circumstances, such as needing money for immediate needs, force a sell decision. Letting such needs influence a selling decision is a sure recipe for losing money. Funds invested in the stock market should be those that will not be needed in the near future. If the investment horizon is short, or the possibility exists that such funds may be required soon, other financial instruments that are more appropriate for holding short-term funds should be used.

Select a Selling Strategy

An investor must have a selling plan for cutting losses, profit taking (short-term), and disposing of long-term winners. Without a specific strategy for individual stocks and the market, an investor will not be able to effectively react to changes. However, an investor with a predetermined strategy is always better equipped. For example, such an investor will be better prepared than one with no strategy when a decision is required to sell or buy more shares if there is an unexpected price decline.

No strategy will work forever. Even good strategies need to be modified and fine-tuned occasionally. Also, it is natural for investors to make mistakes. Therefore, periodic self-analysis should be conducted in order to pinpoint mistakes and subsequently refine or change the strategy.

Set Price Targets

When buying any stock, price targets should be set for loss selling, short-term profit taking, and long-term profit taking. A common tool for this purpose is the limit sell order, which is an order that gets executed only if the stock reaches a specified price. Such an order can be placed with the "good till canceled" condition, which usually remains in effect for two months. If such an order expires, a new order can be placed. If needed, it is possible to increase the target sell price while such an order remains in effect.

Common Reasons for Selling

Profit Taking

Profit taking refers to selling a stock after it has appreciated in price. This can occur after a short price run-up that leads traders to dispose of a stock at a profit. However, the majority of selling involves investors disposing stocks for capital gains—after an appreciable price increase. A fair amount of selling is also done by investors after varying holding periods, even though they may have only modest capital gains.

Loss Exceeds a Percentage

Many market advisers recommend that an investor should sell, no matter what the reason, if a stock declines more than 7% to 10% below the buy price. This makes an assumption that the stock has been bought at the correct (exact) buy price. This may be an acceptable strategy for well-established blue chip companies and utilities, whose price movement in either direction is limited. However, for small growth companies, whose price fluctuations can routinely be 10% or more, such a strategy will not work satisfactorily. An investor in such companies can easily get whipsawed if this method is used. A more practical strategy may be to place a mental stop loss about 10% to 15% below the purchase price. Investors already having profits in a stock can be more flexible when determining the acceptable price fluctuation limits.

Laggard Performance

Sometimes even the best research and analysis does not prevent an investor from picking a stock that fails to meet expectations. Such a stock, despite good earnings and favorable news, does not rise as can be expected of a company posting good results. Herein lies the difference between a good company and a good stock. A good company does not always translate into a good stock. Examples are Seagate Technology and Advanced Micro Devices (AMD) in the early 1990s. Both are good companies that turned in hefty profits for a number of years without exciting investors and rising to their potential. During the period that these two companies underperformed, other companies with far lower profits handsomely rewarded their shareholders.

Portfolio Pruning

Investors buy both losers and winners. While ultimately all stocks need to be sold, some are required to be dumped very quickly, while others can be sold after a long holding period. Periodically, investors should evaluate their holdings and get rid of deadwood; this improves the portfolio performance in the long run. Such pruning should be an ongoing process. When evaluating stocks for pruning, favor selling the losers first. These should be followed by those with small profits and those which failed to meet expectations.

Tax Reasons

Capital gains can be offset by *capital losses*. Therefore, investors sell their losers in order to compensate for the capital gains tax liability generated by selling their winners. Typically, selling losers is done at the end of the year, when the tax situation is more clear than at the beginning of the year. If a decision to sell a winner is reached at year-end, it is advisable to postpone selling until the new year starts. This permits an investor to defer the tax liability and, consequently, take advantage of the time value of money.

Selling Signals

Common Sell Signals

The most important reason to sell a stock is the deterioration of its fundamentals. In such a case, it should be sold without any hesitation or delay. A number of other factors can also indicate trouble for a stock. These need to be analyzed as part of an overall analysis for holding on to a stock. In general, the following signals indicate that a stock might be a candidate for complete or partial selling:

General and Market Reasons
- Stock does not appear to be meeting the investment goal.
- Earnings growth begins to slow or actually decline for two consecutive quarters.
- Reason/factors for buying the stock no longer exist.
- Stock has appreciated significantly:
  Profit taking appears in order.
  Stock has become a larger-than-desired percentage of the portfolio and, therefore, needs to be partially sold.
- Stock continues to decline without any rally.
- Loss exceeds a predetermined percentage.
- Management actions seem irrational.
- Acquisition has had a fundamentally negative impact on the company.
- Market top is recognized.

Technical Reasons
- Uptrending 200-day moving average turns into a downtrend.
- Stock price breaks below its 200-day or 50-day moving average line:

Break below 50-day moving average is a warning.

Break below 200-day moving average is more serious.

- Stock is 70% to 100% above its 200-day moving average line.
- Price drops on heavy volume.
- Stock makes new highs on decreased or poor volume.
- Stock is trading on heavy volume after an advance—without further price appreciation.
- Number of down days in price versus up days in price changes after the stock starts declining.
- Stock is undergoing distribution.
- Decline appears more than a normal decline from a peak (i.e., a correction of 10% to 12%).
- Relative strength rank falls below 70, especially in a rising market.
- Group strength is weak and stock is acting alone.
- Support level fails.
- Trading band: failure swing at the top of the band or support failure at the 30-day moving average line.
- Trendline: occurrence of a trend break through a rising trendline, which signals the probable end of the trend.

Additional Sell Signals for Small Growth, Niche, and One-Product Companies

- Earnings growth rate decreases significantly, which does not justify its high P/E.
- Revenue growth does not meet expectations.
- Market share is being lost very fast.
- Poor financial health is indicated by high or increasing debt.
- New company enters business, which changes the competitive picture materially.
- Competitor introduces killer product.
- Critical product is delayed or gets bad reviews after introduction.
- Litigation is pending whose adverse judgment can materially affect the company.
- Adverse ruling in a major patent lawsuit or other litigation occurs.
- Company starts wasting money on unnecessary, nonproductive assets.

Strong Reasons to Sell

While some sell signals can be ignored and usually need to be analyzed in conjunction with other indicators and signals, others are quite clear-cut.

Such indicators are very strong sell signals and cannot be ignored without increasing the risk factor considerably. These include:

- Company is in trouble: deteriorating financials or business prospects.
- Rate of quarterly earnings increase slows significantly or actually declines.
- Earnings actually decline for two consecutive quarters.
- Market share is lost for two consecutive years.
- Shares start declining due to fundamental weakness.
- No new products are being developed.
- Spending in R&D has been curtailed.
- Company is resting on its laurels and historical performance.
- Company paid too much for an acquisition.
- Better opportunity: A stock with far more favorable prospects has been identified.
- Impending bear market has been recognized.

Market as a Sell Signal

An investor should carefully check the overall market health and direction before leaping out of the market. One should not let some sharp sell-offs, which can be isolated events, lead to bailing out of the market prematurely. This can result in good stocks being sold too early. If that happens, the potential exists for missing a strong upward move following the sell-off.

Warning Signs from the Market

The following are some signals emanating from the market that should raise warning flags:

- Change in direction is accompanied by increased volume.
- Leaders are among the casualties; this is an indication that the market will follow.
- Leaders decline on expanding volume.
- If most declining stocks have low relative strength (RS below 80), it indicates that the weaker stocks are being hit.
- *IBD* mutual fund index falls significantly.
- Yields on long-term bonds exceed the S&P 500 dividend yield by 6% or more; this is a very bearish sign.

Riding Out Sell-Offs

Sharp sell-offs are quite frequent and an investor needs to understand and profit from them. A very good example is the behavior of the market on a very volatile day—when the Nasdaq dropped 1.3% and the DJIA fell slightly less. On the NYSE, losers beat gainers by a five-to-three margin. However, trading volume actually declined on all the three major exchanges: NYSE, Nasdaq, and AMEX. The sell-off subsided in just two days. On subsequent days, the market rebounded and the A/D line moved upward, while volume declined.

Following a sell-off, as in this case, low volume is viewed positively by analysts. Such a drop is more in line with an orderly correction than the start of a major market move in the opposite (downward) direction. Further analysis revealed that the leading stocks had suffered only minor pullbacks on decreasing volume. Investors who bailed out of the market missed the rebound. And as typically happens in such cases, bailed-out investors continued to wait for the market to decline after the rebound in order to reinvest. However, the decline did not materialize.

Mistakes to Avoid

Common Mistakes Preventing Selling

Three of the biggest mistakes that investors make are:

1. Being extremely nervous, resulting in selling a stock prematurely.
2. Continuing to hold a stock for too long even after its mediocre performance becomes apparent.
3. Focusing too much on what was paid for the stock.

A common mistake that many investors make, when deciding whether to sell, is to look at the current loss or profit. Instead of basing a decision on the price paid basis, they should evaluate the stock's future price appreciation potential. They should not be driven by the paper loss. If a stock's fundamentals are sound, a paper loss should not cause an investor to lose confidence. However, a sell decision should be made immediately if the company's future looks cloudy.

Some long-term investors who are paid a dividend do not worry when their stock plunges. They do not consider selling such a stock because of the income it generates. But numbers in such a case do not add up: A 5% dividend yield minus a 30% loss equals a 25% loss! Such an attitude can be very costly if the company's fundamentals are not sound. Firstly, the stock can fail to recover in price. Secondly, the risk increases that the company may ultimately be forced to cut its dividend.

When Avoiding Selling Is Not a Mistake

Some signals appear to indicate selling, but certain stocks should not be sold despite these signals. The following are some guidelines for holding on to a stock, even though a signal indicates that selling might be in order:

- Pessimism is pervasive: Do not be a crowd follower during pessimistic periods.
- Stock has appreciated significantly and appears overvalued: Ride a winner, and do not sell early; do not sell just because of the price appreciation.
- Price target is reached: If fundamentals show an improvement, increase the price target.
- Stock has high P/E: Do not use guideline P/E ratios for selling decisions; realize that winners can have four to five times the market's P/E ratio.
- Price drops: Hold on if the reasons for buying remain valid.
- Leading stock gaps down in price: Do not panic—the drop may be due to a large block being sold by an institution.

Concluding Remarks

Ultimately, every stock needs to be sold. The most common selling reasons are profit taking (profit target is reached or profit exceeds a percentage), laggard performance, portfolio pruning, and tax reasons. However, despite this ultimate need to sell, too many investors confine their attention to buying stocks while ignoring selling—which is a very important aspect of investing.

A common factor preventing selling is emotional involvement with a stock (which should never happen) and unrealistic hopes (which are not based on any sound reasons). Every investor should have a selling strategy and understand the factors that should trigger selling. This will prevent one from just reacting and making ad hoc decisions. Learn to recognize sell signals. Be aware of the common mistakes that investors make. Also, recognize the situations when avoiding selling a stock is not a mistake.

Before a sell decision is made, other factors need to be studied in conjunction. However, there is one scenario which dictates that a stock be sold without any delay—deteriorating fundamentals. Also, once a sell decision has been reached due to fundamental reasons, selling should not be delayed in anticipation of a minor rebound from current levels.

Chapter **18**

Risk and Portfolio Management

Types of Investment Risks

An investor who desires to maximize returns must generally be prepared to assume higher risk. Conversely, if one desires to reduce risk, then one must be prepared to accept a lower return. Therefore, every investor needs to strike a balance between protecting capital while building wealth. This is done by taking measured risks using selected strategies. While the nature of risk varies with the type of investment, the most common types of risks are identifiable. These risks are:

- Market risk
- Inflation risk
- Interest rate risk
- Business risk
- Liquidity risk
- Currency risk
- Specific risks

Market Risk

This is the risk of a loss caused by a declining stock price, which can occur over short or extended periods. Stock prices never remain steady at any one value. They always fluctuate—up and down. The frequency and amplitude of these price fluctuations are affected by many factors including:

- Economic factors (inflation rate, unemployment rate, interest rate changes, etc.).

■ External factors and events (political, international, trade issues, wars, national disasters, etc.).

■ Changing investor expectations for the economy and individual companies.

■ Profitability of the company (performance in terms of profit or loss).

■ Emotional factors (hope, fear, and greed).

■ Speculation.

The overall stock market behavior is also a major factor causing price fluctuations in individual stocks. If the market declines, the risk increases that an individual stock or the portfolio will follow the market's decline and a loss can result. These market declines occur periodically as was shown in earlier chapters. As expected, individual stocks also suffered major declines simultaneously. Hence, due to these wide and unpredictable price swings, stocks tend to be viewed as risky investments.

Inflation Risk

Inflation is an increase in the price level of goods and services, which reduces the purchasing power of consumers. It adversely impacts the cost of living and has a corrosive effect on investments. It reduces the real return of an investment. If the annual inflation rate is 4%:

■ The real rate of return is only 3% if an investment grows at a 7% rate.

■ Purchasing power will be reduced by half in 18 years.

Since stocks have historically protected money against inflation, they are referred to as an "inflation hedge." The average inflation rate from 1926 to 1997 was 3.2%—which offset most of the returns obtained from short-term instruments. During this period the return on Treasury bills averaged 3.81%, while long-term bonds gained 5.59%. However, in each case inflation reduced the real return by 3.2%. Stocks of both large and small companies fared better than bonds and T-bills. After taking inflation into account, large company stocks provided a real average annual return of 9.76%. Small stocks performed even better—with a real return of 14.53%.

In the recent 10-year period, from 1988 to 1997, the annual inflation rate averaged 3.4%. This reduced the real performance of various investments—whose returns are shown in Table 2.1 (Chapter 2). Again, stocks performed far better than long-term bonds and shorter-maturity bills.

Every investor is faced with the risk that the return from investments will not match, or exceed, the inflation rate. In order to beat inflation risk, it becomes imperative that investments grow faster than the inflation rate.

Interest Rate Risk

Interest rates significantly influence the stock market. Both the absolute value and the direction of interest rates affect the stock market to a significant degree. When interest rates go up, they make alternative investments (such as bonds and CDs) more attractive compared to stocks. Additionally, higher interest rates affect the profitability of corporations because their borrowing costs increase—which then drags stock prices down. However, the effect of higher interest rates on individual stocks varies. For example, bank and utility stocks are more sensitive to interest rate movements because of their heavy requirements for borrowed capital. Consequently, when interest rates rise, bank and utility stocks decline.

To reduce interest rate risk, investors try to predict interest rate trends. Predicting the level of interest rates 6 or 12 months down the road is difficult, and forecasting with consistency is even more difficult. However, interest rate trends can be anticipated and predicted, to some extent, if an investor monitors important factors affecting interest rates.

Business Risk

Corporations work in a dynamic environment where business conditions change constantly. Therefore, a risk always exists that a company's business will become obsolete, be decimated by competition, become unresponsive to its customers, or be managed poorly. These risks cannot be eliminated completely. Investing in solid, healthy companies that an investor understands can minimize these risks.

Liquidity Risk

The demand for the shares of different companies varies significantly—with the daily trading volume of individual stocks ranging from a few hundred to tens of millions of shares. Due to insufficient demand for their stock, the shares of some smaller companies can be more difficult to sell. This can result in a seller of a small company stock receiving a lower price than a stock with a higher trading volume would get—under the same conditions. This problem is usually magnified during a declining or panicky market. Investing in companies having a healthy daily trading volume can reduce this risk. As part of their risk strategy, some individual investors do not buy companies with a trading volume under 100,000 shares a day, while large institutional buyers maintain even higher daily trading volume limits.

Currency Risk

A change in the value of the dollar relative to foreign currencies can have a significant effect on the profits of U.S. companies with foreign operations. This, in turn, can affect their stock price. The magnitude of this effect depends on the extent of foreign operations and the percentage change in the value of the dollar. An investor has limited options for eliminating this risk.

Specific Risks

There are three elements to investment risk associated with stocks. They are from the stock market, the industry, and the company itself. The most important risk is from the company itself—because there is always the possibility that it may perform unsatisfactorily. If that happens, the investment can be adversely affected, with the potential for a drastic decrease in its value. This specific risk can be reduced through *diversification* (i.e., by spreading the investment among many companies, sectors, or industries). This ensures that if one company in the portfolio performs miserably, other investments can balance the total returns.

Balancing Risk and Reward

The road to wealth for most investors is through stocks, bonds, or real estate. However, none of these investments is risk free. The bond market loss in 1994, one of the worst ever on record, showed that even low-volatility fixed income funds can lose value significantly. The real estate market suffered significant losses in the early 1990s, especially in California, where home prices dropped 30% in many areas. Therefore, an investor needs to realize that investing in any of these vehicles can put the capital at risk.

Understanding the Implications of Risk

Many investors incorrectly equate risk to an investment's price decline. In reality, risk is a far more complex term, whose nature and implications an investor must understand. The crucial factor in investing success, or failure, is the ability to understand the risks and potential effects associated with the investment being made. Every investor needs to balance risk and reward. The fundamental investing equation is simple: The higher the expected return, the greater will be the investment risk. For example, stocks offer higher returns than cash reserves or CDs. They also expose an investor to a higher risk level. Every investor has to resolve this conflict caused by trying to preserve capital, while simultaneously trying to maximize the return. This risk/reward trade-off is a key consideration in investing and cannot be ignored by any investor. An investor needs to look at the following factors when evaluating risk/reward trade-offs:

∎ Potential return
∎ Ability to meet goals
∎ Investing period
∎ Risk of losing principal
∎ Acceptable fluctuations
∎ Vulnerability to interest rate changes
∎ Alternative investments
∎ Risk if no investing is done

Quantifying Risk

Within each investment type, the degree of risk varies. For example, stocks of smaller companies are usually more risky than those of well-established blue chip companies. In general, investors require about a 4% higher return from equity investments (such as stocks), due to their profits (earnings) risk, than for less risky government-backed securities (such as Treasury bills and bonds).

Volatility

Various measures are used to quantify the risk associated with stocks. The likelihood of a short-term change in price, known as volatility, is the easiest to measure. A gauge called "beta" is used to quantify this risk. It measures the price volatility of a particular stock against the S&P 500 index. Beta indicates how much a stock is expected to move, up or down, relative to the overall market. Usually a stock with a higher beta represents a more volatile and riskier investment.

Every stock is rated for beta relative to the number 1, which is the number used for the S&P 500. A stock with a beta of 1.5 tends to be 50% more volatile than the S&P 500, while a stock with a beta of 0.5 is half as volatile. If a stock with a beta rating of 1 moves 10%, another stock with a beta equal to 2 can be expected to move twice as much (i.e., 20%). This applies to both upward and downward movements. Small and high-technology companies are characterized by high betas.

Using Beta

When the stock market is declining, a stock with a beta rating of less than 1 is preferred. The reason is that such a stock is expected to decline less than the market. Conversely, in a rising market, such a stock will underperform compared to the overall market. Therefore, when the overall market is rising, investors prefer to own a stock with a high beta since it is expected to outperform the market. However, the limitation of using beta to obtain better returns, by timing and switching stocks, is that future market direction cannot be easily or accurately forecasted.

Managing Risk

Risk cannot be eliminated in the stock market. However, it can be managed to some degree in three ways. Firstly, it can be done through reasonable portfolio diversification. However, this does not protect an investor from market or inflation risks. Secondly, it can be managed by investing for the long term. This is far less risky than short-term investing, because it is well established that time has a moderating influence on stock market risk. The longer an investment is held, the greater the probability of earning higher returns. Thirdly, by being an informed investor one can take advantage of opportunities before they become obvious to everyone.

Determining Risk Tolerance

Prior to investing, it needs to be determined whether one is a conservative, moderate, or an aggressive investor. These three terms are relative. Some investors consider themselves conservative because they invest only half their money in the stock market. Others think that conservative means staying away from the stock market altogether. An aggressive investor is comfortable with market swings, invests for the long term, and can withstand considerable short-term losses.

Once a potential investor has accepted the principle of stock market investing, one's risk tolerance should be determined. Just accepting the stock market's short-term fluctuations on an intellectual level is not enough. As an investor you should evaluate yourself on an emotional level through self-examination. Are you the type who will be kept awake by market fluctuations? Are you fearful of losing 10% or 20% of your investment in a few days or weeks? Answering these and related questions will help determine the risk personality, risk tolerance, and suitability for investing in the stock market. In general, an investor should choose investments with a risk level that:

■ Makes one comfortable
■ Is appropriate for the long-term goals

Limiting Risk

Stock market risks cannot be eliminated but they can be minimized. Some investors limit risk by staying away from the stock market altogether. However, for the vast majority, the stock market is the place to be. These investors need to strike a balance between risk and reward based on their individual risk tolerance and profit objective.

A very important way of reducing risk is by staying informed. An informed investor always stays on top, and instead of reacting to tips and events, makes calculated moves. Such an investor comes out ahead. Besides remaining informed, an investor can use a number of methods, explained in the following sections, for limiting the risk faced by stock market investors.

Avoiding Speculation

Every investor should understand the difference between investing and speculating. There is a great difference between picking a winner based on merits and speculating on hunches. The bottom line is that one should not speculate in the stock market. All stock selections should be made based on fundamental research and analysis.

Diversifying

A very common method for reducing risk is by spreading the investment among a number of stocks. This is based on the very old principle—do not place all your eggs in one basket. By buying a number of stocks, an investor does not remain exposed to the fluctuations and performance of any one stock. While this strategy reduces the downside risk, it can also place a damper on any meaningful upside move by a winner.

The following are some diversification guidelines that can be used by investors:

■ In general, five to seven stocks are sufficient for an investment of $50,000.
■ Overdiversification should not be done.
■ Instead of owning a large number of mediocre performers that can only drag down the overall portfolio, it is preferable to own a small number of top-performing stocks.

▪ Stocks with home run potential are inherently riskier than average stocks.

▪ To reduce the risk for those who want to invest in stocks with home run potential, diversification among several home run issues makes sense.

Limiting Risk from One-Product Companies

An important characteristic of a one-product company is that it is very focused. Another advantage is that it can control a niche that larger companies cannot enter profitably. Its stock also has the potential to rise appreciably. However, one-product companies have an above-average risk associated with them. Depending on whether a company's single product succeeds or fails, its stock can soar or crash.

The key to evaluating potential investment in such a stock is to minimize risk while retaining the opportunity for reaping the big reward. A sensible strategy is to avoid having too many one-product companies in the portfolio. Once such a company enters a portfolio, it should be monitored with extra care. A key factor to monitor for such a company is its R&D expenditure. This is an absolute must because only a reasonable amount of R&D investment can ensure that the company maintains or extends its lead in the only product it sells.

Handling a Hot Tip with Care

At some time or other, every investor gets a so-called hot tip. These tips from friends, neighbors, and others should be thoroughly investigated before making any investment. The following is a useful action list for investors when dealing with a hot tip:

▪ Separate the tip from the tipper.
▪ If a story made the stock hot, check it out; the story may already be discounted and the good news may already be reflected in the price.
▪ Study the company and its business.
▪ Analyze the company's fundamentals.
▪ Examine analysts' earnings estimates and other indicators.
▪ Based on earnings estimates, estimate the potential price rise in the next year and then compare it to the current price.
▪ Check out the industry's performance and determine its fundamentals.
▪ Investigate whether any insider buying or selling has taken place.
▪ Invest only if everything investigated is positive and the ROE looks appealing.

Using Cash Substitutes

Many investors prefer to remain invested even if there is uncertainty and worry about the economy (or the market) and the market is volatile. These investors limit their risk by parking their money in the biggest companies, such as the DJIA components, whose price fluctuations are limited even during a volatile or declining market. These mega-stocks, such as GE, which has a float of 3.2 billion shares, can become a cash substitute for such investors. Besides being relatively safe, such companies also pay dividends.

Using Beta to Limit Risk

An investor's objective during the stock selection process is to identify stocks that will:

- Rise faster than the average stock during a bull market.
- Decline less than the average stock during a bear market.

An investor can identify such stocks using software tools, such as Market Guide for Windows, by searching for stocks whose betas are above 1.0 in rising markets and below 1.0 in falling markets. In early April 1999, only 860 out of the 9,199 companies in the Market Guide database were able to meet these desirable attributes.

An investor can use beta as a screening tool to eliminate stocks, even if they have had good price appreciation in the past, if they are too volatile. This can be done by buying a stock having a beta equal to 1 that, on average, will match the market's upside, as well as downside, swings at the same speed.

Each investor has to decide, based on one's personal risk assessment, the acceptable level of volatility. For someone prepared to experience more volatility, a stock with a beta greater than 1 (i.e., with above-average volatility) may be acceptable.

Understanding the Risk of Leverage

Advantage of Leverage

In its simplest form, leverage can be described as "more bang for the buck." Leverage is using borrowed money to buy stocks and can translate into doubling the gain or loss on an investment. Using *margin*, an investor can buy double the number of stocks that can be bought if only the cash in the account is used. Consequently, with double the number of shares, the potential loss or gain will be doubled. An alternative to playing margin is to buy stocks with above-average volatility. The advantage of this technique is explained in the next section.

Alternative to Margin Investing

In a rising market, profits will be made by both techniques: margin investing and investing in high-volatility stocks. During a rising market, a stock with above-average volatility will rise higher. However, while a high-volatility stock will appreciate more than a margined stock that has lower volatility, the margin investor is compensated by having double the number of shares.

However, despite this advantage in a rising market, it is preferable to buy stocks with above-average volatility, even though they tend to be riskier, instead of playing margin. There are a number of reasons for this. With margin, an investor needs to buy double the number of shares (compared to a stock with double volatility). Therefore, a higher commission fee and margin interest will need to be paid. Also, during a declining market, the margin player's loss will be doubled. Another risk is that there always exists the danger of being forced to sell due to a margin call, if the price declines too much. While a riskier, more volatile stock will fall more during a declining market, an investor's overall loss will typically be less with such a stock than with a margined stock, because only half the number of shares will be owned.

Options

Calls and Puts

There are two types of stock options: calls and puts. A call option conveys to the option buyer the right, but not an obligation, to buy the underlying stock from the call seller at a specified price called the strike price. This right expires on the expiration date of the contract. The option buyer pays a premium to the seller for the right to exercise the option.

A put option conveys to the option buyer the right, but not an obligation, to sell the underlying stock to the put seller at a specified price called the strike price. This right expires on the expiration date of the contract. The option seller collects a premium from the option buyer for conveying the right to exercise the option.

A call option buyer expects the stock price to rise, and thus to be able to exercise the right to buy the stock at a price below the market value. If the stock fails to appreciate, the investor loses only the full amount of the option (premium), which is considerably less than the investment required for buying the stock itself. It should be realized that selling a call option does not protect against a price drop. However, buying a put option does protect against a price decline.

How an Option Works

Suppose that an investor owns 1,000 shares of ABC Company currently trading at $22. Let us assume that she sells a call option for 10 contracts, which is equivalent to 1,000 shares, at a strike price of $25 for expiration in March 2000. For getting this right, the call buyer will pay the investor a premium. If this premium is $2 per share, the investor (call seller) will collect $2,000. In March 2000, the call buyer can buy the stock from the call seller for $25 a share. However, if the stock trades below $25 a share on the expiration date, the option becomes worthless and the call buyer will lose the full investment ($2,000). However, if the stock trades at $30, the call buyer can still purchase the stock for $25 from the investor. In this case, it means a net profit of $5,000 minus $2,000 (profit minus premium) for the call buyer.

Options are traded and quoted, just like stocks, with bid and ask prices. Their prices are reported in the newspapers such as the WSJ and IBD.

Advantages and Risks

Stock options, when used correctly, can improve long-term returns and reduce risk. The advantage of using options is that during periods when a stock trades in a narrow range, when its price is not expected to rise appreciably, an investor can receive some income from the stock. However, the flip side is that if the stock makes a big move to the upside during the period that the option contract remains in force, the call writer (seller) will be unable to cash in on the major price move, which benefits the call buyer.

The shorter the expiration time limit, the greater is the risk of buying calls. On the other hand, the longer the term, the less the risk. To lessen the risk of buying options, options can be spread over several months. Risk can also be reduced by buying the options of solid companies. Writing naked calls, without owning the underlying stock, is very risky and should be avoided. Options should not be used by novice investors. When used, they should be used carefully and sparingly.

Hedging

A hedge is a strategy used to reduce investment risk. This technique is used to cushion the risk of a major adverse move in the market or an individual stock. It involves purchasing offsetting long and short positions. A long position refers to buying a stock with the expectation that it will appreciate in price. A short position refers to selling a stock, without owning it previously, based on the expectation that its price will decrease. The buyer of a put option in an individual stock or an index (such as the S&P 500) is considered to be short in that stock or index.

Portfolio Analysis

A very important aspect of investing in the stock market is portfolio management, which includes the following activities:

- Asset allocation, which involves the distribution of assets among different investment types (stocks, bonds, money market funds, etc.).
- Analysis of market conditions, which is used to determine the level of exposure to stocks in asset allocation.
- Managing diversification: determining which, and how much, of various sectors and industries are to be represented in the portfolio of stocks; for example, increasing exposure to interest-sensitive stocks when the interest rate environment turns positive for such stocks.
- Periodic evaluation and review of the portfolio.
- Monitoring stocks in the portfolio.
- Sell decisions: determining whether to let profits run, cut losses, or switch stocks.

Concluding Remarks

The stock market has many risks associated with it, especially in the short term. However, the short-term risks associated with stock price fluctuations are balanced by the superior rewards of being invested in stocks for the long term. While these risks cannot be eliminated, they can be managed and minimized. A number of tools are available to investors for reducing risk to manageable proportions. Two of the most important ways are by becoming an informed investor and diversifying by spreading the stocks among different sectors and groups. While diversifying has its advantages, overdiversification should be avoided.

Investing for the long term in the stock market can reduce the risk caused by price fluctuations. Avoid speculation and select investments based on fundamentals. Be open to hot tips but analyze such companies thoroughly. When investing in one-product companies, be extra careful. They have extra risk and reward associated with them.

No portfolio should remain stagnant. The performance of every stock changes over time and, therefore, every stock in a portfolio should be periodically evaluated. This exercise will enable the pruning of underperformers and the infusion of new, faster growing stocks in the portfolio.

Chapter **19**

Investing Rules and Tips

General Guidelines and Tips

1. Follow a simple investing approach.
Do not be confused by complicated theories on investing. Fancy and sophisticated techniques are for the professionals. For most individual investors, it does not make sense to use them. Follow a few simple, but solid, investing rules. Be aware that the simplest investment techniques can be quite successful. Have a clear objective—the selection of profitable companies characterized by high and consistent growth.

2. Follow a disciplined approach.
Stick with an overall plan and strategy. Do not change your investment strategy based on daily market action. Do not be swayed by day-to-day news unless it affects the fundamentals of the stock. However, the strategy must be periodically reviewed, analyzed and, if required, refined.

3. Be an investor—not a trader.
Be a patient investor and invest for the long term. Do not become a trader who tries to capitalize on the small price changes that characterize stock movements. A trader buys at dips, sells at blips, and holds a stock for a few days or, in some cases, only a few hours. Understand that it takes time to accumulate wealth, which is not built through short-term gains. A little trading might be in order, but overtrading should not be done.

4. Be an informed investor.
Always be informed and alert. Monitor the company and the industry to which your stock belongs. Observe and understand economic, financial, and political news. Analyze their implications because of their potential

impact on your stock. Never stop monitoring either the stock or its environment.

5. Follow a few stocks well.

Do not invest in, or try to follow, too many stocks. Limit the number of stocks that you monitor to a manageable number. Monitoring does not mean checking daily stock prices. Far more important is the requirement to track the indicators and events that influence the fundamentals of the stock.

6. Invest in a company—not the market.

Realize that you are investing in a company, not the stock market. The profit to be made depends on the performance of the company—not the overall stock market. Therefore, it is imperative that you understand the business and fundamentals of the company that you have invested in.

7. Remain invested at all times.

Ride market ups and downs. Aim to be heavily invested when the stock market makes its periodic big moves. Ignore short-term price fluctuations. Be prepared to lose money during market declines. Lighten up just a little when the market is about to decline, rather than unloading all your stocks. Buy more stocks when the market is depressed. Remember that long-term returns from stocks are relatively predictable and far superior to bonds.

8. Keep cash reserves.

Avoid investing all your funds in the stock market except for short periods. Keep some cash reserves handy. They can be very useful for picking up bargains during market or individual stock corrections. The disadvantage is that keeping cash reserves can affect the overall return.

9. Keep in mind that market declines are buying opportunities.

Look at market corrections and bear markets as great buying opportunities. These come occasionally and you should be prepared for them. Maintain cash reserves so that you can pick up bargains while others are dumping. The most profitable time for investors (i.e., when the highest percentage of profits are made) is the first phase of a rebound from a bear market. Rebounds from corrections are also very profitable.

10. Be a leader, not a follower.

Do not follow the crowd for either buying or selling. Be a leader and think for yourself. That will prevent you from buying after prices have already risen or selling after prices have already fallen. Do not buy stocks just because they appear to be current popular picks. Look for undiscovered opportunities missed by Wall Street. However, be aware of the overall market trend. Do not fight the market trend which, besides being very powerful, can point to potentially better buying opportunities in the not too distant future.

11. Be a contrarian.
It pays to be a contrarian. Use your own judgment instead of running with the crowd. Buy when fear is widespread, which typically happens when the market is at the bottom. Sell when there is euphoria, which typically happens at market tops.

12. Do not be overawed by Wall Street professionals.
Do not overestimate the skill and wisdom of professionals. Many amateur investors have performed better than money managing professionals. Do not take at face value what money managers say publicly. A top money manager was selling 10 million shares of Micron Technology in fall 1995—while publicly speaking positively about that company. Carefully evaluate the public utterances, especially stock recommendations, of the pros before using such information for decision making.

13. Know forecasting limitations.
Predicting the state of the economy 12 to 18 months down the road is very difficult. Trying to predict the direction of the stock market, short-term or long-term (one to two years), is a futile exercise.

14. Learn to recognize sentiment extremes.
The stock market is a place driven in cycles by fear, euphoria, pessimism, and greed. Learn to recognize signs of sentiment extremes. This will enable you to become extremely careful when excessive speculation is taking place. On the other hand, at times of panic and pessimism, it will permit you to recognize opportunities.

15. Do not get overexcited by news stories on a company.
Beware if a number of news stories on a company appear in well-known magazines such as *Business Week*. This typically happens when the "story" is already out and known to everyone. At this stage, typically, insufficient buyers remain to push the stock up significantly. Before buying, evaluate the potential impact of news stories that look good. Often, news being reported has already been discounted in the company's

share price. Beware of analysts touting a stock as the next IBM or Microsoft.

16. Beware of the market's discounting mechanism.
Wall Street is forward-thinking. Therefore, future prospects are already priced into the price of a stock. Hence, it is important, when analyzing a stock, to determine how much of the future earnings are already reflected in its current price.

17. Diversify.
Risk and reward levels vary for different stock classifications and groups. To reduce risk, especially from the disastrous performance of a single stock, maintain a diversified portfolio. Diversification should be across industry groups. Try to have about five to seven stocks in your portfolio. However, do not overdiversify. Avoid having more than a dozen stocks in the portfolio. Besides being very difficult trying to monitor so many stocks, overdiversification will typically reduce the overall portfolio return. The lower the number of stocks in a portfolio, the greater is the performance difference compared to a benchmark.

18. Limit exposure to thinly traded stocks.
A daily trading volume of under 100,000 shares is usually considered thinly traded. Avoid buying such stocks because it may not be possible to sell them quickly, especially during a falling market. At times, even routine selling of such stocks may require that the order be broken into many blocks over a number of days. Due to multiple sell orders, the overall commission costs will be very high. In panicky markets, it is possible that a thinly traded stock may not sell at all.

19. Know that small companies make big moves.
Price movements and appreciation can vary significantly based on the type of stock. Big companies have small moves. Small companies make large moves. Invest in small and fast growing companies for the best results.

20. Dollar cost average to avoid mistiming.
One of the biggest mistakes investors make is trying to time the market. Generally, they end up buying when the market is hot (at the top) and selling when pessimism reigns (at the bottom). Few investors are able to jump in and out at precisely the right time, even despite spending an inordinate time studying the market. Timing might be all right for the pros. However, it is not recommended for the individual investor. A better

strategy is to stay invested at all times, while reducing exposure during an expected downturn. Dollar cost average and buy stocks as money becomes available. It is better to average up than average down.

21. Base your decision making on fundamentals.

Always base your buy, hold, and sell decisions on the fundamentals of the company you are investing in. All other factors (such as market behavior, taxes, etc.) are peripheral. While these factors should be part of the overall evaluation process, they must not become the primary criteria—which should be based, without exception, on the company's fundamentals.

22. List specific reasons for buying a stock.

Whenever you buy a stock, list the reasons why you bought it. Also, write down your expectations. When the reason(s) for buying the stock no longer exist, get rid of the stock.

23. Establish and adhere to a price target.

Reevaluate a stock when it reaches its price target. At this stage, evaluate it with the same perspective that you would use for buying a new stock. If there are strong reasons for the stock to continue rising, raise the price target. Raising the target in a bull market can be quite effective. However, be careful in a bear market.

24. Keep your slightly overpriced fast growers.

Do not sell your outstanding fast growers just because they seem slightly overpriced. This is a losing technique. These stocks can be real winners and often appear overpriced as they move up sharply.

25. Understand earnings.

Every investor must understand the earnings indicator thoroughly. Realize that it is the most important factor driving any stock in the long run. Understand various earnings aspects such as annual and quarterly earnings. Evaluate comparable quarters. For example, earnings for the third quarter of 1999 should be compared to the third quarter of 1998 rather than the second quarter of 1999.

26. Winners have strong earnings.

The basic factor that drives up a stock's price is profits. Leaders and winners are characterized by healthy and fast growing earnings. If a company has been exhibiting strong growth for three to five years, and continues to show a 20% annual earnings growth rate, it is a potential winner.

Moderately fast growers (20% to 25%) in slow-growth industries are ideal investments.

27. Focus on revenue growth.
Remember that revenue growth is the only true growth. Look for consistent and above-average growth. Earnings improvement due to cost cutting or other factors is rarely long lasting. For consistent and long-term earnings growth, revenues should continue to grow consistently. Be very wary if revenue growth decreases or is not healthy. Be cautious of companies with growth rates of 50% to 100%. They need to be analyzed with more care.

28. Analyze management ownership in the company.
Favor companies in which management has a reasonably high level of stock ownership. The higher the percentage of management ownership in a company, the better it is for the long-term prospects of the company.

29. Do not focus on the number of shares to be bought.
Some investors only want to buy an even number of shares (in multiples of a hundred shares). This does not permit them to buy the shares of some high-priced companies, and causes them to miss investing in big winners. One should think in terms of dollars invested, rather than even number of shares. The percent price appreciation of a stock is not based on the number of shares. Instead, it is based on the dollar amount invested.

30. Make use of stops.
Stops let your profits run but cut your losses short. Often, a stop loss order about 8% to 15% below the buy price, depending on the stock's volatility, is used. Some investors use the 200-day, or 150-day, moving average line as a stop loss limit. Many traders use the 50-day moving average line, with a 1% to 1.5% margin, for a stop. If a stock continues to move up, raise the stop price to lock in profits already made.

31. Understand seasonal effects.
Be aware of the seasonal patterns of the company's business. For example, it is well known that the semiconductor business is very slow during summer. For retailers, the fall season is the best. Seasonal patterns that affect revenues and earnings should be understood.

32. Be aware of factors causing volatility.
Some factors cause temporary high volatility in the markets. These include triple witching day (when options expire), and end-of-quarter

window dressing by money managers. During these periods, some stocks get hit hard—especially those with recent mediocre performance. The reason is that such stocks get purged from many money managers' portfolios. The aim is to give a misleading impression of a portfolio loaded only with winners and consequently make the manager look good.

Buying Tips

1. Invest in what you know best.
You should understand what you are investing in. Invest in a company, industry, or group that you are most familiar with. The most profitable investment is one where an investor gets in early on a story. Solid fundamental company information is often available at one's job long before it becomes known on Wall Street. Therefore, always keep your eyes open in order to identify a potential investment.

2. Buy into a theme.
One of the most successful techniques for becoming a winner in the stock market is to pick stocks based on an investment theme. For those who get in early on an investment theme, the rewards are significant.

3. Buy low, sell high.
This is a well-known Wall Street rule, which rarely fails. It is what investing is all about: Sell the stock at a higher price than what you bought it for. Following this principle will ensure good profits. The problem with this rule is that it does not indicate how to determine the correct low price for buying.

4. Consider buying more shares of a rising stock.
If a stock continues to appreciate in price and the fundamental reasons remain intact or improve, more buying may be in order after further evaluation. A study of the current value, earnings growth, and historic P/E ratios may show that it makes sense to buy more shares instead of taking profits.

5. Get information before, not after, buying a stock.
Indiscriminate buying will never provide a payoff. Conduct your research prior to buying a stock. Do not buy a stock just because it dropped in price and, consequently, looks very attractive compared to its price prior to the drop. Before buying after a sharp drop, determine the reason for the decline and analyze the fundamentals. If a stock is rising fast, do not jump on the bandwagon prior to doing fundamental research on the company. If

you are evaluating a stock that has not moved for some time, determine the reason(s) for its lack of movement.

6. Buy stocks six months after a recession has started.
Be fully invested when a bull market starts. The reason is that the highest percentage of profits is made early in a bull market cycle. To ensure participation in the strong rebound from a market bottom, start buying stocks approximately six months after a recession has started. This usually coincides with the time when pessimism is extreme and the recession is close to an end.

7. Buy leading companies in an industry or niche area.
Do not buy mediocre companies because their price looks right. Buy high-quality and high-performing companies. It is preferable to buy leaders—the top two or three companies in an industry—rather than average companies. Buying a small company, if it controls a niche market or has some unique or innovative product, is also recommended.

8. Buy companies with some institutional presence.
Try to pick and buy stocks before they get discovered and institutional presence becomes heavy. Buy stocks with a reasonable amount of institutional ownership—preferably over 20%. Avoid buying a small company stock with excessive institutional presence.

9. Buy companies that are already profitable.
Avoid buying companies when they are still in their early development cycle. Buy small companies that are already profitable. The earnings of such companies should have been in a positive trend for at least three to five years, unless there is a good reason for having had an off year. One year of underperformance can be ignored if a quick rebound was made.

10. Buy companies whose estimates are being raised.
More important than the accuracy and level of earnings estimates is the direction in which estimates are moving. Usually, stocks whose estimates are being raised will appreciate the most. Buy such stocks while avoiding stocks whose earnings estimates are being lowered.

11. Find winners among laggards and overlooked companies.
Find companies with good track records of several years that are being ignored. Try to identify stocks that have had excellent EPS growth but their P/E ratios failed to grow. When the P/E ratios of such profitable

companies start expanding, especially for growth stocks, tremendous profits can be realized.

12. Buy "hot tip" stocks only after thorough investigation.
Handle hot tips with extreme caution. Beware of tips from your friend, broker, or neighbor. Separate the stock tip from the tipper. Do not get carried away by hype. Never act on a tip without doing your homework. Do not expect a $1 stock to become a $5 or $10 stock in a short period. Before buying, do your research and be aware of the risks involved.

13. Confirm buying decisions by using the moving average line.
If the fundamentals have been confirmed and the stock is trading over its 200-day moving average line, a buy is indicated. If a stock is trading below its moving average line, buying is indicated after the line has turned upward (i.e., after it has reversed direction). However, buying should be done only if the fundamentals are in confirmation.

Buying Tips Not Based on Fundamentals

1. Buy high, sell higher.
This is the formula that momentum investors use. For them, it does not matter that the price is high so long as the stock continues to move higher. This method is also described as "buying because others are buying." This technique is not based on fundamentals and is risky for most investors.

2. Buy on the rumor—sell on the news.
This well-known Wall Street saying is based on sentiment rather than any fundamental factors. By following this rule, the danger exists that an investor may make a wrong decision based on rumors. Rumors and manipulation are not rare in the stock market.

3. Buy on weakness—sell on strength.
This is another well-known Wall Street rule. However, do not buy a stock on weakness until it has been determined that the company is, and will continue to be, fundamentally sound. Selling on strength is actually a contradiction of the adage "Let your profits run." It makes sense to sell on strength only if a decision has already been made to sell a stock.

Selling Tips

1. Know when to fold 'em.
No stock has to be owned forever. Ultimately, every stock needs to be sold for one reason or another—profit taking, cutting losses, and so on. Cutting losses is an important part in the overall scheme to make money grow in the stock market. Do not underestimate the importance of selling. Make your selling rules and follow them. For example, you can use 12% as the loss limit at which a stock will be sold without any hesitation.

2. Sell if the fundamentals are deteriorating.
When a stock price drops, determine whether this is due to market weakness, a correction, or normal fluctuation. Sell the stock without any delay if the drop is traced to fundamental reasons such as slowing earnings (or revenue) growth or other developments—which can negatively impact future earnings or growth. Evaluate selling when the quarterly earnings growth rate slows materially or earnings actually decline for two consecutive quarters. Selling is not recommended if weakness is due to an overall market decline, a correction, or subsequent to a significant upward move.

3. Clarify what a loss means.
A question that every investor needs to clarify is: "What is a loss?" Is it loss of profits or an actual loss based on the purchase price? No matter which basis is used, never delay selling when it becomes apparent that the stock is a loser whose price appreciation days are over.

4. Cut your losses and let the profits run.
This means selling your losing stocks as soon as possible before losses become too big. On the other hand, it is strongly recommended that you should ride your winning stocks as long as possible. Continue holding winners until the fundamentals that made them winners deteriorate or the price runs way ahead of earnings. Always get rid of your weak stocks first and hold on to the winners, rather than the other way around.

5. Sell on interest rate move.
Sell stocks, or lighten up considerably, if the Federal Reserve raises short-term interest rates above the long-term interest rate. When this happens, stocks will have considerable competition from bonds and other fixed investment vehicles. Therefore, they will be negatively impacted.

6. Sell to switch.
A good reason to sell a stock, even though it may not be a loser, is in order to switch to a newly discovered growth stock with better price appreciation prospects.

7. Sell a disappointing stock.
A stock should be given 6 to 18 months to move—depending on a number of factors. If it does not act as anticipated, and fails to move within the expected period, sell the stock.

8. Do not delay selling for minor gains.
If a decision has been made to sell a stock, do so without unnecessary delay. Do not try to squeeze the last point out of a move. In particular, if a stock's fundamentals are deteriorating, sell immediately. In such a case, do not try to get something extra such as $1/8$ or $1/4$ point. Often, the probability for a large price drop is greater than for a slight upward blip in such cases.

9. Do not delay selling for a rebound or comeback.
Never wait for a rebound of a few dollars to sell if fundamental analysis has revealed that the stock should be sold. Don't believe that if a stock has gone down "so much," it can't decline much further. The reality is that no one can pinpoint the exact low level where a falling stock will stabilize. Also, do not hold a losing stock in the belief that stocks ultimately come back.

10. Use a technical sell signal.
If a stock is overextended, about 70% to 100% above its 200-day moving average line, selling may be in order according to the tenets of technical analysis. Similarly, a stock may be evaluated for selling by those using technical analysis if it surges above its upper channel line.

The Don'ts

1. Never fight the trend.
Never go against the trend of the stock market, or an individual stock, which represents the current buying or selling sentiment of investors. Other well-known sayings that mean the same are "Never fight the tape" and "The trend is your friend." You should know that profits are realized by participating in, not by fighting, major market moves. Therefore, you should determine the trend, which indicates the direction and momentum in the near future, and benefit from it. However, do remember that trends change over time.

2. Never fight the Fed.

The Federal Reserve controls interest rates—a critical variable in the stock market. When interest rates go up, the stock market goes down and vice versa. Therefore, you should monitor current Federal Reserve policies and actions, which will make you aware of the interest rate trend. Using that information, you can choose investment ideas that go along with, rather than fight, the interest rate trend.

3. Do not confuse the company with the stock.

A company's reputation and the price of its stock should not be related for investment purposes. An excellent company can be a mediocre investment because its shares may be overvalued or for other reasons. An investor should focus on the current and potential value of the company's shares, rather than its historical performance.

4. Never get attached to a company.

Remember that you are in the stock market to make money. The aim is to buy the stock of a good company and sell it for a profit after it has appreciated—or sell it sooner if it fails to appreciate. You should never become emotionally involved with a stock, because doing so can affect logical decision making.

5. Do not ignore the market's seasonal nature.

Do not give undue importance to seasonal factors, nor should you ignore them. Avoid pruning your portfolio during the strong seasonal periods. For example, it is well known that January is a very good month for small stocks. During this period, they benefit from the so-called January effect. During such periods, try to hold on to your stocks, especially the small cap stocks.

6. Do not make yield your objective.

Growth, rather than yield, should be your main objective. Do not be complacent when a stock performs poorly just because it provides a good dividend yield. Remember that a 5% dividend yield can never compensate for a 20% price decline! You must never ignore losses and poor fundamentals because the company pays a good dividend.

7. Never use a single indicator.

Always use a number of indicators. Some may be given more importance than others. However, do not use too many indicators because they can give conflicting signals. Also, it is time-consuming and difficult trying to track too many indicators. Avoid using a combination of indicators picked from different investment approaches.

8. Never buy penny stocks.
The risks associated with penny stocks are too high. Usually, investment research material regarding such companies is either unavailable or insufficient. Also, commissions can be too high, as a percentage of the total buying cost, for such stocks. Realize that there are too many good companies—literally thousands—that you can choose from in the stock market. Therefore, unless you are a speculator, why take an unnecessary risk?

9. Do not buy stocks of mediocre companies.
Buying stock of a mediocre company because it is cheap is a losing technique. It is better to overpay for quality than to underpay for junk.

10. Never buy a stock just because it has a low price.
Never buy a stock based on its current price being low compared to its recent, or historical, price. Keep in mind that many such stocks are actually expensive in relation to their earnings. While an oversold or undervalued stock situation may make a stock look attractive, one should review more than just the price and P/E ratio. Determine the potential for future price appreciation based on fundamentals—in relation to the company's projected earnings. A stock's low price must be only a single selection factor at best. The basic determination to be made is whether the company is fundamentally sound, with good products, and likely to recover. Fundamental knowledge about the company is important in determining whether the stock will recover and be a good investment.

11. Do not buy immediately after a big price drop.
Never buy a stock immediately after a major drop in price. Understand the reasons for the price decline. Let the stock base for a while (i.e., trade in a narrow price range) before seriously considering it as a buy candidate. The only exception to this rule applies when you are thoroughly familiar with the company, know its fundamentals, and are reasonably sure that the stock will soon rebound.

12. Do not buy companies embroiled in serious litigation.
Never buy companies, especially those with a single product, that are embroiled in serious litigation. Besides jeopardizing the financial viability of the company if a negative judgment results, such a stock rarely becomes an investor favorite. Therefore, its price appreciation potential is limited.

13. Do not ignore a stock's industry and group.
Never buy a stock without analyzing its industry. A deteriorating outlook for an industry will usually affect the performance of even the best company in that industry—despite the company having very sound fundamentals.

14. Do not become emotional.
The stock market is a unique place where psychology and economics blend. It is a place driven by fear, hope, and greed. An investor has to be very calculating and clinical. One must never become emotional because it can cloud sound judgment based on logic.

15. Do not speculate or short a stock.
Do not speculate in the stock market since gambling does not make long-term winners. Unless you are a very experienced investor, do not engage in shorting—selling a stock first (after borrowing it) and then expecting to buy it back at a lower price after it declines in price. This is a very dangerous game. Also, do not buy options, unless you are an experienced investor. The reality is that small investors who buy options usually end up being losers.

16. Do not give undue importance to taxes.
While taxes should be a part of your investment decision, do not make them a major factor in your decision making, especially when evaluating a stock for unloading. If a winning stock has run its course and needs to be sold, do not delay the sale without good reason. For example, a potential sale of a big winner in December can be delayed until January in order to defer the tax liability to the following year. However, remember that the potential always exists that a delay due to tax considerations can result in the loss of profits that have already been realized. The magnitude of such a loss can be appreciable and, in some cases, can be greater than the tax liability the investor sought to avoid.

17. Do not be plain stupid.
An "investor" asked one of the authors to provide him information about a particular stock that had dropped $10, from $20, in a single day. The investor volunteered the information that he had bought the stock because it had fallen "so much" and, therefore, was a good buy. The author was amazed to discover that even days after buying the stock, the investor knew nothing about the company or its business. This investor had lost over $100,000 in the market a few years earlier and, obviously, had not

learned from his mistakes. That particular stock was trading in the $1 range a few months later.

Analysis and Monitoring Tips

1. Test and evaluate your own decisions.
Make your own independent decisions. You will make mistakes, especially as you navigate your first stock market and business cycles. To come out ahead, you need not be right all, or even a majority, of the time. A few big winners can easily compensate for many small losers if you follow the rule "Cut your losses and let the profits run." From time to time analyze your mistakes and learn from them. Use this analysis to refine your strategy and techniques.

2. Analyze losers.
All investors—including professionals—make mistakes. For success, one needs to learn how to limit losses from losers. When a loser turns up in a portfolio, determine the reasons for its decline (or lack of price appreciation). Then decide whether to sell, continue holding, or buy some more of the stock. If too much damage has already been inflicted, it might not make much sense to sell, especially if the proceeds are going to be limited and cannot be reallocated efficiently. If a sell decision is reached, sell without delay. If the fundamentals are sound, dollar cost averaging might be in order.

3. Never stop monitoring.
Never become complacent, or too confident, about a company or the market. Over time, the business prospects and growth rate of even the best company can change. Also, the market does not move in the same direction forever. Always remember that the stock market never stops surprising investors.

4. Monitor frequently.
Do not limit monitoring to checking daily prices of the stocks in your portfolio. Be on the lookout for any stories relating to your company that can influence its business environment and, consequently, its profitability. Spend a minimum of one to two hours per week on investment research.

5. Know what to monitor.
Understand the company in which an investment has been made and stay informed. Do not monitor stock prices only. Monitor news and develop-

ments affecting the company's fundamentals and its underlying business. Monitor the overall stock market, industry, economy, interest rates, and so on. Focus on earnings. News items affecting the company should be studied prior to, and after, buying the stock. News items can pertain to product announcements, changes in ratings and earnings estimates by analysts, management changes, earnings news, moves and announcements by competitors, and so forth.

6. Monitor earnings releases.
Monitor quarterly earnings for all companies in your portfolio. Be aware of the market earnings expectations by checking the quarterly and annual earnings estimates at least once a month. Be prepared for a stock price to decline after earnings are released, even if the company reports excellent earnings, if there was a good price run-up prior to the announcement.

7. Monitor a stock's group.
Always monitor a stock's industry group and be aware of its pattern and business prospects. When comparing the performance of a stock, match it with a stock in its own group/industry.

8. Monitor market averages.
The overall market should be monitored but it should not be given too much importance. For tracking purposes, more importance should be given to stocks making up your portfolio. Do not base your stock picking decisions on forecasts of where the market is headed made by investment newsletters.

9. Be on the lookout for divergence.
Divergence indicates that the stock price movements of the DJIA (representing 30 companies) and the overall market (as represented by the NYSE stocks) are in opposite directions. Divergence can exist between any pair of indexes such as the DJIA and the Nasdaq. Divergence can be an early warning signal because it typically precedes changes in direction and trend. Observe any divergence in the major market averages.

10. Monitor volume signals.
A very important monitoring indicator is volume. Big moves, in both up and down directions, are accompanied by expanding trading volume. In general, the higher the volume, the stronger the move in either direction.

11. Compare relative performance.
Measure the performance of your portfolio against an appropriate index containing stocks with similar characteristics, such as the Nasdaq or high-technology sector index. A good comparison benchmark is the *IBD* mutual fund index, whose performance is reported daily by the *IBD*. Get concerned if the index is gaining and your portfolio is underperforming. If your portfolio underperforms consistently, reevaluate your strategy and techniques.

12. Evaluate performance over time.
The stock market requires patience. Give your stock 6 to 18 months to perform unless the fundamentals deteriorate prior to the end of that period. If that happens, sell without delay. The actual waiting period should depend on a number of factors including the type of company, industry, market conditions, and the state of the economy.

13. Be on the lookout for stock buybacks.
A stock buyback announcement is good news for a company because it reduces the total number of outstanding shares and, consequently, boosts its stock price. Usually, a buyback is announced if the company believes that its shares are undervalued or they are needed for the employees' stock purchase plan.

14. Monitor Federal Reserve actions and hints.
Always monitor Federal Reserve policy and hints from its officials, which can influence interest rates and move the stock and bond markets. On December 6, 1996, Federal Reserve chairman Alan Greenspan indicated in a speech that "irrational exuberance has unduly escalated asset values." The next day, the DJIA dropped 144 points in early trading. On July 22, 1997, Greenspan hinted that the Federal Reserve was not considering an immediate increase in interest rates. This ignited the stock market and the DJIA rose 154 points, or 1.96%, to a record close of 8,061.

15. Monitor political and economic events.
The Japanese prime minister, Ryutaro Hashimoto, was quoted as saying that Japan might sell U.S. Treasury bonds because of dollar currency fluctuations blamed on the United States. As soon as the news hit the wires on June 23, 1997, it created panic on Wall Street. Concern that any large-scale dumping of bonds would drive U.S. interest rates higher led to a sell-off that caused the DJIA to drop 192 points.

16. Know your rights as a shareholder.
Most companies are very responsive to their shareholders' concerns and requests. As a shareholder, you can call a company's investor relations department to seek information, get clarifications, determine business prospects, and so forth. If you don't get cooperation or satisfactory answers, insist on talking to the CFO or some other high-ranking officer of the company. In 1995, a company's investor relations director did not return the author's calls when he needed to determine why its stock was declining. This prompted him to call the president's office, identify himself as a shareholder, and complain. Within a few hours, he found a message from the investor relations director in his voice mail: "I will continue calling you until I contact you"!

17. Attend shareholders' meetings.
If a shareholders' annual meeting is held in your area, make it a point to attend. These meetings can be very useful for getting good solid information from the formal company presentation. The informal exchanges with the company's officers, and other shareholders, can also be quite productive.

Common Mistakes

1. Lack of patience.
Trying to make money quickly is a very common problem. Do not invest in the stock market if you do not have the temperament to wait patiently.

2. Lack of selection criteria.
Too many investors do not have any stock selection criteria. Many others use poor selection criteria that are not based on sound investing principles and methods.

3. Inadequate research.
Too many investors buy stocks without conducting any research at all. Other investors perform almost negligible, or inadequate, research and analysis prior to buying a stock.

4. Ignoring fundamentals.
This is another common mistake. Many investors ignore fundamentals while being overly influenced by news and inconsequential factors such as stock splits.

5. Buying on tips and rumors.
Buying on tips from neighbors, colleagues, and friends is very common. While there is nothing wrong in being open to receiving tips, you should perform adequate research and analysis prior to investing in a stock that has been recommended.

6. Buying a company just because its P/E ratio is low.
Investors using low P/E as their primary buying criterion have often been unpleasantly surprised if they did not investigate the reason(s) causing the low P/E ratio. In many cases, a company's low P/E is justified due to its poor business and earnings outlook. Consequently, such a stock may fail to appreciate in price for a long time or it may even decline.

7. Buying a stock because its price declined to a lower level.
This is one of the worst mistakes that many investors make. The fact that a company's stock is performing poorly does not mean that it cannot have an even worse performance in the future. Never buy a stock just because its price is relatively low compared to its recent, or historical, price. A stock once trading at $70 may look very attractive at $50. However, the market is littered with the wreckage of stocks that declined from such lofty heights to lows in the 20s and 30s. Base your buying decision on a company's future prospects (i.e., on where it is headed), rather than on where it has been.

8. Mistaken beliefs.
Many investors naively believe that they can tell when a stock has hit bottom. The only time you can be sure of this is when a stock's price goes to zero. Another wrong attitude is to buy a $3 stock and say, "I can only lose a maximum of $3." Using a different angle, a serious investor will view this as a 100% loss.

9. Focusing too much on buy price.
It is a mistake to remain too focused on a stock's current or historical price. Opportunities are missed due to waiting to buy at a fraction of a dollar below the current price. Such investors miss paying attention to the potential level that the stock can rise to, which may be considerably higher than its current price level.

10. Averaging in the wrong direction.
Many investors buy more shares of a stock they own only if it declines in price. They do not buy more shares if the stock appreciates over their buy

price. The view is that such a stock has already made its move and, therefore, should be bought only on a price decline—which never occurs in many cases. Such investors make a mistake by only focusing on where the stock has traded in the past. They do not analyze where the stock can rise to in the future, which might be far higher than its current appreciated price level. Do not hesitate to average up if a stock appears to have good potential to appreciate further. Average down only if you are very confident about the company's future prospects.

11. Buying a company because it is well known.
Many people buy a stock because they are familiar with the company and are aware of its reputation. This hinges on their belief that a good company cannot be a poor stock to own. Such investors, typically, do not base their decision on any investment criteria. Investors should realize that a good company is not necessarily a good stock.

12. Waiting for the perfect scenario.
Some investors delay buying because all the conditions are not right. They wait forever for the right combination of the market, individual stock, and economic conditions. It should be realized that the perfect scenario will never occur.

13. Delay in cutting losses.
Many investors are unable, or unwilling, to cut their losses. Their lack of action is based more on hope than on any logical reason for holding on to their stock. Once it is realized that a stock is a loser, sell it immediately.

14. Selling too early.
Selling winning stocks too early is a common mistake. Typically, investors selling early focus too much on the price appreciation that has taken place. They do not analyze the higher level to which a winner can potentially rise. Do not get caught up in the syndrome "If it has already reached this high, how can it go any higher?" You should let your profits run.

15. Inadequate monitoring.
For many investors, the concept of monitoring means checking daily stock prices. This is grossly inadequate. For each stock in your portfolio, regularly monitor developments and news because they have the potential

to affect the company's business prospects, fundamentals and, consequently, the stock price.

16. Making taxes an important factor.

Selling decisions should primarily be based on fundamental factors and the stock's price appreciation potential. Many investors do not sell, even though they realize that the stock has peaked, because of tax implications. Such investors do not include in their decision making the value of potential profits that could have been earned by investing in a superior stock. Taxes should never become the major consideration in determining whether to hold on to a stock.

17. Placing too much importance on dividends.

Some investors buy stock in a mediocre company only because it pays a dividend. They do not realize that while the company may be paying a dividend, it also has the potential to fall far more, in percentage terms, than the dividend being paid out.

18. Emotional involvement.

Many investors get emotionally involved with a stock that they own, which affects their judgment. You should try to remain very analytical and clinical, without any emotional attachment to the company.

19. Playing long shots.

There is no shortage of speculators in the stock market who try to hit only home runs. Realize that using a conservative approach is better than speculation. Keep in mind that long shots almost never pay off.

20. Trying to time the market.

Many investors try to get out of, or into, the market based on their analysis of the market being high or low. Usually they are wrong and end up buying at the peak or selling at the bottom. Avoid timing the market and remain heavily invested in the stock market most of the time.

Concluding Remarks

The stock market is the only investing choice that leads to wealth for the vast majority of investors. However, it is a place characterized by many forces and undercurrents, including emotions and economics, which pull it in different directions at different times. This can make it very confusing for the average investor. However, investors who are able to filter out the noise and identify important variables affecting the stock market are assured of success.

This chapter introduces investors to the commonly accepted principles, guidelines, and rules for investing in the stock market. The objective is to provide them to investors in a summarized and easy-to-understand format. The guidelines presented embody the basics of buying and selling, the dos and don'ts, performance evaluation, as well as the common mistakes investors are prone to make.

Chapter 20

Select Stocks the Fast Way:
The "Express" Method

Recognizing Investor Limitations

Common Problem: Unable to Conduct Research and Analysis

To be successful in the stock market, investors need to conduct in-depth company research and analysis. Initially, analysis is required when a company is being considered for procurement. After a stock has been bought, it needs to be analyzed periodically—in order to evaluate its performance and determine its future price appreciation potential. However, many investors are either unwilling or unable to put in the time and effort required to conduct in-depth company research and analysis. Such investors base their decisions on tips, hunches, emotions, and sentiments. Consequently, their flawed decision-making process, which lacks any methodology, exposes them to consistent and large losses. Also, they frequently end up selling their winners way too early because, typically, they have no idea about the price appreciation potential of the stocks that they are holding.

The "Express" Solution

The ideal scenario would be for each investor to be a serious researcher. However, the reality is quite different. The number of investors who are unable, or unwilling, to conduct detailed company research and analysis is extremely large and, without a doubt, will continue to remain so. These investors need a fast and easy method for analyzing companies. Therefore, in recognition of this need, this chapter has been written specifically for such investors. The objective is to give casual investors a tool with which they can:

■ Screen a stock that is being considered for procurement based on its potential to meet the profit objective of the investor.

■ Determine the price appreciation potential of a stock that:
Is being considered for procurement.
Has already been bought (as part of a continuous monitoring and evaluation process).

Analyzing Stocks Using the "Express" Method

The "Express" Method

The "Express" method is a procedure to quickly determine if a stock should be bought, based on its price appreciation potential and ability to meet the investor's desired return on investment (ROI). For using this method, only a few data items are required, which are readily available to all investors. The "Express" method is based on three variables:

1. Stock's current price
2. Projected earnings (EPS)
3. Projected earnings growth rate

Assumptions and Basis for Calculations

In the "Express" sample calculations which follow, the following assumptions have been made:

■ Investor's annual profit target (ROI): 18%
Aggressive investor will aim for a higher profit percentage.
Conservative investor will have lower profit expectations.

■ Calculations are based on the formula:

Forecasted price = Projected EPS × Projected earnings growth rate

A conservative investor will use a lower projected earnings growth rate figure in this equation. Typically, this will be lower, by a specific percentage amount, than the projected earnings growth rate. For example, if a conservative investor desires to use a growth rate that is equal to 80% of the projected growth rate, the following equation will be used:

Forecasted stock price = Projected EPS ×
(Projected earnings growth rate × 0.8)

Using the reduction factor of 80%, consequently makes the fore-casted stock price and potential profit proportionately lower. However, such an investor, being conservative, will also have lower profit expectations.

Express Procedure

Collecting the Data

The first step is to obtain an "earnings estimate report" from First Call, Zacks, or any another reliable source. An example of such a report is shown in Figure 20.1. Such reports can be obtained directly from the publishing source or through a broker. Now extract the following data from such a report:

- Current stock price ($).
- Mean earnings estimate ($/share) for the current and next fiscal year.
- Average long-term earnings growth rate predicted by contributing brokers (%).
- Five-year historical growth trend in annual EPS (%).
- Number of brokers included in the earnings estimate.
- Mean of buy/hold/sell recommendations of analysts following the company.

Calculations Procedure

This step involves forecasting how much the stock will rise by the end of the next fiscal year. This forecast is based on the company's projected earnings estimate and projected earnings growth rate. As an example, assume the following data for company XYZ:

- Consensus, or mean, earnings estimate for the next fiscal year (EPS) = $1.20
- Projected average earnings growth rate for the next five years (%) = 30
- Current stock price = $29.50

Based on this data, the stock price at the end of the next fiscal year is forecasted to be:

$$\$1.20 \times 30 = \$36$$

▰FIRST CALL®

Earnings Estimate Report

Orion Capital (OC)

Consensus Recommendation

Buy	Buy/Hold	Hold	Sell/Hold	Sell
1	2	3	4	5

▲

The mean recommendation of 5 brokers is 2.0 with a range of 2.0 to 2.0

Fiscal Year Earnings Estimates

Price as of 09/12/96 .... $50.88
Dividend Yield 2.0%
Beta 0.4

Fiscal Year End is December	Actual 1995	FY 1996	FY 1997
Mean Estimate	$4.22	$4.80	$5.44
Date of Last Revision		08/15/96	08/15/96
Date of Last Confirmation		09/03/96	09/03/96
Brokers Included In Consensus		7	7
Range of Broker Estimates		$4.55-$4.95	$4.95-$5.80
Median Estimate		$4.80	$5.50
Implied P/E ratio		10.6	9.4
Average long-term growth rate predicted by contributing brokers 11.0%			
Five year historical growth trend in annual EPS			4.8%

Current Quarter Earnings Estimates

The next quarterly earnings announcement is expected October 28, 1996.

Quarter End is September	Actual Q3 95	Q3 96
Mean Estimate	$0.94	$1.24
Brokers Included In Consensus		4
Range of Broker Estimates		$1.20-$1.30
Median Estimate		$1.23
Implied Growth Rate Over Comparable Quarter		31.9%

Revision Momentum

The total number of upward and downward estimate revisions received
from all contributing brokers during
the last 90 days.

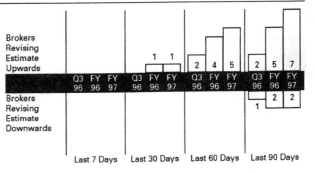

To Order Additional Reports Call: 1-800-544-4699

Figure 20.1 First Call Earnings Estimate Report Orion Capital

Source: First Call Corporation. Reprinted with permission.

Therefore, the stock is expected to appreciate:

$$\$36 - \$29.50 = \$6.50$$

To calculate the return on investment (ROI), divide the forecasted price rise by the current stock price:

$$\left(\frac{\$6.50}{\$29.50} \right) \times 100 = 22.03\%$$

This means that the ROI will be 22.03%—assuming that the stock price appreciates to the forecasted level. Now compare this ROI to the investor's desired rate of return, which is 18%. The positive difference is:

$$22.03\% - 18\% = 4.03\%$$

Obviously, this indicates that the stock has the potential to be a good investment because it exceeds the investor's annual profit target by more than 4%. If the desired profit target had been 25%, this stock would not be considered suitable for investment.

Using the "Express" Table: Proceeding Step-by-Step

In this section, the "Express" method is used to analyze three companies in order to determine if they are good buys. These companies are:

1. Orion Capital (OC)
2. Healthcare Compare (HCCC)
3. Mylan Laboratories (MYL)

The completed "Express" tables, one each for the three cases, are shown in Tables 20.1 through 20.3. For illustration purpose, the following reports have been attached:

■ Orion Capital's earnings estimate report from First Call (Figure 20.1)
■ Healthcare Compare's company report from Zacks (Figure 20.2)

The following sections contain the step-by-step instructions for completing an "Express" table. The example is based on the Orion Capital report. The data source is Figure 20.1. The completed "Express" table is shown in Table 20.1.

Table 20.1   "Express" Table for Orion Capital (OC), Report Month: September 1996

Market capitalization: $694 million
Annual sales: $874.3 million
Business: Insurance holding company specializing in specialty property and casuality insurance

Data from First Call's Earnings Estimate Report

A. Current stock price ($):		50.88
B. Mean earnings estimate ($/share) for the next fiscal year (12/97):		5.44
C. Average long-term growth rate predicted by contributing brokers (%):		11
D. Five-year historical growth trend in annual EPS (%):		4.8
E. Number of brokers included in earnings estimate:		7
F. Mean recommendation of brokers (buy = 1, hold = 3, sell = 5): Note: Zacks does not provide a numeric rating		2
G. Current dividend yield (%):		2

Calculations

H. Months remaining till the end of the next fiscal year (12/97):			16
I. Investor's annual profit target (%):			15
J. Estimated price at the end of next fiscal year ($):	B × C	5.44 × 11	59.84
K. Estimated price appreciation from current level ($): (forecasted – current stock price)	J – A	59.84 – 50.88	8.96
L. Estimated profit till the end of next fiscal year (%):	(K/A) × 100	(8.96/50.88) × 100	17.61
M. Annualized profit (%):	L × (12/H)	17.61 × (12/16)	13.21
N. Annualized profit including dividend (%):	M + G	13.21 + 2	15.21
O. ROI difference compared to investor's objective (%):	N – I	15.21 – 15	**0.21**
P. Implied P/E ratio:	A/B	50.88/5.44	9.35

Analysis

The stock passes the screening test. The projected rate of return exceeds the profit target by 0.21%. The "Express" analysis indicates that this stock is a good buy.

Analysis of the recent earnings history from the S&P report, not included here, showed that the company earned $2.77/share in the prior six months. This was higher than the $2.33/share earned in the comparable period of the previous year. This indicated that the earnings trend was positive—which provided more weight and confirmation to the "Express" analysis.

Table 20.2   **"Express" Table for Healthcare Compare (HCCC),
Report Month: January 1996**

Market capitalization: $1.4 billion
Annual sales: $214 million
Business: Provides a broad range of medical cost management services to
government, corporate, and other health care payers

Data from First Call's Earnings Estimate Report

A.	Current stock price ($):	43.63
B.	Mean earnings estimate ($/share) for the next fiscal year (12/96):	2.21
C.	Average long-term growth rate predicted by contributing brokers (%):	21
D.	Five-year historical growth trend in annual EPS (%):	48
E.	Number of brokers included in earnings estimate:	13
F.	Mean recommendation of brokers (buy = 1, hold = 3, sell = 5):	
	Note: Zacks does not provide a numeric rating	Buy
G.	Current dividend yield (%):	0

Calculations

H.	Months remaining till the end of the next fiscal year (12/96):			12
I.	Investor's annual profit target (%):			15
J.	Estimated price at the end of next fiscal year ($):	$B \times C$	2.21×21	46.41
K.	Estimated price appreciation from current level ($): (forecasted − current stock price)	$J - A$	$46.41 - 43.63$	2.78
L.	Estimated profit till the end of next fiscal year (%):	$(K/A) \times 100$	$(2.78/43.63) \times 100$	6.37
M.	Annualized profit (%):	$L \times (12/H)$	$6.37 \times (12/12)$	6.37
N.	Annualized profit including dividend (%):	$M + G$	$6.37 + 0$	6.37
O.	ROI difference compared to investor's objective (%):	$N - I$	$6.37 - 15$	**−8.63**
P.	Implied P/E ratio:	A/B	$43.63/2.21$	19.74

Analysis

The stock does not pass the screening test due to a negative ROI (−8.63%). The
projected annual profit is only 6.37%—which does not meet the investor's 15%
profit target.

Analysis of the recent earnings history from the S&P report, not included
here, showed that the company earned $1.00/share in the prior six months. This
was higher than the $0.79/share earned in the comparable period of the previous
year. Hence, this indicates that the earnings trend is positive. If the "Express"
analysis had been positive, the recent positive earnings history would have been
used as a confirmation signal to buy the stock.

Table 20.3   **"Express" Table for Mylan Laboratories (MYL), Report Month: September 1996**

Market capitalization: $2.0 billion
Annual sales: $393 million
Business: Manufacturer of generic pharmaceuticals

Data from First Call's Earnings Estimate Report

A.	Current stock price ($):		16.25
B.	Mean earnings estimate ($/share) for the next fiscal year (3/98):		1.07
C.	Average long-term growth rate predicted by contributing brokers (%):		18.3
D.	Five-year historical growth trend in annual EPS (%):		22.6
E.	Number of brokers included in earnings estimate:		9
F.	Mean recommendation of brokers (buy = 1, hold = 3, sell = 5):		
	Note: Zacks does not provide a numeric rating		2.3
G.	Current dividend yield (%):		1

Calculations

H.	Months remaining till the end of the next fiscal year (3/98):			19
I.	Investor's annual profit target (%):			17
J.	Estimated price at the end of next fiscal year ($):	B × C	1.07 × 18.3	19.58
K.	Estimated price appreciation from current level ($): (forecasted – current stock price)	J – A	19.58 – 16.25	3.33
L.	Estimated profit till the end of next fiscal year (%):	(K/A) × 100	(3.33/16.25) x 100	20.49
M.	Annualized profit (%):	L × (12/H)	20.49 × (12/19)	12.94
N.	Annualized profit including dividend (%):	M + G	12.94 + 1	13.94
O.	ROI difference compared to investor's objective (%):	N – I	13.94 – 17	−3.06
P.	Implied P/E ratio:	A/B	16.25/1.07	15.19

Analysis

The stock does not pass the screening test because it is slightly overvalued. The projected annual profit is 13.94%, which does not meet the investor's more aggressive profit target of 17%. However, the stock can pass the screening test if the stock price declines to $15.50 (from its current level of $16.25), or the investor lowers profit expectations to 14% (from 17%).

Analysis of the recent earnings history from the S&P report, not included here, showed that the company earned $0.86/share in the last year. This was lower than the $1.01/share earned in the prior year. This is an indication of a negative earnings trend. Consequently, this would warrant further investigation despite the neutral "Express" analysis.

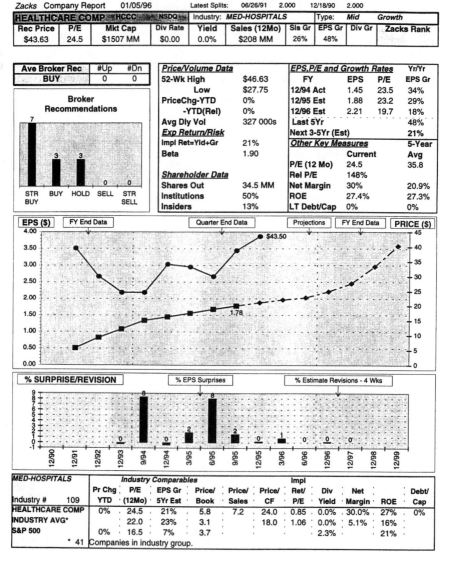

Figure 20.2   Zacks' Company Report Healthcare Compare (HCCC)

Source: Zacks Investment Research, Inc. Reprinted with permission.

Basic Procedure

1. Data is extracted from an earnings estimate report from First Call or another source.
2. Extracted data is plugged step-by-step into the "Express" table.
3. Five simple calculations are performed with a calculator.
4. The result of the test, a "pass" or a "fail," is determined in row "O" of the "Express" table.

Plugging Data into the "Express" Table

Rows A to C

Plug raw data extracted from Figure 20.1 (First Call report). Note that only four items (rows A, B, C, and G) are required for performing calculations in the "Calculations" section—which is the lower half of the "Express" table.

Rows D to F

Plug raw data extracted from Figure 20.1. These items are not used in any calculations. However, they are used to determine the importance to be given to the earnings estimate and to note whether the stock is being recommended, as a buy or sell, by professionals.

Row G

Enter the current dividend yield (%) from Figure 20.1.

Performing Calculations in the "Express" Table

Row H

Count and enter the months remaining till the end of the fiscal year. This is the period remaining, in months, from the earnings estimate report date till the end of the fiscal year for which the analysis is being done. In this case, 14 months remain from September 1996 (report month) to December 1997.

Row I

Enter the investor's desired profit target (15%).

Rows J to M

Perform calculations, for each table row, based on the formula shown:

- Row J: Values in rows "B" and "C" are multiplied to get the value for "estimated price at the end of next fiscal year."
- $J = B \times C = \$5.44 \times 11 = \$59.84$

Similar calculation procedure is followed for the next three rows (K to M):

- K = J − A = $59.84 − $50.88 = $8.96
- L = (K/A) × 100 = ($8.96/$50.88) × 100 = 17.61%
- M = L × (12/H) = 17.61 × (12/16) = 13.21%

Row N
Perform this calculation as follows:

- N = M + G
- N = 13.21 + 2 = 15.21%

Row O
Perform calculations based on the formula shown:

- O = N − I
- O = 15.21% − 15% = 0.21%

Pass/fail decision, to buy or not to buy the stock, is based on the calculated value in row "O"; if:

- "O" row value is zero, or greater, the stock passes the test and is indicated to be a buy.
- "O" row value is negative, the stock fails the procurement test.

Row P
Perform calculations based on the formula shown:

- P = A/B
- P = $50.88/($5.44/share) = 9.35

Compare the calculated value for the implied P/E ratio (row "P") to the long-term earnings growth rate (row "C"):

- Row "P" value should be less than the row "C" value. A lower number for this variable is preferred.
- For Orion Capital, the implied P/E is 9.35. This is less than its projected long-term earnings growth rate of 11% and, hence, is a positive.

Note: Some numbers in the "Express" tables, in the preceding pages, may not add up exactly due to rounding numbers.

Reasons for Rejecting a Stock Using this Rudimentary Analysis

For a stock being evaluated by the "Express" method, the following are good reasons for rejection:

■ Stock has one or more "sell" recommendations.
■ ROI is less than the investor's desired annual profit target (i.e., row "N" is less than row "I").
■ Implied P/E ratio is greater than, or almost equal to, the projected earnings growth rate; in such a case, the stock has already discounted future earnings and is overvalued (i.e., row "P" value is equal to or greater than the row "C" value).

Where possible, a company's financial health should be verified and used for confirmation of the "Express" analysis. For this purpose, a very valuable tool is the company's earnings. The "recent earnings" history indicates the earnings trend. It is preferred that this number be increasing. The higher the earnings increase, the better it is. If earnings for the past two quarters have been decreasing, and the investor is unaware of any factor that can make the earnings turn up in the next couple of quarters, the stock should be rejected.

A company's earnings can be easily obtained from a number of sources. Good sources are the company's annual and quarterly reports as well as various sources listed in Chapter 3.

Limitations of Using the "Express" Method

■ It is based solely on estimates, which can be inaccurate.
■ Recent bad/good news may not be reflected in the earnings estimates.
■ Earnings reports do not indicate the prospects for future business conditions, which can materially affect a company's fundamentals.
■ Analysts are hesitant in using a "sell" recommendation even when a company clearly deserves one; hence, analysts' recommendations can be suspect at times.

When using an earnings estimate report, it is very important to note the number of analysts following the company. If fewer than three analysts are following the company, the earnings estimates should not be considered reliable. In such a case, considerable risk is involved if even one analyst makes a mistake and issues an inaccurate earnings forecast. In general, confidence starts being generated only if four or more analysts are included in an earnings estimate.

Examples Using the "Express" Method

There are three conclusions that can be reached after a stock has been analyzed using the "Express" method. The three scenarios are:

▋ Stock is a buy
▋ Stock fails the procurement test
▋ Stock is a borderline case; may be bought if its price decreases

These three scenarios are shown in the following tables:

▋ Table 20.1: Stock is a buy—Orion Capital
▋ Table 20.2: Stock is not a buy—Healthcare Compare
▋ Table 20.3: Stock is a borderline case—Mylan Laboratories

Actual Performance

The three stocks analyzed in the "Express" tables performed as follows.

Orion Capital
A year later, Orion Capital had exceded the price appreciation expectation for its stock. On September 1, 1997, it was trading at 84^1/_4$, after taking into account a two-for-one stock split on July 8, 1997.

Healthcare Compare
In January 1997, the stock was continuing to trade at its year-earlier price level of January 1996, confirming the "Express" table analysis, which had indicated that the stock was overvalued. On January 11, 1997, the stock was trading at $43.

Mylan Laboratories
By May 1, 1997, Mylan had declined to 12^1/_8$ from $16.25, which was its price on the report date (September 1996). Assuming that the consensus earnings estimate had not changed by May 1, the stock would have been considered a good buy at that price level. The "Express" table analysis and recommendation, to buy on a price pullback, was borne out by the subsequent performance of the stock. After initially

declining, the stock rebounded strongly. By September 1, 1997, it had risen to $21^1/_{16}$—which compared favorably to the "Express" method's forecasted price of $19.58.

Concluding Remarks

The "Express" method is a screening procedure to quickly determine whether a stock should be bought—based on the stock's price appreciation potential and ability to meet an investor's desired return on investment. For using the "Express" method, only a few data items are required, which are readily available. The "Express" method is based on three variables: current stock price, projected earnings (EPS), and the projected earnings growth rate.

To be successful in the stock market, an investor must thoroughly research and analyze a company. Therefore, the "Express" method is no substitute for fundamental analysis. However, it can be a starting point for determining a company's price appreciation potential based on the collective information provided by well-informed stock analysts. It should be primarily used as a screening, rather than a selection, tool.

The "Express" method has the potential to be a very useful tool for investors who cannot afford the time and effort required to perform fundamental analysis. However, before using it, an investor should understand its limitations—especially the fact that it is based on analysts' estimates, which can be inaccurate. Also, at times, some analysts are not very diligent in reporting changes in their earnings estimates to reporting agencies like First Call and Zacks. Investors should realize that even if an "Express" analysis is positive, a negative earnings trend should always be considered a warning flag.

Appendixes

Getting the most from the Value Line Page

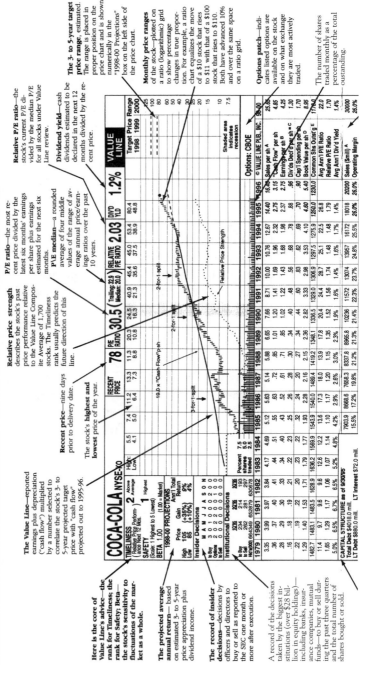

The Value Line—reported earnings plus depreciation ("cash flow") multiplied by a number selected to correlate the stock's 3- to 5-year projected target price with "cash flow" projected out to 1995-96.

Recent price—nine days prior to delivery date.

The stock's highest and lowest price of the year.

Relative price strength describes the stock's past price performance relative to the Value Line Composite Average of 1,700 stocks. The Timeliness rank usually predicts the future direction of this line.

P/E ratio—the most recent price divided by the latest six months' earnings per share plus earnings estimated for the next six months.

P/E median—a rounded average of four middle values of the range of average annual price/earnings ratios over the past 10 years.

Relative P/E ratio—the stock's current P/E divided by the median P/E for all stocks under Value Line review.

Dividend yield—cash dividends estimated to be declared in the next 12 months divided by the recent price.

The 3- to 5-year target price range. The range is placed in proper position on the price chart and is shown numerically in the "1998-00 Projections" box on the left side of the price chart.

Monthly price ranges of the stock—plotted on a ratio (logarithmic) grid to show percentage changes in true proportion. For example, a ratio chart equalizes the move of a $10 stock that rises to $11 with that of a $100 stock that rises to $110. Both have advanced 10% and over the same space on a ratio grid.

Options patch—indicates listed options are available on the stock and on what exchange they are most actively traded.

The number of shares traded monthly as a percentage of the total outstanding.

Here is the core of Value Line's advice—the rank for Timeliness; the rank for Safety; Beta—the stock's sensitivity to fluctuations of the market as a whole.

The projected average annual return— based on estimated 3- to 5-year price appreciation plus dividend income.

The record of insider decisions—decisions by officers and directors to buy or sell as reported to the SEC one month or more after execution.

A record of the decisions taken by the biggest institutions (over $28 billion in equity holdings)—including banks, insurance companies, mutual funds—to buy or sell during the past three quarters and the total number of shares bought or sold.

The capital structure as of recent date showing the percentage of capital in long-term debt (14%) and in common stock (86%); the number of times that total interest charges were earned (20 as of February 1996).

Current position—current assets and current liabilities, the components of working capital.

Annual rates of change (on a per-share basis). Actual past, estimated future.

Quarterly earnings are shown on a per-share basis (estimates in bold type), quarterly sales on a gross basis.

Quarterly dividends paid are actual payments. The total of dividends paid in four quarters may not equal the figure shown in the annual series on dividends declared. (Sometimes a dividend declared at the end of the year will be paid in the first quarter of the following year).

Footnotes explain a number of things, such as the way earnings are reported, wether "fully diluted", on a "primary" basis, or on an "average shares outstanding" basis.

(Total interest coverage: 20x) (14% of Cap'l)

Pension Liability None

Pfd Stock None

Common Stock 1,255,185,525 shs. (86% of Cap'l)

178.1	166.8	153.5	169.8	183.8	243.9	261.4	321.9	360.0	411.0	*460*	*500*	**Depreciation ($mill)**	*650*
677.6	800.3	916.1	1044.7	1192.8	1381.9	1618.0	1883.8	2188.0	2554.0	2985	*3400*	**Net Profit ($mill)**	*5020*
38.0%	39.2%	35.0%	34.0%	32.4%	31.4%	32.1%	31.4%	31.3%	31.5%	31.0%	*31.5%*	**Income Tax Rate**	*31.5%*
8.6%	9.2%	12.0%	12.5%	13.3%	13.5%	14.0%	14.4%	15.7%	15.8%	16.6%	*16.9%*	**Net Profit Margin**	*16.7%*
966.5	984.6	17.7	376.5	d54.4	d153.7	26.6	d1056	d737.0	d972.0	*d1075*	*d1000*	**Working Cap'l ($mill)**	*d1645*
889.2	1011.2	803.4	761.1	548.7	535.9	985.3	1120.1	1428.0	1426.0	*1475*	*1525*	**Long-Term Debt ($mill)**	*1675*
2979.1	3515.0	3223.8	3345.3	3485.5	3849.2	4425.8	3888.4	4584.0	5235.0	*5770*	*6645*	**Net Worth ($mill)**	*10500*
18.7%	18.8%	23.8%	28.2%	30.2%	32.2%	30.6%	38.4%	37.7%	39.3%	*42.5%*	*43.0%*	**% Earned Total Cap'l**	*42.0%*
22.7%	22.8%	28.4%	31.2%	34.2%	35.9%	36.6%	48.4%	47.7%	48.8%	*52.0%*	*51.5%*	**% Earned Net Worth**	*48.0%*
9.7%	11.3%	15.3%	19.8%	22.0%	22.0%	22.1%	29.5%	28.5%	29.6%	*32.5%*	*33.5%*	**% Retained to Comm Eq**	*33.5%*
57%	50%	46%	42%	41%	40%	40%	39%	40%	39%	*37%*	*35%*	**% All Div'ds to Net Prof**	*30%*

CURRENT POSITION ($MILL.)	1993	1994	9/30/95
Cash Assets	1078	1531	1925
Receivables	1210	1470	1648
Inventory (Avg Cst)	1049	1047	1203
Other	1097	1157	1336
Current Assets	4434	5205	6112
Accts Payable	2217	2564	3075
Debt Due	1672	2083	3138
Other	1282	1530	1602
Current Liab.	5171	6177	7815

ANNUAL RATES of change (per sh)	Past 10 Yrs.	Past 5 Yrs.	Est'd '92-'94 to '98-'00
Sales	10.0%	13.5%	*15.0%*
"Cash Flow"	16.0%	18.5%	*16.5%*
Earnings	17.0%	18.5%	*16.5%*
Dividends	12.0%	17.0%	*11.5%*
Book Value	7.5%	9.5%	*17.0%*

Cal-endar	QUARTERLY SALES ($ mill.) Mar.31	Jun.30	Sep.30	Dec.31	Full Year
1992	2771	3550	3507	3246	13074
1993	3056	3899	3629	3373	13957
1994	3352	4342	4461	4017	16172
1995	3854	4936	4895	4333	18018
1996	*4320*	*5530*	*5490*	*4860*	*20200*

Cal-endar	EARNINGS PER SHARE B Mar.31	Jun.30	Sep.30	Dec.31	Full Year
1992	.29	.43	.41	.30	1.43
1993	.35	.52	.45	.36	1.68
1994	.40	.59	.55	.44	1.98
1995	.50	.71	.64	.52	2.37
1996	*.55*	*.85*	*.75*	*.60*	*2.75*

Cal-endar	QUARTERLY DIVIDENDS PAID C ■ Mar.31	Jun.30	Sep.30	Dec.31	Full Year
1992	--	.14	.14	.28	.56
1993	--	.17	.17	.34	.68
1994	--	.195	.195	.39	.78
1995	--	.22	.22	.44	.88
1991	--				

BUSINESS: The Coca-Cola Company is the world's largest soft drink company. Distributes major brands (*Coca-Cola, Sprite, Fanta, TAB*, etc.) through bottlers throughout the world. Foreign (non-U.S.) operations accounted for 67% of net sales and 79% of profits in 1994. Food division, world's largest distributor of juice products (*Minute Maid, Five Alive, Hi-C*, etc.). Coca-Cola Enterprises, 44%-owned soft drink bottler. Advertising costs, 8.1% of sales. Has approximately 33,000 employees; 195,000 stockholders. Berkshire Hathaway owns 7.9% of stock (1995 Proxy). 1994 dep. rate: 6.7%. Estimated plant age: 5 years. Chairman and Chief Executive Officer: Roberto C. Goizueta. Incorporated: Delaware. Address: One Coca-Cola Plaza, Atlanta, Georgia 30313. Tel.: 404-676-2121.

As expected, Coca-Cola had another excellent year in 1995, with sales up 11%, net income up 17%, and earnings per share up 20%. While business was strong in many markets, the U.S., with a gain of 8% in unit case volume in the fourth quarter, was particularly noteworthy. Higher non-operating income, a lower tax rate, and a smaller number of shares outstanding all contributed to the rise in share net to $2.37.

This year and 1997 should again be good ones. Global unit case volume was up 8% in 1995, and we think gains of at least that amount are likely going forward. The percentage gains in China, India, and Eastern Europe have continued to be large, although from a relatively small base, and it is reasonable to think strong growth will continue for a number of years. The current year should get some benefit from Coke's sponsorship of the Olympics to be held in its home town of Atlanta. (The company has also signed up to be a sponsor of the games in 1998 and 2000.) And new packaging will continue to drive the business around the world; new contour *Coca-Cola* bottles in 16-oz. glass and 20-oz. plastic have proven to be extremely popular. New products such as *Powerade* and *Minute Maid Juices To Go* should contribute higher sales, and we expect the company to put some of its marketing muscle behind *Barq's* root beer, which it acquired last year. Our current estimate is that Coke will earn $2.75 a share this year. (*Directors have approved a 2-for-1 stock split; shareholders will vote on it at the annual meeting in April.*)

Prospects out to 1998-2000 also look bright. International opportunities seem almost limitless as Coke continues to spend large amounts to expand its infrastructure around the world. Annual earnings gains in the 15% to 20% range seem to be very achievable.

Coke shares continue to carry an above-average Timeliness rank. While we do have some concern that the price/earnings ratio is high, there is no question that Coke's earnings prospects are about as well defined as is possible. A continuing stock repurchase plan will also provide support for the stock price and help boost share earnings.

Stephen Sanborn, CFA February 16, 1996

(A) Includes Columbia Pictures: 7/82-12/86. (B) Based on average shares outstanding. yext earnings report due late Apr. Excludes special gains: '81, 4¢; '86, 17¢; disc. op. gains (loss): '83, (1¢); '85, 5¢; '89, 3¢; nonrec. gain (loss): '89, 73¢; '92, (17¢). (C) Next div'd meeting about Apr. 17. Goes ex about June 12. Div'd payment dates: April 1, July 1, Oct. 1, Dec. 15. ■Div'd reinvestment plan available. (D) Incl. intangibles. In '94: $660.0 mill., 52¢/sh. (E) In millions, adjusted for stock splits.

Company's Financial Strength	A++
Stock's Price Stability	90
Price Growth Persistence	95
Earnings Predictability	100

Factual material is obtained from sources believed to be reliable, but the publisher is not responsible for any errors or omissions contained herein. For the confidential use of subscribers. Reprinting, copying, and distribution by permission only. Copyright 1996 by Value Line Publishing, Inc. ® Reg. TM—Value Line, Inc.

To subscribe call 1-800-833-0046.

Statistical milestones that reveal significant long-term trends. The statistics are presented in two ways: 1) the upper series records results on a per-share basis; 2) the lower records results on a gross basis. Note that the statistics for the current year are estimated, as are the figures for the average of the years 1998-2000. The estimate would be revised, if necessary, should future evidence require. The weekly *Summary & Index* would promptly call attention to such revisions.

A condensed summary of the **business**, significant shareholders, and the company's address and telephone number.

A 400-word **report on recent developments and prospects**—issued once every three months on a preset schedule.

The date of delivery to the subscribers. The survey is mailed on a schedule that aims for delivery to every subscriber on Friday afternoon.

Value Line's Indexes of **Financial Strength, Price Stability, Price Growth Persistence, and Earnings Predictability.**

Appendix A Value Line Sample Report

Source: Copyright © 1997 by Value Line Publishing, Inc. Reproduced by permission. All rights reserved.

FIRST CALL®

Earnings Estimate Report

Oracle Corp (ORCL)

Consensus Recommendation

Buy	Buy/Hold	Hold	Sell/Hold	Sell
1	2	3	4	5

The mean recommendation of 20 brokers is 1.4 with a range of 3.0 to 1.0

Fiscal Year Earnings Estimates

Price as of 09/09/96 .... $37.50
Dividend Yield .... N/A
Beta 0.8

	Actual 1996	FY 1997	FY 1998
Fiscal Year End is May			
Mean Estimate	$0.95	$1.28	$1.69
Date of Last Revision		08/30/96	09/05/96
Date of Last Confirmation		09/09/96	09/09/96
Brokers Included In Consensus		25	20
Range of Broker Estimates		$1.22-$1.34	$1.55-$1.79
Median Estimate		$1.28	$1.70
Implied P/E ratio		29.3	22.2
Average long-term growth rate predicted by contributing brokers 29.6%			
Five year historical growth trend in annual EPS			62.8%

Current Quarter Earnings Estimates

The next quarterly earnings announcement is expected September 12, 1996.

	Actual Q1 96	Q1 97
Quarter End is August		
Mean Estimate	$0.13	$0.17
Brokers Included In Consensus		25
Range of Broker Estimates		$0.16-$0.20
Median Estimate		$0.17
Implied Growth Rate Over Comparable Quarter		30.8%

Revision Momentum

The total number of upward and downward estimate revisions received from all contributing brokers during the last 90 days.

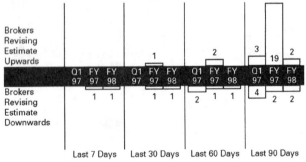

To Order Additional Reports Call: 1-800-544-4699

Appendix B **First Call Earnings Estimate Report for Oracle Corporation**
Source: First Call Corporation. Reproduced by permission. All rights reserved.

370

Oracle Systems   **4876T**

Nasdaq Symbol **ORCL**

In S&P 500

07-SEP-96   **Industry:** Data Processing   **Summary:** Oracle supplies computer software products used for database management, applications development and decision support, as well as end-user and other applications.

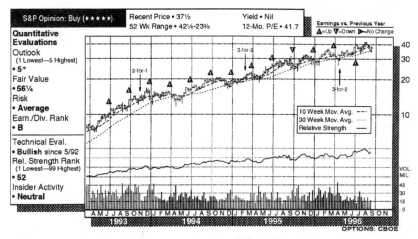

S&P Opinion: Buy (★★★★★)	Recent Price • 37½	Yield • Nil
	52 Wk Range • 42⅛-23⅜	12-Mo. P/E • 41.7

Quantitative Evaluations

Outlook (1 Lowest—5 Highest)
• **5**

Fair Value
• **56¼**

Risk
• **Average**

Earn./Div. Rank
• **B**

Technical Eval.
• **Bullish** since 5/92

Rel. Strength Rank (1 Lowest—99 Highest)
• **52**

Insider Activity
• **Neutral**

OPTIONS: CBOE

Overview - 25-JUN-96

Revenues should increase at a 35% to 40% rate in FY 97 (May), reflecting strong demand for the company's relational database management system, aided by new releases of application products, accelerated growth in software develpment tools, driven by strength in the Windows market, continuing robust demand for services, and continued expansion of worldwide economies. Products for the UNIX and desktop environments (which account for about 90% of total revenues) should continue to grow rapidly, and proprietary systems growth is reaccelerating, led by strength in products tailored for Digital Equipment computers. Net profit margins are expected to be maintained, as volume efficiencies and cost controls are offset by a higher tax rate. Earnings should benefit from the greater revenues, steady margins and absence of the $0.05 a share nonrecurring charge recorded in the FY 96 first quarter.

Valuation - 25-JUN-96

Earnings should rise over 35% in FY 97. The database software segment is growing rapidly, as organizations cope with managing and utilizing the massive data stored on their computer systems. ORCL's leadership position bodes well for future results; the core database server business is strong, applications software revenues should continue to grow rapidly, the database tools business should increase, and there is a continuing need for additional services. The shares, which reached new highs in June, were recently trading at a P/E of about 85% of the projected growth rate over the next several years, based on FY 97 projections. The strong earnings growth that we expect should help the stock outperform the market in coming months.

Key Stock Statistics

S&P EPS Est. 1997	1.25	Tang. Bk. Value/Share	1.87
P/E on S&P Est. 1997	30.0	Beta	0.83
Dividend Rate/Share	Nil	Shareholders	4,000
Shs. outstg. (M)	654.2	Market cap. (B)	$ 24.5
Avg. daily vol. (M)	3.896	Inst. holdings	54%

Value of $10,000 invested 5 years ago: $ 214,258

Fiscal Year Ending May 31

	1996	1995	1994	1993	1992	1991
Revenues (Million $)						
1Q	771.8	556.5	398.0	307.0	245.0	215.0
2Q	967.2	670.3	452.2	353.0	284.0	257.0
3Q	1,020	722.3	482.8	370.0	290.0	269.0
4Q	1,464	1,018	668.1	472.6	235.0	282.0
Yr.	4,223	2,967	2,001	1,503	1,178	1,028

	1996	1995	1994	1993	1992	1991
Earnings Per Share ($)						
1Q	0.08	0.09	0.06	0.02	0.00	-0.05
2Q	0.21	0.14	0.09	0.05	0.02	0.00
3Q	0.22	0.16	0.11	0.04	0.03	0.02
4Q	0.40	0.27	0.17	0.10	0.04	0.01
Yr.	0.90	0.67	0.43	0.21	0.10	-0.02

Next earnings report expected: mid September

Dividend Data

Amt. of Div. $	Date Decl.	Ex-Div. Date	Stock of Record	Payment Date
3-for-2	Mar. 14	Apr. 17	Apr. 02	Apr. 16 '96

Appendix C   S&P Stock Report for Oracle Corporation

Source: Standard & Poor's. Reprinted by permission of Standard & Poor's, one of the McGraw-Hill Companies.

STANDARD
&POOR'S
STOCK REPORTS

Oracle Systems Corporation

4876T
07-SEP-96

Business Summary - 03-JUL-96

Oracle Systems Corporation develops, markets and supports computer software products used for database management, network communications, applications development and end-user applications. Its principal product is the ORACLE relational database management system (DBMS). The company offers its products, along with consulting, education, support and systems integration services, worldwide.

Database management systems software permits multiple users and applications to access data concurrently while protecting the data against user and program errors and against computer and network failures. Database management systems are used to support the data access and data management requirements of transaction processing and decision support systems. The ORACLE relational DBMS runs on a broad range of massively parallel, clustered, symmetrical multiprocessing, mainframes, minicomputers, workstations and personal computers using the industry standard SQL language.

A variety of applications development products, sold as add-ons to the ORACLE relational DBMS, increase programmer productivity and allow non-programmers to design, develop and maintain their own programs. Access tools enable end users and decision support analysts to perform rapid querying, reporting and analysis of stored data.

The company also offers an integrated family of end-user financial applications, including general ledger, purchasing, payables, assets, receivables and revenue accounting programs, as well as manufacturing and human resource applications. These application products use the ORACLE relational DBMS and related development and decision support tools.

ORCL offers consulting, education and systems integration services to assist customers in the design and development of applications based on company products.

Important Developments

Jun. '96—Total revenues in the fourth quarter of FY 96 (May) grew 44%, year to year; core database license revenues rose 49%, applications rose 73%, tools were up 13% and services advanced 44%.
Sep. '95—In the first quarter of FY 96, ORCL recorded a $51 million ($0.05 a share) charge to reflect costs associated with the acquisition of the online analytical processing business of Information Resources.

Capitalization

Long Term Debt: $897,000 (5/96).

Per Share Data ($) (Year Ended May 31)	1996	1995	1994	1993	1992	1991	1990	1989	1988	1987
Tangible Bk. Val.	2.85	1.87	1.15	0.82	0.69	0.56	0.66	0.40	0.25	0.16
Cash Flow	1.23	0.89	0.52	0.30	0.18	0.07	0.25	0.17	0.09	0.04
Earnings	0.90	0.67	0.43	0.22	0.10	-0.02	0.19	0.14	0.07	0.03
Dividends	Nil	Nil	Nil	Nil	Nil	Nil	Nil	Nil	Nil	Nil
Payout Ratio	Nil	Nil	Nil	Nil	Nil	Nil	Nil	Nil	Nil	Nil
Cal. Yrs.	1995	1994	1993	1992	1991	1990	1989	1988	1987	1986
Prices - High	32½	20⅝	16¾	6⅜	3¾	6¼	5¾	2½	2⅛	13/16
- Low	17¾	11⅝	6	2⅝	1¼	1 1/16	2 1/16	1¼	9/16	⅜
P/E Ratio - High	36	31	39	30	39	NM	30	18	29	29
- Low	20	17	14	12	13	NM	11	9	8	13
Income Statement Analysis (Million $)										
Revs.	4,223	2,967	2,001	1,503	1,178	1,028	971	584	282	131
Oper. Inc.	1,124	797	485	297	165	81.0	226	143	75.0	33.0
Depr.	220	148	65.2	56.2	50.9	54.5	35.9	19.7	10.6	4.6
Int. Exp.	6.6	7.0	6.9	9.0	18.6	24.0	12.1	4.3	1.5	1.2
Pretax Inc.	920	659	423	218	96.0	-13.0	173	120	65.0	28.0
Eff. Tax Rate	34%	33%	33%	35%	36%	NM	32%	32%	34%	44%
Net Inc.	603	442	284	142	62.0	-12.0	117	82.0	43.0	16.0
Balance Sheet & Other Fin. Data (Million $)										
Cash	841	586	465	358	177	101	50.0	49.0	49.0	38.0
Curr. Assets	2,284	1,617	1,076	842	641	586	569	337	192	109
Total Assets	3,357	2,425	1,595	1,184	956	858	787	460	250	144
Curr. Liab.	1,455	1,055	682	551	406	479	284	178	102	48.0
LT Debt	0.9	81.7	82.8	86.4	95.9	18.0	89.1	33.5	5.4	9.0
Common Eqty.	1,870	1,211	741	528	435	345	388	231	135	83.0
Total Cap.	1,880	1,321	862	623	541	369	499	276	147	95.0
Cap. Exp.	308	262	251	41.3	46.6	60.7	89.3	68.4	31.0	16.9
Cash Flow	823	589	349	198	112	42.0	153	101	54.0	20.0
Curr. Ratio	1.6	1.5	1.6	1.5	1.6	1.2	2.0	1.9	1.9	2.3
% LT Debt of Cap.	1.0	6.2	9.6	13.9	17.7	4.9	17.9	12.1	3.6	9.5
% Net Inc.of Revs.	14.3	14.9	14.2	9.4	5.2	NM	12.1	14.0	15.2	11.9
% Ret. on Assets	20.9	22.0	20.4	13.2	6.7	NM	18.6	22.6	21.5	15.1
% Ret. on Equity	39.1	45.2	44.6	29.2	15.6	NM	37.5	43.9	38.8	27.4

Data as orig. reptd.; bef. results of disc. opers. and/or spec. items. Per share data adj. for stk. divs. as of ex-div. date. E-Estimated. NA-Not Available. NM-Not Meaningful. NR-Not Ranked.

Office—500 Oracle Parkway, Redwood Shores, CA 94065. **Reincorporated**—in Delaware in 1987. **Tel**—(415) 506-7000. **E-mail**—investor@oracle.com **Website**—http://www.oracle.com **Chrmn**—J. A. Abrahamson. **Pres & CEO**—L. J. Ellison. **EVP & CFO**—J. O. Henley. **SVP & Secy**—R. L. Ocampo, Jr. **Investor Contact**—Catherine Buan. **Dirs**—J. A. Abrahamson, M. J. Boskin, J. Costello, L. J. Ellison, J. Kemp, D. L. Lucas, R. P. McKenna, D. W. Yocam. **Transfer Agent & Registrar**—Harris Trust & Savings Bank, Chicago. **Empl**— 14,830. **S&P Analyst:** Peter C. Wood, CFA

Appendix C Continued

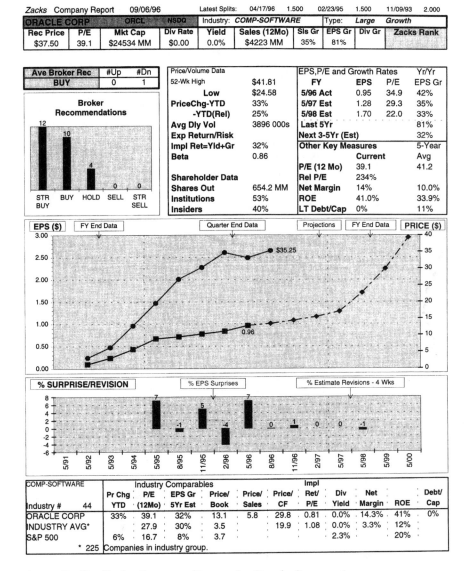

Zacks Company Report   09/06/96   Latest Splits: 04/17/96 1.500   02/23/95 1.500   11/09/93 2.000

ORACLE CORP   ORCL   NSDQ   Industry: *COMP-SOFTWARE*   Type: *Large* *Growth*

Rec Price	P/E	Mkt Cap	Div Rate	Yield	Sales (12Mo)	Sls Gr	EPS Gr	Div Gr	Zacks Rank
$37.50	39.1	$24534 MM	$0.00	0.0%	$4223 MM	35%	81%		

Ave Broker Rec	#Up	#Dn
BUY	0	1

Broker Recommendations

12
10
4
0   0

STR BUY   BUY   HOLD   SELL   STR SELL

Price/Volume Data	
52-Wk High	$41.81
Low	$24.58
PriceChg-YTD	33%
-YTD(Rel)	25%
Avg Dly Vol	3896 000s
Exp Return/Risk	
Impl Ret=Yld+Gr	32%
Beta	0.86
Shareholder Data	
Shares Out	654.2 MM
Institutions	53%
Insiders	40%

EPS,P/E and Growth Rates			Yr/Yr
FY	EPS	P/E	EPS Gr
5/96 Act	0.95	34.9	42%
5/97 Est	1.28	29.3	35%
5/98 Est	1.70	22.0	33%
Last 5Yr			81%
Next 3-5Yr (Est)			32%
Other Key Measures			5-Year
		Current	Avg
P/E (12 Mo)		39.1	41.2
Rel P/E		234%	
Net Margin		14%	10.0%
ROE		41.0%	33.9%
LT Debt/Cap		0%	11%

EPS ($) FY End Data | Quarter End Data | Projections | FY End Data | **PRICE ($)**

$35.25

0.96

% SURPRISE/REVISION | % EPS Surprises | % Estimate Revisions - 4 Wks

7   -1   5   -4   7   0   1   0   0   -1

5/91 5/92 5/93 5/94 5/95 8/95 11/95 2/96 5/96 8/96 11/96 2/97 5/97 5/98 5/99 5/00

COMP-SOFTWARE		Industry Comparables					Impl				
	Pr Chg	P/E	EPS Gr	Price/	Price/	Price/	Ret/	Div	Net		Debt/
Industry # 44	YTD	(12Mo)	5Yr Est	Book	Sales	CF	P/E	Yield	Margin	ROE	Cap
ORACLE CORP	33%	39.1	32%	13.1	5.8	29.8	0.81	0.0%	14.3%	41%	0%
INDUSTRY AVG*		27.9	30%	3.5		19.9	1.08	0.0%	3.3%	12%	
S&P 500	6%	16.7	8%	3.7				2.3%		20%	
* 225 Companies in industry group.											

Appendix D   **Zacks Company Report for Oracle Corporation**

Appendix E Range of P/E Ratios and Corresponding Growth Rates

Company	Symbol	Industry	P/E ratio	% annual earnings growth
Altera	ALTR	Semiconductors	40.05	0.5
Amgen	AMGN	Major drugs	34.40	17.8
Celestial Seas	CTEA	Food processing	36.12	30.8
Cerner Corp.	CERN	Computer networks	50.47	52.9
Coca-Cola Bottling	COKE	Beverages (nonalcoholic)	36.86	24.6
Dollar Tree	DLTR	Retail (department & discount)	47.49	36.8
Federal Express	FDX	Air courier	25.56	0.2
Gateway 2000	GTW	Computer hardware	26.12	65.7
Gymboree	GYMB	Retail (apparel)	10.99	−87.7
Healthcare Services	HCSG	Business services	12.33	20.6
Intel Corp.	INTC	Semiconductors	36.48	−12.6
Lindsay Mfg.	LNN	Const. & agricultural machinery	10.66	−38.8
OfficeMax	OMX	Retail (speciality)	15.91	11.1
Orion Capital	OC	Insurance (property & casualty)	9.37	−11.7
Palm Harbor Homes	PHHM	Construction services	16.25	23.5
Papa Johns Intl.	PZZA	Restaurants	37.71	37.4
Pool Energy Svcs.	PESC	Oil well services & equipment	7.67	−13.1
Precision Cast	PCP	Aerospace & defense	9.79	19.0
Remedy Corp.	RMDY	Software & programming	19.63	−21.4
Starbucks Corp.	SBUX	Food processing	74.83	36.8
Sun Microsystems	SUNW	Computer hardware	43.91	21.0
Swift Transportation	SWFT	Trucking	23.76	26.3
Tuboscope	TBI	Oil well services & equipment	7.07	−11.3
USBancorp Inc.	UBAN	Regional banks	12.74	−0.2

DJIA Companies

Company	Symbol	Industry	P/E ratio	% annual earnings growth
AT&T	T	Communication services	21.52	28.5
Caterpillar	CAT	Const. & agricultural machinery	10.27	−2.9
Philip Morris	MO	Tobacco	20.42	8.5
American Express	AXP	Consumer financial services	22.78	13.9
Alcoa	AA	Metal mining	15.19	9.2
Exxon	XON	Oil and gas—integrated	24.46	−19.0
AlliedSignal	ALD	Auto and truck parts	19.69	15.5
General Electric	GE	Conglomerates	37.78	13.8
McDonald's	MCD	Restaurants	33.54	9.4
Merck	MRK	Major drugs	35.46	15.0

Source: Zacks Investment Research and Yahoo! Inc. (Yahoo!'s web site, January 1, 1999). Reproduced with permission. Yahoo! and the Yahoo! logo are trademarks of Yahoo! Inc.

AOL Personal Finance
Investment Research

Oracle Corporation
NASD : ORCL
Sector : Technology
Industry: Software & Programming

Market Guide

The Benchmark for Quality Financial Information

Comparison

RATIO COMPARISON				
Valuation Ratios	**Company**	**Industry**	**Sector**	**S&P 500**
P/E Ratio (TTM)	35.74*	59.23	49.51	34.75
P/E High - Last 5 Yrs.	50.86	69.60	51.65	40.37
P/E Low - Last 5 Yrs.	24.40	23.04	16.04	14.31
Beta	1.34	1.27	1.32	1.00
Price to Sales (TTM)	4.88*	17.00	8.72	4.56
Price to Book (MRQ)	12.40	15.19	13.25	8.40
Price to Tangible Book (MRQ)	12.81	15.98	13.77	11.75
Price to Cash Flow (TTM)	29.23	44.08	34.40	22.74
Price to Free Cash Flow (TTM)	28.24	48.23	53.60	47.72
% Owned Institutions	48.58	46.30	48.78	63.12

Dividends	**Company**	**Industry**	**Sector**	**S&P 500**
Dividend Yield	0.00	0.31	0.62	1.59
Dividend Yield - 5 Year Avg.	0.00	0.02	0.39	2.03
Dividend 5 Year Growth Rate	NM	10.68	9.31	9.85
Payout Ratio (TTM)	0.00	0.59	6.14	32.75

Growth Rates(%)	**Company**	**Industry**	**Sector**	**S&P 500**
Sales (MRQ) vs Qtr. 1 Yr. Ago	27.40*	31.59	23.04	10.87
Sales (TTM) vs TTM 1 Yr. Ago	26.39*	31.54	21.81	10.89
Sales - 5 Yr. Growth Rate	36.59	35.89	32.77	14.80
EPS (MRQ) vs Qtr. 1 Yr. Ago	50.54*	111.88	36.81	14.38
EPS (TTM) vs TTM 1 Yr. Ago	52.57*	51.34	24.43	11.49
EPS - 5 Yr. Growth Rate	41.60	35.46	36.92	19.44
Capital Spending - 5 Yr. Growth Rate	38.48	30.34	32.66	13.31

Financial Strength	**Company**	**Industry**	**Sector**	**S&P 500**
Quick Ratio (MRQ)	1.64	2.66	1.97	0.94
Current Ratio (MRQ)	1.85	2.80	2.43	1.45
LT Debt to Equity (MRQ)	0.10	0.08	0.25	0.68
Total Debt to Equity (MRQ)	0.10	0.09	0.37	1.03
Interest Coverage (TTM)	NM	12.87	10.77	8.91

Profitability Ratios (%)	**Company**	**Industry**	**Sector**	**S&P 500**
Gross Margin (TTM)	66.98	83.24	52.42	49.34
Gross Margin - 5 Yr. Avg.	72.75	81.18	52.26	48.98
EBITD Margin (TTM)	24.08	37.09	21.71	22.46

Appendix F   Market Guide's Ratio Comparison Report
Source: AOL and Market Guide. Reprinted with permission.

EBITD - 5 Yr. Avg.	25.72	32.96	22.21	22.33
Operating Margin (TTM)	19.58	32.21	16.56	17.52
Operating Margin - 5 Yr. Avg.	20.79	26.93	16.38	17.94
Pre-Tax Margin (TTM)	20.45	12.65	12.48	14.78
Pre-Tax Margin - 5 Yr. Avg.	21.26	29.55	17.33	15.89
Net Profit Margin (TTM)	13.65*	22.39	11.31	10.86
Net Profit Margin - 5 Yr. Avg.	13.84	19.37	11.11	10.29
Effective Tax Rate (TTM)	35.00	35.71	33.41	34.38
Effective Tax Rate - 5 Yr. Avg.	35.02	35.38	35.64	35.88

Management Effectiveness (%)	Company	Industry	Sector	S&P 500
Return On Assets (TTM)	20.68*	18.49	10.98	8.29
Return Of Assets - 5 Yr. Avg.	19.89	18.92	12.67	8.33
Return On Investment (TTM)	34.03*	26.16	16.16	13.21
Return Of Investment - 5 Yr. Avg.	34.99	24.88	17.43	13.17
Return On Equity (TTM)	38.53*	28.64	21.80	22.75
Return Of Equity - 5 Yr. Avg.	39.68	28.84	21.28	21.77

Efficiency	Company	Industry	Sector	S&P 500
Revenue/Employee (TTM)	216,466*	446,627	384,817	395,728
Net Income/Employee (TTM)	29,536*	144,255	71,409	61,452
Receivable Turnover (TTM)	5.44*	10.28	7.89	9.35
Inventory Turnover (TTM)	NA	27.57	10.52	9.11
Asset Turnover (TTM)	1.52*	0.92	1.18	1.07

50 Companies in the Software & Programming industry listed in order of descending market capitalization.

MSFT	ORCL	CA	SAP	CPWR	HBOC	BMCS	NETA	CDN
NSCP	PMTC	INTU	PSFT	CTXS	SNPS	INKT	SE	DOX
ADBE	VRTS	ERTS	LHSG	SEBL	JDEC	RATL	TLC	KEA
ITWO	LGTO	BAANF	SSW	EFII	ADSK	PLAT	CSKKY	IFMX
CHKPF	MACR	IDXC	CBR	MAST	WANG	RNWK	TSAI	VRSN
ASDV	WIND	VSIO	NEON					

Alphabetical Listing of all Industries in theTechnologySector

Communications Equipment

Computer Hardware

Computer Networks

Computer Peripherals

Computer Services

Computer Storage Devices

Electronic Instr. & Controls

Office Equipment

Scientific & Technical Instr.

Semiconductors

Software & Programming

TTM: Trailing Twelve Months
MRQ: Most Recent Quarter
Mil: Millions

Appendix F Continued

Appendix G Financial Statements for Oracle Corporation

Annual balance sheet (thousand dollars)

Fiscal year (ending)	05/31/98	05/31/97	05/31/96
Assets			
Cash	1,273,681	890,162	715,742
Marketable securities	645,518	323,028	125,166
Trade receivables	1,857,480	1,540,470	1,084,858
Other current assets	546,371	517,436	358,699
Total current assets	4,323,050	3,271,098	2,284,465
Net property	934,350	868,948	685,754
Long-term cash investments	186,511	116,337	41,963
Deferred charges	99,012	98,981	99,072
Deposits & other assets	276,088	268,953	245,989
Total assets	5,819,011	4,624,315	3,357,243
Liabilities & shareholders' equity			
Notes payable	2,924	3,361	5,623
Accounts payable	239,698	185,444	169,895
Accrued expenses	1,063,502	804,912	663,012
Income taxes	181,354	203,646	181,999
Other current liabilities	996,687	724,776	434,435
Total current liabilities	2,484,165	1,922,139	1,454,964
Deferred income taxes	15,856	7,402	9,207
Long term debt	304,337	300,836	897
Other long term liabilities	57,095	24,226	21,726
Total liabilities	2,861,453	2,254,603	1,486,794
Common stock net	976,275	696,018	475,833
Retained earnings	2,023,056	1,686,170	1,382,203
Other equities	−41,773	−12,476	12,413
Shareholders equity	2,957,558	2,369,712	1,870,449
Total liabilities & stockholders' equity	5,819,011	4,624,315	3,357,243

Annual income statement (thousand dollars)

Fiscal year (ending)	05/31/98	05/31/97	05/31/96
Net sales/Total revenues	7,143,866	5,684,336	4,223,300
Cost of goods	4,644,913	3,520,860	2,645,244
Gross profit	2,498,953	2,163,476	1,578,056
R&D expenditures	886,197	592,276	440,024
Gen & admin expenses	368,556	308,215	233,141
Operating income	1,244,200	1,262,985	904,891
Non-operating income	100,277	27,348	21,251
Interest expense	16,658	6,806	6,632
Income before tax	1,327,819	1,283,527	919,510

Annual income statement (thousand dollars)—(Continued)			
Fiscal year (ending)	*05/31/98*	*05/31/97*	*05/31/96*
Provision for income taxes	514,124	462,070	316,231
Net income	813,695	821,457	603,279
Outstanding shares	973,337	651,980	655,828

Cash flow statement (thousand dollars)			
Fiscal year (ending)	*05/31/98*	*05/31/97*	*05/31/96*
Cash flow provided by operating activity			
New income (loss)	813,695	821,457	603,279
Depreciation/amortization	328,563	264,773	219,494
Net incr (decr) assets/liab.	198,352	−185,161	−48,959
Other adjustments, net	273,969	129,435	115,343
Net cash prov (used) by oper	1,614,579	1,030,504	889,157
Cash flow provided by investing activity			
(Incr) Decr in prop, plant	−328,358	−390,741	−308,392
(Incr) Decr in securities Inv.	−392,664	−272,236	−61,469
Other cash inflow (outflow)	−201,499	−114,404	−181,627
Net cash prov (used) by Inv	−922,521	−777,381	−651,488
Cash flow provided by financing activity			
Issue (purchase) of equity	−285,531	−354,127	−3,121
Incr (decr) in borrowing	2,685	297,005	−85,170
Net cash prov (used) by finan	−282,846	−57,122	−88,291
Effect of exchange rate on cash	−25,693	−21,581	−13,794
Net change in cash or equiv	383,519	174,420	235,584
Cash or equiv at year start	890,162	715,742	480,158
Cash or equiv at year end	1,273,681	890,162	715,742

Sources: Oracle Corporation and AOL.

Summary of Brokerage EPS Estimates and Recommendations
from Zacks Investment Research

ORACLE CORP (NSDQ: ORCL)
last updated 12/11/1998
Price: $37.250   1999 P/E: 29.81
Industry: Comp-Software
Estimated Industry Earnings Growth: 31.1%

Number of Brokers Recommending:	
Strong Buy	8
Moderate Buy	13
Hold	9
Moderate Sell	0
Strong Sell	0

Earnings Per Share	
Last Quarter (Nov-98)	0.28
Surprise	16.67%

Consensus Estimates	
This Quarter (Feb-99)	0.29
This Year (May-99)	1.25
Next Year (May-00)	1.49
Last Updated: 12/11/1998	
Next Earnings (Approx.): 3/12/1999	

Average Recommendation	
(strong buy) 1.00 - 5.00 (strong sell)	
This Week	1.95
Last Week	2.06
Change	0.11

Industry: Comp-Software
Ranked 162 of 288

Summary of Consensus EPS Estimates

	MEAN	HIGH	LOW	NUMBER EST	MEAN CHG LAST MNTH
($)					
FISC YR END May-99	1.25	1.33	1.18	28	0.04
FISC YR END May-00	1.49	1.60	1.40	20	0.04
VS ACTUAL May-98	0.92				
QUARTER END Feb-99	0.29	0.32	0.26	25	0.01
VS ACTUAL Feb-98	0.22				
QUARTER END May-99	0.50	0.56	0.46	24	0.01
VS ACTUAL May-98	0.41				
NEXT 5 YR GRTH (%)	23.73	35.00	15.00	22	0.57

*ESTIMATES & ACTUALS ARE BOTH EPS BEFORE XTRAS & OTHER NRI'S

Company Estimate Profile

buy	buy/hold	hold	hold/sell	sell
	1.95			
8	13	9	0	0

Current consensus recommendation of 30 brokers.

Appendix H   Summary of Brokerage EPS Estimates and Recommendations from Zacks Investment Research

Source: Zacks Investment Research, Inc. Reprinted with permission.

	QTR Feb-99	QTR May-99	FY May-99	FY May-00
CURRENT MEAN EPS ESTIMATE	0.29	0.50	1.25	1.49
Number of Brokers	25	24	28	20
Year Ago EPS	0.22	0.41	0.92	1.25
Report Date	3/12/1999	6/17/1999	6/17/1999	6/17/2000
Current High Estimate	0.32	0.56	1.33	1.60
Current Low Estimate	0.26	0.46	1.18	1.40
Standard Deviation	0.014	0.022	0.045	0.061

	QTR Nov-98	QTR Aug-98	QTR May-98	QTR Feb-98
Previous Quarters' Estimates	0.24	0.16	0.38	0.19
Previous Quarters' Actual EPS	0.28	0.20	0.41	0.22
% Difference	16.67	25.00	7.89	15.79

EARNINGS ESTIMATE REVISIONS AND TRENDS

	QTR Feb-99	QTR May-99	FY May-99	FY May-00
Current Mean	0.29	0.50	1.25	1.49
7-days ago Mean	0.28	0.49	1.22	1.45
30-days ago Mean	0.28	0.49	1.21	1.45
60-days ago Mean	0.27	0.49	1.20	1.44
90-days ago Mean	0.27	0.49	1.17	1.49
Up Revisions last 7 days	8	7	12	8
Up Revisions last 30 days	8	8	15	9
Down Revisions last 7 days	0	0	0	0
Down Revisions last 30 days	0	0	0	0

CONSENSUS RECOMMENDATIONS

Current Mean Recommendation	1.95
Number of brokers	30
7-days ago Mean	2.06
30-days ago Mean	2.10
60-days ago Mean	2.17
90-days ago Mean	2.24

SECULAR EARNINGS GROWTH RATES

Next 5 years - Median	24.000
Number of Brokers	22
Next 5 years - High	35.00
Next 5 years - Low	15.00
Last 5 years actual	40.6

Appendix H Continued

	QTR Feb-99	QTR May-99	FY May-99	FY May-00
Company EPS estimate	0.29	0.50	1.25	1.49
Current vs. Year Ago Change	29.64	22.36	35.83	19.27
Industry - Comp-Software	3.611	3.719	13.099	16.695
Current vs. Year Ago Change	29.71	23.00	28.32	27.45
Sector - Computer and Technol	18.762	16.288	61.241	67.886
Current vs. Year Ago Change	9.65	30.25	10.85	39.73
S&P Index	10.68	11.77	44.74	45.30
Current vs. Year Ago Change	-4.81	2.31	10.88	1.26

Ratios:	Company	Industry	Sector	S&P
P/E on 1999 Calendar Year Mean	29.81	22.79	16.64	25.75
PEG on 1999 Calendar Year Mean	1.26	0.74	0.76	3.68
Recommendation	2.04	1.99	1.96	2.15
Earnings Growth Rate	23.73	30.64	27.04	7.00

Appendix H   Continued

Research By Industry I Upgrades & Downgrades I **Research Abstracts** I Finance Home

Detailed Research - Oracle Corp (Nasdaq:ORCL)   **As of 25-Jan-99**

More Info: Quote I Chart I News I Profile I SEC I Basic Research I Messages I Insider I Up/Downgrades

Important Disclaimer Information

Earnings Estimates & Recommendations

	This Quarter (Feb 99)	Next Quarter (May 99)	This Year (May 99)	Next Year (May 00)	Number of brokers recommending as:	Months Ago			
						0	1	2	3
Earnings Estimates									
Avg Estimate	0.29	0.51	1.28	1.54	Strong Buy	8	8	8	5
# of Analysts	25	22	28	24	Moderate Buy	14	15	13	13
Low Estimate	0.27	0.47	1.19	1.32	Hold	8	8	9	12
High Estimate	0.33	0.54	1.34	1.71	Moderate Sell	0	0	0	0
Year Ago EPS	0.22	0.41	0.92	1.28	Strong Sell	0	0	0	0
EPS Growth	31.82 %	24.06 %	39.64 %	20.07 %	Mean*	1.90	1.90	1.97	2.17
Consensus EPS Trend					* (strong buy) 1.00 - 5.00 (strong sell)				
Current	0.29	0.51	1.28	1.54	Industry: COMP-SOFTWARE				
7 Days Ago	0.29	0.51	1.28	1.53	Ranked 156 of 274				
30 Days Ago	0.29	0.51	1.28	1.52					
60 Days Ago	0.28	0.49	1.21	1.46	Next Earnings (Approx.): N/A				
90 Days Ago	0.28	0.49	1.20	1.54					

Earnings Growth

	Last 5 Years	This Year (May 99)	Next Year (May 00)	Next 5 Years	Price/Earn (May 99)	PEG Ratio (May 99)
Oracle Corp	40.6 %	39.6 %	20.1 %	23.7 %	n/a	n/a
COMP-SOFTWARE	17.8 %	18.0 %	32.7 %	31.0 %	53.3	2.96
S&P 500	13.9 %	1.1 %	4.1 %	7.2 %	27.4	24.91

Appendix I Detailed Brokerage EPS Estimates and Recommendations: Zacks/Yahoo!

Source: Zacks Investment Research and Yahoo! Inc. Reproduced with permission. Yahoo! and the Yahoo! logo are trademarks of Yahoo! Inc.

Glossary

Acquisition: The procurement of all, or enough, shares of another company for taking control of its operations.

Annual report: A comprehensive annual financial statement issued by every public company. Mandated by the SEC, this report indicates the financial health of the company.

Ask price: The lowest price that a stock is being offered for sale. Also called the "offer" price. Ask price is higher than the bid price.

Assets: Items of value owned by a company such as cash, inventory, land, buildings, and equipment.

Average down: To buy more shares of a company after its price declines. This results in the average cost of all the shares decreasing to a value somewhere between the purchase prices of the two transactions.

Balance sheet: A company's financial statement indicating what it owns (assets), what it owes (liabilities), and their difference (known as stockholders' equity or net worth).

Bear: A pessimistic investor who expects stock prices to drop.

Bear market: A market that declines steadily for an extended period; the usual decline is 20% to 30%, and it can last months or years.

Bearish: Price expected to decline.

Beta: A measure of a stock's price volatility compared to the market as represented by the S&P 500 index. A beta equal to 1 is equivalent to the market's volatility. Beta higher than 1 means that the stock is more volatile than the market, while beta less than 1 means that the stock is less volatile than the market.

Bid price: Highest price at which a market maker is willing to buy a stock from a seller. Bid price is lower than the ask price.

Board of directors: A small but powerful group, elected by shareholders every year, who are empowered to make important decisions including acquisitions, appointing officers, issue shares, increase/decrease dividends, and so on.

Bond: A debt instrument maturing in a period extending over a year from the date of issue.

Book value: The per share value of an outstanding share of stock, calculated by subtracting a company's liabilities from its assets and then dividing the resulting number by the outstanding shares.

Broker: A brokerage company's registered (licensed) representative who handles customer accounts and executes orders.

Brokerage: A company licensed to execute investor orders for securities.

Bull: An optimistic investor who expects stock prices to rise.

Bull market: Stock market characterized by rising prices over a period of months or years.

Bullish: Price expected to rise.

Call option: An agreement that gives the buyer the right to buy a stock at a predetermined price, known as the strike price, before the expiration date of the agreement. Agreements are made in terms of "contracts," where each contract is equivalent to 100 shares.

Capital gain: Net profit resulting from the sale or exchange of securities.

Capital loss: Net loss resulting from the sale or exchange of securities.

Capitalization: Capital that is invested in a company. Includes common stock and preferred stock, long-term debt (bonds), and retained earnings.

Cash flow: The amount of internally generated cash that can be used for paying dividends, financing growth, or purchasing assets. Commonly defined as net income plus depreciation.

Commission: The fee that a brokerage company charges an investor for buying or selling a security.

Common stock: The unit of ownership in a corporation which is represented by a share.

Corporation: The most common entity through which business is conducted in a free market capitalistic economy.

Covering: Buying back the shares of a stock that has been sold short in order to close the position.

Depreciation: A decrease in the value of an asset over a period of time.

Discount: The amount below the list price or face value of a security. Such a security is said to be "selling at a discount."

Discount rate: Interest rate that the Federal Reserve Bank charges on loans to member banks.

Discounted: Already taken into account; for example, a stock may not react to good earnings because the expectations may already have been factored (discounted) into the stock price by investors.

Diversification: To spread out the investment in stocks, or other securities, of different companies and/or sectors/industries.

Dividend: The payment a corporation makes, usually quarterly, to its stockholders. The payout amount is decided by the company's board of directors. It is usually related to the level of profits earned by the company. Payment is usually made in cash though it can be distributed in the form of additional shares.

Dollar cost averaging: Investment technique that involves buying shares, at regular intervals, in a fixed dollar amount irrespective of the price. This enables the purchase of more shares at a lower price than when prices are higher.

Dow Jones Industrial Average (DJIA): A measure of the market based on the price of 30 stocks making up the Dow Jones Industrial Average.

Earnings: The net profit of a company after all costs, expenses, and taxes have been paid. Typically reported as earnings per share, which is calculated by dividing the earnings by the total number of outstanding shares. Reported for each quarter and annually.

Equity: This represents the ownership of the company which, for a publicly traded company, is synonymous with its common stock.

Expiration date: The date on which an option—put or call—has expired. Stock options expire on the third Friday of the month. The next Saturday is designated as the expiration date.

Float: The number of shares of a company currently available for trading. Float is calculated after reducing, from the total number of outstanding shares, the shares held by the founding family, management, and/or institutions.

Fundamental analysis: A comprehensive study of a company, which covers its financial statements, management, and the industry of which it is a part.

Growth stock: The stock of a company that is growing at an above-average rate and, hence, is expected to appreciate in price at a faster rate.

Income statement: A document that reports a company's financial results for a specific period. Includes revenues, costs, expenses, taxes, and earnings.

Index: A measure for representing the combined value of a group of stocks.

Inflation: The phenomenon of rising prices for goods and services.

Initial public offering (IPO): The initial offering of shares to the public, in the stock market, of a company that has been held privately so far.

Insider: An officer or director of a company who has access to confidential information that is not available to ordinary investors.

Insider trading: Illegal stock trading by an individual (such as a company's officer or director) who has access to information about the company that is not available to the public.

Institutional investor: A large organization that invests in the stock market, such as mutual and pension funds, insurance companies, and so on.

Leading economic indicators: A group of economic variables that help economists forecast the direction of the overall economy six to nine months down the road.

Liabilities: What a company owes, including all debts and other claims against the company.

Limit order: An order that instructs that the transaction be executed at a specific price or better.

Liquidity: The ability of a stock to meet all buy and sell demands without causing the stock price to be moved appreciably. Lack of liquidity can cause the stock price to swing considerably or even prevent the shares being sold when required.

Long-term debt: Liabilities that need to be repaid after one year.

Margin: Money borrowed from a broker for buying stocks, which are kept as collateral by the broker.

Market breadth: A measure of the extent to which stocks are participating in a market advance. Often indicated by the number of stocks that advance or decline during a specified period. Also measured by the number of stocks hitting new highs or new lows.

Market capitalization: Total shares outstanding at the end of the most recent quarter multiplied by the stock's closing price.

Merger: Friendly takeover of a company by another.

Money market fund: A fund whose investments are made only in short-term debt securities.

Mutual fund: An open-ended investment company through which investors can invest in the stock market. These funds are safer and less volatile, due to diversification, than individual stocks.

Mutual funds cash: The cash held by mutual funds as a percentage of their assets.

Nasdaq: National Association of Securities Dealers automated quotations system, used for trading stocks in the over-the-counter market.

Net earnings: see "earnings."

Net income: see "earnings."

Net profit: see "earnings."

New York Stock Exchange (NYSE): The most important stock exchange in the United States where buyers and sellers can trade stocks.

Option: An agreement that gives the buyer the right to buy, or sell, a stock at a predetermined price, known as the strike price, before the agreement's expiration date. Options are written in terms of contracts, where each contract is equivalent to 100 shares.

Over-the-counter (OTC): Network of brokers/dealers who mostly buy/sell stocks that are not listed on the major exchanges.

P/E ratio: See price/earnings ratio.

Penny stock: The shares of a company that sell for under a dollar per share. Some investors classify stocks selling under $3 per share in this category.

Portfolio: The basket of stocks that an investor owns.

Premium: The amount above the list price or face value of a security. Such a security is said to be "selling at a premium."

Price/earnings (P/E ratio): The ratio obtained by dividing a stock's price by its earnings per share for a specific period like a quarter or the year. A stock trading at $24 having an earnings per share equal to $2 per share has a P/E equal to 12.

Prime rate: The interest rate that commercial banks charge their most creditworthy customers.

Profit margin: A measure of the profitability of a company that relates profits to revenues. Commonly used profit margins are operating, pretax, and net profit margins.

Profit taking: The selling of shares to lock in profits that have been realized in a stock.

Put option: An agreement that gives the buyer the right to sell a stock at a predetermined price, known as the strike price, before the expiration date of the agreement. Agreements are made in terms of "contracts," where each contract is equivalent to 100 shares.

Quote: A stock's current highest bid and the lowest offer (ask) price for buying or selling.

Rally: Significant upward price movement of a stock or the overall market.

Retained earnings: A company's earnings that are not distributed to the shareholders as dividends. Instead, they are reinvested in the company.

Return on equity (ROE): Rate of investment return that is earned by a company on its stockholders' equity. Calculated by dividing net earnings by the total stockholders' equity.

Revenues: Income derived by a company through sales and other sources before the deduction of costs and expenses.

Sales: The value of goods/services sold by a company.

Securities and Exchange Commission (SEC): Regulatory authority that oversees and regulates the stock market.

Shares outstanding: The number of authorized shares that have been issued for a company.

Short selling: The technique of selling a stock by borrowing it from a broker. The expectation is that the stock price will decline and, consequently, the investor will be able to buy back the stock at a lower price. The repurchased shares are then returned to the broker (or other lender). The difference between the sale and procurement price is the investor's profit.

Specialist: A member of the stock exchange assigned the responsibility of maintaining an orderly market for a particular stock by balancing its supply and demand.

Specialist short sales: Short sales made by an exchange specialist.

Speculator: Someone who takes on far higher risk with the expectation of far greater profit than an ordinary investor. Investment decisions made by speculators are often made on hopes and hunches rather than on solid research.

Split: The division of a company's shares into a greater number of shares, with the most common being a 2-1 split. Its result is to double the number of shares, while halving the price per share.

Spread: The difference between the bid and ask prices of a stock.

S&P 500 (Standard & Poor's 500): An index comprising 500 of the largest U.S. companies. It is widely considered to be a measure of the financial health of corporate America.

Stock exchange: A market that facilitates the trading of stocks that are registered there.

Stockholders' equity: The stockholders' ownership in the company. Also known as "net worth." It is the difference between the total assets and total liabilities of a company.

Stop order: An order to buy at a price above, or sell below, the currently quoted price for a stock. An order becomes a "market order" when the stock sells at or below the stop price. A stop sell order is used to protect profits or limit a potential loss.

Strike price: A stock option's predetermined exercise price.

Technical analysis: A technique for analyzing stocks. It is based on the study of the price fluctuations with the objective of predicting future price movements.

Volatility: The degree to which a stock's price moves up or down, especially in the short term.

Volume: The total number of shares traded, of an individual stock or the entire market, in a specified period.

Yield: The annual return on an investment, from dividends or interest, expressed as a percentage of the current price.

Yield curve: The difference in the yield between short-term Treasury notes and long-term Treasury bonds.

Index